Shakespeare and
The Two Noble Kinsmen

Shakespeare and
The Two Noble Kinsmen

by PAUL BERTRAM

RUTGERS UNIVERSITY PRESS

New Brunswick   *New Jersey*

For
R. A. and R. P.

This general theory is to the following effect: there are not poems, pictures, instances of natural beauty, passages of prose and so forth, which exist as such in themselves and can be assessed by themselves, but there are men, who in various situations make poems and paintings and the like, and who experience other things made by other men or naturally existing; and it is impossible to understand or assess any of these unless we take into account explicitly the whole of the epistemological situations in which they occur, even though it is convenient for more superficial purposes to refer to a poem or a painting or an explanation or the like by itself without explicit reference to the man who made it and to the men who experience it.

Angus Sinclair

ADVERTISEMENT

The Two Noble Kinsmen, probably acted in 1613, was first published in 1634. The original title-page ascribed the play to Shakespeare and Fletcher. Despite the absence of external evidence that Shakespeare ever collaborated, and despite the uncertainty and confusion that have long attended study of the play, a majority of interested critics since the time of Lamb and Coleridge have come to accept that dual attribution. The present study seeks to show, however, that the play must have been entirely the work of Shakespeare.

Partly as a consequence of the problem of authorship, the play has seldom received close attention as a dramatic work. Yet among the critics who have become familiar with it, De Quincey went so far as to call it "perhaps the most superb work in the language," and more recently Kenneth Tynan has called it "the last of the great plays of the time." There is a close relation between questions of critical interpretation or evaluation and the historical problem of authorship, and this relation is explored in the discussion of the play itself.

The Introduction offers a synoptic description of the contents and organization of the study as a whole. In addition to historical, bibliographical, and critical chapters on *The Two Noble Kinsmen,* the contents include a chapter on Shakespeare's *Henry VIII,* a play first brought into discussions of *The Two Noble Kinsmen* by several Victorian critics who asserted that it too represented a joint effort of Shakespeare and Fletcher.

The present study offers the most coherent and reasonable explanation yet brought forward to resolve one of the most long-standing and formidable problems in English literary scholarship and criticism. Whether or not the reader accepts its thesis, he will find in *Shakespeare and "The Two Noble Kinsmen"* the most comprehensive and detailed examination of the relevant historical and textual evidence ever published.

CONTENTS

Any book that sets out to extend the limits of the Shakespeare canon is bound to engender suspicion. I have tried, of course, to give a reasonably fair presentation of earlier critical opinion as well as of the relevant evidence. The conclusions drawn from this evidence may seem surprising, but no one has attempted to examine all of it together before; given the evidence, the conclusions are neither willful nor arbitrary. "Every event, before experience," wrote Hume, "is equally difficult and incomprehensible; and every event, after experience, is equally easy and intelligible."

Portions of the book have already been published in different form. An article on the date of *The Two Noble Kinsmen* appeared in *Shakespeare Quarterly* (1961). An essay on *Henry VIII* appeared in the critical anthology *In Defense of Reading,* ed. Reuben A. Brower and Richard Poirier (New York: E. P. Dutton & Co., 1962). I am grateful to the editors and publishers for permission to reprint.

Except where otherwise noted, references to *The Two Noble Kinsmen* follow the line-numbering of the 1876 New Shakspere Society type-facsimile of the 1634 quarto (see page 21 below); when mainly textual points are at issue, quotations follow the quarto; when mainly literary points are at issue and the peculiarities of early punctuation and spelling might be distracting, the text has been conservatively modernized. References to *Henry VIII* follow the edition by R. A. Foakes in the new Arden Shakespeare (1957). Other references to Shakespeare follow the standard line-numbering of the Globe edition (1894). Citations from Fletcher are drawn from the Cambridge University Press edition of Beaumont and Fletcher prepared by Arnold Glover and A. R. Waller (1905-12).

To the Research Council of Rutgers University I am indebted for grants in aid both of research and publication. I am grateful to Francis A. Johns and H. Gilbert Kelley for help in obtaining rare books. And I must also express my sense of deep indebtedness to those who have offered valuable criticisms of the manuscript at various stages of composition—especially to Gerald E. Bentley, Reuben A. Brower, Daniel F. Howard, Harry Levin, Charles F. Main, and Richard Poirier. I alone take credit for all that is wrong with the book.

P. B.

New Brunswick, N.J.
June 1965

Shakespeare and
The Two Noble Kinsmen

Introduction

Most of the collected editions of Shakespeare since the end of the eighteenth century, when modern editors began regularly to add *Pericles* to the plays contained in the First Folio of 1623, have included a total of thirty-seven plays. A number of Shakespearean editors during the past hundred twenty years have also included a thirty-eighth play, *The Two Noble Kinsmen,* and it is this play and the issues related to its place in the canon with which the present study is mainly concerned.

The Two Noble Kinsmen, thought to have been first acted in 1613, was first published in 1634. The title-page of the 1634 quarto, printed for the bookseller John Waterson, attributed the play to Shakespeare and to John Fletcher. The play was subsequently reprinted, in 1679 and thereafter, in collected editions of Fletcher's works. Its authorship has been a matter of dispute for over two hundred years, and its admission to editions of Shakespeare from 1841 to the present has been more the exception than the rule.

Previous attempts to resolve the problem of authorship are examined in some of the chapters that follow, but the most widely held theories of past and present may be identified briefly. (1) A hypothesis put forward by George Steevens in 1780 that the play had been written by Fletcher alone, and that in it Fletcher sought deliberately to imitate Shakespeare, commanded occasional support during the nineteenth century. (2) A hypothesis invented by Robert Boyle in 1882 that the play had been written by Fletcher and Massinger (with Massinger imitating Shakespeare) attracted a few supporters during the later years of the nineteenth century and the earlier years of our own. (3) A majority of critics since the time of Lamb and Coleridge, including virtually every critic to comment at length on the play in the past forty years, has held that internal evidence tends to confirm the title-page attribution to Fletcher and Shakespeare. Although several modern editions of Shakespeare omit the play, this belief in Shakespeare's partial authorship—indorsed by Bradley, Chambers, Kittredge, Greg, Bentley, and other equally prominent scholars and critics—may fairly be taken to represent received opinion at the present time.

A fourth view concerning the authorship of the play has been expressed by a few men of letters, among them Pope and De Quincey, namely that the entire play was written by Shakespeare. This hypothesis has never been developed or explored in any previously published discussion of the play. The present study seeks to show that this bold-sounding hypothesis works very well, that in fact it provides the most reasonable explanations for nearly all the many puzzles attending previous inquiries into the problem of authorship, that it leads to the observation of a good deal of hitherto overlooked evidence relevant to that problem, that in short it is true.

The Two Noble Kinsmen has been described as "perhaps the most superb work in the language" (De Quincey), and it has also been damned as intolerable trash. Questions of critical analysis and evaluation are, of course, intimately bound up with the historical problem of authorship. "Far more than we like to admit, we take a hint for our response from the poet's reputation. Whether we assent or dissent, the traditional view runs through our response like the wire upon which a climbing plant is trained" (I. A. Richards). Critics have sometimes believed they could read and interpret the play without being affected by whatever assumptions they held about its authorship, but that belief is not wholly credible; the present study shows that the problem of authorship has interfered with nearly every recorded critical observation on the play. Conversely, the new solution to that problem is not an end in itself; it alters our view of the play, leading to the recognition of its dramatic unity and disclosing more fully its considerable charm and power. De Quincey's estimate of the value of the play is no doubt excessive, but it is not ridiculous.

It may be helpful to indicate the disposition of materials in the six chapters of this study. Although the paragraphs that follow seek neither to summarize nor even to identify all the classes of evidence examined in the book as a whole, in a general way they let the reader know what to expect.

I. After a review of the earlier publishing history of the play, the opening chapter traces the origins of current opinion on the question of authorship and re-examines some of the evidence on which that opinion rests. It shows that the belief in dual authorship is much less solidly grounded than most readers have been led to suppose.

The problem of authorship first came in for serious study in the later eighteenth century, but not until Lamb and Coleridge had popularized the view that Shakespeare's hand could be seen in the play did anything like the modern critical consensus begin to form itself. Victorian critics, attempting to determine which scenes could safely be claimed for Shakespeare and which might be left to Fletcher, worked out a fairly precise division of authorship based largely on metrical grounds. The twelve scenes most often ascribed to Shakespeare today are those which had first been marked off by Samuel Hickson in 1847 and which were again defended in 1876 by Harold Littledale in his influential New Shakspere Society edition of the play. The later theory by Boyle that these scenes had been written by Massinger (a theory which assumed the same lines of division between the two writers) helped to set the direction for subsequent scholarship; post-Victorian students of the play have usually devoted themselves to re-defending Shakespeare's authorship of the scenes championed by Hickson and Littledale. Although now long out of fashion, the Boyle theory is largely responsible for inhibiting any very fundamental inquiry into the original grounds of the division between authors postulated by the Victorians.

The assumptions of divided authorship and of Fletcher's presence, in short, have seldom been re-examined; for the past eighty years they have been treated as if they had been proved conclusively by the metrical evidence compiled by the Victorians (as may be seen, for example, in the recent comments by Kenneth Muir cited below on page 20). The singularly influential metrical tests, however, have been based on texts in which the verse-lineation follows the arrangements of Thomas Seward, an eighteenth-century editor notorious for his metrical licenses—texts in which (to pick but one example) several hundreds of lines of prose are printed as verse. The recognition of these and other surprising deficiencies in the evidence for divided authorship and for Fletcher constitutes the necessary first stage in any careful re-examination of the problem of authorship. The extensive inaccuracies that survive in modern editions of the text, moreover, point up the superficiality of much of the scholarship devoted to this play. The naturally skeptical reader would perhaps do well to turn at once to Chapter I and satisfy himself on these points before proceeding further into the present Introduction.

II. The 1634 quarto has only recently begun to attract attention from bibliographical analysts, and the first published findings indicate that previous studies of the play have overlooked a mine of evidence relevant to the authorship problem. There are strong signs, for example, that the quarto was printed at least in part from Shakespearean autograph copy.

The many arresting features of the quarto text include an exceptionally full complement of stage directions—both of the kinds normally employed by authors and of the kinds commonly added to theatrical manuscripts by book-keepers for prompting purposes. Sir Walter Greg has observed briefly that the quarto was "almost certainly" printed from the original prompt-book of 1613. The first detailed analysis intended to determine the nature of the manuscript used by the printer appears in an essay by F. O. Waller published in 1958; Waller has called attention to some of the features pointing to an authorial manuscript and has noted several features suggesting that this manuscript consisted of Shakespeare's autograph (e.g. anomalous spellings found also in early Shakespeare quartos or in the Shakespearean manuscript Addition to *Sir Thomas More*). Committed to the traditional assumption of divided authorship, Waller postulates a manuscript composed of two sets of authors' foul papers (or some species of transcription thereof)—i.e. a rough-draft manuscript too irregular to have served as the theatrical prompt-book. (The prompter's directions noted by Greg are interpreted by Waller as book-keeper's annotations on the foul papers prior to the making of a prompt-book.) As for transcription, Waller suggests that the printer's copy may have been some sort of hastily prepared scribal transcript of the foul papers which would somehow have preserved the authorial features surviving in the quarto and which might at the same time account for the absence from the quarto of features distinctive of Fletcher's hand (features the scribe must presumably have removed). The theory is an interesting attempt to reconcile as much of the bibliographical evidence as Waller has observed with received opinion on the question of authorship.

After reviewing Waller's analysis, Chapter II introduces additional evidence of a prompt-book, of authorial fair copy, and of Shakespearean autograph. (With respect to the last, for example, one portion of the evidence consists of several distinctive misprints identical with or strikingly similar to examples found in earlier Shakespeare texts and attributable to idiosyncrasies of Shakespeare's handwriting and spelling.) The presentation greatly extends the range of evidence already observed by Greg and Waller, and the analysis shows that the many peculiarities of the quarto are best explained by postulating a fair copy in Shakespeare's hand which had served as the company prompt-book. With respect to the problem of authorship, this explanation would imply that, whether or not there had been dramatic collaboration, Shakespeare was responsible for the final draft of the play. (The puzzling absence of the play from the 1623 Folio could then be accounted for by assuming that, as in several other known cases, the company prompt-book had been temporarily lost.) [1] The recognition of biblio-

---

[1] It is admittedly highly arbitrary to assume the play was absent from the Folio because the manuscript was unavailable; such an assumption can be justified only if literary and historical evidence of the kinds considered in later chapters prove alternative explanations to be impracticable. But the bibliographical evidence for a single prompt-book consisting of an author's fair copy facilitates that explanation of the crucial Folio question, and it is for this reason that the subject is introduced in a chapter dealing with the copy used by the printer.

graphical evidence for Shakespeare's hand in the scenes commonly assigned to Fletcher does not necessarily contradict the testimony of the title-page, but it does require drastic modifications in current views on the authorship of the play.

III. The presence of a chapter on *Henry VIII* in a study of *The Two Noble Kinsmen* calls for some explanation. There is no known item of historical evidence older or stronger than the 1634 title-page of *The Two Noble Kinsmen* to link the names of Shakespeare and Fletcher as collaborators; but it has nevertheless been thought by many scholars that Shakespeare collaborated with Fletcher on *Henry VIII*. This belief goes back directly to the arguments first offered in 1850 by James Spedding and popularized a generation later by the New Shakspere Society. Spedding attacked the play on moral grounds—its dénouement, he felt, amounted to "little less than the ultimate triumph of wrong"—and he then proceeded, silently following some leads given by Hickson in his 1847 essay on *The Two Noble Kinsmen,* to divide *Henry VIII* into two sets of scenes, to assign one set to Shakespeare and the other to Fletcher on metrical grounds, and to argue that Fletcher had taken an abandoned play by Shakespeare and completed it badly. Spedding's analysis did not allow for active collaboration between Shakespeare and Fletcher, but once the notion of dual authorship had attained wide currency it was often used to support the assumption of dual authorship or collaboration in *The Two Noble Kinsmen.* During the past generation the theory of dual authorship in *Henry VIII* has been reviewed and rejected by a growing number of editors and scholars, and a majority today regards the play as entirely the work of Shakespeare.

The critics who during the past forty years have been most active in refuting the theories set in motion by Spedding, and who by this and other means have in effect reaffirmed the integrity of *Henry VIII*, have generally tended to ignore *The Two Noble Kinsmen.* The critics who have written at length on behalf of Shakespeare's partial authorship of the latter play, meanwhile, have usually made reference to the view that *Henry VIII* was a collaboration (again, without detailed analysis) as one of their supporting arguments. Perhaps this is not surprising.

The presumption of dual authorship in *Henry VIII* gave rise to a good deal of serious misinterpretation of the play, and the history of the controversy over its authorship affords a favorable opportunity to observe the intricate and often unsuspected relationships between the examination of a "problem of authorship" and literary criticism proper. The later sections of Chapter III offer an interpretation of *Henry VIII*. Designed primarily to show its theatrical coherence and its imaginative integrity, the discussion at the same time draws attention to the ways in which many normally acute readers appear to have been misled, as a direct consequence of assuming divided authorship, into overlooking important elements of dramatic design.

IV. Students of *The Two Noble Kinsmen* have usually had to deal with the little known and decidedly peculiar problems of a third play on which Shakespeare and Fletcher are sometimes thought to have collaborated. A play known as *Cardenio* was acted by the King's men in 1612, and in 1653 a manuscript copy was recorded in the Stationers' Register with an attribution to Shakespeare and Fletcher. The attribution itself would carry little weight (especially as the same entry ascribed two other lost plays to Shakespeare and Davenport), but *Cardenio* is now thought to have been the original Jacobean play adapted as *Double Falsehood* by Lewis Theobald and acted in 1727. The Theobald adaptation (based ultimately on the Cardenio story in *Don Quixote*) was published in 1728, and it is the text of this play, and Theobald's statements about its provenance, from which scholars have sought to learn more about *Cardenio*.

Before it was publicly performed *Double Falsehood* was advertised by Theobald as nothing less than a previously unknown play "written originally by William Shakespeare" which he had acquired in manuscript and then adapted to the requirements of the contemporary stage. In the Preface to the published text Theobald reiterated his claim and spoke of himself merely as an "editor"; he also referred to several unidentified critics who (he said) had charged that the language of *Double Falsehood* sounded more like Fletcher than Shakespeare, and he remarked coolly that this charge was not worth the trouble of a reply. Theobald's actions and statements with respect to *Double Falsehood* in 1727-28, and the remarkable silence he maintained on the subject throughout the rest of his distinguished scholarly career, have led many critics to find his whole performance an "ironic mystification." No one has been able to credit his claim that *Double Falsehood* was based on an entire play written by Shakespeare—or to maintain that any part of it in its present form was written by Shakespeare—although many critics from Theobald's day to our own have thought Fletcher's presence likely enough.

Since the connection between *Cardenio* and *Double Falsehood* was first pointed out in 1909, however, a number of critics (notably, critics who have championed Shakespeare's partial authorship of *The Two Noble Kinsmen* and thought that establishing collaboration on *Cardenio* would strengthen their case) have interpreted certain of Theobald's statements along with a few metrical phenomena in the text of *Double Falsehood* as evidence supporting the dual attribution of the 1653 entry in the Stationers' Register. The lack of verbal evidence for Shakespeare in the text of *Double Falsehood* has been explained away as the result of Theobald's "levelling" in the process of adapting the piece to the stage—although those who have used this argument have ignored the fact that Restoration and eighteenth-century adaptations of Shakespeare, however mangled, usually preserve large portions of Shakespeare's dialogue verbatim, and they have also ignored the fact that Theobald's one adaptation of Shakespeare, *Richard II,* is unusually faithful to the original in this respect.

Careful review of the problems connected with *Cardenio* and *Double Falsehood* shows that the many curious aspects of Theobald's behavior, like the text of his play, can be fully and satisfactorily explained only if the assumption that Shakespeare had anything to do with *Cardenio* is abandoned. It is perhaps unfortunate, but it is necessary, that a chapter in a book about *The Two Noble Kinsmen* should be devoted to explaining why the subject it discusses, *Cardenio,* is wholly irrelevant to *The Two Noble Kinsmen.*

V, VI. The last third of the book seeks finally to establish that *The Two Noble Kinsmen* was written entirely by Shakespeare and at the same time to show that this play—to borrow a comment of De Quincey's on several scenes within it—is "finished in a more elaborate style of excellence than any other almost" of Shakespeare's finest works. Chapter V is concerned mainly with what critics of the past have observed in the play, Chapter VI with a fresh analysis of the text.

The statement that Fletcher was author or part-author of *The Two Noble Kinsmen,* since it has been repeated virtually without question or challenge for a few hundred years, has naturally tended to be regarded by many as a statement of fact. Even before literary scholars began to examine the play, the circumstances of its publishing history attached it to the Fletcher canon. The first professional scholar of repute to look closely into the problem of authorship was Steevens. He could see no sign of divided authorship. More positively, he observed that "the language and images of this piece coincide perpetually with those in the dramas of Shakspeare," and he documented this observation carefully with a sizeable collection of parallel passages. Combining what he had seen with what he had been led to assume in advance, however, he was brought by this evidence to the conclusion that, although Fletcher had nowhere else made a like attempt, the entire play must have been written by Fletcher in silent imitation of Shakespeare. Although Hazlitt and Halliwell-Phillipps were later to express similar opinions, Lamb and Coleridge thought the possibility remote that Fletcher could have achieved so close an imitation of Shakespeare's language and they rejected Steevens' argument; as remarked earlier, the assurances they offered that parts of the play were genuinely Shakespeare's encouraged later scholars to adduce a variety of proofs in support of that judgment. The possibility of answering the question of authorship along the line taken by Steevens has become increasingly remote since the time of Lamb (as stylistic evidence for Shakespeare has been accumulated), and the bibliographical evidence—even the partial evidence already published by Waller—is today decisive against any theory of imitation; for it would be hard to maintain that Fletcher set out to imitate Shakespeare's handwriting and spelling as well as his literary habits.

Although Lamb and Coleridge rejected the theory of imitation in their few comments on the play, they unwittingly helped to foster the development of the metrical tests (by drawing attention to versification as a criterion of authorship) and thus to encourage the division which those tests established as orthodox during the nineteenth century. Once the play had been divided into two separate compartments, critics usually commented on Shakespearean highlights and generally neglected whatever they were led to regard as not-Shakespeare; yet when on occasion they did try to account for the text of one or another of the scenes described by editors as "known" to be "certainly" Fletcher's, their comments followed a curious but consistent pattern. One critic would take up only the scenes involving Gerrold and the Countrymen, but would remark that in them Fletcher was evidently imitating the language and comic characterizations of *A Midsummer Night's Dream* and *Love's Labor's Lost;* another critic would take up only the dialogue of the prison scene, and to him it would seem an "imitation" of dialogues in *Cymbeline;* the quarrel between Palamon and Arcite would appear to a third critic to represent Fletcher's "imitation" of the quarrel between Brutus and Cassius; and so forth. Even the ablest among the Victorian professional scholars, searching diligently through works of the Fletcher canon for verbal parallels to scenes in the play assigned to Fletcher, have unwittingly offered similar testimony; their most substantial parallels were taken from, of all plays, *Henry VIII,* and the only other play from which a number of supposed parallels could be collected, *The Lover's Progress,* although regarded by the Victorians as a work of Fletcher, is now recognized to have been thoroughly rewritten by Massinger—apparently rewritten, moreover, shortly after the quarto of *The Two Noble Kinsmen* had been printed, so that Massinger, characteristically, was able somewhat mechanically to echo phrases from it. In short, the repeated assertions that Fletcher was author or part-author of *The Two Noble Kinsmen,* whenever they have been explained or defended by reference to the text, have usually been joined with observations and evidence testifying to precisely the opposite view. Critics and scholars who would have been startled by Pope's observation that the play bears little resemblance to Fletcher might have been even more startled to learn that they themselves have provided testimony, the more valuable perhaps for being unintentional, supporting his further observation that the play looks more authentically Shakespearean than several plays in the Folio. Since one of the principal obstacles that any argument on behalf of Shakespeare's single authorship must overcome is the *apparent* weight of received opinion against it, it is noteworthy that a less superficial examination of that opinion actually reveals a surprising degree of support for that argument.

The final chapter presents a considerable body of direct evidence, both internal and external, for Shakespeare's single authorship. It opens with a study of the treatment of sources to show that elements from *The Knight's Tale* are taken over into the play and redistributed or transmuted in ways suggesting a single mind at work. The major part of the chapter is given to analysis of the text—to questions of philosophic theme and of character-development, to imagery that cuts across the received lines of divided authorship, to continuities in the language of the play that constitute decisive evidence of poetic and dramatic integrity. This unfamiliar play about the chivalric values arising from a series of contests over "the name of men" offers an impressive dramatic experience, and the final proof of Shakespeare's authorship lies in a careful and responsive reading of the text.

If a theory concerning the authorship of *The Two Noble Kinsmen* is to gain credence, it ought to make coherent and manageable a body of evidence larger and more various than any rival theory has been able to reduce to order. It must be able in fact to interpret satisfactorily all the critical evidence—down to and including such data as the little known statement of Leonard Digges (who was in a position to know) that Shakespeare did not collaborate, or the reference to a single writer in the Prologue to *The Two Noble Kinsmen*. Advocates of dual authorship have usually ignored all but a fraction of the evidence and often conceded their inability to clarify the fraction they did deal with. Yet the theory maintained in the last two chapters and supported by the study as a whole, if it is to engage the attention of anyone other than the writer who expounds it, will naturally have to deal, whether directly or by implication, with certain wider issues, issues of more general significance than the authorship of a single play—even if that play happens to be a neglected masterpiece. Some of the wider issues touched

on in the present study are intrinsic in the subject of a problem of authorship. One such issue can be suggested indirectly by citing a passage from
T. S. Eliot's famous attack on *Hamlet:*

The *Hamlet* of Shakespeare will appear to us very differently if, instead of treating the whole action of the play as due to Shakespeare's design, we perceive his
Hamlet to be superposed upon much cruder material which persists even in the
final form.

("Hamlet and His Problems")

Of course it will, and the fact that Eliot in 1919 accepted J. M. Robertson's
thesis about non-Shakespearean material in *Hamlet* led him at that time to
look at the play very differently from the way in which most men look at
it today. "Perceiving" collaboration with Fletcher, critics have looked at
The Two Noble Kinsmen in ways the present study would seek to correct.
The study of a problem of authorship is, among other things, a study in
ways of reading, and a study also, more generally, of certain of the relationships between knowledge and experience, of the ways in which our assumptions and expectations may set or remove the limits around the data we are
able to observe and may affect for worse or better our ability to interpret
them.

I

The Division of Authorship

How odd it is that anyone should not see that all observation must be
for or against some view if it is to be of any service!

Darwin

Many engaging modern studies of the authorship of *The Two Noble
Kinsmen* have dealt with Shakespeare's responsibility for about half of the
play. The scenes usually believed to be by Fletcher have, understandably
enough, received less attention. The purpose of the present chapter is to
inquire into several of the less frequently examined points in the division
of authorship, and in particular to review the most important evidence for
Fletcher's authorship of the twelve scenes commonly assigned to him. Those
scenes are II.ii–vi, III.iii–vi, IV.i–ii, and V.ii; a few passages elsewhere in
the play have occasionally been attributed to Fletcher, of course, and it
should be understood that the ascriptions just given are simply the least
contested. The chapter as a whole amounts, in effect, to a detailed explanation of how (and by whom) agreement has been reached on so precise a
division of authorship.

Recent scholarship holds that the play was first acted in 1613—probably
at Blackfriars in the autumn of that year. The dating evidence (reviewed
in Appendix A) also indicates that performances were probably given about
1619 and that a revival took place about 1626. Other early performances may
have been staged, but those of 1613, c.1619, and c.1626 are the only ones for
which any evidence is known to survive.

The play was first published—and the first direct reference to its authorship recorded—in 1634. A manuscript was entered to John Waterson in
the Stationers' Register on 8 April of that year:

8 Aprilis.

M^r. Io: Waterson Entred for his Copy vnder the hands of S^r. Hen: Herbert & m^r Aspley warden a TragiComedy called the two noble kinsmen by Io: ffletcher & W^m. Shakespeare vj^d.

(Greg, *Bibliography*, I, 43)

The title-page of the quarto does not call the play a "TragiComedy," but its wording is otherwise sufficiently arresting:

THE

TWO

NOBLE

KINSMEN:

Presented at the Blackfriers

by the Kings Maiesties servants,

with great applause:

Written by the memorable Worthies

of their time;

{ M^r. *John Fletcher,* and } Gent.
{ M^r. *William Shakspeare.* }

[Device: McKerrow 283]

Printed at *London* by *Tho. Cotes,* for *Iohn Waterson:*

and are to be sold at the signe of the *Crowne*

in *Pauls* Church-yard. 1 6 3 4.

Shakespeare had been dead for eighteen years, Fletcher for nine, and Waterson—a bookseller who published seven other plays owned by the King's company—was presumably responsible for describing the dramatists as "memorable Worthies of their time." Thomas Cotes, successor to the Jaggard firm and one of the busiest of Caroline printers, is perhaps best known as printer of the Shakespeare Second Folio of 1632 and of the Sixth Quarto of *Pericles* (in which he then owned the copyright) in 1635. Waterson would be more likely than Cotes to have been responsible for the wording of the title-page, and the entry in the Stationers' Register implies that the attribution to Shakespeare and Fletcher derived either from the manuscript or from Waterson; the occasional suggestion by critics that Cotes's other ventures in Shakespearean publication might have some bearing on the problem of authorship seems to be without substance.

Title-page attributions do not always carry much weight. Chapman's *The Ball* was attributed to Chapman and Shirley in the quarto of 1639, Shirley's *The Coronation* was attributed to Fletcher in the quarto of 1640, and both of these false ascriptions have been blamed in part upon errors in Cotes's printing-house.[1] In addition to *The Two Noble Kinsmen,* John Waterson issued only two other King's company plays by a dramatist no longer alive at the dates of publication, *The Elder Brother* (1637) and *Monsieur Thomas* (1639); the title-pages attributed both to Fletcher alone, although some critics believe Massinger to have been co-author of *The Elder Brother.*[2] The title-page ascriptions to Shakespeare of *The London Prodigal* in 1605 and *A Yorkshire Tragedy* in 1608 are as famous as they are wildly improbable. But since the title-page of *The Two Noble Kinsmen* records an attribution which most present-day critics accept, there is perhaps little now to be gained by speculation on its inherent reliability or on Waterson's probity, and the dual attribution may be allowed to serve as our starting point.

Our present concern, however, is with the actual determination of the supposed shares of the two authors. The most commonly accepted assignments have had to rely, obviously, on various analyses of internal evidence. To review the circumstances within which those analyses were first conducted may prove convenient, and a brief chronological survey of the entire subject—first of the earlier publishing history of the play, then of the more influential scholarly studies—will therefore precede our first examination of the text.

Waterson transferred his rights in the play to Humphrey Moseley in 1646; the record of the transfer in the Stationers' Register makes no mention of Shakespeare, listing the play along with other properties (Waterson had been half-owner of the first) as below:

The 31th. of October 1646

M[r] Moseley. Assigned ouer vnto him by vertue of a Note vnder the hand & seale of M[r] Waterson & both the wardens All the Estate right Title & Interest w[ch] the said M[r] Waterson hath in these Playes following (viz[t])

> The Elder Brother   his part ⎫
> Mounsieur Thomas.   ⎬ by M[r] fflesher
> The Noble kinsman   ⎭

(Greg, *Bibliography,* I, 57)

Moseley's most famous publication, the Beaumont and Fletcher First Folio of 1647, excluded plays that had previously appeared in print, but it was presumably through Moseley that *The Two Noble Kinsmen* eventually found its way into the Beaumont and Fletcher Second Folio of 1679 (the second appearance of the play in print) and thence into the Fletcher canon. Mose-

---

[1] A. H. Stevenson, "Shirley's Publishers: The Partnership of Crooke and Cooke," *The Library,* 4th Ser., XXV (1945), 147–150. Cf. also *SB,* XVIII (1965), 265–266.

[2] Cf. Gerald E. Bentley, *The Jacobean and Caroline Stage,* III (1956), 332–336.

ley advertised copies of the play—no doubt the stock he had acquired from Waterson—during the 1650's, and presumably he retained the rights to it until his death in 1661. Although no transfer records have been found, Moseley's property must have passed from his widow into the hands of the booksellers who published the 1679 Folio.[3] It was a matter of course for the play to appear thereafter in collected editions of Beaumont and Fletcher.

Three such collected editions, and therefore three editions of *The Two Noble Kinsmen,* appeared during the eighteenth century. Jacob Tonson reprinted the contents of the Second Folio in 1711. The Theobald-Seward-Sympson edition of Beaumont and Fletcher was published in 1750; Theobald had died in 1744, and Volume X of this edition, in which the first formally edited text of our play appeared, was mainly the work of Thomas Seward. Another edition, prepared by George Colman (the elder) and others, was published in 1778; the Colman edition contained a but slightly revised reprint of the Seward text and was distinguished mainly for the annotations that Colman and his colleague Isaac Reed added to the notes of the 1750 editors.

Charles Lamb printed extracts from the play in his popular *Specimens of the English Dramatic Poets* (1808), and his confident assertion that Shakespeare was part-author was seconded by the next editor of the play, Henry Weber, in his Beaumont and Fletcher of 1812. Lamb's opinion no doubt also influenced Charles Knight to include the play in his Pictorial Edition of Shakespeare—in the undated volume of *Doubtful Plays* which appeared about 1841. This was the first edition of Shakespeare's works to include the play, although Knight appended an essay (to be described later) expressing his belief that Shakespeare could not have written any of it. Many later nineteenth-century editors, however, came to accept the play, and Dyce, Skeat, Collier, Rolfe, and Hudson were among those whose editions of Shakespeare included it.

The acceptance of the play by several Shakespearean editors was a reflection of its wider acceptance among critics in general. We might now turn back to the origins of this acceptance in the history of critical opinion.

Serious attempts to arrive at a division between authors were not undertaken before the middle of the eighteenth century, and the division now most generally accepted was not settled before the middle of the nineteenth.

---

[3] For these reasons the play would presumably not have been available to Philip Chetwinde if he had wished to include it among the other works—*Pericles* and six minor apocrypha—which he added to the second issue (1664) of his Shakespeare Third Folio. Critics of the past who sometimes treated the omission of *TNK* from the Chetwinde Folio as relevant to the problem of authorship did not take the question of copyright into account.

Pope once remarked that to him the play bore "little resemblance of *Fletcher*," and in fact that it more resembled plays by Shakespeare "than some of those . . . received as genuine"; his comment in the Preface to his 1725 edition of Shakespeare was so brief and casual that it has usually been ignored—especially as the play was omitted from his edition—but perhaps any comment by Pope should be recorded in full:

we may conclude him [Shakespeare] to be . . . conversant with the Ancients of his own country, from the use he has made of *Chaucer* in *Troilus* and *Cressida,* and in the *Two Noble Kinsmen,* if that Play be his, as there goes a [play-house?] Tradition it was, (and indeed it has little resemblance of *Fletcher,* and more of our Author than some of those which have been received as genuine.)
(vol. I, p. xi)

Twenty-five years later the editor Seward suggested in the opening notes to his 1750 text that "it will be an Entertainment to the curious to distinguish the Hand of *Shakespear* from that of *Fletcher*"; Seward himself did not try to account for the authorship of every scene in the play, although in several of his notes he ascribed to Shakespeare a number of scenes now widely regarded as Fletcher's and to Fletcher certain scenes usually regarded as Shakespeare's. A different view was expressed by the editor Colman, who held in 1778 that the play should be regarded as the work of Beaumont and Fletcher. The next scholar to deal with the subject took still another tack; in an essay on *Pericles* published in 1780 George Steevens digressed at length on *The Two Noble Kinsmen* to argue that the whole play had been written by Fletcher. The observations that led Seward, Colman, and Steevens to their conclusions are not without interest, but since they had little perceptible influence on the later critics who worked out the division that has come down to us, they (and the remarks of Lamb as well) may be more fittingly reviewed in another chapter. It should, however, be remarked that the three editions of the play previous to Seward's (1634, 1679, and 1711) presented substantially similar texts, but that Seward introduced certain novelties into his 1750 edition which perhaps had more to do with the subsequently accepted division than his direct comments on authorship would suggest; Seward's was the first modernized text, and to its peculiar features and their significance we shall return presently.

The first comprehensive division was proposed in 1812. Appended to the text of the play in Weber's edition of Beaumont and Fletcher were sundry "Observations on the Participation of Shakspeare in the *Two Noble Kinsmen*" (XIII, 151–169); after citing the views of his predecessors, Weber proposed a particular assignment for each scene to one or the other dramatist. Lamb had been helpful in leading him to identify Act I and part of Act V as the work of Shakespeare, and the rationale of Weber's division appears to have been simply to assign to Shakespeare those scenes in Acts I, III, and V whose sustained rhetoric and ceremonious character make a strong immediate impression, and to assign to Fletcher most of the scenes in which the underplot of the Jailor's Daughter is worked out or in which low-comedy dialogue predominates. Specifically, he attributed to Fletcher the twelve scenes listed at the outset of the present chapter as well as II.i and III.ii. His discussion of these assignments in a few notes and in the final paragraphs of the "Observations" was quite cursory, however, as the following extract may illustrate:

The second act bears all the marks of Fletcher's style. Of the third, I should be inclined to ascribe the first scene to Shakspeare, and in the fourth, the third scene, which is written in prose; while the other scenes, in which the madness of the Jailor's Daughter is delineated, are in verse, according to the usual practice of Fletcher.

(p. 169)

The first complete division of the play to be proposed, in short, seems to have been little more than a mere outgrowth of the lengthening commentaries.

Although Weber offered little defense of his proposal, the want was supplied by the next student of the subject. A young Scotsman named William Spalding published a book-length study of the play in 1833, *A Letter on Shakspeare's Authorship of "The Two Noble Kinsmen"; a Drama commonly ascribed to John Fletcher.*[4] To the scenes Weber had given to Fletcher, Spalding added IV.iii and a brief passage in V.iv (the dialogue in which the Jailor converses with Palamon and his knights)—so that all of the underplot of the Jailor's Daughter would be assigned to Fletcher. Although Spalding thus did not much depart from Weber's division, his *Letter on Shakspeare's Authorship* was still the first major contribution to reasoned analysis of the subject—or at least it was the first contribution that later scholarship came to regard as consequential. Spalding's division was not very different from that which has come down to us, and the differences—they amount to three scenes—can be accounted for by the next item to be described.

In an essay printed by the *Westminster Review* in 1847, Samuel Hickson, reviewing Spalding's *Letter,* pointed out certain intricacies of dramatic

---

[4] The first edition (Edinburgh, 1833) is not widely accessible, but the *Letter* was republished by the New Shakspere Society in 1876 (N.S.S. Ser. VIII, no. 1) with marginal annotations and a Foreword by F. J. Furnivall. Subsequent references, given in the text, are to the reprint.

construction which made it difficult for him to regard the story of the Jailor's Daughter as a separately conceived unit. Hickson also observed several errors in Spalding's analysis; Spalding had evidently known only Weber's text, and Weber had arbitrarily combined two scenes into one in a way calculated to confuse the question of authorship; Hickson argued that Spalding was misled in assigning both II.i and II.ii (printed as a single scene by Weber) to Fletcher, and most later commentators and editors followed Hickson in assigning the first to Shakespeare. A fuller consideration of Spalding and Hickson may be reserved until later; here it need only be noted that, despite their early dates, these studies (both republished by the New Shakspere Society in the 1870's) remain among the most influential in the scholarly literature on the play. Later scholarship in general sought to corroborate Hickson's division by developing the evidence he had cited briefly in its support; the scenes listed in our opening paragraph are those which Hickson assigned unambiguously to Fletcher, and the few scene-ascriptions that some later scholars treated as uncertain have usually been those on which Hickson differed from Spalding.

Whatever the rightness of a view, one might expect to find it occasionally contested—if only from sheer perversity. While the main explanation of the success of Hickson's division is naturally to be sought in the character of the evidence brought forward to support it, a brief résumé of the scholarship between Hickson's time and our own may suggest other factors in its success and at the same time provide a needed context for the presentation of the evidence itself. During the later nineteenth century and the earlier decades of our own—the years during which disintegrationism flourished in Shakespearean scholarship—a few substitutes for Shakespeare as Fletcher's partner were sometimes proposed, the chief of whom was Massinger (advocated principally by Robert Boyle and H. Dugdale Sykes).[5] Shakespeare's participation in the play was of course defended vigorously and often, and in recent years has seldom been challenged. Studies by Willard Farnham, A. C. Bradley, Alfred Hart, Theodore Spencer, Kenneth Muir, and others—employing the most diverse criteria for judging the question—have argued on behalf of his partial authorship, and many of our leading Shakespearean authorities—including Chambers, Kittredge, Greg, Bentley, and McManaway—have concurred in this defense. But while no serious argument against Shakespeare's presence in the play has been

---

[5] Boyle and Sykes are cited elsewhere; probably more influential than either of them, however, was Tucker Brooke, who edited the only critical edition of *TNK* in our century and who indorsed Boyle's views in his Introduction to that edition, *The Shakespeare Apocrypha* (1908), pp. xl–xlv. But Brooke later recanted and accepted Shakespeare as co-author; cf. Baugh, Brooke, *et al., A Literary History of England* (1948), pp. 540, 576.

made for about forty years,[6] virtually all scholars who have supported the Shakespearean authenticity of about half the play have nevertheless felt obliged, whether out of historic necessity or considerations of tact, to adopt a defensive attitude, and this may help to explain the odd fact that Fletcher's responsibility for twelve scenes has usually been conceded with a minimum of explanatory discussion. To say that Hickson's views on the authorship of the play met with full success would be misleading, since Hickson was as deeply concerned as recent scholars have been to establish Shakespeare's presence, but those who urged a case for Massinger were at one with their opponents in treating the basic lines of division as a settled matter.

The most recent study of authorship, an effective presentation by Kenneth Muir of new evidence for Shakespeare, illustrates the characteristic procedure of critics with respect to evidence for Fletcher and will serve at the same time to introduce the first important class of this evidence.[7] The essay begins:

Littledale, in what is still the best edition of *The Two Noble Kinsmen* [1876–85], made two preliminary assumptions: (1) that two authors are discernible in the play; (2) that Fletcher is one of them. Every modern critic would, no doubt, make the same assumptions. The difference of style in the two portions is apparent even to the casual reader; and general impressions are substantiated by more objective tests. Littledale, for example, applied four metrical tests to the scenes he supposed to be by two different dramatists, and arrived at the following conclusions:

	Fletcher	Non-Fletcher
Light endings	3	52
Weak endings	1	35
Light + weak	4	87
Percentage of feminine endings	52.9	28.6
Percentage of unstopt lines	24.6	56.1

The above table alone would establish the fact that the play was written by more than one dramatist.

(p. 50)

A note adds, appropriately, that "metrical tests are no longer fashionable—it has become the fashion rather to sneer at them"; Muir proceeds to offer a

---

[6] The last fresh arguments for Massinger were advanced by W. J. Lawrence in 1921; but Lawrence, like Tucker Brooke, later changed his mind and indorsed Shakespeare as co-author; cf. pp. 295–296 in Appendix A.—There are nevertheless several contemporary scholars who privately hold that Shakespeare wrote none of the play, and this view was expressed publicly by Una Ellis-Fermor in a brief paper given orally in 1948 and posthumously published in her *Shakespeare the Dramatist* (1961); she does not undertake to examine evidence but merely proposes that the "mystery" of the play—a "dazzling imitation of Shakespeare's hand"—be accorded fresh investigation.

[7] Muir, "Shakespeare's Hand in *The Two Noble Kinsmen*," *Shakespeare Survey 11* (1958), pp. 50–59. Reprinted in Muir, *Shakespeare as Collaborator* (1960).

cautious defense of their merits as one possible means of substantiating the assumed division. It is probably true that all the criteria that have been cited and discussed, no matter how significant or trivial they seem to different observers, deserve attention; in any case, whether one holds metrical tests in high or low regard, Muir is justified in giving them prominence— for most of the scholars who were first concerned with the "objective" analysis of this play held such evidence in very high regard indeed. We shall therefore consider the tests in the next few pages, and incidentally glance at several related issues in the scholarly history of the play.

Metrical Tests and Lineation

Fletcher's versification, his heavy use of end-stopped feminine lines in particular, had been mentioned in connection with *The Two Noble Kinsmen* by Lamb in 1808, discussed again at somewhat greater length by Spalding, and received prominent attention in Hickson's article. Hickson did not actually compute metrical statistics on the play in 1847, but (as explained in Chapter III) it was his observations on the distinction between Shakespeare's and Fletcher's versification that seem to have prompted James Spedding to invent the metrical table in 1850. Spedding had appended a tabulation of verse measurements to his famous essay proposing the division of *Henry VIII* between Shakespeare and Fletcher, and he indicated his debt to the Hickson essay; the metrical test became the instrument by which Hickson's division of *The Two Noble Kinsmen* (as well as Spedding's counterpart division of *Henry VIII*) was verified for scholars later in the nineteenth century. The following comment by Harold Littledale, who prepared the important three-part New Shakspere Society edition of the play,[8] is characteristic of a surprisingly large proportion of other editorial

---

[8] The parts were issued as follows:

(a) 1876. *Reprint of the Quarto, 1634* (N.S.S. Ser. 2, no. 7). An exact type-facsimile to which line numbers have been added. Also contains an annotated Bibliography of editions to 1876 (pp. v–xii) and a Collation of the 1679 Folio text (pp. 91–107).

(b) 1876. *Revised Text and Notes* (N.S.S. Ser. 2, no. 8). The Littledale edition proper. An old-spelling text, modernized in punctuation and verse-lineation. Variant readings. Copious annotations.

(c) 1885. *General Introduction and List of Words* (N.S.S. Ser. 2, no. 15). Discussion of source and date (pp. 9*–29*). Review of authorship scene-by-scene (pp. 30*–68*). Summary of critical opinion to 1880 (pp. 69*–81*). Concordance (pp. 85*–197*).

Subsequent references are given in the text, with the parts identified as "1876 Q Reprint," "1876 Text," and "1885 Introduction" respectively.

and scholarly comment on the division of authorship and on Fletcher's share in the play:

> The metrical evidence is conclusive of two things already assumed. It clearly divides the verse-scenes between two distinct and dissimilar styles of versification, and shows that one part agrees absolutely with the known metrical peculiarities of Fletcher.
>
> (1885 Introduction, p. 18*)

Most commentators from Victorian times to the present have, like Muir, abandoned further analysis of Fletcher's versification once the metrical statistics have been referred to. Our present line of inquiry demands that we look more closely at this evidence.

A rather novel subject, however, claims precedence at this point. The metrical statistics collected from this play have not been based on the original quarto text but on one or another of the various nineteenth-century editions; with respect to such matters of immediate concern as the lineation of verse, these editions were in turn based largely upon Seward's. A comparative study of the 1634 quarto and the post-1750 editions reveals that there are many irregularities of lineation in the quarto, that some of these have been widely noted, and also that many others have not—that, in fact, Seward and later editors have introduced irregularities of their own. Their relevance to the metrical tests should soon become obvious.

Nearly all modern editors have been led to agree that the quarto incorrectly prints as verse two scenes that were evidently intended by the author as prose. All of II.i and most of IV.iii were set by the 1634 compositor in highly irregular long lines.[9] These lines are neither metrical as they stand nor susceptible to metrical rearrangement.[10] An example from one of these

---

[9] The text of II.i, still lined as verse in the editions of Seward and Colman, was first printed as prose by Weber in 1812. The case of IV.iii is a bit different; two speeches by the Jailor's Daughter had actually been set as prose by the 1634 compositor (reasons for his inconsistency will be suggested in Chapter II) and they may have led Seward to recognize the entire scene as prose. Seward's text was right, but Colman (perhaps in line with Augustan predilections for metrical order, or perhaps partly in reaction to an editorial predecessor whom he held in contempt) printed the entire scene—even the speeches printed as prose in 1634—as verse. Weber and later editors, however, have printed it correctly.

[10] A reader desirous to see an attempt to treat these scenes as verse may compare the transcription below of IV.iii.64–77, a wholly characteristic passage, with the same lines as printed by Colman. Observing that the quarto lines were hopelessly unmetrical, Colman sought to produce the appearance of verse (without verbal alterations) by redividing them, ending each as follows: distemper'd/ again/ faculties;/ vagary./ light/ permitted./ name/ her,/ attention,/ objects,/ eye,/ madness;/ she . . .

scenes (a speech by the Doctor to the Jailor and the Wooer on a cure for the madness of the Jailor's Daughter) should suggest that the editorial decision was virtually inescapable, for capitalized initial letters and a jagged right-hand margin seem to be all the evidence of verse to be found:

(the

Do. That intemprat surfeit of her eye, hath distemperd
Other sences, they may returne and settle againe to
Execute their preordaind faculties, but they are
Now in a most extravagant vagary. This you
Must doe, Confine her to a place, where the light
May rather seeme to steale in, then be permitted; take
Vpon you (yong Sir her friend) the name of
Palamon, say you come to eate with her, and to
Commune of Love; this will catch her attention, for
This her minde beates upon; other objects that are
Inserted tweene her minde and eye, become the prankes
And friskins of her madnes; Sing to her, such greene
Songs of Love, as she sayes *Palamon* hath sung in
Prison . . .

(IV.iii.64–77)

Although editors have not had to be persuaded that the lines are indeed prose, perhaps the reader will not find an attempt to account for the original errors purposeless; other material soon to be presented will seem less surprising if the recognized peculiarities in the quarto text of II.i and IV.iii can be explained.

The text is verbally excellent in both scenes, suggesting good copy, and the erroneous arrangement as verse is most easily attributed to a compositor. The length of the lines suggests that each printed line reproduces literally one line of prose, extending approximately to the right-hand side, in the manuscript. The first lines of most speeches, as in the example above, usually go farther to the right in the quarto than other lines (and must often therefore be printed, again as in the example above, as turn-overs), but this would be caused by the compositor's indentation of speech-prefixes, which in the manuscript would normally be written in the left-hand margins (so that, for example, *that* in line 64 would be written directly above *other* in line 65). Most dramatic manuscripts did not ordinarily distinguish between prose and verse through capitalization; dramatic verse was normally capitalized only when it came to be set in type. One possible explanation for the compositor's treatment of his copy in these scenes, although not a very satisfactory one, would be to regard the arrangement as an honest error due to his inexperience with dramatic poetry; coming to prose in II.i (all of Act I had been in regular verse), he may simply have failed to recognize the difference and continued to reproduce manuscript lineation and add capitals. An alternative and somewhat more plausible explanation (suggested originally in another connection by W. A. Jackson) might be that a printing-house employee, paid according to the number of pages or formes he composed, would be tempted deliberately to space out prose as verse in order to increase his earnings. But whatever the explanation for his behavior, the total of more than one hundred forty lines of prose-printed-as-verse in the quarto text of these two scenes alone well exceeds the total number of similarly spurious lines of verse in the entire text of any of the Shakespearean "good quartos" or in the entirety of any Folio text.

Two further points might be added regarding the text of II.i and IV.iii. The first is that these two scenes are the only ones printed as prose in modern editions of the play. The second is that both scenes contain speeches of considerable length (one speech exceeds thirty lines), and that this circumstance must have helped to make the quarto errors obvious to most editors; if some capricious editor had attempted to rearrange the speeches to make them appear to conform to some sort of metrical pattern (as Colman [cf. note 10] tried in IV.iii), their length alone would probably have sufficed either to deter him or to expose him at once (as in effect Weber exposed Colman). If on the other hand the scenes had been composed largely or entirely of briefer speeches, a misguided editor might have been able to pass off prose as verse with less trouble; he might, for example, contract or expand a few expressions in his text to make his quasi-metrical lineation appear more plausible, and even if his alterations were noticed, few scholars before the recent past would have raised their eyebrows at such practices. That these reflections are more than airy speculation should become clear as we turn to other scenes in the play.

Act II scene iii opens with a blank verse soliloquy by Arcite (lines 1–23); it closes with another such soliloquy by Arcite (lines 89–97). Between these two speeches four Countrymen enter and converse with one another and with Arcite; the entire middle episode (lines 24–88) appears to have been written as prose, but the quarto compositor has printed it as a mixture of prose and verse—verse which appears suspiciously like the mislined prose of II.i and IV.iii; the following passage (in which the Countrymen are

speaking of the May Day entertainments they plan to present before Theseus) illustrates:

> Doe we all hold, against the Maying?
> 4. Hold? what should aile us?
> 3. *Arcas* will be there.
> 2. And *Sennois.*
> And *Rycas,* and 3. better lads nev'r dancd under green Tree,
> And [ye] know what wenches: ha?
> But will the dainty Domine, the Schoolemaster keep touch
> Doe you thinke: for he do's all ye know.
> 3. Hee'l eate a hornebooke ere he faile: goe too, the mat-
> ter's too farre driven betweene him, and the Tanners daugh-
> ter, to let slip now, and she must see the Duke, and she must
> daunce too.
> 4. Shall we be lusty.
> 2. All the Boyes in Athens blow wind i'th breech on's,
> and heere ile be and there ile be, for our Towne, and here
> againe, and there againe: ha, Boyes, heigh for the wea-
> vers.
> 1. This must be done i'th woods.
> 4. O pardon me.
> 2. By any meanes our thing of learning s[ay]s so: where he
> himselfe will edifi[e] the Duke most parlously in our behalfes:
> hees excellent i'th woods, bring him to'th plaines, his lear-
> ning makes no cry.
> 3. Weele see the sports, then every man to's Tackle: and
> Sweete Companions lets rehearse by any meanes, before
> The Ladies see us, and doe sweetly, and God knows what
> May come on't.
> 4. Content; the sports once ended, wee'l p[e]rforme. Away
> Boyes and hold.

(II.iii.37–65)

Modern editions (exemplified here by the Kittredge text of 1936) print the
passage and re-number the lines as follows:

> Do we all hold against the Maying?
> 4.   Hold?   [36
> What should ail us?
> 3.   Arcas will be there.

    2.   And Sennois.
And Rycas; and three better lads nev'r danc'd
Under green tree; and ye know what wenches, ha?
But will the dainty domine, the schoolmaster,   [40
Keep touch, do you think? for he does all, ye know.
    3. He'll eat a hornbook ere he fail. Go to!
The matter is too far driven between
Him and the tanner's daughter to let slip now;
And she must see the Duke and she must dance too.   [45
    4. Shall we be lusty?
    2.   All the boys in Athens
Blow wind i'th'breech on us; and here I'll be,
And there I'll be, for our town, and here again,
And there again. Ha, boys, heigh for the weavers!
    1. This must be done i'th'woods.
    4.   O, pardon me!   [50
    2. By any means; our thing of learning says so—
Where he himself will edify the Duke
Most parlously in our behalfs. He's excellent i'th'woods;
Bring him to th' plains, his learning makes no cry.
    3. We'll see the sports; then every man to's tackle!   [55
And, sweet companions, let's rehearse by any means
Before the ladies see us, and do sweetly,
And God knows what may come on't.
    4.   Content. The sports
Once ended, we'll perform. Away, boys, and hold!   [59

Although the verbal changes (*matter's* to *matter is* in line 43, *on's* to *on us* in 47) are quite inconsequential in themselves, the editorial license they represent was characteristic of the Seward text; these changes were almost as common in the nineteenth-century texts on which the metrical tests were based, and—along with the suspicious verse-lineation they were designed to facilitate—they survive, as we have just seen, in more recent editions.

Another example, from a later scene which also appears to be prose that the quarto misprinted as verse, illustrates further the Seward method:

    Doct. Has this advice I told you, done any good upon her?
    Wooer. O very much; The maids that [k]ept her company
Have halfe perswaded her that I am *Palamon;* within this
Halfe houre she came smiling to me, and asked me what I
Would eate, and when I would kisse her: I told her
Presently, and kist her twice.

                                            (V.ii.1–6)

The same passage is printed as follows by Littledale in the 1876 Text of the New Shakspere Society edition:

> *Doct.* Has this advice I told you done any good upon her?
> *Woo.* O very much; the maids that kept her company
> Have halfe perswaded her that I am Palamon;
> Within this halfe houre she came smiling to me,
> And asked me what I'ld eate, and when I'ld kiss her;
> I told her presently, and kist her twice.

The new lineation and the contraction "I'ld" originated with Seward but were retained by most later editors.

The longest of the few prose speeches that were actually printed as prose in 1634 is the speech by Gerrold the Schoolmaster at the beginning of Act III scene v:

> *Sch.* Fy, fy, what tediosity, & disensanity is here among ye? have my Rudiments bin labourd so long with ye? milkd unto ye, and by a figure even the very plumbroth & marrow of my understanding laid upon ye? and do you still cry where, and how, & wherfore? you most course freeze capacities, ye ja[n]e Iudgements, have I saide thus let be, and there let be, and then let be, and no man understand mee, *proh deum, medius fidius,* ye are all dunces: For why here stand I. Here the Duke comes, there are you close in the Thicket; the Duke appeares, I meete him and unto him I utter learned things, and many figures, he heares, and nods, and hums, and then cries rare, and I goe forward, at length I fling my Cap up; marke there; then do you as once did *Meleager,* and the *Bore* break comly out before him: like true lovers, cast your selves in a Body decently, and sweetly, by a figure trace, and turne Boyes.

> (III.v.1–16)

There seems no reason to believe that the manuscript had been arranged as verse that the compositor misread as prose. A reader might amuse himself by attempting to dispose these lines into iambic pentameter (or any other meter), but he would probably soon find himself obliged to introduce rather drastic variations into whatever measure he had chosen, and he might also find it difficult to justify either the initial choice of a verse-arrangement or the variations needed to sustain any such arrangement. Seward nevertheless wrenched the passage into lines ranging from tetrameter to hexameter and editors have followed suit ever since. The passage is highly rhythmic, to be sure, but much other dramatic prose of the period is no less rhythmic, and

Seward's rearrangement has never, as a matter of fact, been defended on this or any other ground during all the years since it first appeared.[11]

Seward did, however, provide hints in one or two notes as to the way in which he thought about lineation. Apart from the opening prose speech just cited, a song by the Jailor's Daughter, and Gerrold's prologue and epilogue to the morris dance, the text of III.v consists of short speeches which in the quarto are printed indifferently as prose or (highly improbable) verse. These speeches were usually rearranged by Seward, and in one rare instance he commented upon his rearrangement. The speech in question is this:

> 3. Ther's a dainty mad woman M^r. comes i'th Nick as
> mad as a march hare: if wee can get her daunce, wee are
> made againe: I warrant her, shee'l doe the rarest gambols.
>
> (III.v.73–75)

Seward printed the following revision—

> 3. There is a dainty mad Woman, *Magister,*
> Comes i'th'Nick, as mad as a March Hare;
> If we can get her dance, we're made again:
> I warrant her, she'll do the rarest Gambols.

—and explained in a note:

As most, and I believe all the Countrymens Speeches are in Verse, I fancy *Mr.* stood for *Magister* here. [Editors since 1812 print *master.*] The Schoolmaster's first Speech and the greatest Part of this Scene was printed as Prose. But I have found it running easily into Measure, which *Fletcher*'s Drollery . . . frequently does . . .

Since Seward assigned several underplot scenes to Shakespeare, the reason he gave this one to Fletcher might be noted:

This Schoolmaster and his Fellow-Comedians seem very like the Farcical Clowns in *Midsummer-Night's Dream,* and other Plays of *Shakespear;* yet it seems probable that *Fletcher* had the greatest Share of this, as the Quotation from *Tully*'s Oration against *Catiline* [referring to Gerrold's exclamation *Quo usque tandem* at line 38], and all the Latinisms of the *Schoolmaster* seem wrote by one who was more ready in *Latin* Quotations than *Shakespear;* who . . . seems to have had no more *Latin* than falls to the Share of a very young Schoolboy . . .

Seward's opinion of Holofernes is not recorded.

[11] Littledale once spoke of Seward as a "metrical Procrustes" whose text had been "stretched or lopped" (1876 Q Reprint, p. viii), but he himself corrected only the very worst of Seward's extravagances and other editors seem to have ignored the matter of lineation entirely.

"The question of lineation . . . has emerged lately into the 'live border' of Shakespeare study" (C. J. Sisson), and our final examples of editorial lineation in *The Two Noble Kinsmen* may be thought to bear on editorial procedures still current elsewhere. In scenes which are on the whole written in regular verse one often finds extended passages of dialogue composed mainly or entirely of speeches less than ten syllables in length which editors commonly rearrange into pentameter verse. The dialogue below from Act II scene ii represents nine short lines (lines 192–200) in the 1634 quarto; editors from Dyce to Kittredge have stepped them into four:

Palamon. You love her then?
Arcite.   Who would not?
Palamon.   And desire her?   [158
Arcite. Before my liberty.   [159
Palamon. I saw her first.
Arcite.   That's nothing.
Palamon.   But it shall be.   [160
Arcite. I saw her too.
Palamon.   Yes, but you must not love her.   [161

In metrical tests this passage would count as three feminine endings and one irregular half-line. It is not clear, however, that such passages were originally conceived as part of any kind of five-foot measure; the decision to treat them as such has been characteristic of editorial taste for two centuries, but the irregular line 159 is a witness to the arbitrariness of the decision. The same questions about the presence of a metrical norm may arise when one observes similar dialogue in the canonical plays (especially the later plays) which editors likewise insist on treating as pentameter; the following passage from *Antony and Cleopatra* II.ii, for example, constitutes "line 28" in most editions:

Caesar. Welcome to Rome.
Antony.   Thank you.
Caesar.   Sit.
Antony.   Sit, sir.
Caesar.   Nay, then.

But such curiosities are less widespread in modern editions of Folio plays than in the editions of *The Two Noble Kinsmen*. The extensive printing of prose as verse in II.i and IV.iii of the Cotes Quarto may serve as an index to the extent of the errors elsewhere—errors compounded by Seward and subsequent editors. Specifically, a conservative estimate of the erroneous lineation in the post-1750 editions would be that approximately four hundred lines of prose are misprinted as verse, and that about two hundred additional lines constructed by editors out of such brief speeches as those cited above represent verse lineation too dubious (and lacking in authority) to serve as a sound basis for metrical tests. Passages of twenty or more quarto lines which ought to be printed as prose but which modern editors print as verse are to be found at II.iii.24–88 (lines 24–73 in the Kittredge text), III.iii. 21–71 (16–53 in Kittredge), III.v.1–61 (1–58), III.v.73–105 (72–99), IV.i.18– 70 (16–51), IV.i.127–196 (105–152), and V.ii.1–163 (1–112). Extended passages of short-line dialogue turned by editors into artificial pentameter occur at II.ii.135–162 in the quarto (122–136 in Kittredge), II.ii.175–200 (146– 161), II.ii.319–342 (259–274), and III.vi.56–91 (49–69). There are, in addition, many doubtful shorter passages, but the examples just listed should suffice to indicate the extent of the trouble.

Nearly all the erroneous and doubtful lineation is found within scenes ascribed to Fletcher, which together comprise about 1450 lines in modern editions. The remaining scenes in these editions are generally free of such errors; they include the two scenes inaccurately printed as verse in 1634 but now corrected to prose, and ten scenes of regularly lined verse in which a few questionable details about half-line speech-endings and the like may be regarded as negligible. Every modern text, moreover, introduces into the scenes ascribed to Fletcher a host of minor verbal alterations (contractions or expansions of the sort we observed earlier) whose purpose is clearly to render the metrical arrangements more plausible; yet even with recourse to such liberties, not one modern edition has failed to print as pentameter many lines that the most broad-minded reader would be forced to reject, and whose authority does not go back farther than Seward. A final brief example may be cited from Gerrold's prose speech at III.v.1–16 (quoted earlier); editors print the following passage as lines 11–13:

> Proh deum, medius fidius, ye are all dunces!
> For-why here stand I; here the Duke comes; there are you
> Close in the thicket. The Duke appears; I meet him . . .

The metrical tests do not stand up very well on close inspection.

It should be recalled that there have been relatively few editions of *The Two Noble Kinsmen*—many fewer, for example, than of *Pericles*. There was, of course, no Cambridge, Globe, or Variorum text. The metrical liberties found in many pre-Cambridge editions of Folio plays (presumably owing something to the misapplication of the classical conventions within which both the best and worst of early editors were trained) have been reduced somewhat in more recent years. The original mislineation in the

Cotes Quarto not only provided a more generous invitation to this sort of editorial liberty than did most Folio texts, but the scholar who set the initial standards was, almost by common consent, one of the least adept of all eighteenth-century editors. Among those who have observed his work, R. B. McKerrow has remarked (in his Introduction to *Wit Without Money*) on the "very numerous and daring alterations" with which Seward brought his texts "into metrical form." A century earlier Coleridge had commented: "Mr. Seward! Mr. Seward! you may be, and I trust you are, an angel; but you were an ass." [12] If in addition it is recalled that *The Two Noble Kinsmen* was merely one play among the more than fifty in the Beaumont and Fletcher collections in which it was most often published, it should not seem merely presumptuous to say that it has seldom been edited with adequate care.

The most carefully prepared modern text, as the remark by Muir quoted earlier rightly suggests, is that edited by Littledale, and it is from this text that most of the generally accredited metrical statistics were gathered. Although Littledale was not wholly ignorant of the bearing of lineation on those statistics, his decisions on the subject were remarkable, and they help to indicate to us something of the climate of opinion within which Victorian scholarship came to general agreement on the division of authorship. The following paragraph is Littledale's opening note on II.iii, the second scene of the play in which the presence of prose is unquestionable and the first in which (as we saw earlier) even the versifying compositor gave up and printed a few speeches as prose:

"In my paper on Fletcher, I have shown that Fletcher never wrote *prose* in any of his plays."—Rev. F. G. Fleay, *N.S.S. Trans.*, pt. I. 1874, App. p. 62*. I follow Dyce's arrangement, in the hope that these lines may appear metrical: certainly not a few seem to me *prose*.

(1876 Text, p. 136)

Littledale evidently allowed his deference to the authority of Dyce and Fleay to count for more than the evidence before his eyes.

During the next few years Littledale prepared his *General Introduction* to the New Shakspere Society edition. Metrical statistics had already been published in 1874 to confirm Hickson's division of the play, but—as Littledale noted in the 1885 Introduction (p. 21*)—they were not wholly reliable.[13] To replace them he included a full new set of verse measurements

---

[12] *Literary Remains of Samuel Taylor Coleridge,* ed. H. N. Coleridge, II (1836), 290.
[13] F. G. Fleay and F. J. Furnivall prepared metrical tables from Weber's and Dyce's texts for *TNK* which were published in the N.S.S. *Transactions* for 1874 (Appendix, pp. 61*–65*). The leading N.S.S. statistician had been Fleay—it was he, for example, who

(the same ones given in Muir's table) based on his own text of 1876. Commenting on the discrepant figures for the "two parts" of the play, Littledale said that "such divergences, consistently preserved throughout, cannot be lightly scorned as the frenzied fancies of maniacal metremongers" (p. 23*). One may suppose that Littledale had never become fully alert to the extent of the lineation problems involved, and that whatever he had perhaps once become aware of while working on the text he had since dismissed or forgotten. It should be added that no later figures have been compiled from a more reliable text; the figures newly compiled by Chambers in 1930 for the Metrical Tables in *William Shakespeare,* for example, were based, as Chambers noted (II, 408), on the 1897 "Temple Dramatists" edition of the play by C. H. Herford, a text virtually identical with Littledale's with regard to lineation and one which retains quite as many Sewardisms (e.g. contractions of "I would" to "I'd") as any other modern edition.

If, furthermore, the metrical tests did not have to be dismissed on the ground that they were based on inaccurate texts and sometimes on bad arithmetic, they would still be open to the objection that the kind of data they record are not very sensitive indicators of differences in dramatic style. They may measure the number of syllables to a line, but they are hardly able to measure with precision those particular personal cadences and rhythms that one is sometimes able to experience as characteristic of a particular writer. To devise a mathematical representation of a writer's style adequate to the purposes which the Victorians claimed to achieve by their tests would require—if indeed such a representation could be achieved at all—the gifts of a Von Neumann; the belief held by Muir and others that a small table of unexamined statistics "alone would establish the fact that the play was written by more than one dramatist" does not compel assent.

Before we advance to a new subject, the odd-sounding remark by Fleay "that Fletcher never wrote *prose* in any of his plays" (cited above in Littledale's note) deserves a moment's notice; for it embodies yet another argument about the authorial division which seems once to have been regarded

---

had published in the 1874 *Transactions* the metrical data on Fletcher to which Littledale alluded when he spoke of Fletcher's "known metrical peculiarities" (cf. p. 22 above)—and the following observation on Fleay's work may therefore be worth noting. Commenting in 1930 on the metrical statistics for Shakespeare which Fleay had collected from the Globe edition, Chambers (*William Shakespeare,* I, 257) had this to say:

Unfortunately Fleay's . . . totals often do not add up to anything like the Globe lines and sometimes diverge to the extent of hundreds. It is not very creditable to modern scholarship that these figures have been constantly reproduced down to Professor Tucker Brooke's *Shakespeare of Stratford* in 1926.

with respect. The supporting evidence (no doubt more satisfactory to Fleay's generation than to us) is that there appears to be virtually no prose in the plays which have been accepted as Fletcher's unaided work—or at least that editors have rarely printed prose in the texts of those plays. This point was made as early as 1812 by Weber in connection with questions of authorship in the Beaumont and Fletcher canon; it was cited by Hickson (along with other evidence) to support his ascription of II.i and IV.iii to Shakespeare; it seems to have hardened into dogma by the later nineteenth century; and it survives in modified form in present-day scholarship.[14] If a scrupulously edited text had appeared in Victorian times, perhaps a few scholars of the period would have felt constrained to reassign certain scenes from Fletcher to another dramatist. But attention has been drawn to this altogether trivial issue merely for the sidelight it may be thought to cast on earlier scholarly approaches to problems of authorship.

Few scholars today would regard either the metrical tests or the arguments from the use of prose with quite the solemnity with which they were once taken. Yet for at least two generations they were the principal evidence alleged by Victorian literary science and its post-Victorian adherents on behalf of the Hickson division; by the common standards of what constituted objective evidence for the Victorians, in fact, they were almost the only such evidence cited before the present century. Whoever has had occasion to examine the *Transactions* of the New Shakspere Society will not be surprised at this statement; the hundreds of pages devoted to tabulating and discussing metrical statistics were a normal manifestation of the notions of objectivity held in their culture; Lord Kelvin was a more typical Victorian scientist than Darwin. In our own time the scientist and the literary critic are more likely than their predecessors to take into conscious account how broadly they share certain premises; the meaning of any expression is to be found by examining the criteria from which it derives, and our educated technician is apt to regard his simplest measuring instruments as "subjective" (as E. B. Wilson describes the voltmeter), while our literary critic is accustomed to describe in far greater detail than his predecessors the criteria for his judgments. If we turn to the Victorian critics who regarded the metrical data as sufficient confirmation for their literary opinions, we should not be surprised that they did not often make explicit the other criteria that lay behind those opinions. This is not to say, however, that it is always difficult to determine what those criteria were; the non-metrical arguments which helped to establish the received division of authorship were based on a limited number of clearly identifiable assumptions. After a short

[14] Cf. Milton Crane, *Shakespeare's Prose* (1951), p. 42.

discussion of a small but essential detail in Act II of the play, we shall go
on to consider those arguments and assumptions.

The Staging of II.i and II.ii

Critics have sometimes argued about a detail of staging in Act II—specifically, about the location of Palamon and Arcite in the second scene. The
nineteenth-century interpretation of this staging question has something to
do with the evidence for authorship, and an explanation of that question
may provide a useful connective thread to trace through our later review
of the more comprehensive arguments and evidence. The staging question
has a certain additional interest, moreover, for it has apparently not yet
been solved.

The most relevant part of the quarto text is the concluding episode in II.i
and the opening of II.ii. Near the end of II.i, the Jailor and his Daughter,
standing presumably on the main platform (the "outer stage"), are talking
of the imprisoned Palamon and Arcite; the prisoners then make a brief,
mute appearance at what editors have called the windows of their prison
tower:

> *Iailor.* The Duke himselfe came privately in the night,
>
>   *Enter Palamon, and Arcite, above.*
> And so did they, what the reason of it is, I
> Know not: Looke yonder they are; that's
> *Arcite* looks out.
> *Daugh.* No Sir, no, that's *Palamon: Arcite* is the
> Lower of the twaine; you may perceive a part
> Of him.
> *Iai.* Goe too, leave your pointing; they would not
> Make us their object; out of their sight.
> *Daugh.* It is a holliday to looke on them: Lord, the
> Diffrence of men.   *Exeunt,*
>
>   Scæna 2. *Enter Palamon, and Arcite in prison.*
>
> *Pal.* How doe you Noble Cosen?
> *Arcite.* How doe you Sir?
> *Pal.* Why strong inough to laugh at misery. . . .

The conversation continues for over a hundred lines in which the young
men ring changes on the theme of their captivity. Then, after line 127 in
the quarto, *"Enter Emilia and her woman."* The ensuing dialogue indicates
that Emilia and her companion have entered on the main platform, which

here represents the garden outside the prison; they are observed by Palamon and Arcite from the prison but do not themselves see the cousins.

Editors to the present day add *below* to Emilia's entrance direction, assuming that Palamon and Arcite are seen *"above"* not only in scene i but also in scene ii—i.e. that the cousins leave the upper-level windows or gallery at the end of the first scene and return a moment later on the same stage. Weber, to avoid this apparently awkward departure and re-entrance, was moved to combine the two scenes into one, and the next few editors of the play (Dyce, Darley, Skeat) followed him in eliminating the intervening stage directions, leaving Palamon and Arcite on stage, above, to begin their dialogue as the Jailor and his Daughter depart. Littledale and subsequent editors restore the original scene-division and the intervening stage directions, but they also keep *below* in Emilia's entrance direction,[15] and they comment in their notes on the anomalous re-entrance which they believe the original text entails and which Weber had sought to correct. In short, editors have felt bound to choose between a difficulty of staging and abandonment of the original text. It seems that no one has ever suggested that the prison dialogue of the second scene might have taken place at the rear of the main platform or on the so-called "inner stage."[16]

When the cousins make their brief appearance *"above"* during the last moments of scene i (perhaps at a window, or perhaps at two separate windows), the audience is required to assume that they are so remote that the Jailor and his Daughter cannot clearly distinguish their features (as shown in the dialogue from "Looke yonder they are" through "leave your pointing"). Their long prison dialogue is easy and familiar in tone, creating the dramatic effect of intimacy and closeness with the audience. If the actors must actually be supposed to have played this scene on an upper stage, a re-entrance—anomalous or not—would seem the minimum requirement for sustaining dramatic illusion. But this is to invent unnecessary difficulties; the prison is the main focus of attention throughout II.ii, a scene which runs to 342 lines, and to present it on an upper stage, physically as well as

[15] The brief and somewhat vague note in Rolfe's edition of 1883—"In the old theatre the platform of the stage would be the garden, while the raised balcony at the back would be the interior of the prison"—typifies editorial comment in the nineteenth century. More recent editors (from Brooke in 1908 to Kittredge in 1936) say nothing about the staging question but retain Weber's *below* in their direction at Emilia's entrance.

[16] Or "enclosure" or "pavilion" or "recess" or "discovery space" (depending on the theory one holds about early staging): G. E. Bentley's admirably neutral term is "curtained place." It might be mentioned that at the Blackfriars, where *TNK* was probably first performed, the main platform was almost certainly shallower than that of the Globe, and most authorities agree that there was probably a larger "curtained place."

psychologically distant from the audience, would be a pointless piece of stupidity. The mass of textual evidence reviewed in theatrical scholarship in recent years supports the view that upper-level appearances in plays acted at both the Globe and Blackfriars were rare and usually brief; [17] the placing of the prison chamber toward the rear of the main platform would seem to be recommended by simple common sense; and the wording of the original directions—first *"above,"* then *"in prison"*—makes a dramatically appropriate distinction whose authority appears to have been abandoned without its ever having been considered. There may be a further small confirmation of this distinction in the text; late in the scene—Emilia and her woman have now left the garden—the Jailor returns, entering the prison chamber to release Arcite and to remove Palamon to a more cloistered part of the prison because, in the chamber represented here, "the windows are too open" (line 323).

If there is insufficient warrant for assuming that *above* and *in prison* were originally both intended to mean *above*,[18] there would seem to be even less warrant for basing arguments about the division of authorship on any such assumption. The actual instances in which this question of scene-transition has entered into the authorship question will appear as we proceed. Strictly speaking, however, the staging problem has been the creation of uninformed scholarship, and the quarto text creates no difficulty at all.

Spalding, Hickson, and the Later Victorians

Before Spalding, it will be recalled, the arguments about the authorship of the play had come to no settled agreements. The various opinions of Pope, Seward, and Steevens referred to earlier indicate that the authorship of individual scenes was by no means regarded as self-evident before the nineteenth century. When Weber offered a complete scene-by-scene breakdown, he provided his successors with a useful lead; even so, in 1828 De

---

[17] Even at the time Chambers published *The Elizabethan Stage* (1923) it was recognized that in plays given at Blackfriars action taking place "above" was "generally a very slight action, amounting to little more than the use by one or two persons of a window or a balcony. . . . The importance of the upper stage in the plays of the King's men sensibly diminishes after their occupation of the Blackfriars" (III, 153).

[18] Even a critic who would insist on placing the second-scene prison chamber in a gallery would be justified only in assuming that the brief and more distant first-scene appearance of the cousins took place at a still higher level (e.g. in a third-level musicians' gallery); he cannot assume that the distinction between *above* and *in prison* is no distinction at all and then go on to complain that the text fails to provide a distinction which is theatrically necessary. That, in effect, is what critics who have complained of an "anomalous re-entrance" have done.

Quincey asserted his conviction that the play was entirely the work of a single writer—in his view Shakespeare (cf. page 263 below)—and it was not until the middle years of the century that, largely through the efforts of Spalding and Hickson, the clear disparity of two styles in the play came to be regarded as axiomatic.

Spalding's 1833 *Letter* reviewed what little was then known about the provenance of the play, compared the versification of Shakespeare and Fletcher, and concluded with a general philosophic essay on poetry and drama. A scene-by-scene analysis of the play occupied about one quarter of the 111-page *Letter,* and most of Spalding's energies here and elsewhere went as one would expect to arguing the case for Shakespeare; in 1833, as Spalding's sub-title suggests, the play was still often ascribed in its entirety to Fletcher. The Spalding division itself, as stated earlier, gave to Fletcher the twelve basic scenes still generally accepted as his, as well as II.i, III.ii, IV.iii, and the brief passage in V.iv in which the Jailor speaks with Palamon; the division made Fletcher responsible for all of the underplot and most of the more colloquial passages in the play. The assignments resembled some of those which used to be proposed by disintegrationist scholars for canonical plays, though statistical evidence for such a division was not yet deemed necessary in 1833 and Spalding relied on more personal arguments to carry his points.

On the scenes he assigned to Fletcher he seldom had much to say, although what he said was enough to make clear that he disliked nearly every one of them: "Neither [II.iii or II.iv] . . . have any thing in them worthy of particular notice" (p. 40); "the essential dulness of [II.i helps to] . . . absolve Shakspeare from the charge of having written it" (p. 35); and so forth. He calls the Jailor's Daughter a vulgar imitation of Ophelia, and his comment on V.ii illustrates the degree to which Fletcher served as a whipping-boy (a role he continued to play in later discussions of divided authorship); the scene, Spalding wrote,

is disgusting and imbecile in the extreme. It may be dismissed with a single quotation:
  Doctor. What stuff she utters!

(p. 49)

From frequent comments of this sort (Palamon and Arcite undergo "needless degradation" in III.iii, Emilia's indecision over which lover to choose in IV.ii shows "a want of insight into the nicer shades of association," and so forth), one is led to conclude that Spalding's criteria for the rejection of Shakespeare in parts of the play were largely moralistic—in the simplest possible sense of that tricky term. At one point Spalding asked his reader, in looking at the play, to "view its elements of thought and feeling less as the qualities of a literary work, than as the signs and results of the mental constitution of its author" (p. 82), and this way of thinking appears to have encouraged a certain exaggeration of moral differences in the two parts as Spalding distinguished them. Present-day opinion, at any rate, appears to be quite different—as typified by Kittredge's comment in his 1936 edition that, "Apart from one or two characteristic Fletcherian touches, there is nothing in the underplot to justify the heroics with which some critics have assailed it."

A few of the passages Spalding assigned to Fletcher were excepted from his general disapproval. Whether as a matter of independent judgment or as a result of prompting from Lamb or Hazlitt, he found much to praise in the prison dialogue between Palamon and Arcite at the beginning of II.ii. Coming to that part of the play which (following Weber's text) he identified as Act II scene i, he spoke admiringly of "the versified portion of this scene [i.e. our II.ii], which follows the prose dialogue among the inferior characters"; seeing no irony in the high-minded dialogue of the cousins, Spalding felt that Fletcher had for once "gathered no small portion of the flame and inspiration of his immortal friend and assistant" (p. 36). If the thought had crossed Spalding's mind that Fletcher's "assistant" might have written this scene, perhaps its erroneous appearance (in Weber's text) of unity with the preceding episode involving the Daughter and other "inferior characters" was a factor (however minor) in persuading him otherwise. In any case, it was at this point—regarding the relative merits of II.i and II.ii and the authorship of the former—that Hickson parted company with Spalding.

Hickson's 1847 essay on the play was printed as a review of three books, of which one was the Spalding *Letter* and the others were the editions of the play by Dyce (in his Beaumont and Fletcher of 1846) and Charles Knight (in the *Doubtful Plays* volume of his Pictorial Shakespeare).[19] Dyce generally followed Weber in his text and Spalding in his judgments on the problem of authorship, but Knight argued for a different view—one which calls for some attention at this point if Hickson's performance is to be fully intelligible. The Pictorial was a popular edition which enjoyed a much wider circulation than Spalding or Dyce. As mentioned earlier, although Knight was the first editor to include the play in a Shakespearean

---

[19] Hickson's review, untitled when first published in the 1847 *Westminster Review*, was reprinted with the title "The Shares of Shakspere and Fletcher in *The Two Noble Kinsmen*" in the N.S.S. *Transactions* for 1874 (Appendix, pp. 25*–61*). Subsequent references to Hickson, given in the text, are to the reprint.

collection, he appended to his text an essay attributing it to Fletcher and Chapman and attacking much of it for moral grossness. "It is perfectly evident that this underplot was of a nature not to be conceived by [Shakespeare]," he insisted, "and further not to be tolerated in any work with which he was concerned" (p. 178). Knight's widely disseminated essay provoked Hickson to a spirited and skillful reply. But while Hickson succeeded in demolishing the case for Chapman—it has never been seriously revived—the rather raucous middle-class proprieties for which Knight had been a spokesman continued to exert influence on later studies of the play, and they appear also to have played a curious part in Hickson's own proposals about the division of authorship. To this matter we shall return in a moment.

Between Spalding's and Knight's views on authorship, Hickson naturally favored those of Spalding, his difference from them appearing chiefly in his efforts to reassign II.i, III.ii, and IV.iii to Shakespeare. With regard to the first of these scenes, he had an advantage over Spalding in that Coleridge, in a statement published posthumously in 1835, categorically asserted that Shakespeare must have written it (cf. page 211 below), and as Hickson observed, "his authority will . . . weigh with some" (p. 38*). He also quoted from the scene admiringly and called attention to parallels elsewhere in Shakespeare, meanwhile commenting that the prison scene which follows had in his opinion "been over estimated" (p. 59*). But of equal importance with his other arguments concerning all three scenes, and indeed of greater importance for the entire division of authorship which he postulated, were the various moral factors on which he concentrated. It is in this connection that the Knight edition apparently best served his critical purposes.

The attitudes toward the play expressed in Knight's essay were reflected in his treatment of the text; his edition was the first to be considerably bowdlerized. Hickson's treatment of Knight involves some apparent contradictions, but with a bit of historical imagination they should not prove difficult to reconcile. One of the mad speeches of the Daughter in IV.iii begins, "Lords and courtiers that have got maids with child, they are in this place [Hell] . . ."; Hickson quoted the speech but deleted the words "that have got maids with child," adding a note at the point of deletion in which he remarked that "in the original a qualifying phrase here occurs, very shocking to Mr. Knight" (p. 49*). Hickson's own attitude, however, was more complex than his parody of the Knight text would suggest, for elsewhere in his essay he sounds almost as stuffy as Knight himself. In answering Knight's rejection of Shakespeare, for example, he referred to several parallels between the Daughter's speeches in IV.iii and certain of Lear's mad speeches, went on to chide Knight for his editorial inconsistency in expurgating the former and printing intact the latter, but nonetheless refrained from reproducing the passages from either play in his own article; they could not be exposed to public view detached from context, he said, for they contained "expressions, perhaps harmless in themselves, but repudiated by modern conventionalism" (p. 52*). Perhaps this was the tact of a debater addressing an audience he regarded as largely pharisees. Similarly, in defending II.i as Shakespeare's, he evidently felt constrained to reassure his readers that it exhibited "not a single gross word, or gross thought" (p. 38*).

Such language is familiar enough from popular Victorian dramatic commentaries, and wherever the kind of thinking it implies may once have encroached upon serious scholarship, the damage has probably since been undone and the subject is now best forgotten. But if Hickson himself shared few of the prejudices of his contemporaries, the pressures they exerted on him in a public discussion cannot be ignored in assessing his reasons for attributing certain scenes to Fletcher. Nor did these pressures diminish; it was a scholar writing for scholars who, a generation later, solemnly announced that although Shakespeare in his view was certainly the author of I.i, "assuredly Shakspere never wrote 1.27:—'And as you wish your womb may thrive with fair ones.'" This was Littledale (1885 Introduction, p. 31*), addressing himself primarily to his fellows in the New Shakspere Society. Scholars may occasionally be able to escape the values of their time and place, but they are usually too prudent to burn their passports.

On the whole Hickson was almost as brief as his predecessors in citing non-metrical evidence for Fletcher; he appears to have allowed to Fletcher those scenes which, under the circumstances in which he wrote, he found least amenable to public defense, and his method in general appears to have been to concede much to Fletcher in order to salvage more for Shakespeare. His fullest critical comment on a scene he assigned to Fletcher is confined to a few sentences in his comparison of the final two scenes—IV.iii and V.ii— in which the Daughter appears. In IV.iii the Doctor had advised the Wooer to disguise himself as Palamon (the speech is given on page 23); by the opening of V.ii the Wooer had carried out the advice (cf. page 26). Spalding and Knight had given both scenes to Fletcher, and Knight had impartially condemned both, having been shocked by the "unnatural and revolting union" between the girl and her disguised fiancé. After giving in detail his reasons for assigning the former scene to Shakespeare, Hickson sought to distinguish it from its sequel as sharply as possible; "it could never be imagined," he asserted, that the Doctor's words in IV.iii had been intended to convey meanings similar to those Hickson found in his words in V.ii:

That insight into the nature of his patient's disorder, displayed in so remarkable a manner by the doctor in [the] . . . former scene, in this has left him; and his business here seems to be to recommend and nurse up a sensual idea into an alliance with better feelings.

Hickson then sums up the differences:

We should observe that the former scene is in prose wholly, while this is in Fletcher's verse; but, in short, the tone and moral effect of the two scenes are so different,—the same characters have so altered an aspect,—the language, sentiments, and allusions are so unlike,—that the case of any one who can read and deliberately compare them, and still believe them to be by the same writer, we must give over as hopeless.

(pp. 53*–54*)

Our present concern is not to determine whether or not the two scenes are by the same writer, but it might be remarked that the alleged distinctions between the scenes have not seemed so sharp to all present-day critics (cf. Tynan on page 273 below), that the later scene also appears to be written in prose, and that Hickson's quotations from IV.iii failed to include those lines which most specifically connect it with V.ii—the Doctor's advice to the Wooer to "crave her, drink to her, and still among, intermingle your petition of grace and acceptance into her favor" (IV.iii.82–84).

The tone of Hickson's comments on V.ii is unlike anything else in his essay except the quotations he repeats with mocking scorn from Knight. His echo of Spalding's opinion of V.ii—"disgusting and imbecile in the extreme"—may therefore be due to the fact that he was defending IV.iii and might have undermined his assurances that no "gross thought" could be found in the scenes he claimed for Shakespeare had he not attributed the later scene to Fletcher as emphatically as possible. This is hardly to say that V.ii is morally gross, but the concluding part of this scene, probably the most chilling episode in the play to a typical English audience of 1847, may suggest the relevance of social factors to the Victorian division of authorship:

Doctor. I'll warrant you, within these three or four days I'll make her right again. You must not from her, but still preserve her in this way.
Wooer. I will.

Doctor. Let's get her in.
Wooer. Come, sweet, we'll go to dinner. And then we'll play at cards.
Daughter. And shall we kiss too?
Wooer. A hundred times.
Daughter. And twenty?
Wooer. Aye, and twenty.
Daughter. And then we'll sleep together.
Doctor. Take her offer.
Wooer. Yes, marry will we.
Daughter. But you shall not hurt me.
Wooer. I will not, sweet.
Daughter. If you do, love, I'll cry.   *Exeunt.*

Surely the critics who found an appeal to prurient interests in this lovely episode brought to the play a grotesquely inappropriate set of standards.

Little further discussion of divided authorship was published during the next few decades. The kind of scholarly attention the play did receive can best be indicated by the following small but representative example from the contributions of a textual critic and an important editor who adopted many of this critic's proposals. In III.vi Emilia begs Theseus to cancel his sentence against the lives of the kinsmen; the dialogue at this point may seem more characteristic of Shakespeare than of Fletcher:

> *Emilia.* Oh my noble brother,
>   That oath was rashly made, and in your anger;
>   Your reason will not hold it; if such vows
>   Stand for express will, all the world must perish.
>   Beside, I have another oath, 'gainst yours
>   Of more authority, I am sure more love,
>   Not made in passion neither, but good heed.
> *Theseus.* What is it, sister?
> *Pirithous.* Urge it home, brave lady.
> *Emilia.* That you would ne'er deny me anything
>   Fit for my modest suit and your free granting:
>   I tie you to your word now; if ye fall in't,
>   Think how you maim your honor . . .
>   Shall anything that loves me perish for me?
>   That were a cruel wisdom. Do men proin
>   The straight young bows that blush with thousand blossoms
>   Because they may be rotten? Oh Duke Theseus,
>   The goodly mothers that have groan'd for these,
>   And all the longing maids that ever lov'd,   [*]
>   If your vow stands, shall curse me and my beauty,

And in their funeral songs for these two cousins
Despise my cruelty, and cry woe worth me,
Till I am nothing but the scorn of women. . . .

(III.vi.276–288, 292–301)

In his *Critical Examination of the Text of Shakespeare* (posthumously published in 1860), William Sidney Walker proposed a number of alterations, both verbal and metrical, for the play. Typical among them was the suggestion that *them* be added to line 297 (marked above with an asterisk): "Both sound (the Fletcherian rhythm especially) and sense require 'that ever lov'd *them*.'" (III, 344). Dyce, who re-edited the play when he added it to his 1866 edition of Shakespeare, adopted this and various other proposals of Walker, and the notes in many later editions (Littledale, Skeat, Hudson, *et al.*) document the ways in which Walker and Dyce, in effect, gave the finishing touches to the metrical rearranging begun by Seward. As for the particular line in our passage, several later editors have wisely abandoned the addition, but it reappears—contracted to the presumably more "Fletcherian" *'em*—in Kittredge's text, and perhaps it would therefore be well to add with regard to its meaning that although we do indeed learn in III.iii that Palamon and Arcite have gone out with girls, Walker's reading (no doubt unintentionally) converts the young heroes' earlier experience into something of a debauch.

It is odd enough that such "Fletcherian" verse-reconstructions could be adopted by editors of the texts from which metrical statistics would then be gathered to verify the Fletcher assignments, but equally notable is the confidence about the scene-assignments that such scholars as Walker and Dyce attained as early as the middle years of the century; it testifies to the efficacy of the kind of arguments used by Spalding and his immediate successors. If we recall again that Pope and Steevens (among others) had agreed that the play was by a single dramatist, even though they disagreed on his identity, it was clearly not the inner light of individual taste that established the lines of division so distinctly and decided Fletcher's responsibility for certain scenes so easily. The element common to Spalding's, Knight's, Hickson's, and other Victorian treatments of the problem, but infrequent in earlier and later discussions, is the reliance on puritan attitudes we have been examining. Similar attitudes were not widely shared by readers of a century earlier (at least there is little trace of them in the notes of the eighteenth-century editions); they were surely alien to most Jacobean theatrical audiences; one piously hopes they are absent from present-day historical scholarship; but they were widespread when the play was first divided, and without taking the social context into account it would be hard to understand how the division came about. The contexts within which arguments are accepted appear almost to be among the conditions for the validity of the arguments themselves.

Since many lesser Jacobean dramatists—including, in criticism not concerned with either this play or *Henry VIII,* Fletcher himself—escaped the worst morality-mongering of the middle and later nineteenth century, it may be the special institutional character of Shakespeare's name that led to the peculiar treatment of this play. This point is merely speculative, but it is prompted by recollection of disintegrationist attempts to expunge passages from Folio plays as "spurious" when they could not be reinterpreted to render them acceptable to the tastes of the time—for example, *Troilus and Cressida,* as Chambers observed, was once "the happy hunting-ground of disintegrators"—and the dual ascription on the title-page of *The Two Noble Kinsmen* must have presented a powerful invitation to many Victorians to exercise the talents for moral discrimination on which they prided themselves. The issue for us is not, of course, the moral tastes of the Victorians, but whether or not those tastes were historically enlightened or critically adequate when they operated on this play, and part of the answer might be found in the later criticism that offered to verify the Hickson division.

The last quarter of the ninetenth century, the years after the New Shakspere Society began operations in 1874, saw renewed interest in the examination of the play. The discussions that appeared in publications of the Society were by far the most influential, especially those by two scholars, of somewhat different points of view, who were particularly concerned with this play—F. J. Furnivall and Harold Littledale.

Furnivall, the Director of the Society, was a leading exponent of what he himself (adapting the term from Biblical scholarship) called "the higher criticism." One of his comments on the authorship of a remarkable 67-line speech in V.i typifies much of the aesthetic criticism of the play at the time. Such criticism has never, of course, been wholly divorced from the problem of authorship. Part of the speech must be given first. The time is shortly before the final tournament; Palamon kneels with his attendant knights before the altar of Venus:

> Hail Sovereign Queen of Secrets, who hast power
> To call the fiercest tyrant from his rage
> And weep unto a girl; that hast the might,
> Even with an eye-glance, to choke Mars's drum
> And turn th'alarm to whispers; that canst make

A cripple flourish with his crutch, and cure him
Before Apollo; that mayst force the King
To be his subject's vassal, and induce
Stale gravity to dance. . . .
                            Take to thy grace
Me thy vow'd soldier, who do bear thy yoke
As 'twere a wreath of roses, yet is heavier
Than lead itself, stings more than nettles;
I have never been foul-mouth'd against thy law,
Ne'er reveal'd secret, for I knew none; would not,
Had I kenn'd all that were; I never practic'd
Upon man's wife, nor would the libels read
Of liberal wits; I never at great feasts
Sought to betray a beauty, but have blush'd
At simp'ring sirs that did; I have been harsh
To large confessors, and have hotly ask'd them
If they had mothers: I had one, a woman,
And women 'twere they wrong'd.   I knew a man
Of eighty winters—this I told them—who
A lass of fourteen brided; 'twas thy power
To put life into dust: the aged cramp
Had screw'd his square foot round,
The gout had knit his fingers into knots,
Torturing convulsions from his globy eyes
Had almost drawn their spheres, that what was life
In him seem'd torture: this anatomy
Had by his young fair fere a boy, and I
Believ'd it was his, for she swore it was,
And who would not believe her? . . .
                                (V.i.83–91, 100–124)

Perhaps the most ambitious and explicit speech in Shakespeare on the powers of love, Palamon's prayer to Venus annoyed a number of Victorians. Even in 1833 Spalding, evidently reacting more to subject matter than to dramatic purpose, referred to the last twelve lines cited (from "I knew a man/ Of eighty winters" to the end) as a "sketch of the deformity of decrepit old age" which he found "unpleasing," although he did not doubt but that the entire speech was "distinctly Shakspeare's" (p. 47). Furnivall, in his comments accompanying the Society's 1874 reprint of Hickson, had also accepted the scene as Shakespeare's, but in his Foreword to the Society's 1876 reprint of Spalding's *Letter* he recorded his own discomfort with the same passage that had displeased Spalding and claimed to find there a fault of characterization:

Is it likely, . . . at the end of his career, with all his experience behind him, that Shakspere would make his hero Palamon publicly urge on Venus in his prayer to her, that she was bound to protect him because he'd believd a wanton young wife's word that her old incapable husband was the father of her child? Is this the kind of thing that the Shakspere of Imogen . . . would put forward as the crown of his life and work? . . . It can hardly be.

(pp. vi–vii)

One marvels at the clairvoyant ability of the higher criticism to perceive essences of character directly, undistracted by mere words and unconcerned with mere drama. The line between moral and aesthetic criteria is as hard to draw as most imaginary lines, and comments such as Furnivall's show how one kind of criticism inevitably shaded off into the other. By 1876, moreover, metrical testing had dominated the activities of the Society for two years, and disintegrationist analysis of plays might now be based on supposedly objective investigation. Furnivall concluded his Foreword to the Spalding reprint as follows:

My own words [of two years earlier, indorsing Shakespeare's authorship] . . . were incautiously strong. . . . If it could be shown that Beaumont or any other author wrote the suppos'd Shakspere parts, and that Shakspere toucht them up, that theory would suit me best.

(p. ix)

To this Furnivall added a brief note hinting that Beaumont's "run-on lines, &c." (sic) ought to be investigated for evidence to support a case against the attribution to Shakespeare; needless to say, the Director's invitation was taken up—by Boyle on behalf of Massinger in the 1880's. But the late-Victorian attempts to exclude Shakespeare from the play can be omitted from the present discussion, not merely because they are no longer a live issue, but because they were not addressed to the division of authorship; Fletcher's share in the play they took for granted,[20] and their principal effect was to contribute confusion and distraction, but no new evidence.

No less important than Furnivall was Littledale. His familiarity with the play was much greater than that of most of his contemporaries, and the elaborate commentaries in his notes and Introduction to the Society edition probably made him as influential as Spalding or Hickson in guiding opinion on the problem of authorship. With the negligible exception of a few passages he thought might be Fletcherian insertions in scenes by Shake-

[20] The Boyle article in the N.S.S. *Transactions* for 1882, for example, opened as follows: "Amongst the candidates put up as Fletcher's literary partners in the *Two Noble Kinsmen,* it is singular that nobody has as yet hit upon Massinger" (p. 371).

speare, Littledale accepted the division whose general lines had been traced by Hickson, and he tried in several of his notes to draw those lines still more sharply by bringing forward fresh corroborative evidence.

It will be recalled that V.ii had been singled out for special attack by Spalding and Hickson, and it might be suggested that Victorian critics, forewarned of "disgusting" behavior in this scene (as in the passage cited on pages 41–42), might have been predisposed to overlook anything that would conflict with their expectations. This possibility was actually perceived by Littledale in a comment on V.ii (although he applied his perception only to other scenes):

> It is this scene in particular—as it is the basest—which has given rise to the undue depreciation of any potentialities of merit which may be in the underplot.
>
> (1885 Introduction, p. 65*)

Whether or not the scene is "base," his recognition that the effect of one passage may lead to "undue depreciation" of others is notable; but Littledale was unfortunately not much warier of the effect of such interaction than most of us are normally likely to be. In any case, the operation of such psychological leads, not merely in shaping critical opinion but also in the process of gathering evidence to support an assumed division of authorship, can be illustrated with a minimum of conjecture. The leads for Littledale came most strongly from Hickson. It was Hickson, we may recall, who first drew a clear line of division between II.i and II.ii; Littledale referred to Hickson's discussion and went on to offer his own corroboration that "the two scenes do not fit together exactly," for "in the prose scene the kinsmen are referred to as if in conversation, but in the verse dialogue which ensues they are made to begin with mutual salutations" (1876 Text, p. 132). Accordingly, he asserted that the two scenes "overlap in point of time . . . and the juncture is confusing" (p. 133). It appears, oddly enough, to have been for this reason that he restored the original scene-division in his text; "the Quarto rightly makes a distinction" and "the very fact of the scenes overlapping in point of *time* goes to prove the separate authorship" (pp. 107–108).

One hesitates to assert so categorically that the cousins did not converse during their brief appearance in the first scene as Littledale asserted that they did, but the dialogue (cf. page 34) does not indicate that they were talking or even that they were together at a single window. The conviction Littledale held on this point recalls the characteristic Victorian search for absolute certainty and the dangerous ease with which those who sought for certainty were usually able to arrive at it. No doubt the quasi-scientific metrical tests helped too in permitting such "proof" as the "fact" of the "overlapping scenes" to be added to the self-generating evidence of Sidney Walker's verse-relineations. But perhaps just as potent a factor in establishing the Hickson-Littledale division was the unremittingly tendentious language used in most commentaries on the play; thus the rest of the general comment on V.ii in Littledale's 1885 Introduction—"one has only to compare this [scene] with Act IV. sc. iii. to see that it is by a different and immeasurably inferior hand"—echoes the sharp comments by Hickson quoted earlier and treats as perfectly obvious what not even Spalding had given any sign of noticing.

During a large part of the nineteenth century, "Fletcher" appears to have served as a convenient label for those scenes of the play that several critics particularly disliked; given the label and the intimidating assumptions that were attached to it, many readers seem to have had their responses to the drama itself distorted by their presumed knowledge of the division of authorship.[21] "Knowledge" and "response," to be sure, are merely two abstractions we find it convenient to make from the whole of our experience; but it seems doubtful whether this later and wider view of language was sufficiently well understood in the nineteenth century to prevent the compounding of serious errors. The present chapter is written in the conviction that a more constructive approach both to the problem of authorship and to the play must depend, at least in part, on the recognition of these errors.

Post-Victorian Contributions

The post-Victorian scholarship on the problem of authorship may be divided generally into two varieties—that produced by the disintegrators and that produced by those who upheld Shakespeare's part in the play. Virtually all of this scholarship has taken the traditional lines of divided authorship (sanctioned repeatedly by the editors who followed Littledale) for granted at once. The attribution of a few short scenes has sometimes been debated,[22] but most discussions of the play have set out with the announced

[21] The degree to which readers were once expected to be continuously conscious of authorship, however much it distracted them from dramatic values, may be suggested by a typographical novelty in the edition of Hudson (1881), whose text conspicuously placed an asterisk beside every line of every scene ascribed to Fletcher.

[22] For example, disagreements over the authorship of III.ii (going back to Spalding versus Hickson) led A. C. Bradley to single out this scene for special notice in his short essay defending Shakespeare's presence in the play; cf. Bradley, *A Miscellany* (1929), pp. 218–224.

intention of determining the authorship of the "non-Fletcherian" parts. Thus in 1916 the arguments of Boyle on behalf of Massinger (then being revived by Sykes) [23] were answered by Willard Farnham in an essay on "colloquial contractions" as a test of authorship.[24] This essay, well known to students of *The Two Noble Kinsmen,* illustrates a number of important features of the post-Victorian studies of the play and might appropriately be considered in some detail.

In the section of his essay entitled "Shakespeare and Massinger," Farnham pointed out the high incidence in the text of *The Two Noble Kinsmen* of the thirty-seven contracted forms (*i'th', o'th', on's,* and the like) which he had selected for his test.[25] These forms were to be found throughout all the scenes in the play, but they were found rarely or not at all in the Massinger texts examined by Farnham, and the net result of his analysis was to reduce the claims for Massinger. Subsequently uncovered evidence (cited in Appendix A) further reduced those claims to the vanishing point, but Farnham's contribution was by no means negligible. His essay also made a point about the division of authorship, however, and this point calls for further notice.

After leaving out three brief scenes on the grounds that their authorship was still subject to dispute, Farnham counted 44 of his chosen contractions in 1060 lines assigned to Fletcher and 82 contractions in 1322 lines assigned to Shakespeare. (His line-totals were based on the numbering of Tucker Brooke's text in *The Shakespeare Apocrypha.*) These figures led him to observe that "the non-Fletcherian parts of this play are much more colloquial than the Fletcherian" (p. 356); while this conclusion was merely incidental to the main subject of his article, naturally it has sometimes been assumed that Farnham's analysis helped to verify the established division. The facts, however, are different.

The dramatic contexts of the forms counted by Farnham would be immaterial to a comparison between Shakespeare and Massinger, since these forms rarely occur in Massinger. Texts of both Shakespeare and Fletcher provide numerous examples, however, and Farnham therefore felt obliged to consider whether their use might not be determined by dramatic factors that would affect the results of his tests:

[23] H. Dugdale Sykes, "The Authorship of *The Two Noble Kinsmen,*" *MLR,* XI (1916), 136–148. Reprinted in Sykes, *Sidelights on Shakespeare* (1919).

[24] Farnham, "Colloquial Contractions in Beaumont, Fletcher, Massinger, and Shakespeare as a Test of Authorship," *PMLA,* XXXI (1916), 326–358.

[25] Farnham's statistics are included in the more comprehensive statistics subsequently compiled by Cyrus Hoy and F. O. Waller and tabulated in Chapter II.

Obviously, if subject matter is to influence colloquial contractions, it will be the colloquial scenes and colloquial characters which will show the most contractions. . . . [One expects that] the low comedy character will use a sort of dialect speech full of contractions [and so forth] . . .

(p. 356)

But, Farnham noted, one's expectations were upset in the case of Shakespeare's later plays, "where almost every character is made to use contractions in almost any situation"; Fletcher, on the other hand, "seems to have felt some slight connection between low comedy and colloquial speech" (p. 357). Again, these observations were not addressed to Farnham's main issue (Massinger), but it is not difficult to see how later investigators were led to believe that his figures (the contrast between 82/1322 contractions for Shakespeare and 44/1060 for Fletcher) tended to strengthen the case for the traditional division. It is with this later impression in mind, not with Farnham's own more modest claims, that one feels bound to note certain flaws in his analysis.

The distinction between verse and prose was evidently not considered by Farnham, and a comparison of two examples from the play—the first from a passage given to Shakespeare, the second given to Fletcher—will clarify the "much more colloquial" character of the scenes ascribed to Shakespeare:

Thou, oh jewel
O'th'wood, o'th'world, hast likewise bless'd a place
With thy sole presence . . .

(III.i.9–11)

Let the plough play today; I'll tickle't out of the jades' tails tomorrow.

(II.iii.28–29)

Two of the contractions counted by Farnham were *o'th'* and *'t;* the first of these passages, therefore, is found to be twice as "colloquial" as the second. Apparently the expectations upset by the study were expectations set up by the author's use of the word "colloquial." The contractions are often due to metrical elision, and the contrast between their incidence in the two "parts" of the play (even if certain errors in Farnham's figures remain uncorrected) [26] is hardly significant—especially since the ratio of verse to prose is higher in the part assigned to Shakespeare.

[26] In the Brooke text which Farnham cited as his source, Act II is correctly divided into six scenes. Farnham's tables, however, list only five scenes, and his line-totals and word-citations show that he counted II.i and II.ii together as "II.i" and assigned its combined total of 411 lines to Shakespeare. Since Farnham professed to exclude scenes whose authorship was in dispute, it seems strange that he should silently as-

Writing in 1916, Farnham was directly concerned with answering dis-integrationist claims, not with verifying the received division. Although the disintegrators have long been silent, most of the essays published during the past forty years or so have also been concerned with adding to the evidence for Shakespeare in the once disputed scenes. Several discussions—the essays by E. H. C. Oliphant [27] and Theodore Spencer, [28] for example, or the brief but highly influential statements by such leading Shakespeareans as Chambers and Kittredge—have not presumed to offer fresh confirmation for the division or for Fletcher's part in the play; clearly assuming that these matters have already been proved, they have stressed the case for Shakespeare and then gone on to deal with questions other than authorship. Inevitably, however, a few articles on the play printed in recent decades have mentioned various criteria (incidence of "rare words," for example) by which the two "parts" of the play have been said to be distinguishable. [29] Usually this evidence has not been pressed, perhaps again because it was cited under the conviction that the received division had already been conclusively proved. The essay by Kenneth Muir cited earlier in this chapter is a particularly interesting case in point.

Following a method proposed by E. A. Armstrong, Muir offers a skillful analysis of "image-clusters" in the scenes he holds to be Shakespeare's, pointing out that groups of as many as ten images recurring in close con-junction in various passages of canonical plays are also to be found in vari-

---

sign II.ii to Shakespeare when nearly all critics for a century had given it to Fletcher. By Farnham's professed standards, the scene should have been reassigned, the 82 con-tractions listed for Shakespeare reduced by nine, and the 44 for Fletcher increased by nine.

[27] Oliphant, *The Plays of Beaumont and Fletcher* (1927), pp. 325–348.

[28] Spencer, "*The Two Noble Kinsmen*," MP, XXXVI (1939), 255–276. Part of this essay is given to conjecture on the unexplained and puzzling phenomenon of Shake-speare's supposed retirement as a writer (the documentary evidence for his retirement relates only to his career as an actor), but Spencer also deals at some length (as few other modern critics have done) with literary and dramatic values in the play.

[29] Cf. Alfred Hart, "The Vocabulary of *The Two Noble Kinsmen*," RES, X (1934), 274–287. Reprinted in Hart, *Shakespeare and the Homilies* (1934). Dividing the play as usual, Hart gives statistics on various "rare words" in the play (words new to our language, seldom-used words, etc.) to show that the percentages in "Part A" are consistent with his figures from Shakespeare's later plays. His findings with respect to Fletcher are harder to credit, however, since he gives no tabulations of Fletcher's vocabulary and since few of the words counted in his *TNK* tables are precisely iden-tified in his text; his brief discussion of selected words from "Part B" (assigned to Fletcher), moreover, unfortunately presumes to assess isolated words without regard to context; for example, compound words in "Part B" (*honest-hearted, freckle-faced,* etc.) are described as "not unsuitable to drama but merely descriptive and without any poetic quality" (p. 280).

ous passages of *The Two Noble Kinsmen*.[30] With regard to his case for Shakespeare, the reader must be referred to the article itself, but it might be remarked that simple considerations of statistical probability make the conjunction-of-images argument particularly forceful and, unlike simpler image-tests or the traditional discussions of parallel passages, hard to assail on the grounds that the parallels may be due to chance. It might also be remarked that there is some irony in the very circumstance that such demonstrations are still offered, since it now seems hard to see why Fletcher's role in the play should be treated as obvious and Shakespeare's not; it is the more and not the less distinguished writer who is the more easily distinguishable, and although the majority of critics who have discussed the question of authorship have felt they had to begin by conceding the presence of Fletcher's hand in the play, their essays have in most cases been inspired by a much deeper conviction of a wholly different sort. When Muir observes that "the case [for Shakespeare] seems to me to be so strong that the onus of proof really rests on the sceptics" (p. 54), the student familiar with studies of authorship recognizes one of the peculiar conditions involved in dealing with this play—namely, that much of his energy must be devoted at the outset to combatting the confusions carried over from the disintegrationist era. The dangers inherent in starting from the usual concessions about Fletcher, however, can be illustrated from the Muir essay itself.

We observed earlier that Muir opens with a frank acknowledgment of prior assumptions about the division of authorship and a citation of metrical statistics to support those assumptions. Elsewhere in the article Muir devotes a few sentences to fresh confirmation of the received division; the evidence he cites in this connection has to do with imagery in the play (not the complex "image-clusters" cited in his elaborate case for Shakespeare, but mere single images):

---

[30] Although condensation of "image-cluster" evidence cannot do it justice, a brief illustration might be offered from the review of Muir's article by James G. McManaway in *Shakespeare Survey 12* (1959), p. 149: "Muir finds in the scenes usually attributed to Shakespeare two of the image-clusters (*kite* and *hum*) isolated by Armstrong [in *Shakespeare's Imagination*], and two or three others. One of the more interesting of these involves a reference to the osprey (I, i) in a context of *war, c[o]rds, knives, lords, Kings, beds* (=graves), *graves, shadows* and *actions,* that is to be compared to a similar reference in *Coriolanus* (IV, vii) in a context of *war, breaking the neck, sword, lord,* and *sovereignty,* with *tomb, darkened* and *action* in nearby lines." This "strong confirmation" of Shakespeare's presence (as McManaway calls it) will naturally appear even stronger to those who watch Muir trace a group of eleven closely associated images through thirteen passages in ten canonical plays and then show its recurrence in a 15-line passage in *TNK* I.iii. (Cf. also Armstrong, *Shakespeare's Imagination*, rev. edn. [1963], pp. 94–97, 203–217.)

The fields from which the imagery is drawn in the two parts of the play show some striking differences. There is less imagery drawn from nature in the Fletcher scenes, much less from business and wealth, and none at all from sickness and medicine.

(p. 53)

Muir would probably be willing to grant that a precise counting of images from any particular field is difficult and rather arbitrary—just as all classifications must be arbitrary, so that (for example) an "image of surfeit" might not seem related to an "image of medicine" unless both were reclassified under "sickness imagery." Since Muir does not illustrate his first two categories—nature, business and wealth—they will have to be passed over; but "none at all" from "sickness and medicine" is most definite, and Muir cites a few brief examples from scenes assigned to Shakespeare to indicate clearly what he means this class to comprise:

> cure their surfeit
> That craves a present med'cine . . .
>
> (I.i.212–213)

> that heal'st with blood
> The earth when it is sick, and cur'st the world
> O'th'plurisy of people . . .
>
> (V.i.70–72)

In IV.ii (assigned to Fletcher), Emilia may surely be said to employ an image drawn from sickness and medicine in the opening lines, in which she refers to choosing between Palamon and Arcite so as to make their fifth-act combat unnecesary:

> Yet I may bind those wounds up, that must open
> And bleed to death for my sake else; I'll choose,
> And end their strife . . .
>
> (IV.ii.1–3)

The wounds she would bind (the estrangement and strife between the cousins) are purely metaphoric; if they were not, perhaps they might not qualify as imagery drawn from medicine, but the requirements for classifying an expression as an image are not always self-evident. The line at which literal language leaves off and metaphoric language begins would also seem to depend partly on verbal contexts and partly on the purposes of the critic who draws the line; one might well question whether the scenes ascribed to Fletcher concerning the Daughter do not furnish even more than the "seventeen images derived from sickness and medicine" counted by Muir in the scenes he regards as Shakespeare's; the Daughter's madness is spoken of as illness, of course, and is attended by a doctor. (Emilia's "I am sotted, utterly lost . . . ," later in IV.ii, incidentally reminds us that her growing distraction over Palamon and Arcite parallels the Daughter's feelings about Palamon.) But to cite instances apart from interpretive discussion of the play seems pointless, and such discussion is rendered more difficult than the reader may suppose by the hanging question of authorship. The present remarks are merely intended to show how a critic committed to the assumption of divided authorship may be misled by this assumption into overlooking contradictory evidence.

A note of apology should be entered at this point with respect to the one-sided kind of attention so far accorded in these pages to nearly every scholar from Spalding to Muir. Without the solid achievements of their century-long defense of Shakespeare the present book could never have been written. To single out for special notice just those parts of their work in which they touch on the supposed evidence for Fletcher or for divided authorship is bound to give a distorted picture of the genuine merits of their work as a whole. But those impressive merits lie in that much larger part of their work concerning the parts of the play they assign to Shakespeare, and it is what remains—the relatively little which remains—to which the present chapter has of necessity been confined. One or two further points related to the arguments about Fletcher's role in the play remain to be considered, however, before the purpose of reviewing those arguments in such detail can be made fully clear.

Critics have usually credited the original design of the play to Shakespeare, since nearly all of the lines of action in the plot begin and end in the scenes ascribed to him and all of the major characters except Gerrold make their first (and usually their final) appearances in those scenes. But although the principal nineteenth-century critics from Spalding to the late Victorians agreed that Shakespeare must have been responsible for the original design, they nevertheless found the notion of an active collaboration between Shakespeare and Fletcher quite inadmissible; the following remarks by Littledale (sometimes paraphrasing others) should suffice to illustrate the curious way in which many Victorians chose to imagine the play had been written:

Shakspere cannot be accused of tolerating the trash . . . which abounds in the underplot.

Fletcher has perverted the original design.

The only valid hypothesis [is] . . . that Shakspere, when he retired from the stage, left this play . . . incomplete, and that [it was] . . . worked up by Fletcher afterwards.

Why Shakspere left [it] . . . unfinished seems hopeless to inquire. He may have himself regretted his choice of subjects, or may, at the close of his career, have thrown aside various fragments and sketches, . . . leaving them for subsequent completion by Fletcher, or other playwrights of the company.

(1885 Introduction, pp. 23*, 25*, 37*, 27*)

No evidence—unless the literary tastes of the 1870's and 1880's constitute evidence—ever substantiated these speculations, but the rhetoric in which they were couched naturally helped to inhibit further inquiry for many years afterwards; the assumption that Shakespeare "cannot be accused of tolerating" the parts assigned to Fletcher was capitalized by disintegrators and by adherents to the more orthodox position alike, and those who saw Shakespeare's hand in the play but might have been reluctant to accept the theory of cast-off fragments were, in effect, expected to grant that the whole question was so irremediably confused (". . . hopeless to inquire . . .") that no respectable purpose could be served by exploring other possibilities.

The late-Victorian view of how the play had been put together could not, of course, be demonstrated with the aid of statistical tables, and it naturally proved to be somewhat less durable than the orthodox view of the division between authors. Changes in literary taste, along with an accumulation of evidence pointing to the completion and first performance of the play in 1613, gradually led modern scholars to take a different view of its composition; the following observation from Chambers' *William Shakespeare* (1930) is representative of most opinion on the subject today:

The distribution of the Shakespearean matter shows that it is a case of collaboration and not of the completion by Fletcher of a Shakespearean fragment.

(I, 532)

And although present-day critics continue to accept the prescriptions of earlier critics on the identification of Fletcher's share in the play, they may also differ from their predecessors on more than the question of when those scenes were written. For example, when Marco Mincoff, an authority on Fletcher, argued at length for Shakespeare's partial authorship, he added several comments on the so-called Fletcher scenes to which none of the earlier critics who divided the play would have been prepared to assent:

One further piece of evidence [for Shakespeare's authorship] I shall only touch on very briefly, since it concerns Fletcher's share rather than Shakespeare's. It is that both here and in *Henry VIII* Fletcher rises so far above his usual level in poetic and dramatic imagination, his style and metre have undergone such changes as to presuppose some very strong influence at work upon him. His figures are more finely modelled, nearer to human flesh and blood than anywhere else. In his work with Beaumont a parallel veiling of style and metre can be observed, though not in his collaborations with other authors; and in his work with Beaumont his art does not rise as high as in these plays. Even more, in the Fletcher parts of both plays distinctly Shakespearian images can be found. It seems hard to avoid the conclusion that he was working here under the guidance of Shakespeare himself.[31]

The critics who first divided *The Two Noble Kinsmen* between Shakespeare and Fletcher had the initial excuse of the original title-page, while those who divided *Henry VIII* had (as Chapter III will argue) no excuse at all. None of these critics, however, was prepared to observe that Fletcher's "style and metre have undergone such changes," nor did they speak so favorably of the scenes they gave to Fletcher; had they done so, they might have found it difficult to allege very strong grounds for their arguments for dual authorship.

The present chapter has, it is hoped, shown that the common assumptions about divided authorship and Fletcher's presence in *The Two Noble Kinsmen* rest in part upon very shaky evidence. A reader unfamiliar with the ways in which those assumptions came to be taken for granted, however, might not feel prepared to abandon them *even if he were persuaded that the so-called Fletcher scenes looked decidedly more like the work of Shakespeare than of Fletcher:* he might seek to account for such a phenomenon along lines similar to that followed by Mincoff. Hence the need—or so it seems to the present writer at least—for so long-winded a probing into the grounds for the received division. No further progress toward resolving the problem of authorship, in any case, is likely to be made as long as the usual assumptions about Fletcher's part continue to be accepted without question. Later chapters will try to show several of the consequences that follow from questioning those assumptions. The evidence examined in the next chapter, for example, implies that Shakespeare, whether or not he collaborated with Fletcher, was probably responsible for the final version of the play as it has come down to us.

One significant study of the play to deal with evidence of divided authorship has been neglected in the present chapter. The first detailed analysis of the manuscript copy supplied to the printer in 1634 has only recently been published, and it has suggested the strong probability of Shakespearean

[31] Mincoff, "The Authorship of *The Two Noble Kinsmen*," *English Studies*, XXXIII (1952), 115.

autograph behind the text of at least some scenes in the play. That analysis—
by F. O. Waller—appears to have proceeded on the conviction that the traditional division between authors is correct; moreover, it also claims—explicitly, as few modern studies of the play have done—to provide a strong
confirmation of that division, this time with palpable bibliographical and
linguistic evidence. Even the transition between II.i and II.ii, it is claimed,
serves to confirm the lines of division on bibliographical grounds. The evidence for Fletcher presented in the Waller essay is considered along with
the more important subject of the printer's copy itself in the next chapter.

II

The Manuscript

We shall merely replace what is unknown and unintelligible by possibilities that are at least comprehensible.

Freud

To try to ascertain the nature of the manuscript that lay behind the printed text of a given play may be to enter "a land of shadowy shapes and melting outlines," but as long as we recognize that certainty is quite unattainable, Greg adds, "we may at least hope to form an idea of the manuscript . . . that can claim to be reasonable and to possess a measure of plausibility." [1] The only text of *The Two Noble Kinsmen* possessing critical authority is the quarto printed by Cotes for Waterson in 1634. Fortunately it presents an unusually rich array of bibliographical evidence from which "we may at least hope to form an idea" of the underlying manuscript.

The quarto has not attracted wide notice from modern scholarship. Sir Walter Greg has published a few brief but valuable observations in various of his books, and these will be cited as we proceed. More importantly perhaps, F. O. Waller, author of a doctoral dissertation on *The Two Noble Kinsmen,* has recently offered the first extensively detailed analysis of the text to appear in print; his essay, published in the 1958 *Studies in Bibliography,* [2] calls attention for the first time to certain features of general interest to Shakespearean scholarship, and his findings must be given careful examination in this chapter. There is, nevertheless, no very comprehensive account as yet of the bibliographical data relevant to the printer's copy. The

[1] W. W. Greg, *The Shakespeare First Folio* (1955), pp. 105–106. Hereafter cited as *Folio.*

[2] Waller, "Printer's Copy for *The Two Noble Kinsmen,*" *SB,* XI (1958), 61–84. Subsequent references given in the text. (The Waller dissertation—unpublished, but available on microfilm, University of Chicago, 1957, Thesis No. 3662—is an annotated edition of the play.)

mislineation of prose as verse described in the preceding chapter, for example, is ignored in the Waller essay (and the traditional relineations are adopted in his unpublished edition of the text); Waller accepts the customary Victorian division of authorship, refers to "metrical evidence" (apparently without having closely examined it) as support for this division, and works out his own theory of the copy within the rigid limits imposed by his acceptance of this dubious evidence. These circumstances actually enhance the value of his essay in one respect: they permit us to observe how well or ill the bibliographical data may be used to support the assumption of divided authorship.

A few speculative points will help to introduce our subject. As we set out to consider the quarto, we inevitably make a few preliminary assumptions about what we might expect to find. If we start from the title-page attribution, for example, we adopt the tentative assumption that the manuscript used by the printer may have been entirely in the hand of Fletcher, entirely in the hand of Shakespeare, entirely in the hand of a scribe, or—leaving aside the question of theatrical additions in another hand for prompting purposes—in some combination of author's sheets and scribal copy. The complication hardly ends here, of course; Dr. Johnson's supposition that plays were multiplied by transcript after transcript, out of favor for so much of the present century, has undergone a good deal of conjectural reconstruction in recent years. But at this point we might turn from thinking about the printer's copy to further preliminary speculation about the original draft that would have to precede any kind of scribal transcription. Only three varieties of such a draft need be imagined—a manuscript consisting of some scenes in Shakespeare's autograph and others in Fletcher's, a manuscript written entirely by Shakespeare, or a manuscript written entirely by Fletcher. It should be added that this pedantic speculation, based on the most literal-minded gloss of the word "writer," is not intended to prejudice the question of authorship; all that is meant is that one collaborator may have given his share of the play to his partner, and that a single autograph draft might in this way have stood between whatever previous collaboration and whatever later transcription may be assumed to have taken place. Simplicity is perhaps always to be distrusted, but it is nevertheless worth bearing in mind, as we go on to the actual printed evidence in the quarto, that this evidence may point either to single or to double autograph.

The Revival

Certain details in the quarto have been related by Greg and others to a revival production of the play which must have taken place about 1626. This matter might be dealt with first.

In the manuscripts surviving from Elizabethan playhouses we occasionally find warning notes written in the margins by the theatrical book-keepers for prompting purposes. Such notes seldom survive in printed texts, but the Cotes Quarto is unusual in that it prints nine stage directions in outer page-margins and three of these unambiguously reproduce warning notes for the prompter. The first appears next to a speech of Emilia to Hippolyta in I.iii and anticipates the entrances in I.iv (with which it is concerned) by about forty lines:

> You talke of *Pirithous* and *Theseus* love;
> Theirs has more ground, is more maturely seasond,
> More buckled with strong Iudgement.and their needes

2. Hearses rea- The one of th'other may be said to water
dy with Pala- Their intertangled rootes of love, but I
mon:and Arci- And shee (I sigh and spoke of) were things innocent,
te:the 3. Lou'd for we did, and like the Elements
Queenes.
Theseus: and That know not what, nor why, yet doe effect
his Lordes Rare issues by their operance; our soules
ready. Did so to one another; what she lik'd,
> Was then of me approov'd, what not condemd

(sig. C3ᵛ)

The other two warning notes appear as follows:

3. Hearses rea- (abreast I.iv.30–31 on sig. C4ᵛ, anticipating I.v by 24
dy. lines)

Chaire and (abreast III.v.67–68 on sig. G2ᵛ, anticipating "Ladies sit
stooles out. downe" at line 105)

Equally clear signs of a book-keeper's hand appear in the addition of actors' names to two of the regular stage directions. Following IV.ii.74 we find:

> *Enter Messengers. Curtis.*

(sig. I4ᵛ)

And the entrance direction for V.iii reads as follows:

> Scæna 3. *Enter Theseus, Hipolita, Emilia, Perithous: and*
> *some Attendants, T. Tucke: Curtis.*

(sig. L4ᵛ)

The abbreviated names have been identified (cf. Appendix A) with two actors, Thomas Tuckfield and Curtis Greville, who were together present in the King's company only *circa* 1626, and the appropriate assumption appears to be that the names were added to the manuscript when at that time it was used as the prompt-copy for a revival of the play.

The actors' names would have been added by the company book-keeper; the book-keeper for the King's men from about 1623 until at least 1633 was Edward Knight,[3] whose hand has been identified (and whose work as scribe or annotator may therefore be studied) in four surviving dramatic manuscripts.[4] Greg has observed that the peculiarities of punctuation in the first of the warning notes cited earlier (beside Emilia's lines in I.iii) are paralleled in some of the notes written by Knight in those manuscripts.[5] It is in any case a reasonably safe assumption that Knight was responsible for at least the first of the three warning notes, the addition of the actors' names, and at least a few of the many other prompter's directions we shall review later.

The present discussion has been intended merely to dispose of the tangential matter of the revival, to distinguish certain details in the quarto associated with the use of the manuscript at the time of the revival. We may now go on to consider the nature of the manuscript that came into Knight's hands about 1626.

Approaches to the Printer's Copy

The most convenient procedure will be to deal first with F. O. Waller's theory of the copy and then move on to an independent analysis of the

[3] In his Introduction to *The Honest Mans Fortune: A Critical Edition of MS Dyce 9 (1625)* (1952), Johan Gerritsen provides the most complete information on Knight now available, showing that he must have become book-keeper for the company at some date between 1619 and 1624—probably in 1623 or 1624 (pp. xxv–xxvi).

[4] In addition to the 1625 MS of *The Honest Mans Fortune* cited above (a prompt-book in Knight's hand), these are:

Bonduca (Brit. Mus. MS Add. 36758), a transcript by Knight from Fletcher's foul papers (as Knight states in a note), prepared c.1625–35 for a private collector. Ed. W. W. Greg (Malone Society), 1951.

Believe as You List (Brit. Mus. MS Egerton 2828), a prompt-book in Massinger's autograph, 1631, extensively annotated by Knight for theatrical use. Ed. C. J. Sisson (Malone Society), 1927 (1928).

The Soddered Citizen (MS in private collection), a prompt-book in the hand of an unidentified scribe, c.1631, bearing annotations by Knight for theatrical use. Ed. J. H. P. Pafford (Malone Society), 1935 (1936).

[5] Cf. Greg, *The Editorial Problem in Shakespeare* (3rd edn., 1954), p. 39 n. It is not, of course, the idiosyncratic punctuation alone that identifies the hand of Knight; it is this evidence along with that of date, parent company, etc.

quarto. In order to avoid prejudicing Waller's case, it will be best to avoid presenting any evidence not considered by him until after we have worked through his analysis. Yet two salient facts about the quarto should be mentioned at once in order to keep the discussion reasonably clear: it contains evidence strongly suggestive of one or more authors' hands in the manuscript, and it also contains evidence strongly suggestive of one or more book-keepers' hands. On this point Greg, Waller, and the present writer are in agreement. How these two kinds of evidence are to be reconciled may be disputed, but that both kinds are present and must be accounted for is not itself a matter of dispute. With respect to evidence that the manuscript may have seen service as a prompt-copy, we have already observed a few examples in the discussion of Knight and the revival; we might at this point, therefore, glance briefly at some of the evidence suggesting an authorial manuscript. The following examples constitute a few of the stage directions which must for the most part have derived from an author of the play:

> *Enter a Schoole master. 4. Countrymen: and Ba[vian]. 2. or 3.*
> *wenches, with a Taborer.*
>
> (III.v.1)

> *Enter.4. Country people, & one with a garlond before them.*
>
> (II.iii.23)

> *Enter Palamon as out of a Bush, with his Shackles: bends his fist*
> *at Arcite.*
>
> (III.i.30)

> *Here Musicke is heard, Doves are seene to flutter, they fall againe*
> *upon their faces, then on their knees.*
>
> (V.i.135)

> *Still Musicke of Records.*
> *Enter* Emilia *in white, her haire about her shoulders, a wheaten*
> *wreath: One in white holding up her traine, her haire stucke*
> *with flowers: One before her carrying a silver Hynde, in whic[h]*
> *is conveyd Incense and sweet odours, which being set upon the*
> *Altar her maides standing a loofe, she sets fire to it, then they*
> *curtsey and kneele.*
>
> (V.i.142)

The indefinite "2. or 3." in the first direction; the introduction of the mute garland-bearer (who theatrically is not strictly necessary) in the second; [6]

---

[6] The garland is a prize in the games discussed by Arcite and the Countrymen in II.iii, and Arcite enters wearing it in II.v. Book-keepers often eliminated such minor characters as the garland-bearer, evidently as a matter of economy.

the fact that several details in the directions can be traced back to the literary source in Chaucer;[7] the unusual fullness of specific details about managing the production—all these pretty strongly suggest the hand of a playwright, and few of the details could have originated with (or would be of use to) a prompter. More extensive evidence of authorial manuscript will appear both in our review of Waller's arguments and in the later discussion, and further evidence for a prompt-copy will also be presented in that discussion. These are the two kinds of evidence most strikingly apparent in the quarto.

If a printed text exhibits many signs of having been printed from authorial copy, if it also exhibits many signs of the prompter, and if there is no other significant evidence to inhibit our interpretation of these data, we should assume that the manuscript used by the printer had been an author's fair copy that had been augmented and corrected by the book-keeper and had served as the prompt-book. (About six of the eighteen or so surviving manuscript prompt-books consist of authors' fair copies of this sort.) If, however, a printed text shows evidence of so much confusion and irregularity that the manuscript behind it would probably have been inadequate for the needs of a prompter, we might have to assume that the printer had been provided, not with the prompt-book, but with the author's foul papers which had been annotated by a book-keeper prior to their transcription into a prompt-book. (One surviving manuscript, Heywood's *The Captives,* appears to consist of annotated foul papers.) Waller seeks to explain the Cotes Quarto by postulating annotated foul papers (or something very similar) as the printer's copy. We turn now to the evidence and interpretations given in his 28-page essay on the play.

The Divided Manuscript Theory

Waller adheres to the traditional division of authorship, giving to Fletcher the usual twelve scenes assigned to him (II.ii–vi, III.iii–vi, IV.i–ii, V.ii); in addition he regards four brief passages elsewhere as interpolations by Fletcher in scenes written by Shakespeare. The interpolations (each of which was first suggested by some earlier critic) are alleged to occur at I.i.25–29, I.iv.29–43, V.i.1–19, and V.iv.25–48—or, in the line-numbering of the 1936 Kittredge edition cited by Waller, at I.i.25–28, I.iv.25–38, V.i.1–17, and V.iv.22–38.[8] (When the Kittredge line-numbers must be used in this chap-

---

[7] Palamon's angry entrance at III.i.30 follows *The Knight's Tale* 1576 ff., Emilia's entrance direction at V.i.142 adapts details from *KT* 2275 ff., etc.

[8] A reader checking the passage in I.iv may be puzzled when he notes that l. 29 or 25 commences with a reply by the Herald to a question asked by Theseus in the

ter, they are distinguished by italic type.) [9] Waller's grounds for accepting
the traditional assignments, in addition to majority consensus and the metrical statistics that helped bring about that consensus, include certain bibliographical data in which he claims to find strong confirmation for the theory
(a) that Shakespeare and Fletcher "divided the scenes between themselves"
and wrote their respective shares "simultaneously but in no very close collaboration," (b) that Fletcher handled the play last to give the text "a final
reworking," and (c) that Fletcher's "revisory attentions" appear to have
been "haphazard and incomplete," amounting "only to the addition of some
new matter"—namely, the interpolations—"with a number of irregularities,
some quite obvious, left untouched" (p. 84). The "irregularities," of course,
constitute the bibliographical evidence that supposedly confirms the division
between writers and proves that Fletcher handled the copy last to give "a
final reworking" to the text as it has come down to us. Waller adds that the
irregularities were presumably smoothed out before the play was first performed, but that their survival in the quarto is one among other indications
that the printer's copy consisted of the foul papers of the two authors.

We might begin with one of the more interesting and less controversial
elements in the Waller analysis. One area of evidence touched on by Waller
consists of idiosyncratic Shakespearean spellings. After quoting Greg's observation that "if we find any considerable number of eccentric or archaic
spellings in a print, the likelihood is great that it was set from the author's
own manuscript and not from a scribal copy," Waller offers a list of the
anomalous spellings he has observed:

The list which follows is drawn from his [Shakespeare's] scenes and also represents spellings which are paralleled in various texts of his acknowledged plays,
thought to have been printed from authorial manuscripts: *angle* (i.e., *angel*),
Asprayes, boudge, cease (i.e., *seize*), *Cizard, cizd, mervaile, right* (i.e., *rite*), and
Wrinching (i.e., *rinsing*). In addition, I conjecture the anomalous form, *a eleven,*
at I.iii.*54,* to be a compositorial misreading . . . of an original copy spelling,
a leven. Spellings of *eleven* with *a* occur, of course, in a number of the Shakespeare good quartos and in Addition D of *Sir Thomas More.* In the Fletcherian

---

preceding line, and that l. *43* or *38* is grammatically wedded to the lines that precede and follow; but Waller does not explain. Editors have noted, moreover, that
Theseus' command at ll. *30–31* ("All our surgeons/ Convent in their behoof!") must
be in our minds if his later and more general command at ll. *46–47* ("All our
best/ Their best skill tender!") is to be intelligible; the dramatist would have written
the latter with the former in mind, but on Waller's hypothesis ll. *46–47* were
written first by Shakespeare and ll. *30–31* were added later by Fletcher.

[9] In citations from the Waller essay, the Kittredge numbers have accordingly been
italicized by the present writer.

scenes I note only *stoa* (i.e., *stow*), *aborne* (i.e., *auburn*), and *take* (i.e., *tack,* in both Prologue and [twice in the] text).

(pp. 82–83)

"Supposing that there is a one-in-ten chance of a peculiar spelling being reproduced by a scribe or a compositor, the chance of its surviving in a print set up from a transcript is only one in a hundred" (Greg). Waller's examples, moreover, are not (as we shall see later) exhaustive for the quarto as a whole; his list is impressive nonetheless. By way of contrast, only about half a dozen of Shakespeare's anomalous or "old fashioned" spellings have been noted by Dover Wilson in the 1600 Fisher Quarto of *A Midsummer Night's Dream*—a text believed on other grounds than spellings to have been printed from autograph copy—and even those half a dozen (cited in Wilson's editorial notes) are less striking than most of the examples cited by Waller. A further and most important point—one which Waller seems to have overlooked but which decidedly enhances the value of the evidence he cites—concerns the date of the Cotes Quarto; normalization or modernization of spellings had proceeded far enough in Caroline printing houses to make the survival of distinctive Shakespearean forms in a text printed in 1634 even stronger evidence for Shakespearean autograph copy than the appearance of the same forms in books printed a generation earlier. The evidence of spellings, of course, is evidence neither for foul papers nor for a fair copy, but merely for Shakespearean autograph.

If a few pieces of evidence were conclusive for foul papers, then it would no doubt be legitimate to regard every other neutral indication of authorial copy (such as author's spellings) as corroboration for foul papers. The principal evidence Waller regards as decisive for foul papers is the same evidence alluded to earlier with which he believes the division between authors is confirmed and by which he thinks "a final reworking" by Fletcher is proved. His decisive evidence for two different authors' hands in the copy is found in the transition between Act II scenes i and ii; his decisive evidence for Fletcher's final handling of the text has to do with the supposed interpolation in V.iv. We turn next to these two issues.

The Transition between Scenes in Act II

Waller sees two irregularities in the transition between II.i and II.ii. The first is the "anomalous re-entrance" discussed in the preceding chapter; Waller assumes that the quarto text requires Palamon and Arcite to leave the upper stage near the end of II.i (which is true) and that it requires them to reappear on the same stage a moment later (which is not true), while in the Jacobean theater the two scenes must actually "have been played as a single scene, with Palamon and Arcite remaining on the upper stage after the departure of the Jailer and his company at the *'Exeunt'* of scene i" (p. 72). Waller does not explain why they "must" have remained nor why we cannot credit the quarto distinction between *above* in scene i and *in prison* in scene ii. For the reasons already discussed (pages 34–36), we may conclude that the text is perfectly sound.

The other irregularity Waller cites in connection with II.ii is quite real. The Jailor makes his first appearance in II.i (assigned to Shakespeare) and is there called *Iailor* in the entrance direction and speech-prefixes. Upon both of his appearances toward the end of II.ii, however, he is called *Keeper* in the directions and prefixes. The discrepancy is there, and Waller regards it as evidence of two hands in the text (as well as an indication of foul papers); he recognizes, however, that the evidence is not quite so clear as he might have hoped:

In II.iv Fletcher has the Jailer's Daughter, there so called, speak of her father as the "meane Keeper of his Prison". When the Jailer reappears in Acts IV and V, in both Fletcherian and non-Fletcherian scenes, he is regularly *Iailor* (or *Iaylor*). The likeliest explanation is that Fletcher himself realized the discrepancy after writing II.ii.

(pp. 71–72)

After completing II.ii, presumably, Fletcher looked at a copy of the outline he and Shakespeare had agreed upon, noted that the character was to be called "Jailor," wrote *Iailors Daughter* accordingly in the entrance direction for II.iv, vacillated three lines later when he had the Daughter call her father "Keeper," but scrupulously reverted to "Jailor" in the later acts. The trouble with this discrepancy in names as evidence for a division of authorship is that it fails to coincide with the division it is supposed to confirm and that it thereby demands an effortfully fanciful defense.

In the 1599 quarto of *Romeo and Juliet* the inconsistencies in identifying Lady Capulet—*Lady of the House, Old Lady, Lady, Wife, Capu. Wi., Mother*—are, like much else in that text, clear evidence of foul papers; they might prove seriously inconvenient in a prompt-book. With respect to the reason for their occurrence, Greg suggests "it may be the relation of a character to others on the stage that is uppermost in the author's mind" (*Folio*, p. 114). As for the *Keeper* in the prison scene, perhaps the fact that in this scene alone he is seen *vis-à-vis* his prisoners rather than as elsewhere in relation to his Daughter would sufficiently account for the shift. But the discrepancy in names is even less likely as a source of ambiguity to a prompter than the distinction between *Macbeths Wife* and *Lady* in the Folio *Macbeth;* in contrast to *Macbeth*—which most critics, despite much more serious irregularities than the detail just cited, believe to derive from a prompt-book—the quarto of *The Two Noble Kinsmen* is generally consistent in identifying its thirty-three speaking roles, and the single exception could not possibly have caused confusion, hence is not evidence for foul papers.

Waller writes:

Had the authors composed their work in close collaboration, it is unlikely that the discrepancy in character-names or the re-entry of Palamon and Arcite would have occurred. Nor would these irregularities be likely to have persisted in a fair copy made either by one of the authors or a competent theatrical scribe. The implication is that the printer's copy was the *two* authors' foul papers. . . . It also seems to be implied that the two authors wrote their shares simultaneously but without close consultation; had, for example, Shakespeare written his share (and to Fletcher's collaborator goes the initiation [and the resolution] of all the major lines of action) from retirement in Stratford, . . . as some scholars have postulated, we should expect Fletcher to have achieved a closer meshing of his scenes than appears here.

(p. 72)

Evidently a good deal of Waller's reasoning about the copy depends upon his interpretation of *in prison* to mean *above* and on his treatment of the point about the Keeper. Waller does, however, offer an additional item of bibliographical evidence to support his theory of how the play was put together. It concerns the alleged interpolation in the closing scene.

Arguments for Interpolation

Waller's argument for an interpolation at V.iv.25–48 (22–38), by far the most fully documented case for a Fletcherian interpolation ever to be published, is meant not only to show a division between two hands but also (as noted earlier) to prove that it must have been Fletcher who was responsible for the final text of the play as printed:

Differences of style or metre in scattered passages in certain of the non-Fletcherian scenes have led a number of critics to suppose that such scenes had been reworked by Fletcher. Thus Chambers . . . found no evidence of revision but suggested that "in fitting the scenes together, Fletcher may possibly have added a few lines to Shakespeare's." For at least one . . . interpolated passage . . .

some visible "seams" remain in Q, to provide further evidence of the authors' method of collaboration. The passage is V.iv.22–38; it presents no conclusive linguistic or metrical evidence for or against Fletcher's authorship, but the exaggerated courage Palamon displays in it is strongly suggestive of Fletcher, and it incidentally resolves the sub-plot involving the Jailer's Daughter, the development of most [?] of which had been in Fletcher's hands. There is no mark of textual disarrangement at line 22, but at the other end there are two significant features. Q prints lines 21–23 and 37–40 as follows:

> 3.*K.* Come? who begins?   21
> *Pal.* Ev'n he that led you to this Banket, shall
> Taste to you all: ah ha my Friend, my Friend,
>
> . . . .
>
> *Pal.* Adiew; and let my life be now as short,   37
> As my leave taking.   *Lies on the Blocke.*
> 1. *K.* Leade couragiou[s] Cosin.
> 1.2.*K.* Wee'l follow cheerfully.
> *A great noise within crying, run, save hold:*
>   *Enter in hast a Messenger.*
> *Mess.* Hold, hold, O hold, hold, hold.

Line 39 is not only metrically defective but the speech-prefixes show a manifest error; the dramatist hardly intended that the first knight should answer himself. But if lines 22–38 are excised, . . . then the first and second knights' declaration in line 39, "Wee'l follow cheerefully", becomes a natural answer to the *third* knight's question in line 21, "Come? who begins?" Significantly, the question and answer make up one full line.

An alternative explanation for the confusion . . . must ascribe the apparent relation between divided authorship and textual irregularity to sheer coincidence. It is more probable that the repetition of prefixes is an inadvertent seam resulting from an imperfect fusing of Fletcher's addition with an originally non-Fletcherian scene. It would appear that after the initial draft was complete, Fletcher went through his collaborator's scenes . . . not to effect a thoroughgoing revision . . . but here and there to insert slight additions, making little or no attempt to remove the marks of jointure.

After referring to Chambers and identifying the passage in question as V.iv. 22–38, Waller appends the following footnote:

Actually, Chambers puts the passage at lines 23–38, rather than 22–38. The points of division Chambers indicates apparently go back to William Spalding's *Letter* . . . of 1833 . . . and Harold Littledale's introduction to his edition. . . . Line 23 is the second line of a new speech, and Spalding put the point of division in the very middle of the line without explaining why; since there is nothing particularly un-Fletcherian about line 22, there is no reason why Fletcher should not be given the whole of the speech . . . and [in the point about the question and answer making up a full line] . . . there is reason to assign it all to him.

(pp. 80–81)

The nature of the material we are dealing with seems to call for a certain pettifogging precision, and a few points about Waller's footnote must be mentioned first. Spalding made quite clear his reason for suggesting an interpolation in the scene, and although he mentioned no particular line of division his reason pointed to line *23;* he had assigned every scene concerning the Daughter to Fletcher, and finding "several lines" in V.iv that resolved her story, he thought either that Fletcher had interpolated them or else that Shakespeare "may have inserted them" on Fletcher's suggestion (*Letter*, pp. 52–53). Few critics have ever found Spalding's division satisfactory—Waller himself recognizes three important scenes concerning the Daughter (II.i, III.ii, IV.iii) as Shakespeare's—but the reference to a possible interpolation has occasionally been repeated in editorial notes. Littledale mentioned it casually in his 1885 Introduction only to speak of it as "open to doubt" (p. 67*). Chambers took it up (without discussion) and specified line 23 no doubt because it is here, at "ah ha my Friend," that Palamon turns to the Jailor and begins to speak of his Daughter. One may, in short, question the weight of the tradition behind the alleged interpolation. We come next to the weight of Waller's evidence.

Even the narrowest subject of textual research may involve wider issues, and the reader's patience is begged for an attempt to draw attention to some that are involved in the present case. The dramatic context of the disputed passage, first of all, is highly relevant. The playwright who wrote III.vi, altering the Chaucer original, had made Theseus decree, as a condition of the fifth-act tournament between Palamon and Arcite, that not only the loser, but also the knights who would second him—"gallant idiots" as Seward called them—were to be brought to execution. Although the latter half of IV.ii is given over to long heroic descriptions of these knights, they do not appear on stage until V.i, where they accompany Palamon and Arcite at the altars of Venus and Mars but do not speak. They appear again, and speak, only in the final scene. Two other actions more closely precede V.iv: near the end of V.ii the Jailor is summoned to attend the tournament, while his Daughter, her mind beginning to clear, remains behind with her Wooer; then the off-stage combat in V.iii, and the report of Arcite's victory. Now V.iv begins:

Enter Palamon and his Knights, pinioned; Jailor, Executioner, Guard,
and others.

Palamon. There's many a man alive that hath outliv'd
 The love o'th'people, yea i'th'selfsame state
 Stands many a father with his child; some comfort
 We have by so considering; we expire,
 And not without men's pity; to live still,
 Have their good wishes. We prevent
 The loathsome misery of age, beguile
 The gout and rheum, that in lag hours attend
 For gray approachers. We come towards the gods
 Young and unwapper'd, not halting under crimes   [10
 Many and stale: that, sure, shall please the gods
 Sooner than such, to give us nectar with 'em,
 For we are more clear spirits. My dear kinsmen,
 Whose lives for this poor comfort are laid down,
 You have sold 'em too too cheap.
1ˢᵗ Knight. What ending could be
 Of more content? O'er us the victors have
 Fortune, whose title is as momentary
 As to us death is certain; a grain of honor
 They not o'er-weigh us.
2ⁿᵈ Knight. Let us bid farewell,
 And with our patience anger tott'ring Fortune,   [20
a] Who at her certain'st reels.
b] *3ʳᵈ Knight.* Come! Who begins?
Palamon. Ev'n he that led you to this banquet shall
 Taste to you all—ah ha, my friend, my friend,
 Your gentle daughter gave me freedom once;
 You'll see't now done forever. Pray, how does she?
 I heard she was not well; her kind of ill
 Gave me some sorrow.
Jailor. Sir, she's well restor'd,
 And to be married shortly.
Palamon. By my short life,
 I am most glad on't; 'tis the latest thing
 I shall be glad of, prithee tell her so.   [30
 Commend me to her, and to piece her portion,
 Tender her this.
1ˢᵗ Knight. Nay, let's be offerers all.
2ⁿᵈ Knight. Is it a maid?
Palamon. Verily I think so,
 A right good creature, more to me deserving
 Than I can 'quite or speak of.

All Knights. Commend us to her.   *They give their purses.*
Jailor. The gods requite you all,
   And make her thankful.
Palamon. Adieu, and let my life be now as short
   As my leave-taking.   *Lies on the block.*
c] *1ˢᵗ Knight.* Lead, courageous cousin.
d] *All Knights.* We'll follow cheerfully.
   A great noise within crying 'run,' 'save,' 'hold' . . .

   10 *unwapper'd* = unwasted, unspoiled
   12 *such:* i.e. the *gray approachers* (line 9)
   39 *All Knights:* Dyce's emendation for "1.2.K." in Q.

The banquet at which Palamon shall act as taster (line 22) is one at which he and the young knights, by one of those startling imaginative reversals common in Shakespeare's final acts, are to be food for the gods and at the same time honored guests at the table of their hosts (lines *9–13*). Other plays by Shakespeare offer a wealth of analogies for the complex associations here, from the "feasting presence full of light" that is Juliet's vault, to the fineness of the vision of Katherine—with its "blessed troop" robed in white and vizarded in gold, garlanded with bays, casting "thousand beams" upon her as they perform their reverend dance and invite her "to a banquet."

   But what Waller alleges that Shakespeare wrote is this:

   2ⁿᵈ Knight. Let us bid farewell,
      And with our patience anger tott'ring Fortune,
a]   Who at her certain'st reels.
b] *3ʳᵈ Knight.* Come! Who begins?
d] *1ˢᵗ & 2ⁿᵈ Knights.* We'll follow cheerfully.

The effect produced by this sequence is of a kind that some vaudeville comedian might try for. We must assume that Shakespeare in this context would not.

   Minor points that might be added are these: (1) If one were to accept Waller's premises on meter and lineation in drama, whatever they are, the significance claimed for [b] and [d] making up a full line is threatened by what then becomes the left-over [a]; the charitable construction to place on Waller's failure to quote [a] would be that his zeal led him to overlook it. (2) the "sheer coincidence" Waller would urge us to reject in favor of his own explanation is the coincidental tally between his own metrical restoration of [b] and [d] with his own rearrangement of Spalding's assumed interpolation. (3) Whatever Shakespeare "hardly intended," [d] is not an "answer" to [c]; both lines are obviously addressed to Palamon. (4) The dubious prefix is replaced by some editors with 2nd *Knight* (by others with 2nd & 3rd *Knights*) perhaps with more plausibility than the more commonly preferred *All,* but the error in any case is rather slight evidence for a 17-line interpolation or for anything else. Waller's use of this fly-speck as proof that "the play went through Fletcher's hands last, not for general revision but for the insertion of additional matter" (p. 77) merely points up the awkward consequences of conducting bibliographical analysis with too little attention to literary values.

A reader not closely familiar with the text of *The Two Noble Kinsmen* might approach the Waller essay with some knowledge of the usual authorial assignments, and since he would therefore find little in the essay to upset his expectations, he might be led to accept Waller's theory of how the play was written. That would seem to be how received opinion, so undisturbing and so easy to rationalize, endures like tribal superstition; once an ascription has been made, it is widely recorded and remembered long after the original reasons for it have been forgotten; fresh reasons are then invented to sustain it. Possibly the word *reason* is being used rather casually here, since we naturally demand evidence before we credit any theory; nevertheless, most of the evidence for the majority of our assumptions inevitably consists of the words of other men—a circumstance that becomes troublesome only when the assumptions are about matters of genuine concern or interest to us, and when the words issued from men whose knowledge and experience were more limited than we have had opportunity to recognize. A scholar wishing to credit some of the traditional assumptions about *The Two Noble Kinsmen* may be able to find the evidence he seeks in the play, but perhaps he will find that the real evidence for those assumptions, equally verbal if less poetic, lies elsewhere. He might, for example, wonder if he should give credence to another interpolation referred to by Chambers and by Waller, alleged to occur at I.i.25–28. Chambers offers no explanation whatever, and Waller, immediately after having dealt with the "metrically defective" line 39 in V.iv, has only the following to say: "One of the other passages Chambers cites—I.i.25–28—is also marked by defective lineation" (p. 81). The passage comes at the very beginning of the action (after the 24-line bridal song) and is introduced by a remarkable stage direction; the line-numbering that follows is traditional:

> Enter 3. Queenes in Blacke, with vailes staind, with impe-
> riall Crownes. The 1. Queene fals downe at the foote of
> Theseus; The 2. fals downe at the foote of Hypolita. The
> 3. before Emilia.

    1. *Qu.* For pitties sake and true gentilities,   [*25*

Heare, and respect me.

    2. *Qu.* For your Mothers sake,   [*26*

And as you wish your womb may thrive with faire ones,   [*27*

Heare and respect me,   [*28*

    3 *Qu.* Now for the love of him whom *Ioue* hath markd   [*29*

The honour of your Bed, and for the sake   [*30*

Of cleere virginity, be Advocate

For us, and our distresses: This good deede

Shall raze you out o'th Booke of Trespasses

All you are set downe there.   [*34*

    Theseus. Sad Lady rise.

    Hypol. Stand up.

    Emil. No knees to me.   [*35*

What woman I may steed that is distrest,

Does bind me to her.   [*37*

    Thes. What's your request? Deliver you for all.

    1 *Qu.* We are 3. Queenes, whose Soveraignes fel before

The wrath of cruell *Creon* . . .   [*40*

The original reason for regarding lines 25–28 as an interpolation was Little-dale's presumption that Shakespeare was incapable of writing line 27 (cf. page 40 above); the aptness of the line at Hippolyta's wedding would hardly register on the minds of those who thought it indecent; but the reason given for the interpolation today is "defective lineation." The symmetry of the stage business and the incantatory rhythm of the three prayers, reflected throughout the pageantry and formality of this scene, should suggest that Shakespeare is not likely to have opened the scene with the single speech of the Third Queen; and when in the replies by Theseus to the First Queen, Hippolyta to the Second, and Emilia to the Third, we note the rhythmic balance (as in the respective length of each) to the corresponding supplication, we may conclude that the composition is all of a piece. "Three minutes' thought would suffice to find this out," Housman once remarked *à propos* an editorial absurdity, "but thought is irksome and three minutes is a long time."

    We may, then, dismiss Waller's theory of how the play was put together and pass on to a new class of evidence, called linguistic, that figures prominently in his theory of the printer's copy. Waller believes that it helps to confirm the division of authorship and even to identify the hand of Fletcher in the appropriate parts of the play. It also incorporates the findings of other twentieth-century scholars who have dealt with the problem of authorship, and it deserves patient consideration.

Linguistic Tests and Intermediate Transcripts

Many critics have said that the text of the play, as Waller puts it, "shows two distinct linguistic habits which correspond to the authorial divisions indicated by other areas of evidence—metrical, stylistic, *etc.*" (p. 65). The habits referred to concern the presumably more or less unconscious preferences of the two writers for certain pronominal forms (e.g. for *ye* over *you* in Fletcher's case), predilections for certain linguistic contractions, and so forth. Before we look at Waller's statistics for the "two parts" of *The Two Noble Kinsmen,* however, a few words about the application of these stylistic tests in studies of authorship must be offered for readers who have perhaps not before had occasion to explore this curious field.

Statistical tabulations of authors' apparent or supposed linguistic preferences have been employed during the past sixty years, modestly or ambitiously, by such different scholars as A. H. Thorndike, R. B. McKerrow, Willard Farnham, and A. C. Partridge.[10] The most elaborate tables so far devised for use in problems of authorship are those offered in a series of seven articles by Cyrus Hoy in *Studies in Bibliography.*[11] Hoy's first article gives the results of his work on fourteen plays generally accepted (usually on the basis of sound historical evidence that G. E. Bentley has set into intelligent order) as the unaided work of Fletcher, together with his findings on fifteen plays by Massinger. Hoy's figures were gathered from printed and manuscript texts of the twenty-nine plays, printed in many different shops or transcribed by different hands over a wide span of years in the first half of the seventeenth century. The results may be summarized in tabular form; with one minor exception [12] Hoy found no significant chronological variation in the frequency of the forms he counted—the authors were generally consistent about their usage throughout their

[10] Thorndike in 1901 invented an *'em-them* test (*The Influence of Beaumont and Fletcher on Shakspere,* pp. 24 ff.). McKerrow in 1905 counted the occurrences of *ye* in different acts of one Fletcher-Massinger play (*The Spanish Curate,* Variorum Beaumont and Fletcher, II, 104). Farnham's "colloquial contractions" test of 1916 has already been cited. Partridge's work on *Henry VIII* is discussed in Chapter III. The tests of Thorndike and Farnham were applied to *TNK;* their findings are included in the Waller table cited on p. 78 below.

[11] Hoy, "The Shares of Fletcher and his Collaborators in the Beaumont and Fletcher Canon," *SB,* VIII (1956), 129–146 (dealing with Fletcher's and Massinger's unaided plays), and IX (1957), 143–162 (dealing with Fletcher-Massinger collaborations and Fletcher plays revised by Massinger); five later installments in *SB* XI–XV (1958–62) deal with the other plays of the canon.

[12] All instances of *i'th'* in Massinger occur in five plays that Hoy dates after the death of Fletcher.

careers—and it should therefore do no harm to combine his separate totals for the fourteen Fletcher plays and the fifteen by Massinger into a single table:

	ye	o'th'	a(= he)	's(= his)	h'as*	'is**	let's	i'th'	i'the	t'	of't
Fletcher	4507	126	28	52	83	19	200	187	1	0	0
Massinger	2	0	0	2	1	0	19	18	20	31	44

* *h'as = he has.* Hoy does not say whether he includes in his count the alternate forms of this contraction found in Fletcher, *'has* and *Has.* (These forms should be distinguished from *ha's,* a Jacobean spelling for *has.*)

** *'is = he is.* Hoy does not say whether he includes in his count the alternate forms in some Fletcher texts, *Is* and *His.*

A few forms counted by Hoy but showing less clear-cut distinctions have been omitted. Clearly there is more than entertainment value in the statistics cited. Their value in cases of disputed authorship, and the ways in which Hoy applies them to plays known or presumed to have been the joint work of Fletcher and Massinger, are not, however, matters with which we need now concern ourselves. They have been cited for another purpose (as well as to suggest the sort of work being done in this field); specifically, they are relevant to the question of scribal and compositorial interference with copy and they are only slightly less relevant to Waller's analysis of the Cotes Quarto. The first question, fidelity to copy, must involve us in a brief digression, but perhaps we shall soon find that the digression has not been irrelevant to the quarto.

Whatever else Hoy's figures may or may not be used to prove, distinctions such as 4507 *ye*'s and no instances of *of't* in fourteen texts by one writer, as against 2 *ye*'s and 44 instances of *of't* in fifteen texts of another, amount to presumptive proof that Jacobean and Caroline scribes were reasonably faithful to their copy (more so, in general, than their Elizabethan predecessors).[13] There must, of course, have been exceptions; yet Hoy's twenty-nine texts comprise a sufficiently broad sample to suggest that interference with copy could not in general have been as widespread as

[13] For comparison: In his facsimile edition of the 1594 First Quarto of *Titus Andronicus* (1936), J. Q. Adams tabulates the minor changes made by the compositor of Q2 (1600) when he reset Q1; these include 4 instances of *yee* altered to *you* and 15 other changes involving either pronouns or such verb-forms as *hath* (altered to *have*) or *doth* (to *do*)—items of the sort commonly used in linguistic tests of authorship. While Alice Walker's researches have shown how widely the degree of fidelity to copy varies with individual compositors, the changes in *Titus* and in other Elizabethan reprints do suggest that earlier printers were generally less conscientious than their successors.

sometimes supposed. Certain recent discussions of textual transmission (including the influential writings of Fredson Bowers) have, however, used as a basis for their arguments the conjecture that scribes may sometimes have intervened with copy to the extent that, for example, they would alter one or two hundred of Fletcher's *ye*'s to *you*'s in a single play—presumably out of distaste for *ye*. This conjecture has been based almost wholly upon a single case, Fletcher's *Bonduca,* and the two surviving texts of *Bonduca* are the subject of our digression.

In each of the fourteen Fletcher texts counted by Hoy, the pronoun *ye* appears from 133 to 543 times, the average being 322. Hoy's count for *Bonduca* is based on the text in the 1647 Folio, in which *ye* occurs 352 times. The other text of *Bonduca* survives in manuscript—the transcript made in 1625 or thereabouts by the book-keeper Edward Knight for a private collector (cf. note 4 above)—and it contains only 147 instances of *ye*. Since it is hardly conceivable that a Folio compositor gratuitously altered so many *you*'s to *ye*'s, the low figure in the manuscript has led such critics as Hoy, Bowers, and Waller to conclude that Knight gratuitously altered *ye*'s to *you*'s and then to cite *Bonduca* in postulating analogous scribal transcripts behind certain other printed texts.[14]

But perhaps the other differences between the two texts of *Bonduca* should be considered in connection with the difference in pronouns. A famous note by Knight near the end of his manuscript explains that he is copying the play from the foul papers; "the booke where by it was first Acted from is lost: and this hath beene transcrib'd from the fowle papers . . . wch were found." The 1647 Folio text, on the other hand, is apparently printed from the recovered prompt-book; i.e. first there was Fletcher's

---

[14] Hoy's first article, for example, states that the 1647 Folio text of *A Wife for a Month* (the only substantive text) contains tangles and false starts which provide "clear indication of author's foul papers" as the printer's copy; nevertheless, having found an average of 322 *ye*'s in Fletcher's plays and having noted only 176 *ye*'s in *A Wife for a Month,* Hoy sets aside his own evidence of foul papers in favor of the supposition that the copy had been a "not too careful transcript" of the foul papers— one in which "Fletcher's favorite pronoun [had] . . . been given much the same treatment as Knight accorded it in his *Bonduca* manuscript." Similarly, having noted only 213 *ye*'s in the single text of *Rule a Wife* (Q1640), Hoy suggests that "the diminished number of *ye*'s . . . may be traced to . . . intervention in the transmission of the text" (*SB,* VIII, 141–142). The alleged reduction in the supposedly higher original number of *ye*'s in these two plays is Hoy's only reason for postulating scribal transcripts, and his only reason for supposing that Fletcher had in each case written a larger number of *ye*'s which had been reduced by a scribe is that the numbers 176 and 213 are lower than the number 322. (For Bowers, who indorsed Hoy's findings before they were published, cf. pp. 79–80 below.)

very rough draft, then his revision of this foul-papers version into the prompt-book version, then the loss of the prompt-book, the transcription by Knight from the foul papers, the recovery of the prompt-book, and the use of the prompt-book as copy for the Folio text.[15] The foul papers were frequently so illegible that Knight was forced to leave numerous blanks where he could not make out Fletcher's hand. The printed version of the play, moreover, provides "authentic examples of author's revision more definitely and frequently than any of the other plays" in the 1647 Folio for which we have two texts; [16] it clears up the many dramatic confusions taken over by Knight in copying from the foul papers. About 400 lines of text (containing several dozen of the *ye*'s) are, furthermore, wholly missing from the manuscript and found only in the Folio. In view of the state of the foul papers, it is not necessary to assume that Fletcher added the larger number of *ye*'s when he revised the play into the version printed in the Folio —although that is surely possible—but it is hardly self-evident that Knight, copying what may conceivably have been mere abbreviations in Fletcher's rough draft, should be credited with "reducing" the number of *ye*'s to be found in the Folio text; we do not, after all, attribute to Knight the dramatic confusions which he took over from the foul papers but which were corrected by Fletcher in the text printed from the prompt-book. In any event, the text containing the *ye*'s that Knight is alleged to have altered to *you*'s was not the text Knight had before him as he made his copy, and it therefore seems most incautious to base any theory of wholesale scribal interference in textual transmission on a mere arithmetical comparison between the *ye*'s in the two versions of *Bonduca*.

Waller, however, regards it as "demonstrably true" that "scribal influence" accounts for the lower number of *ye*'s in the *Bonduca* manuscript (p. 75). We shall soon observe that this assumption accounts for certain key features in his theory of the copy behind the Cotes Quarto.

"The *Kinsmen* is marked by two sets of linguistic characteristics which may be presumed authorial; one is certainly Fletcher's." To demonstrate this, Waller offers a table of the forms he has counted; the figures for Fletcher are drawn from the twelve scenes and four alleged interpolations listed earlier, 1517 lines in the Kittredge text; the figures for Shakespeare (or "non-Flet.") are drawn from the remaining 1257 lines:

[15] Cf. Greg, ed. *Bonduca* (as in n. 4 above), pp. x–xiii.
[16] R. C. Bald, *Bibliographical Studies in the Beaumont & Fletcher Folio of 1647* (1938), pp. 83–84. Hereafter cited as *Beaumont & Fletcher Folio*.

	hath	has	*'em*	*them*	*ye*	*y'*	*you*	*i'th*	*o'th*
Flet.:	1	26	44	9	38	8	252	10	8
non-Flet.:	15	10	11	24	0	2	129	12	21

	other contractions in th' (e.g. to th', th'offense, etc.)	's (contractions of us & his; e.g. in's, told's, between's)	let's
Flet.:	12	4	10
non-Flet.:	27	6	3

(p. 75)

Waller explains the significance of these data as follows:

> When projected against the average Hoy gives for Fletcher's unaided plays (322), the incidence of *ye*'s in his part of the *Kinsmen* is decidedly low. The occurrence of *'em*'s, *i'th*'s, and *o'th*'s in Fletcher's parts is about what should be expected, and according to W. E. Farnham's examination of colloquial contractions . . . , the rate of occurrence of these and other contractions in the non-Fletcherian scenes of the *Kinsmen* identifies these scenes as Shakespeare's. If scribal intervention has been at work, it has manifested itself only in a diminution of Fletcher's *ye*'s, . . . and even at the lower rate, *ye* serves to distinguish the shares of the two authors.
>
> (pp. 75–76)

Leaving aside all objections to the philosophic presuppositions underlying Waller's selection and interpretation of these data, one may begin by wondering at the presence of certain items on his chart. Choosing at random, the present writer went down to the hot gates and found twenty examples of *let's* in the Folio text of *Antony and Cleopatra*. Other items are equally suspicious. For example, Hoy says there are very few examples of *y'* in Fletcher's unaided plays; [17] there are more in Shakespeare. Three of the *ye*'s and seven of the *'em*'s, moreover, occur in passages in I.iv and V.i which are alleged to be interpolations—largely on the strength of the incidence of *ye*'s and *'em*'s; while perhaps all human reasoning may in a sense be circular, one might hope that the circles would always be kept as large as possible. And a comparison with Hoy's application of the particle-tests leads one to note a further point: whenever Hoy (in his second article) found as few as 70 or 80 *ye*'s in the scenes assigned to Fletcher in a Fletcher-Massinger play, he was led to conclude that Massinger had given the play

---

[17] He finds one *y'ave* in *The Chances,* one *y'have* in *Bonduca,* and two examples of *y'are* in each of four plays (*SB,* VIII, 142–143). But perhaps it should be mentioned that his treatment of this contraction varies in his later articles on collaborative plays, as in one case he appears to regard "14 instances of *y'* " as notably "Fletcherian" (*SB,* XI, 96), while in another he cites "35 *y'*s" as part of a "language pattern . . . uncharacteristic of Fletcher" (*SB,* XIII, 78).

its final form (a conclusion occasionally supported by external evidence); but the analogous conclusion is ruled out for Waller, of course, because of the evidence of sharply divided copy that he found in the II.i–ii transition and the V.iv interpolation.

Waller says that "*ye* serves to distinguish the shares of the two authors." Leaving aside the alleged interpolation in V.i, there are 35 *ye*'s in the scenes assigned to Fletcher. But in six of those twelve scenes there are no *ye*'s at all. In the scene with the largest number, III.vi (with 308 lines by modern numbering, 372 in the quarto), there are only 10 *ye*'s—along with 93 instances of *you, thou,* and *thee;* in most of Fletcher's plays (for what this is worth) *ye* usually outnumbers *you, thou,* and *thee* combined in scene after scene. One must doubt, therefore, that "*ye* serves to distinguish the shares." Waller himself, in fact, seems to have doubted it, for he not only acknowledged that the incidence of *ye*'s was "decidedly low," but he also went to great lengths to account for so low a figure. He postulates a very special kind of manuscript as printer's copy to account for the missing *ye*'s.

Throughout his essay Waller describes the evidence he sees in the quarto text as evidence for foul papers; nevertheless, he suggests that the printer's copy may have been a "literal transcript" of the foul papers, hastily made in 1613 for use perhaps while the play was being rehearsed. This "literal transcript"—a scribal manuscript intermediate between author's foul papers and scribal prompt-copy—is a curious species of manuscript recently hypothesized by Fredson Bowers, to whom we must turn for an explanation.

Bowers first supposes that a dramatist may sometimes have failed to deliver a fair copy of his play to a dramatic company; if he delivered only his foul papers, then,

in some cases, especially if the papers were not in very good shape, it could well have been expedient, in lieu of the author's fair copy, for a theatrical scribe to make an intermediate transcript of them for consideration, revision, submission to the censor, copying of the parts, or sometimes for marking and cutting in preparation for the final prompt book.

Bowers describes the kind of manuscript he believes would then result:

In the circumstances some scribes might attempt to clean up difficulties in the act of transcribing, but . . . it is more probable that he would usually concentrate on making a more or less faithful copy of the foul papers before him, and would reproduce many of the very authorial characteristics which in printed form are taken as indicating foul papers.

And he defends these speculations as follows:

The idea that on some occasions an intermediate scribal fair [?] copy of author's true foul papers was made is not idle speculation only, for there is some evidence in its favor. For example, various tangles in the 1647 Folio text of Fletcher's *Wife for a Month* suggest the unlikelihood that a prompt copy stood behind the text. On the other hand, according to Dr. Hoy's recent study there is a considerable diminution in some classes, though not in all, of Fletcher's linguistic characteristics, . . . which resembles the situation found in the preserved transcript of Fletcher's *Bonduca* made by the book-keeper Edward Knight from autograph.[18]

The "diminution in some classes . . . of Fletcher's . . . characteristics" in *A Wife for a Month* was, however, purely a conjecture on the part of Hoy and was based *solely* on the presupposition that the 176 *ye*'s in the Folio text were not enough to warrant the assumption of foul papers as copy even though the text otherwise looked to Hoy as if it derived from foul papers (cf. note 14). Hoy too, of course, cited the Knight manuscript of *Bonduca,* a copy made for a private patron, to support his theory that an intermediate transcript of *A Wife for a Month* may have stood behind the Folio text. The Bowers-Hoy speculations, however, have by no means been "idle"; they have been very active indeed, as may be inferred from the following remark by Philip Edwards in his generally favorable review (for *Shakespeare Quarterly*) of the Waller essay:

It is now generally recognized [!] that a number of the dramatic manuscripts secured by publishers must have been "transitional": that is to say, a draft or copy of the play at one stage of its development marked and annotated as a prelude to the writing out of the next stage.[19]

The idea of such transcripts is not altogether new, of course, for casual references to "a rough copy of the play which had been carelessly transcribed for some subordinate purpose of the playhouse" [20] were once the commonplaces of bad scholarship, although many had hoped that the reformation in textual studies of the past fifty years had put an end to this sort of thing.[21]

---

[18] Bowers, *On Editing Shakespeare and the Elizabethan Dramatists* (1955), pp. 20–21. Although this theory presupposes that an author had submitted foul papers, Bowers elsewhere (pp. 14–16, 111–114) imagines circumstances that might require an intermediate transcript to be produced even when an author submitted *fair* copy. Bowers' two intermediate transcripts are wholly separate (and equally conjectural), but in support of his theory on *TNK* Waller cites passages from Bowers' arguments on both varieties.

[19] Edwards, rev. of *Studies in Bibliography* Vol. XI, *SQ,* X (1959), 228.

[20] Sidney Lee, Introd. to Oxford facsimile of the 1623 Folio (1902), p. xii.

[21] Cf. F. P. Wilson, "Shakespeare and the 'New Bibliography'," *The Bibliographical Society, 1892–1942: Studies in Retrospect* (1945), pp. 76–135.

In any case Waller postulates a transcript; "no very clear alternative to the intermediate transcript presents itself, to account for the diminished number of *ye*'s in Fletcher's scenes" (p. 77). This manuscript is regularly treated by Waller as so literal a copy of authorial autograph as to amount to a virtual facsimile or a Malone Society edition (making the suggestion of haste in its preparation not merely difficult to accept but even to grasp); it was faithless only in removing the evidence for Fletcher that Waller cannot find. There is, as Waller acknowledges, no actual evidence in the Cotes Quarto that points to a transcript—and later we shall see some positive evidence that seems decisive against any kind of transcript—for "if scribal intervention has been at work, it has manifested itself only in a diminution of Fletcher's *ye*'s."

Waller's longest comment on the *ye*'s in the text concerns the fact that *ye* occurs seven times in the Epilogue but not at all in the Prologue:

If the printer's copy for the dramatic text proper were a transcript, it is quite possible that the Epilogue, at least, was still printed from Fletcher's original draft. The [three] *you*'s in the Prologue, however, may denote [!] that it was set from a transcript.

(p. 78)

Texts of the Prologue and Epilogue are reproduced in Appendix A; even a casual reading—with some attention to the uses to which *I, we,* and *you,* as well as *ye,* are put—should suggest that purely literary considerations in the tone of the speaker to his audience account for the pronouns in each; the greater part of the Epilogue is, as with most Shakespearean and other plays of the period, less formal—more intimate and personal—than the Prologue, and substitution of *ye* for *you* or of *you* for *ye* in either speech would at most points be difficult to imagine (e.g. at Prologue 25: "Do but you hold out/ Your helping hands, and we shall tack about . . ."). Similar considerations apply to other parts of the text, as the reader may find if he turns to Gerrold's speech to the Countrymen in III.v (cf. page 27), in which six of the *ye*'s in the play occur in the first eight lines; over half of the *ye*'s in the play are, like these, commonplace plurals. And elsewhere, in a note to a discussion of the dramatic development of Palamon and Arcite (page 277), we shall have an opportunity to observe how second-person pronouns follow a certain consistent pattern through a representative cross-section of dramatic scenes, and this should make clear that the printed pronouns must reproduce pretty faithfully the actual words spoken on the stage and that the likelihood of serious scribal or compositorial interference in this text is negligible. Literary considerations take precedence over the mechanical interpretation of arbitrarily chosen statistics. The "linguistic evidence" for a division of hands in the copy is feeble, and the hypothesis of a transcript to account for its feebleness is willful and unwarranted.

Orthography and a Compositorial Division

One who proceeds on a given hypothesis is not very likely to overlook evidence which would support that hypothesis (whatever else he may overlook), and Waller did not fail to look down every avenue that might have led to corroborative evidence for the supposed division in the copy. It occurred to him, for example, that there might be a general distinction in spellings between the "two parts" of the play, for he was undoubtedly aware that such distinctions do often appear in manuscripts and books produced from mixed copy and that such a distinction might be expected to be especially apparent in the hands of authors so different from each other in most of their spelling habits as Shakespeare and Fletcher. On this point he reported as follows:

I had hoped that a tabulation of various morphological groups according to the authorial divisions might be possible, but any significant variation which might have once appeared seems to have been almost hopelessly obscured by the compositorial pattern.

(p. 83)

Another class of evidence which tradition implies should be present, but which is not, is thus explained away—this time by reference to "the compositorial pattern." Perhaps we should therefore look next at this "pattern."

Waller has worked out a division of labor between two compositors:

An analysis of certain spellings and of the spacings around punctuation shows that the quarto was set by two compositors, Compositor A doing B1-C1, C2^v-E4, F3^v-G2^v, G4^v, I1-I4^v, K3, and L4^v-M2^v, and Compositor B, C1^v-C2, E4^v-F3, G3-G4, H1-H4^v, I4^v-K2, K3^v-L3^v, M3^v-M4^v, and the Prologue and Epilogue on A1^v and N1. [*sic*]

(p. 78)

Apart from the opening clause in the sentence just quoted, Waller publishes none of the evidence by which he arrived at these assignments. The amount and the complexity of the other material comprehended by his essay will perhaps justify the omission to some extent. Yet the assignment of I4^v to both compositors and the failure to assign K2^v, L4, and M3 to either compositor would surely seem to call for explanation or at least brief notice. The proposed division, moreover, would mean that the compositors, if pages had been set seriatim, would have exchanged labor no less than thirteen times, or if the quarto had been set by the forme, that they would have shared work on no less than ten formes—C(i), E(o), F(o,i), G(o,i), K(o), L(o), M(o,i)—or if the I4^v assignment is accurate on eleven. Minor irregularities in the printing that cut across Waller's assignments (e.g. a setting of the running-title distinguished by the misprint *Foble* that appears both on sigs. H3 and I4, a peculiar broken *e* that appears both on sigs. E3^v [14th line] and K1 [6th line]) cast further doubt on his division. But this matter is not very important, and further reference to the compositorial question may be deferred until, very soon, we complete our review of the Waller theory as a whole. In any case, the "significant variation" in spellings which "might have once appeared" but which has since been "almost hopelessly obscured" is merely another minor instance of the presumptuousness that characterizes so many writings on this play.

History of the Hypothetical Transcript

We may finally attempt to trace the history of the manuscript that Waller believes was used by the printer in 1634. Placing the original production of the play at some date prior to 10 April 1613 (too early by several months),[22] Waller thinks that the play probably "had to be written and put together under some pressure" that would account for "carelessness" and "irregularities . . . left untouched" in the manuscript (p. 84). Early in 1613, then, "initial plans for production of the *Kinsmen*" were laid with a manuscript consisting either of the two authors' foul papers or, more probably, a "very literal transcript of them," and "with the marginal annotations representing notes the prompter made during this planning stage" (pp. 76–77). Since this literal transcript would not have been adequate for use as a prompt-book, it must have been used only temporarily (during rehearsals) and a prompt-book would later have been transcribed from it for use at the 1613 performances. The intermediate transcript would then have gone back into the company archives.

Between 1613 and 1626 the first prompt-book must have gone astray. At the time of the revival about 1626 the intermediate transcript would have been taken from the archives by the book-keeper Knight as he made plans for the new production. "All" the marginal annotations, as well as the

---

[22] Ignoring *Henry VIII* and ignoring all of the dating evidence for *TNK* except the borrowing from the Beaumont *Masque* (cf. Appendix A), Waller suggests the play was staged "before the festivities attendant upon the wedding of Elizabeth and Frederick were over" (p. 84); the royal couple left London on 10 April.

actors' names, would probably have been added to the 1613 manuscript at this time by Knight. (This assertion appears on page 64 of Waller's essay, and is not reconciled by him with the apparently contradictory assertion on page 77, quoted in the preceding paragraph, that the marginal notes were probably made in 1613.) A new prompt-book would then have to be transcribed from the intermediate transcript for use at the revival performances, and the 1613 transcript would go back again to the archives.

For one reason or another—perhaps because the second prompt-book too was lost—the intermediate transcript, that hastily prepared facsimile of the foul papers in which some scribe had purged away the evidence of Fletcher's hand, was the copy the company provided to John Waterson in 1634.

A. W. Pollard once made reference to "the theory that rocks were created with fossils in them to tempt proud geologists to unbelief." That theory was held by the elder Gosse, and it served to keep his world coherent for him by reconciling the fossil-evidence he had been forced to observe with the presuppositions he carried with him from his fundamentalist faith.

Although further reference will be made to Waller's views on some points to be discussed, the remainder of the chapter is given over to the exposition of a hypothesis quite different from his. In the view of the present writer, the Cotes Quarto can be satisfactorily explained only by assuming that the printer's copy consisted of an author's manuscript which had served as a prompt-book and that this manuscript was in Shakespeare's hand. The order of the discussion will be to begin with two subsidiary matters—the numbering of scenes in the quarto text and the compositorial question—and then go on to the main areas of evidence, including speech-prefixes and stage directions, the text of the dialogue, and the relevant printed and manuscript texts of Shakespeare's and Fletcher's work which provide us with criteria for judging the quarto.

Scene-numbers

The play is fully divided into acts and scenes in the quarto, each new scene beginning after a stage-clearing *exeunt*. Three scenes, however, are wrongly numbered; scenes iv–vi of Act II are numbered 4, 4, and 6 respectively, and scenes iv–vi of Act III are numbered 4, 6, and 7 respectively. (The first scene in Act I, also, is left unnumbered.) Waller is correct in observing that "the errors do not seem to have resulted from an alteration of the play's original structure," and he appears to be correct in his further observations (a) that "we would expect accuracy if the divisions were intro-

duced . . . as a means of articulating the shares of the two authors" and
(b) that the errors suggest the scene divisions were probably introduced at
the time the play was published (p. 73). This last point would accord with
the historical evidence; the earliest surviving playhouse manuscript to be
fully divided into scenes, the scribal prompt-copy of *Sir John van Olden
Barnavelt,* dates from 1619; formally numbered scene-division, more a literary than a theatrical convention, seems to have become common only by
Caroline times. There may also be some direct bibliographical evidence
that the manuscript was originally undivided, for at the end of IV.iii appears a *"Florish"* which clearly belongs (and is so placed by some editors)
with the entrance of Theseus and his train, after the act-heading, at the
beginning of V.i; another such *"Florish"* is similarly misplaced on the
wrong side of the scene-division between V.ii and V.iii (and is similarly
corrected by Kittredge and several other editors).

The errors in scene-numbering, as Waller agrees, do not appear to be
related to any hypothetical division of labor between two compositors. The
typography of act- and scene-headings, it may be added, is uniform
throughout. Act-headings are centered, spelled out (e.g. *"Actus Tertius."*),
and set off between rules above and below. Scene-divisions are indicated
only by the numbers at the left of the first entrance direction in each scene;
for example:

> Scæna 2. *Enter Palamon, and Arcite in prison.*

The scene-headings invariably include the spelling *Scæna* in roman type,
the arabic numeral, the point, with the direction afterward in italic. The
headings may simply have been added to the entrance directions in the
printing house, and the misnumbering of three scenes appears on the whole
to be insignificant.

The Compositor Question

The Cotes Quarto appears to have been set by a single compositor. As in
every book whose setting is not perfectly uniform, various minor distinctions may be observed on the basis of which one might postulate a division
between two compositors, but a thorough application of tests developed by
Hinman, Alice Walker, and others reveals no reliable evidence (to the present investigator at least) sufficient to establish such a division. The next
few pages will summarize the evidence examined; a reader not interested
in this question may simply skip to the next section.

Many inconsistencies in the quarto provide leads to evidence of a compositorial division. Initial entrance directions (and one mid-scene entrance)

are more generously spaced (separated from the dialogue by lines of quads) in the first eight scenes (through sig. E3) than afterwards. Variant abbreviations appear in speech-prefixes (e.g. *Hipol./Hyp.*). Distinctions in the relative frequency of certain variant spellings are easy to find; for the record, those checked include *do(e)* and *go(e)*; *we(e)* and other pronouns; *-es(se)*, *-ew(e)/-ow(e)*, and *-ie/-y* endings; words with medial *-ea-/-ie-* and *-ou-/-ow-;* and certain words which are more or less common in this text such as *Cosen/Cosin*. In no pair of variants (with one apparent exception noted below) is the observable distinction statistically very sharp, and no pattern derived from any of the pairs (by finding a moderate preference for one form on some pages and for its variant on others) appears to correspond with a pattern derived from the others. The evidence for two compositors, in short, is tenuous in itself, and the counter-evidence to be summarized in a moment, although not decisive, is substantially stronger.

One class of spellings calls attention to itself as soon as one begins to examine the text; one notes a number of *-nck* spellings in the early pages followed by an apparent increase in *-nk* spellings. Waller has noted this point too, and in the case of this single variant he gives statistics:

The ratio of spellings in *-nck* and *-nk* in the non-Fletcherian scenes is 8:16, but in the Fletcherian scenes, 3:48; however, in the second half of the text only one *-nck* spelling occurs.

(p. 83)

Waller hints at an authorial rather than a compositorial distinction; the table below will perhaps suggest that the *-nk/-nck* variant proves upon analysis to be relevant to neither (and at the same time may suggest how an initial impression otherwise may arise):

	-nck	*-nk*	*thinke(s)* & *thanke(s)* *	
B1	Pinckes (Act I sc.i)		B1–B4^v	3
B2^v		shrunke (I.i)		
B3	wrinckled (I.i)			
B4^v	banckes (I.i)			
	sincke (I.ii)			
C1	Cranckes (I.ii)		C1–C4^v	2
C2^v	Thanckes (I.iii)			
D3	sincke (II.ii)		D1–D4^v	10
			E1–E4^v	5
F1	rancke (II.v)		F1–F4^v	4

F2	bancke (III.i)			
G1$^\text{v}$		trinkets (III.iii)	G1–G4$^\text{v}$	7
G3		Tinker [3x] (III.v)		
G3$^\text{v}$	twinckling (III.v)			
			H1–H4$^\text{v}$	7
			I1–I4$^\text{v}$	3
K3		prankes (IV.iii)	K1–K4$^\text{v}$	8
K4$^\text{v}$		ore-rank (V.i)		
L4$^\text{v}$		winke (V.iii)	L1–L4$^\text{v}$	9
M2	banckes (V.iii)		M1–M4$^\text{v}$	6

* These figures include 57 instances of *thinke(s)* or *thanke(s)*, 3 of *think*, 1 of *thinkst*, 2 of *thankefull*, and 1 of *thank'd*. *Banket*, always so spelled, also occurs 3 times (on B4, F3$^\text{v}$, & M3), but is omitted from the count as irrelevant.

Most of the *-nk* words are variants of the common *think* and *thank;* as the table shows, few examples of these words appear in the earlier pages, with the result that the first half dozen or so less common *-nck* spellings catch the eye.

Apart from the difficulty in finding any solid evidence for two compositors, several features in the quarto look like positive evidence for just one. Swash-italic capitals are mixed with the regular italic font in stage directions, pre-fixes, and names throughout the text; but this may be insignificant. More important is a general consistency in make-up—in the uniformity of act- and scene-headings mentioned earlier and in the regularity in the setting of the normal stage directions. Also significant is the widespread treatment of prose as verse, described in Chapter I, in II.i, II.iii, III.iii, III.v, IV.i, IV.iii, and V.ii; it is hard to imagine two compositors falling into the same error or else deliberately padding the text this way in collusion with each other. There is, finally, the evidence of spellings; a number of slightly unusual spellings that reappear frequently throughout the quarto suggest (if, that is, they are not author's spellings) a single compositor—e.g. *lose,* so spelled twice, is spelled *loose(s)* seventeen times. An attempt to determine whether or not the spellings of common recurrent words are generally consistent requires, of course, that one select a sufficiently broad sample according to some non-literary criterion; for this purpose, the past participles of weak verbs provide a good stock of evidence—there are 429 in the quarto—and their analysis shows hardly anything that would support the assumption of two compositors. The less commonplace examples, naturally, are the most instructive. In words such as *died,* for example, the most common Caroline spellings would be *died* or *dyed; di'd* (or *dy'd*) and *dide* (or *dyde*) would be less common; in the Cotes Quarto we find *dide* (once, *dyde*), *tide* (once, *tyde*), *cride, tride, denide,* wherever *died, tied,* etc., appear in modern texts. Other general classes are analogously consistent throughout. It is quite possible that spellings such as *loose* for *lose* and *dide* for *died* reproduce the forms found in the copy and are not compositorial choices, but that would further strengthen the assumption of a single compositor, since two compositors who faithfully reproduced copy-spellings would be less likely than one. In short, if there were two compositors, the evidence of typography, of format, of verse lineation, and of spellings suggests that each had strikingly similar habits and treated his copy in much the same fashion as his partner. It will therefore have to be assumed that, as in the first quartos of *King Lear* and *Othello*,[23] there was probably but a single compositor.

General consistency in spellings may of course point to a single hand in the copy. Although the question of authorial spellings will be examined later, we might revert to Waller's supposition that two compositors could have "obscured" a hypothetical distinction between two hands in the copy. The supposition that two compositors could do so is twice as improbable as the supposition that one compositor would do so, as the following example may suggest. One of the most common Elizabethan spellings of *been* is *bin,* and *bin* is the most common spelling in nearly all texts of Shakespeare printed from autograph copy. Although *bin* had not become rare by 1634, *bene* or *been* were the more common Caroline forms, and they seem to have been the forms preferred by Fletcher throughout his career.[24] In the Cotes Quarto, however, *bin* is the consistent choice, and it would be doubly improbable for two compositors to depart from a more modern copy-spelling in identical ways and revert to the Elizabethan form. It would

---

[23] Cf. Philip Williams, "The Compositor of the 'Pied Bull' *Lear*," *Papers of the Bibl. Soc. of Virginia* [*SB*], I (1948), 59–68, and Charlton Hinman, "Principles Governing the Use of Variant Spellings . . . ," *The Library,* 4th Ser., XXI (1940), 78–94 (cites *Othello* Q1). Division of labor on short dramatic quartos may have been exceptional, and recent articles claiming to show such divisions have not always presented conclusive cases; the analysis of spellings in *Hamlet* Q2 in Vol. VII of *SB* (1955), for example, shows only a single statistically notable distinction—which, as Hinman has pointed out, is not sufficient to establish a division—and the companion essay by Fredson Bowers in the same volume, purporting to identify two sets of running-titles in that quarto, gives no measurements and thus actually cites no evidence whatever.

[24] The spelling *bene* is found in the earliest printed Fletcher text, the c.1609 quarto of *The Faithful Shepherdess* (e.g. in the author's lines "To the Reader" on sig. ¶2ᵛ), as well as in the later texts identified on pp. 107–108.

therefore be gratifying to find that two compositors had worked on the quarto, but the evidence does not seem to warrant it.

Greg on the Cotes Quarto

The most recent comment by Sir Walter Greg on *The Two Noble Kinsmen* is his statement, published in 1956, that the play "was produced about 1613 . . . and was printed in 1634 from what was almost certainly the original prompt-book." [25] The context in which this statement appeared— a study of licensing and copyright—precluded the discussion of specific textual evidence, and Greg's earlier comments on the play were not themselves sufficient to explain so decisive a conclusion; they went no farther than the occasional citation of a few stage directions as typical examples of a book-keeper's work, a few references to Knight's connection with the copy at the time of the revival, and a single citation of one stage direction— the entrance direction for "2. *or* 3. *wenches* . . ." in III.v—as a typical author's direction "which Knight did not alter" (*Folio,* p. 136). The evidence from which Greg concluded that the printer's copy had "almost certainly" been "the original prompt-book," however, is manifest on almost every page of the quarto, and any impartial review of that evidence—any review, that is, which is not misled by the supposition that signs of authorial copy are to be equated with signs of foul papers (copy too poor, by definition, to serve as a prompt-book)—will bear out Greg's conclusion. Our review will begin with the speech-prefixes, go on to the stage directions, and move finally to the text of the dialogue.

Speech-prefixes

Meticulous accuracy in the speech-prefixes of a printed play is often a sign that the source copy had been a prompt-book, just as serious defects, confusions, and omissions in the prefixes may point to foul papers. The prefixes in the Cotes Quarto show six irregularities which may be regarded as defects,[26] and probably from two to four of these were inherited from the manuscript. Their description follows:

[25] Greg, *Some Aspects and Problems of London Publishing between 1550 and 1650* (1956), p. 111.

[26] Another irregularity in the prefixes—although not a defect—occurs at III.v.63, where the prefix *"Daughter."* is printed (like the nine stage directions cited elsewhere) in the outer page-margin of sig. G2^v; it appears next to a song rather than a speech, and it may have been omitted by the dramatist and added later, perhaps unusually far to the left, by a book-keeper.

(1) The prefix "1.2.*K.*" at V.iv.49 ("Wee'l follow cheerefully.") has already been discussed.

(2) The line, "This garden has a world of pleasures in't" (II.ii.130), concludes a speech by Arcite in the quarto, and Emilia begins to speak at line 131, "What flowre is this?" Editors reassign line 130 to Emilia; if they are right, the prefix has been placed a line too late by the compositor—possibly owing to an imperfectly aligned prefix in the margin of the manuscrift, an error which is common enough and without significance.

(3, 4) At IV.i.177–178 in the quarto we find:

1. *Fr.* Do's she know him?
1. *Fr.* No, would she did.

Editors naturally reassign the answer to "*2ⁿᵈ Friend.*" A similar error appears at III.v.104, at which "*Per.*" is repeated from line 103 and corrected by editors to "*Theseus.*" Since both cases of repetition look like the result of "eye-skip," both are somewhat more easily attributable to a compositor than an author.

(5) The prefix for Palamon is omitted at V.iv.1. If the manuscript rather than the compositor were at fault, this error would perhaps be the most notable of the six. But it would not be troublesome at a performance, since the lines for which the prefix is lacking make up the long speech by Palamon at the opening of the scene (printed on page 70), and about the assignment of this speech not even the most muddle-headed prompter could have been confused; the entrance direction for Palamon would suffice in lieu of a prefix, just as (for example) the stage directions at *Troilus* II.iii.1 (Q & F) and V.vii.1 (Q) or at *Julius Caesar* III.i.254 double quite satisfactorily as prefixes for the speeches they precede.

(6) Another omission occurs at III.v.143, a line belonging to Gerrold the Schoolmaster. In this case, however, the omission points toward rather than away from a prompt-copy. In the left-hand margin of sig. G3ᵛ, adjacent to lines 143–145, we find the note, "Knocke for/ Schoole. Enter/ The Dance." The prefix for Gerrold—"Sch." throughout the scene—might have been obliterated in the manuscript margin and "Schoole." made to double as a prefix, or else it may simply have been obscured by the note (leading the compositor to overlook it), just as similar marginal notes in several extant prompt-books sometimes obscured adjacent speech-prefixes. The prompter's note on the left, moreover, partially duplicates an authorial direction—"*Musicke Dance.*"—at the right of line 142, so that with two strong pieces of evidence for a prompt-book at this point (the note itself and the duplication it contains), it would be straining to regard the omitted prefix as a sign of foul papers; [27] Waller cites it as such (p. 74), but fails to say that it occurs together with the marginal note and duplication.

[27] Another possibility should be mentioned, for still another irregularity occurs near the note: Gerrold's epilogue for the morris dance (ll. 144–153) is printed in italic

Before summarizing the evidence of the speech-prefixes, it may be useful to draw comparisons with two other more widely known texts. In the exceptionally clean and accurate Folio text of *Julius Caesar,* thought by nearly all critics to have been derived from a prompt-book, no less than five speech-prefixes are missing (at III.i.254, IV.ii.34–36, V.iv.7) and from two to four others are erroneous (at I.i.16, III.i.101, III.ii.208 & 213); all but one or two of these seven to nine errors are textually insignificant and no critic has suggested that they constitute evidence for foul papers; the prefix errors in the Cotes Quarto (all of which Waller cites as evidence for foul papers) are fewer in number and quite as trivial as those in *Julius Caesar.* For prefix irregularities typical of a text generally agreed to derive from foul papers, we might consider the 1600 quarto of *2 Henry IV,* in which Falstaff in the space of a single scene is variously *John, Sir John, Falstaff,* and *Oldcastle,* where *John* serves also for Prince John, where both Prince John and Prince Henry are sometimes simply *Prince,* where the Boy is *Page* and *Boy,* where the Chief Justice is *Justice* and *Lord,* where Mowbray is *Marshal* in one scene and *Mowbray* in another, where Doll Tearsheet is variously *Doll, Dorothy, Tearsheet,* and *Whore;* in the Cotes Quarto, however, there is only a single inconsistency—the *Keeper/Jailor* discrepancy discussed earlier —and only the six defects just described. On the whole, (3) and (4) are probably attributable to the compositor, (5) and (6) probably to the manuscript, and (1) and (2) are a toss-up. None of the errors could give serious trouble to a prompter, who was, moreover, probably responsible for one of them (6) himself; extant prompt-books, in fact, sometimes contain irregularities in their prefixes more troublesome than any of these six.[28] Since

---

type (the only piece of dialogue—if it *is* dialogue and not a song!—so printed in the play), suggesting that the epilogue may have been written on a separate slip of paper in a different (Italian) hand and the slip then "flown" on the manuscript at this point (like the example in the prompt-book described in n. 28 below); this hypothesis would account for the other irregularities and would again point not to foul papers but to a prompt-book.

[28] In the 1619 scribal prompt-book of *The Tragedy of Sir John van Olden Barnavelt* (ed. W. P. Frijlinck, 1922) consecutive speeches are given to the same speaker at ll. 791 ff. and 796 ff. (cf. Frijlinck, pp. xii, 22, 23); a prefix is omitted at 2041, and the assignment of 2696 to *Orange* is evidently an error. Another kind of difficulty may be seen in the otherwise clean book of the 1611 play known as *The Second "Maiden's Tragedy"* (ed. Greg, Malone Society, 1909) in which an 11-line speech designed to follow l. 1724 was written on a separate slip of paper (in the same scribal hand as the original dialogue) and then "flown" on the original leaf (fol. 48ᵃ); the speaker is unidentified. Near the insertion-slip, in the left-hand margin of the original leaf, and in a different hand, the direction *"Enter mʳ Goughe"* has been added—from which Greg is led to assign the inserted lines to the character Memphronius. The King's company prompter in 1611 would know what was what, but if the MS had gone to a printer without further annotation, the compositor would have known less than Greg and the probable result would have been textual confusion.

each error is trivial, and since there are approximately 830 prefixes correctly assigned to the thirty-three speakers in the play, one cannot regard the errors as evidence for foul papers unless "foul papers" were newly defined e.g. as "a carefully prepared author's copy in which the always inevitable omissions and inconsistencies that remained had been dutifully corrected and regularized by one or more book-keepers." If we attribute three, say, of the errors to the manuscript rather than to the compositor, the prefixes in the manuscript would have been 99.64% perfect. On balance, the evidence of the speech-prefixes strongly favors the assumption of a prompt-book as copy.

Stage Directions

The stage directions in the quarto are unusual both in their quantity and in their variety. Their elaboration of detail, comparable to what we find in the Folio texts of *Coriolanus* and *Antony and Cleopatra,* suggests a very carefully prepared authorial manuscript, although the full complement of book-keeper's annotations suggests that, unlike those Folio texts, the manuscript had also been thoroughly prepared for use as a prompt-book. (A reader who wishes to observe the volume, range, and variety of the directions as a whole and to compare them generally with those in other texts will find that an edition such as Kittredge's, with bracketing to distinguish editorial changes or additions, will serve almost as well as a copy of the quarto.) The evidence for authorial copy is to be sought also, of course, in the body of the text (outside the stage directions) to be examined later, but a number of clearly authorial directions in addition to those already reproduced (pages 62, 70–71, and 72) will be cited as we proceed with a review of irregularities and other noteworthy features in the stage directions as a whole. The adequacy of the directions for prompt-book purposes, partly because it has been denied by Waller, is the issue which ought perhaps to be given major emphasis in these pages.

The most immediately arresting bibliographical oddities of the quarto are no doubt the marginal annotations—one speech-prefix (cf. note 26 above) and nine stage directions. Four of these directions have already been cited—the three warning notes (page 60) and the duplication of an authorial direction at III.v.143–145 (page 90); all four are pretty clearly the work of a book-keeper. Five others remain.

Two of these five are sufficiently unusual to merit reproduction with the adjoining text. One is printed abreast III.vi.123–125; Palamon and Arcite, preparing for their duel, have just helped each other don their armor:

Arc. Take my Sword, I hold it better.

Pal. I thanke ye: No, keepe it, your life lyes on it,
Here's one, if it but hold, I aske no more,
For all my hopes: My Cause and honour guard me.

They bow se-
verall wayes:
then advance
and stand.

Arc. And me my love: ★ Is there ought else to say?

Pal. This onely, and no more: Thou art mine Aunts Son.
And that blood we desire to shed is mutuall,
In me, thine, and in thee, mine . . .

(sig. H1ᵛ)

The star printed in line 123 indicates the point at which they bow, and the direction is apparently authorial. The other unusual direction, next to the heading for Act III, begins at a point opposite the last line of the Daughter's soliloquy in II.vi, although it provides for the sounds which open III.i:

. . . farewell Father;
Get many more such prisoners, and such daughters,
And shortly you may keepe your selfe. Now to him:

Cornets in
sundry places.
Noise and
hallowing as
people a May-
ing.

Actus Tertius.

Scæna 1. *Enter Arcite alone.*
Arcite. The Duke has lost Hypolita; each tooke
A severall land. This is a solemne Right
They owe bloomd May . . .

(sig. F2)

The indefinite "sundry places" and the phrase "as people a Maying" strongly imply another author's direction, and if we follow the usual assumption that the position of a printed direction probably reflects its approximate position in the copy, it would seem that II.vi (usually assigned to Fletcher) and III.i (assigned to Shakespeare) appeared on the same manuscript leaf.

The three remaining marginal directions are as follows:

(1) Florish.   (on sig. A1ᵛ, in upper left margin, just above first line of Prologue)

(2) This short flo-   (on sig. E4ᵛ, abreast the entrance direction and first
rish of Cor-   three lines of II.v)
nets and
Showtes with-
in.

(3) *Sing.*   (on sig. G1ᵛ, abreast III.iv.19)

Most of the marginal annotations are printed in roman; possibly the two exceptions (the third item above and the speech-prefix cited in note 26) reflect additions to the original copy made in an Italian hand. Ordinarily, however, the compositor maintained a high degree of uniformity in his style; the regular stage directions throughout the text, as stated before, are set in italic, although in the Prologue and Epilogue, where the speeches themselves are printed in an oversized italic, the directions are printed conversely in an oversized roman.

Scholars and editors dealing with this play for the past two hundred years have often remarked, on the evidence of some of the marginal directions, that the quarto was apparently printed from a prompt-book. Insofar as this traditional conclusion rests mainly on the few warning notes and actors' names, it is not quite solidly grounded; such details might conceivably (if improbably) represent, as Waller suggests, mere annotations on foul papers. There is, however (as we have already seen in the speech-prefixes), much wider evidence of a prompt-book. Part of it is to be found in the stage directions that call for musical effects, flourishes, noises, and miscellaneous other sound effects. There are no less than thirty such directions in all.

Comparisons may be helpful. In the excellent Folio text of *Cymbeline* the stage directions provide for all essential business and are sufficient, along with other factors, to satisfy many observers that the copy may have been a prompt-book; yet they include only two sound-effect directions, both of which (at IV.ii.186 and V.iv.30) are requests for "Solemn Musick" and look as if they were supplied by the author; even when Cymbeline enters "in state" at III.i.1, there is no direction for a "flourish" or "trumpets" or any other of the proclamations that usually accompanied ceremonial entrances and which book-keepers often added to the manuscripts they prepared for performances. In *The Two Noble Kinsmen,* every ceremonial entrance for Theseus is accompanied by a direction for a flourish. (In the case of I.i the flourish appears at the end of the Prologue and for V.i and V.iii the direction for the flourish is printed with the final *exeunt* of the preceding scene.) In the prompt-book of *Believe as You List,* a manuscript in Massinger's autograph which has been about as heavily annotated by the book-keeper (Knight) as any dramatic text that survives, there are, in addition to a single direction for music (later deleted) by Massinger, only four flourishes added by Knight and a single further direction by Knight that a lute be sounded at the beginning of a song. In *The Two Noble Kinsmen* there are, in addition to four directions simply for music, ten directions for a flourish without specification of instruments, two calling for flourishes of cornets, eight others calling for cornets to be sounded, five for horns, another for both horns and cornets (possibly an error), another for both trumpets and cornets, one for recorders, and a few others for such special sound effects as "clanging of Armor."

Several of these directions, especially the longer ones, are almost certainly authorial—as, for example, when Emilia's prayer to Diana in V.i is interrupted by a sign from the goddess: *"Here is heard a sodaine twang of Instruments, and the Rose fals from the Tree."* Or during the offstage combat between Palamon and Arcite in V.iii, when the audience is to hear trumpets *"sound as to a charge."* Other directions, however, imply that the manuscript had been amended wherever necessary for prompting purposes, as the following set of examples will illustrate. We find a *Florish* directed at the beginning of the Prologue and another at the end of the Prologue; still another appears at the end, but not at the beginning, of the Epilogue on sig. N1; although we need not therefore have expected another such *Florish* at the beginning of the Epilogue, it is interesting to note that such a direction would have been superfluous, for on the preceding page of the text, sig. M4^v, we find there is already a *Florish* accompanying the final *exeunt* of the last scene in the play. The implication is that a book-keeper had carefully integrated the theatrical directions for Prologue and Epilogue with the text; it would be unusual for a dramatist to bother himself with these minor duties of a book-keeper. In any case, the record of sound-effect directions in the printed text is as lavish as the most diligent book-keeper might have supplied. That is the essential point.

There remain a few special points to be noted about the sound-effect directions. Printed at III.i.105 we find *"Winde hornes of Cornets."* Dyce changed the direction to *"Horns winded within."* Kittredge gives it as *"Wind horns [within]."* Many editors retain the anomalous original direction without offering any explanation; neither Dyce nor any of the editors who followed him in changing it has offered any comment. The dialogue at line 107 ("You heare the Hornes") indicates that it is the cornets which are superfluous. The word *off* was sometimes spelled *of* in the earlier seventeenth century (e.g. by Knight in the direction "Pull of their disguises" at line 2210 of *The Soddered Citizen*) and it appears spelled so in several printed Shakespeare texts. *"Winde hornes of[f]"* may therefore have been substituted for an erroneous *"Cornets"* by some book-keeper between 1613 and 1634, and the compositor, as would not be unusual, failed to observe a deletion and printed the strange double direction.

W. J. Lawrence has shown that the delicate, almost flute-like seventeenth-century cornet was preferred to the trumpet for sounding flourishes and the like at indoor theatrical performances, and he has pointed out that the exclusive or predominant appearance of the cornet rather than the trumpet in a printed text may indicate a manuscript prepared or adapted for use at an indoor playhouse.[29] The likelihood that *The Two Noble Kinsmen* was written with performance at Blackfriars specifically in mind is based in part on the evidence for dating the play after the burning of the Globe and in part upon internal evidence (the many songs, the pageantry, the use of incense in the altar scene). It may therefore be worth repeating in this connection that cornets rather than trumpets are specified in ten stage directions. Trumpets are specified once, but the same direction calls for cornets also and raises the suspicion of another substitution; at V.iii.66 we find *"Cornets. Trumpets sound as to a charge."* On the other hand, this direction occurs at the height of the combat between Palamon and Arcite, and the startling sound it calls for may be no error but a deliberate and effective dramatic stroke.

With regard to the possible use of the manuscript as a prompt-book, entrance and exit directions would of course be more important than sound-effect directions. There are a few inconsistencies in the text with regard to entrances, and Waller naturally finds that they "point to an authorial manuscript of a species closer to foul paper[s] than fair copy" (p. 70). Specifically, three scenes fail to provide entrances for a few actors to whom speeches are nevertheless assigned in the text. In each case the text makes clear that the actors in question must have entered at the beginning of their respective scenes—I.i, I.iv, and III.v.

The entrance direction for I.i offers a very long description of the marriage procession of Theseus and Hippolyta, part of which reads, *"Then* Theseus *betweene two other Nimphs . . . Then* Hipolita *the Bride, lead by* Theseus *. . ."* No entrance is given for Pirithous, who speaks later in the scene; editors replace the erroneous repetition of Theseus with the intended Pirithous, and the error, as Waller states, is best explained by "compositorial eye-skip." The errors in the other two scenes, however, are more readily attributable to the manuscript.

The entrance for I.iv (which incidentally looks like an author's direction augmented by a book-keeper) reads as follows:

> *Cornets.*
> Scæna 4. *A Battaile strooke withi[n]: Then a Retrait: Florish.*
> *Then Enter Theseus (victor) the three Queenes meete*
> *him, and fall on their faces before him.*

[29] Lawrence, *Shakespeare's Workshop* (1928), pp. 48–74.

Later in the scene Theseus spies the bodies of the wounded Palamon and Arcite lying on stretchers and asks who they are. A Herald gives a brief reply. The presence of the Herald (as well as that of the mute cousins) created no problem at the time of the revival, since the warning-note at I.iii.68 (page 60 above) provided the necessary arrangements. Unless we arbitrarily re-assign that note to one of Knight's predecessors, however, the manuscript must be assumed to have been deficient in the entrances for I.iv in 1613.

The entrance for III.v (cf. page 62) is also deficient, since it introduces—in addition to Gerrold, the Bavian, a taborer, and four Countrymen—only "2. *or* 3. *wenches*" and the action and dialogue make clear that five wenches must appear on stage (all five are named, although only Nell speaks). Such a defect might have been corrected if the authorial manuscript had been transcribed by a careful book-keeper, and the errors in this direction and in the entrances for I.iv appear at first sight to be the strongest evidence that can be adduced against the use of the manuscript as a prompt-book. They also raise an interesting question concerning the analysis of entrance directions in general.

Although Greg points out that indefinite numbers in authors' directions could neither originate with nor commend themselves to a book-keeper, he has also remarked on the "curious" fact that book-keepers did not often bother to correct such numbers when they found them, and he has gone on to illustrate this point by citing a number of examples (including the entrance for "2. *or* 3. *wenches*" in the Cotes Quarto) both from printed texts and from manuscript prompt-books (*Folio,* pp. 135 137). This evidence leads him to conclude that "it is little use arguing that indefinite and optional directions must have been cleared up in the prompt-book when we have reason to suppose that in fact they were often left standing." In the same discussion, however, Greg has also provided what may be the appropriate explanation for this paradox. Citing numerous instances of imprecise *prompt-book* entrances for "a company of countrymen," "ladies," "others," "a crew attending," and so forth, Greg notes that "the exact composition of the groups would doubtless be settled in production and presumably noted in the 'plot,' as all 'attendants' must have been." And elsewhere, in analyzing the surviving stage-plot of Peele's *Alcazar,* Greg has shown how this would work; where the prompt-book of the play might have read (as the printed text does read at the entrance to III.i) "Enter the king of Portugall . . . ," the stage-plot, which must have served the cast as a kind of backstage bulletin-board, would read "Enter 2 bringing in a chair of state . . ." and would name the two supers whom the author would not have needed to imagine.[30]

The offending entrance directions in *The Two Noble Kinsmen* both precede scenes which call for groups of actors so large that they could not easily be brought rapidly together by the most efficient of prompters during a performance, and precision in prompt-books would in such cases be unnecessary; the prompting of the actors in these cases would have to come from their memory of rehearsals, from their colleagues, from their consciences, and from the stage-plots.

Apart from the two exceptions noted, entrances are wholly adequate. Since Waller's published assertions to the contrary have gone unchallenged by reviewers, however, a few further details must be added. There is, as Waller notes, no specific entrance for the "Artesius" to whom Theseus addresses a command at I.i.176, but Artesius is a mute lieutenant, theatrically indistinguishable from any anonymous minor attendant who might appear in the train of a prince. And at V.iv.98 we find the direction *"Enter Theseus, Hipolita, Emilia, Arcite, in a chaire."*—in which the supernumeraries who carry the chair of the wounded Arcite on stage are not specified; Waller, without quoting it, presents this direction as another inadequacy: "The transport of the dying Arcite in his chair at V.iv.85 is left up to Theseus, Hipolita, and Emilia" (p. 70). Waller also seems to regard as insufficiently specific those directions which call for "attendants" or "others"; by the same criterion, every one of the directions that we find for "soldiers" or "others" or the like in the many surviving manuscript prompt-books would have to be interpreted as evidence that these prompt-books could never have served as prompt-books.

Presumably in order to give themselves warning of the action to come, book-keepers occasionally marked entrances a few lines earlier than dramatists had indicated; Knight, for example, did this at several points in the prompt-book of *Believe as You List,* usually deleting Massinger's original entrance directions and replacing them, one to four lines earlier, with more eye-catching directions of his own (as with Antiochus at line 513 rather than 516 or Flaminius at 1844 rather than 1846). A few mid-scene entrance directions in *The Two Noble Kinsmen* also occur a bit earlier than the characters need to appear; the Messenger at IV.ii.74 (on sig. I4ᵛ) enters four

---

[30] Greg, *Two Elizabethan Stage Abridgements: The Battle of Alcazar & Orlando Furioso* (Malone Society, 1923), pp. 32–33. On the relation between the prompt-book and the stage-plot, and especially on the details of casting that normally found their place in the plot but not in the book, cf. Greg, *Dramatic Documents from the Elizabethan Playhouses* (1931), I, 70–93. Certain directions might also be marked only in the actors' parts, on which cf. *Dramatic Documents,* I, 180–181.

lines early; entrances for the Daughter in II.i (sig. D1ᵛ), the Keeper in II.ii (sig. E1ᵛ), and the Second Friend in IV.i (sig. I1ᵛ) appear to be one or two lines early; editors usually move these entrances forward, perhaps restoring what a book-keeper altered.

Exits in the text of the play are complete. A complete record of exits in a manuscript consisting of foul papers is virtually unimaginable. Exits are not always complete, moreover, in prompt-books themselves, and they are certainly not complete in the one surviving example of annotated foul papers.[31] The record of exits in the Cotes Quarto (of which Waller says nothing) is another clear indication of a very carefully prepared manuscript. If that manuscript was not the prompt-copy, it must have been so like the prompt-copy as to be indistinguishable from it.

Two irregularities in entrance and exit directions call for special notice. In addition to the directions already reviewed, the quarto prints one entrance (for Emilia in IV.ii) and one exit (for the Daughter in IV.iii) that appear to be superfluous. Each case probably arose from a different cause and must be dealt with separately.

The superfluous entrance for Emilia appears at IV.ii.54. The scene opens as follows:

> Scæna 2. *Enter Emilia alone, with 2. Pictures.*
> *Emilia.* Yet I may binde those wounds up, that must open
> And bleed to death for my sake else; Ile choose,
> And end their strife . . .

Her soliloquy before the pictures of Palamon and Arcite continues to line 54, after which she is apparently directed to enter again:

> . . . What a meere child is *Fancie,*
> That having two faire gawdes of equall sweetnesse,
> Cannot distinguish, but must crie for both.   [54
> *Enter Emil. and Gent:*
> *Emil.* How now Sir?
> *Gent.* From the Noble Duke your Brother
> Madam, I bring you newes: The Knights are come . . .

The direction is naturally cut down to "Enter Gentleman" in most editions. Waller offers two alternative explanations for the irregularity:

We can only guess whether the [duplicate entrance represents] . . . addition or deletion. The whole scene in which Emilia's soliloquy appears is unquestion-

[31] *The Captives* (Brit. Mus. MS Egerton 1994, art. 3), ed. Arthur Brown (Malone Society, 1953).

ably Fletcher's, so if there has been addition it was Fletcher's; on the other hand, in 54 lines of soliloquy Emilia protests too much, so that deletion is equally possible, by Knight or any one else through whose hands the manuscript passed in the playhouse.

(p. 82)

One's guess need not really be restricted to addition or deletion. The dramatic necessity for the soliloquy and the Shakespearean integrity of the scene must await demonstration in another place, but the superfluous entrance direction can be made intelligible if one may question the unquestionable. Emilia's soliloquy with the pictures is an episode as intimate in character as any in Jacobean drama and would be particularly well suited for playing on the "inner stage" (which at the relatively small Blackfriars theater would be fairly close to the audience). The entrance of the Gentleman at line 54 is succeeded by the entrance of Theseus, Hippolyta, Pirithous, and others at line 67 and of Messengers at line 74. Unless the "inner stage" at Blackfriars were very large indeed, the additional entrances would suggest that Emilia moves forward to the main platform when the Gentleman appears. Superfluous entrances are found in a few other Shakespeare texts; they are identified and described in *The Shakespeare First Folio,* where Greg indexes them, appropriately, under the heading " 'enter' meaning come forward." (An example may be seen at *Coriolanus* II.i.220.) Such an explanation for the second entrance direction satisfies the staging requirements of the scene and eliminates any need to postulate alteration or deletion.

The superfluous exit for the Daughter is a different matter. A question of censorship by the Master of the Revels may be involved. Sir George Buc was the Master in 1613, and the characteristic standards employed by him, as exemplified in his treatment of the King's company play known as *The Second "Maiden's Tragedy,"* seem to be relevant; Buc was particularly sensitive to "impertinence toward persons of rank," as Greg points out in his neat summary of the censorship wrought by Buc on the prompt-book of that play in October 1611:

Buc comes to the defence of the nobility when he insists that it shall be 'some' rather than 'great' men who fear death (l. 1354); of 'your ladies', striking out the jibe that 'theile sooner kill them selues with lust, then for it' (l. 1426) and making it not 'most' but only 'many' who will sacrifice honour before life (l. 1841)—a nice point this!—and of majesty itself when he will have the Tyrant say 'I am poisoned' and not 'your kinges poisond' (l. 2403). . . .

(*Folio,* p. 150)

The superfluous exit in *The Two Noble Kinsmen* comes at IV.iii.36 and is immediately followed by speeches in which the Daughter's ever-present class-consciousness is expressed in what would no doubt seem to Buc a distasteful series of mordant reflections on courtiers and great ladies:

> *Dau.* Faith ile tell you, sometime we goe to Barly breake, [27
> We of the blessed; alas, tis a sore life they have i'th
> Thother place, such burning, frying, boyling, hissing,
> Howling, chattring, cursing, oh they have shrowd
> Measure, take heede; if one be mad, or hang or
> Drowne themselves, thither they goe, *Iupiter* blesse
> Vs, and there shall we be put in a Caldron of
> Lead, and Vsurers grease, amongst a whole million of
> Cutpurses, and there boyle like a Gamon of Bacon
> That will never be enough.   *Exit.* [36
>   *Doct.* How her braine coynes?
>   *Daugh.* Lords and Courtiers, that have got maids with
> Child, they are in this place, they shall stand in fire up to the
> Nav'le, and in yce up to'th hart, and there th'offending part
> burnes, and the deceaving part freezes; in troth a very gree-
> vous punishment, as one would thinke, for such a Trifle, be-
> leve me one would marry a leaprous witch, to be rid on't
> Ile assure you.
>   *Doct.* How she continues this fancie? Tis not an engraffed
> Madnesse, but a most thicke, and profound mellencholly.
>   *Daugh.* To heare there a proud Lady, and a proud Citty
> wiffe, howle together: I were a beast and i'ld call it good
> sport: one cries, o this smoake, another this fire; One cries, o,
> that ever I did it behind the arras. and then howles; th'other
> curses a suing fellow and her garden house.
> Sings. *I will be true, my stars, my fate, &c.*   *Exit. Daugh.* [52

The two speeches of the Daughter printed as prose seem almost perfectly calculated to have invited deletion by Buc when the prompt-book was submitted for licensing. Possibly some difficulty in making out scored-through passages would have led the compositor to abandon for a short while his habit of padding out prose as verse; certainly a censor's deletion would account for the addition of the exit at line 36.

Although most of the more significant stage directions have already been noticed, the uncommon variety of the directions will be adequately appreciated only by the reader who will trouble to examine the text for himself. He will there find detailed specification of action (as in *"Strew Flowers"* or *"turnes away"* or *"kneele to Emilia"* in I.i), of manner (as when Pirithous enters *"in haste"* in V.iv), and of gesture (as when Palamon, entering *"as out of a Bush"* and wearing his prison Shackles, *"bends his fist at Arcite"* in III.i); he will find such unusual precision as the arrangement of separate exits for Palamon and Arcite, one line apart, at the end of III.iii; he will find exact provision for properties (as when Arcite enters *"with Meate, Wine, and Files"* in III.iii and *"with Armors and Swords"* in III.vi or when Emilia enters *"with 2. Pictures"* in IV.ii); he will even find references to scenery [32] (as in *"Exeunt towards the Temple"* in I.i or *"Enter Palamon from the Bush"* in III.vi). Of the directions which have not yet been cited, the list that follows, although not exhaustive, provides a representative selection: *"Musicke./ Scæna 5. Enter the Queenes with the Hearses of their/ Knightes, in a Funerall Solempnity, &c."* (I.v.1); *"Exeunt severally."* (I.v.16); *"Enter Theseus, Hipolita, Pirithous,/ Emilia: Arcite with a Garland, &c."* (II.v.1); *"Fight./ Hornes within: they stand."* (III.vi.138); *"Fight againe. Hornes."* (III.vi.168); *"Scæna 1. Enter Iailor, and his friend."* (IV.i.1); *"Here they fall on their faces as formerly, and there is heard/ clanging of Armor, with a short Thunder as the burst of/ a Battaile, whereupon they all rise and bow to the Altar."* (V.i.67); *"Enter Iaylor, Daughter, Maide."* (V.ii.53); *"(Cornets.a great cry and noice within crying a Palamon.)"* (V.iii.75).

To sum up: The stage directions provide ample evidence of an authorial manuscript, while the indications that this manuscript had served as a prompt-book—warning notes, actors' names, early entrances, duplications, a nearly complete record of entrances (and of speech-prefixes), a full record of exits, extensive provision for flourishes and other special effects, signs of censorship—are about as substantial as can be found in any dramatic text of the earlier seventeenth century. In the volume and variety of such evidence few printed plays come even close to the Cotes Quarto.

The Text of the Dialogue

We come finally to the body of the text—evidence in the dialogue which bears on the nature of the copy and which may point to the identity of the hand or hands responsible for that copy. This evidence is found in misprints, misreadings, idiosyncratic spellings, and other special irregularities.

Most editors and scholars have found little fault with the quarto text. Chambers calls it "a good one, requiring little emendation"; Kittredge calls it "excellent" and remarks that it was printed "with unusual accuracy"; even Waller, before going on to argue that it was printed from foul papers (or from a hastily made but literally faithful transcript of foul papers), con-

---

[32] Cf. Allardyce Nicoll, *Stuart Masques* (1937), p. 142.

cedes that, "so far as the sense of the spoken word is concerned," the text is "generally fair" (p. 67). The most serious defect in the quarto is a missing half-line at V.i.56,[33] perhaps due to illegibility in the manuscript, but a prompt-book used repeatedly during performances over a period of twenty years would be subject to accidental damage, and this single three-syllable hiatus in a text of nearly three thousand lines is hardly to be construed as evidence against what must on the whole have been a quite fair copy. There are no signs of the confusions, false starts, or other deficiencies normally associated with foul papers.

There are nevertheless certain irregularities pointing more to an authorial than to a scribal fair copy. One case in point, a peculiar typographical arrangement at V.iv.89–90, has drawn as much editorial attention over the years as the marginal notes, and with these lines we shall begin.

Pirithous rushes in to interrupt the execution of the defeated Palamon in V.iv with a breathlessly excited description of the accident by which Arcite was thrown from his horse. Increasing in pace and urgency through its first twenty-three lines, Pirithous' account reaches its climax as it tells how the horse

> seekes all foule meanes
> Of boystrous and rough Iadrie, to dis-seate
> His Lord, that kept it bravely: when nought serv'd,
> When neither Curb would cracke, girth breake nor diffring
> Dis-roote his Rider whence he grew, but that   (plunges
> He kept him tweene his legges, on his hind hoofes   [89
>   on end he stands   [90
> That *Arcites* leggs being higher then his head
> Seem'd with strange art to hang: His victors wreath
> Even then fell off his head: and presently
> Backeward the Iade comes ore . . .
>   (sig. M4)

Weber was the first to suggest that part of line 90 may have been omitted by the compositor. Rolfe suggested that the first part of the line may have

---

[33] The hiatus occurs in l. 56 of Arcite's prayer to Mars on sig. K4:

> Thou mighty one, that with thy power hast turnd
> Green Neptu[n]e into purple.   [56
> Comets prewarne, whose havocke in vaste Feild
> Vnearthed skulls proclaime, whose breath blowes downe
> The teeming Ceres foyzon . . .

Editors insert Seward's emendation: "Green Neptune into purple, whose approach . . ."

"dropped out" after it had been set in type, or alternatively that "on end he stands" may represent an author's revision intended to replace "on his hind hoofes" in the preceding line. The 1679 Folio printed "on end he stands" as a turn-over from line 89, moving it to the right-hand margin and putting a parenthesis before it. Nearly all editors have done much the same, printing it either as part of line 89 or (moving it to the left and capitalizing "on") as a separate half-line. Weber himself remarked that the sense is "perfect as it stands," to which Skeat added: "In fact, the half-line is rather effective."

A little noted variant reading in a neighboring line occurs in some copies of the quarto and has some bearing on the setting of lines 89–90. The transcription above is taken from a copy with sheet M(i) in a corrected state; the uncorrected sheet is distinguished by the reading *victoros* at line 92.[34] A press-correction at this point rules out the chance that part of a line could have "dropped out" unnoticed, and the failure of the compositor to alter "on end he stands" into a turn-over at the time he corrected *victoros* implies that his first decision was deliberate and the arrangement attributable to whatever he found in his copy. Although Waller prefers to assume revision, no editor (not even Rolfe) has been willing to substitute "on end he stands" for "on his hind hoofes"; the ugly elliptical reading that results is one count against the assumption, and another is that it still does not satisfactorily explain the printed arrangement. Hudson alone undertook to replace what he regarded as a hiatus in line 90 with a conjectural emendation; he printed "Quickly uprearing, so on end he stands," but this reading merely points up the superiority of the text as it stands, and the longer one considers the lines the more one prefers the decision of all other editors to leave the words unchanged. A guess about the copy, then, would be that its appearance was the result of an alteration *currente calamo*, with the writing of a complete line 90 followed by the deliberate deletion of whatever preceded "on end he stands"—a deletion thorough enough so that it could not be read but one which still left sufficient trace of underwriting for the compositor possibly to adopt the arrangement he did with the hope of making out what was underneath on a later try (analogous perhaps to *Julius Caesar* V.iv.7 in the Folio). The rush and impact of Pirithous'

---

[34] The uncorrected sheet is found, for example, in the Harvard Univ. and N.Y.C. Public Lib. copies of the quarto; "victors" in the Rutgers Univ. and both Boston Pub. Lib. copies.—Although no complete census or collation has been published, nearly 40 copies of the Cotes Quarto are known to survive and about a dozen variant readings have so far been noted among them by various editors. Only one—"succard" at I.iv.18 on C4 (Rutgers copy), corrected to "smeard" (Harvard and N.Y.C. copies)—implies a misreading corrected by consultation of copy.

speech recommend an editorial arrangement of "on end he stands" as part of line 89; the resulting line would be hypermetrical, but so also is line 87, and other examples occur elsewhere in the play (e.g. at II.iii.17). In any case, the indications are for authorial copy, and the further evidence for such copy in the pages that follow should confirm these indications in the present case.

Spellings constitute one important area of evidence. It should first be recalled that the spellings used in early seventeenth-century books underwent a good deal of change between Elizabethan and Caroline times; the comparative uniformity of Restoration spellings did not come all at once. By way of illustration, the two quarto editions of *A Midsummer Night's Dream,* the Fisher Quarto and the so-called Roberts Quarto, exhibit a decided contrast in the relative modernity of their spellings; both are dated 1600 on their title-pages, and scholars who had no reason to doubt the honesty of the Roberts title-page used long ago to observe that "the principal difference" between the texts "is in the spelling, which is more modern in the Roberts than in the Fisher"; [35] they made this observation long before Pollard, Greg, and Neidig became suspicious of the Roberts Quarto and went on to prove that it had been falsely dated by Pavier and Jaggard when it was printed in 1619.[36] Old-fashioned or abnormal spellings may be relative to a short span of years; we should be surprised, for example, to see the spelling *extatic* in one of our own books, but it is not very long out of date. Even the 1632 Shakespeare Folio had already begun to modernize some of the 1623 Folio spellings (especially in plays printed from manuscript in 1623, in which a higher proportion of older forms had survived than in plays reprinted from quartos); the following examples are among those chosen by Shaaber and Black to afford "a rough index to changes of taste and usage or at least a series of straws showing the way the wind was blowing": *banket* (1623): *banquet* (1632), *cease:seize, winch:wince, angles: angels, shrowd:shrewd, strook:struck, wadg'd:wedg'd, reuerent:reverend, were:wear, militers:muleters, loaden:loaded, bloud:blood, whether: whither.*[37] Certain of the older forms were of course still to be found in

[35] William Reynolds, ed. *A Midsommer Nights Dreame* (Bankside Shakespeare, Vol. VIII, 1890), p. 2. The same point was examined by Alfred E. Thiselton, *Some Textual Notes on "A Midsommer Nights Dreame"* (1903), *passim,* and was noted by other editors of the time.

[36] Cf. Greg, *Folio,* pp. 8–17, and Edwin E. Willoughby, *The Uses of Bibliography* (1957), pp. 81–88.

[37] Matthew W. Black and Matthias A. Shaaber, *Shakespeare's Seventeenth-Century Editors* (1937), pp. 48, 106, 111, 135, 136, 143, 170, 208.

Caroline books, but a few (e.g. *were, angle*) were of a sort that even a pre-1600 compositor would normally alter if he understood them. Many of the anomalous Shakespearean spellings to which Dover Wilson and others have called attention were of course merely old-fashioned at the time they found their way into print; certain of the spellings in Shakespeare's manuscript Addition to *Sir Thomas More* are early sixteenth-century in character, and Shakespeare's spellings in general were, as Pollard noted long ago, "more archaic" than those of the compositors who set the earliest of the early quartos.[38] (The various materials which indicate that Fletcher's spellings were generally much more modern will be described shortly.)

One of the most significant facts about the Cotes Quarto, as suggested earlier, is its date of publication. On superficial inspection it may first appear to be a normal text of the 1630's, partly because Cotes's printing house had switched over from medial *u*'s to medial *v*'s a few years before the quarto was printed,[39] and partly because it exhibits the somewhat greater regularity in spellings one would expect of so late a book. Yet more careful inspection reveals in both ordinary and unusual words a quite liberal sprinkling of generally old-fashioned spellings, as in the following examples (which no doubt include a few misprints): *a fire* (=*afire*), *a foote, a loofe, armenypotent* (=*armipotent*), *banket, cestron, chastice, coynadge, descider, dombe, doombe, dussons* (=*dozens*), *feed* (=*fed*), *freats, gate* (=*gait*), *gerland, girlond, gon, heard* (=*herd*), *howlet* (=*owlet*), *humaine* (=*human*), *jengling, kight, leaprous, loden, ly, Marsis, noice, obbraidings, on* (=*one*), *onely, peobles, plumb* (=*plum*), *proyne* (=*prune*), *quight* (=*requite*), *raze* (=*erase*), *retrait, shrowd, sees* (=*says*), *sith-tuskd-bore* (=*scythe-tusked-boar*), *soldiresse* (=*soldieress*), *solempne, solempnity, spincsters, strooke, tallents* (=*talons*), *time* (=*thyme*), *vittails, undon, waygh, wer* (=*were*), *were* (=*wear*), *whoobub,* and so forth. Many of these spellings must represent copy-spellings, although perhaps imperfectly; *peobles,* for example, is so odd that one suspects it results from a misreading of *peebles* (a form found in the early quartos, *pibbles* being more common in the 1623 Folio and in later books). A spelling like *solempnity* looks familiar from its frequent appearance in earlier books; while it might still occur in manuscripts, it was no longer common in printed texts issued a generation before 1634 and is therefore unlikely to have originated with the compositor. Some words on this list

[38] A. W. Pollard, "Elizabethan Spelling as a Literary and Bibliographical Clue," *The Library,* 4th Ser., IV (1923), 7.

[39] Medial *u*'s, still to be found e.g. in the anonymous *Pathomachia* printed by Cotes in 1630, were generally replaced with *v*'s by the time Cotes printed the 1632 Folio. Most London printing-houses changed over about the same time.

and others in the text probably follow copy exactly because of misunderstanding (*ly* for *lie* appears to be such a case); [40] wherever the poetry is most difficult we find a larger number of archaic forms attributable to misunderstanding, just as we find four misprints for classical names, the context being of no help where the compositor was ignorant. It is hardly possible to date archaic spellings with great precision (the O.E.D. dating assignments are broad and sometimes unreliable), and the list inevitably mixes a few forms that were merely obsolescent in 1634 with a few that were long since obsolete; *sees* for *says* at II.iii.56 (cf. *sed* at I.ii.117 and III.v.70) would be one example of the latter, although it survives also at V.iii.293 in the 1608 *Lear* Q1 (F *saies*) and is analogous to *feed* for *fed* in the Daughter's soliloquy at III.ii.19 and to *steed* for *stead* at I.i.39, a spelling common elsewhere in Shakespeare texts. A few quarto spellings that might be regarded as unusual, such as *wrighter,* or *on* for *one,* were used by both Shakespeare and Fletcher and therefore weigh little in this discussion, and a number of others that seem to have been used by Shakespeare—e.g. *agen, inough, comming*—still occurred frequently enough in Caroline books to be negligible, but the fact remains that old-fashioned spellings of the sorts preserved in a variety of Shakespearean texts must have been widespread in the manuscript; this evidence must be considered in more detail and in relation to certain complementary evidence of misreadings which will shortly be introduced. But the subject of Fletcher's spelling and handwriting should be given some attention first.

The materials relevant to our consideration of Fletcher include the manuscript verse letter to the Countess of Huntingdon, at least part of which is holograph, [41] and the printed and manuscript texts of fifteen plays, written between 1608 and 1625, [42] which are generally agreed to represent Fletcher's unaided work. These include the quarto of *The Faithful Shepherdess* printed about 1609; a private transcript of *Demetrius and Enanthe* (alternate title of *The Humorous Lieutenant*) made in 1625 by the scribe Ralph

---

[40] The opening song contains the lines, "All dear Nature's children sweet/ Lie 'fore bride and bridegroom's feet" (I.i.13–14), but the compositor printed ". . . sweete-/ Ly . . ."; cf. *Lear* Q1 for a similar error at V.iii.147: "hell hatedly" for "hell-hated lie."

[41] Cf. Samuel A. Tannenbaum, "A Hitherto Unpublished John Fletcher Autograph," *JEGP*, XXVIIII (1929), 35–40; Greg, *English Literary Autographs . . . Part III* (1932), plate XCIII; and correspondence between Greg and Tannenbaum (indexed) in various issues of *PQ* for 1934–36.

[42] Based on the summaries of the dating evidence in Chambers, *Elizabethan Stage* and Bentley, *Jacobean and Caroline Stage*. On the date of *The Woman's Prize,* cf. Baldwin Maxwell, *Studies in Beaumont, Fletcher, and Massinger* (1939), pp. 29–45.

Crane, probably from a good author's copy,[43] and the 1647 Folio text of *The Humorous Lieutenant;* the Knight transcript of *Bonduca* from Fletcher's foul papers, and the 1647 Folio text of *Bonduca;* the 1639 quarto of *Monsieur Thomas;* the 1640 quarto of *Rule a Wife and Have a Wife;* the 1647 Folio texts of *The Chances, The Island Princess, The Loyal Subject, The Mad Lover, The Pilgrim, Valentinian, A Wife for a Month, The Woman's Prize* (also extant in a scribal transcript),[44] and *Women Pleased;* and the 1652 text, printed in folio, of *The Wild-Goose Chase* (omitted from the 1647 Folio because the manuscript was temporarily lost). The copy for the Folio had been distributed by the publisher Moseley among several different printing houses, and the Folio texts listed above were produced by at least four different shops. Thus the fifteen printed texts were produced over a 43-year span by at least eight different printers and the principal manuscripts came from at least three different hands. The recurrence of an idiosyncratic spelling or linguistic form in a number of these texts therefore provides good assurance that the form is attributable to Fletcher rather than a scribe or compositor; the contraction *'um* for *them,* for example, must have been used by Fletcher, since it may be found in such diverse texts as the manuscript letter to the Countess of Huntingdon, the Knight transcript of *Bonduca,* the author's lines "To the Reader" in the c.1609 quarto of *The Faithful Shepherdess,* and again in the 1640 quarto of *Rule a Wife.*

With respect to Fletcher's orthography, the most significant observation relevant to our discussion is the negative one that, in the eighteen documents under review, the spellings are generally unexceptional, modern, run-of-the-mill Jacobean and Caroline forms; even the early text of *The Faithful Shepherdess* more nearly resembles a Caroline than a typical Elizabethan book in its spellings, and it rarely invited modernization when it was reprinted in 1629. These eighteen texts, as well as the manuscripts and printed texts of those collaborative plays whose authorship has been responsibly accounted for by such scholars as Bald and Bentley, indicate that the spellings used by Fletcher, as well as his handwriting (with his fashionable proficiency in both Secretary and Italian hands),[45] were characteristic of an up-to-date Jacobean gentleman-author educated at one of the universities; apart from the often illegible rough early draft of *Bonduca,* his manuscripts must have been generally somewhat easier to read than

[43] *Demetrius and Enanthe* (Brogyntyn MS), ed. M. M. Cook and F. P. Wilson (Malone Society), 1950 (1951). Cf. Bald, *Beaumont & Fletcher Folio,* pp. 64–65.

[44] On this unpublished manuscript, dating perhaps from the 1640's and now in the Folger Library, cf. Bald, *Beaumont & Fletcher Folio,* pp. 50–52.

[45] The signature, the address, and several other details in the verse-letter are in Fletcher's Italian script.

Shakespeare's, and his spellings could not often have puzzled or arrested the attention of the scribes and compositors who dealt with them. There are nevertheless a number of idiosyncratic forms to be found in Fletcher's texts which are totally absent or exceedingly rare in Shakespeare's; but of those which Bald, Hoy, Gerritsen, and others have observed (e.g. *eather* for *either, neather* for *neither, heather* for *hither, theather* for *thither, wheather* for *whether, thorow* for *through, 'um* for *them, 'is* or *Is* or *his* for *he is, 'has* or *Has* or *h'as* for *he has*), not one is to be found in the Cotes Quarto. Nor are any of the misprints in the quarto attributable to the kinds of misreading to which Fletcher's handwriting (where its idiosyncrasies may be distinguished from Shakespeare's) [46] might give rise. Although the absence of such spellings or contractions or misreadings is hardly conclusive evidence against the hypothesis of Fletcher's responsibility for any of the manuscript copy, it does make that hypothesis more difficult to sustain than Waller, for example, has been willing to allow, and the presence of distinctive Shakespearean forms in the text (to the more interesting examples of which we shall now proceed) will perhaps suggest the sterility of that hypothesis more effectively than did the earlier demonstration of the degree to which it depends on assuming wholesale scribal suppressions of *ye*, an "anomalous re-entrance" in II.ii, "interpolations" by Fletcher, and the like.

Misreadings and idiosyncratic spellings of course are frequently interrelated. The series of linked examples that follows will begin with an anomalous spelling in the Cotes Quarto, take us then into earlier Shakespeare texts, and return finally to a strange misprint (in a scene ascribed to Fletcher) which Cotes's compositor seems to have produced through a misreading of his copy. The first example is a spelling unusual enough to have caused editorial comment even in the nineteenth century; it appears at I.i.170:

> we stand before your puissance
> Wrinching our holy begging in our eyes
> To make petition cleere.

Following Pope's emendation of *wrenching* at *Henry VIII* I.i.167, most editors since Seward modernize *Wrinching* into *Rinsing*. The medial *ch* need not concern us here (although of course it invites comparison with

---

[46] Bald provides lists of those idiosyncrasies he has found (*Beaumont & Fletcher Folio*, pp. 96–99) and conveniently distinguishes between those which occur also in Dover Wilson's Shakespearean lists (*Essays and Studies*, X [1924], 41–45) and those which do not.

winch),[47] but the initial *wr* must be followed up. There is another such *wr*-spelling in another of the scenes usually assigned to Shakespeare: "I wreake not if the wolves would jaw me" (III.ii.7). Editors naturally print *reck*. *Wreake* is not extremely rare, but (along with *wreaking* for *recking* and *wreakeless* for *reckless*) it is the most common form for *reck* in Shakespeare texts in particular (on a few occasions levelled to *reake*), and the conjunction of two *wr*-spellings in this text does raise the suspicion that Shakespeare spelled with initial *wr* a number of words that had generally come to be spelled, even before the turn of the seventeenth century, with initial *r*. The hypothesis, that is, is that he used such spellings more than has been noticed, that some may have been levelled by compositors in setting the early quartos, and that perhaps a few more disappeared in the setting of the Folio texts.[48] This suggestion should not seem very startling, since occasional examples of *wr*-spellings for words normally spelled with *r* may be found in books by such older Elizabethans as North; it is presumably for this reason, as well as the fact that no abnormal spellings with *wr* occur in the Addition to *Sir Thomas More,* that no special notice of the matter seems to have been taken by textual critics in connection with Shakespeare. Once one does notice it, examples are naturally not difficult to find, one of the most peculiar appearing in Sonnet 6 (Q1609): "Then let not winters wragged hand deface . . ." The most common examples in the plays, along with *wreake* and *wreakleless,* would seem to be instances of suffering on the *wrack*. Since Shakespeare texts frequently print *rite* for our word *right,* perhaps *write* at *All's Well* III.v.69 (emended to *right* in the Second Folio and by many editors) is one of the few Shakespearean spellings to survive in this Folio text which is often thought to derive from autograph copy. A different but possibly related kind of example occurs at *Hamlet* III.ii.253; the Second Quarto prints "our withers are vnwrong" and the Folio prints *vnrung;* the change hints at a scribe or compositor used to levelling such spellings and going too far. But further examples would be similarly trifling in themselves; the 1634 compositor, in any case, preserved two *wr*-spellings, and they are suggestive of more than the frail and inessential hypothesis just ventured. What they suggest will appear if we turn now to the subject of misreadings.

---

[47] *Winch* at *Hamlet* III.ii.253 (Q2 & F, but *wince* in the Bad Quarto) and at *King John* IV.i.81 (but *wince* in F2 and later texts).

[48] Shakespeare was inconsistent about the spelling of his own name; he spelled *sheriff* five different ways in a 5-line passage in *Sir Thomas More;* editors find it difficult to restrict *rack, wrack, wreck* and *wreak* to isolated meanings when they find these words in his plays; and it is therefore hardly the intention of this discussion to imply that any particular spelling with initial *r* can be singled out and identified as a probable instance of compositorial levelling.

Since Theobald's celebrated emendation for "a Table of greene fields" has come under suspicion or attack from many different quarters in recent years,[49] the resolution of the great crux at *Timon of Athens* IV.iii.12 seems to be taking its place in editorial admiration; the Folio, presumably set from Shakespearean autograph at this point, reads as follows:

> It is the Pastour Lards, the Brothers sides,
> The want that makes him leaue:

The 1632 Folio unturned a letter in *leaue,* Rowe modernized the spelling of *Pastour,* and Singer proposed to replace the bewildering *Brothers* with a word meaning *ox* that has since been universally approved:

> It is the pasture lards the rother's sides,
> The want that makes him lean.

Or rather, almost universally, for C. J. Sisson has reasonably objected:

It verges upon impertinence to be dissatisfied with so happy and successful an emendation, from which none today dissents. Is there not a Rother Street at Stratford? Yet the emendation presupposes a compositor who could insert a superfluous *B* in order to make nonsense. We might fairly seek some more intelligible reason for the error, a more plausible misreading of a Secretary hand, and so find in the corruption a clue to the possible original text in Shakespeare's hand. There is no difficulty about *leaue* for *leane.* But there is difficulty about *Brother* for *rother.* The capital *B* need not be considered an essential part of the written pattern, for the compositor is lavish with capitals. But the initial *b* cannot be ignored. And the pattern permits readily of the reading *wether* as an alternative to *brother.* . . . Printed patterns are of course very unsafe guides to plausibility. . . . [The reading *wethers*] is as certain as one could wish graphically, and in sense. The initial downstroke of a *w,* with its first minim, is very easily misread as *b.*[50]

Wethers is surely not inadmissible, but a *w-b* confusion with *brothers* as a misreading of *wrothers* in the copy is the sort of error Sisson himself teaches us to regard as more plausible; by Sisson's own graphic criteria, that is, the assumption of *wrothers* in the manuscript would work better than the assumption of *wethers* to explain the puzzling *Brothers* in the

---

[49] In place of Theobald's *'a babbl'd* at *Henry V* II.iii.18 many scholars now prefer *talk'd* or would defend the Folio *Table.* Cf. *SQ,* IX (1958), 492 n.

[50] Sisson, *New Readings in Shakespeare* (1956), I, 12; II, 174.—More recently another distinguished editor has rejected *rother's.* H. J. Oliver, in his superb new Arden edition of *Timon* (1959), follows F and reads *brother's,* explaining it as a reference to a landed elder brother and treating *him* in l. 13 as a reference to a deprived younger brother. The distinction is clever, but is more easily asserted in a note than visible in the grammar of the text.

Folio. There may be other instances in Shakespeare (e.g. at *Hamlet* I.iii.109, or possibly at *King Lear* II.ii.172) where the assumption of a *wr*-spelling in the copy might help to clear up some long-standing textual question. But to return to *The Two Noble Kinsmen*.

Palamon speaks to Arcite in the prison scene (assigned to Fletcher):

> our good Swords, now
> (Better the red-eyd god of war nev'r were)
> Bravishd our sides, like age must run to rust,
> And decke the Temples of those gods that hate us . . .
>
> (II.ii.23–26)

Were is easily emended to *wore*. There is no such word as *bravishd*, and all editors since Seward emend it to *ravished* and gloss it as "snatched from":

> our good swords, now
> (Better the red-eyed god of war ne'er wore)
> Ravish'd our sides, like age must run to rust . . .

"The initial *b* cannot be ignored," and the supposition of Seward that the compositor had picked up the initial *b* from the preceding line was a gallant try in the absence of evidence to explain the misprint. A copy-spelling of *wravishd* is no more outlandish than *wragged* or *wrinching,* and the misprint bears a strong family likeness to *Brothers* (whether *rother's* or *wether's* be preferred).

None of the other misprints in the quarto is individually as striking as *Bravishd,* but many of them do tell us more about the copy. The next few pages will review the minor misprints, and we shall then proceed to the remaining major cruxes.

Although the quarto gives us the usual sprinkling of misprints clearly the fault of the printer (errors of fatigue such as *crtaine* for *certaine* or of foul case such as *ípare* for *spare*), the majority of readings which editors have had to emend are more easily attributable to misreading of the manuscript or even to faithful and accurate reproduction of anomalous Shakespearean spellings. The relationship between Shakespearean spellings and supposed misprints is sometimes ambiguous, and each case must be decided on its merits. When, for example, the 1623 Folio compositor set *were* for *wear* at *Coriolanus* II.i.195, it is possible that he misread *weare* in the manuscript, but it seems more likely that—without time for literary reflection, and forced to give his copy the fragmented kind of second-to-second a printer must—he found the line "Such eyes the Widowes in Carioles were" a bit puzzling and reproduced *were* as it stood in his copy; the same spelling occurs in Sonnet 77 (Q1609), it is analogous to *bere* and *beres* in the Addition to *Sir Thomas More* and to such examples as *tere* and *swere* in various of the good quartos, and it is identical with *were* for *wear* at *Two Noble Kinsmen* I.iii.83.

Similarly, the misprint *jave* at III.v.6 may be due to the misreading of a Shakespearean spelling; Dyce's emendation of *jave* to *jane* (=*jean*) makes excellent sense in the line "You most coarse frieze capacities, ye jean judgments," and has been generally adopted.[51] If the quarto had been printed four years earlier, the compositor would have printed *jaue* and we might have supposed a turned letter at fault, but *jave* indicates a misreading of *jane,* and such spellings as *lane* for *lean* at *1 Henry IV* II.iv.520 (Q1) point to *jane,* rather than the more common *jene,* as Shakespeare's likely spelling of *jean.* In still another case, a long-standing crux at III.v.137, "the beast eating Clowne" (referring to a character in the morris dance), has been satisfactorily resolved by Kökeritz' explanation of *beast* as a variant spelling for *beest* (beestings); only a country boor would eat beestings, and the clown is the dramatic counterpart of the "rude country clown" in the *Masque* from which the morris dance was borrowed.[52]

On the other hand, the reading *misicall* at I.iii.86 is explicable with about equal plausibility on the assumptions (a) of a mechanical error by the compositor, (b) of a misreading of a minim-letter in the copy, or (c) of an accurate reproduction of a legitimate spelling, reflecting Shakespearean phonology, of the word *musical.*[53] Before we proceed with other misprints, therefore, it must be acknowledged that a few of the examples to be cited are similarly ambiguous; a few errors attributed here to misreading or to Shakespearean spelling (or both) may be due to mere mechanical slips, and it is merely for brevity that this qualification is not repeated in every ambiguous case.

The misprints *Nenuan* for *Nemean* at I.i.72, *Anly* for *Aulis* at I.i.237, *Creou* for *Creon* at I.i.164, and *Love* for *Jove* at IV.ii.16 suggest that the compositor was, unsurprisingly, ignorant of classical names, and these errors, along with the *n/r* misreading in *ore* for *one* at I.iii.37, raise the sus-

---

[51] Seward noted that *jave* must stand for "some sort of coarse cloth" but settled on *sleave.* Some editors compare III.v.6 with "russet yeas and honest kersey noes" (*LLL* V.ii.413).

[52] Cf. p. 284 below.

[53] Kökeritz treats it as such, citing it together with such other examples as *militers* (= *muleteers*) at *Antony* III.vii.36, in *Shakespeare's Pronunciation* (1953), pp. 210–211.

picion that *Nepture* at V.i.56 represents another *n/r* misreading by a compositor who never heard of Neptune. *Nenuan, Anly, Love,* and *Nepture* are, incidentally, printed in roman type, and along with the occasional failure of the compositor elsewhere to italicize proper names, they indicate a manuscript written in a Secretary hand. The misprint of *Love* for *Jove* in IV.ii, it should be added, is strikingly similar to the misprint *Loue* for *Joan* (apparently *Jone* in the copy) at *Love's Labor's Lost* IV.iii.182 (Q);[54] the minim errors are obvious enough, and the ease with which a compositor might confuse Shakespeare's majescule *J* (or *I*) with *L* is readily apparent in the Addition to *More,* in which five of the ten *J*'s are quite indistinguishable from the *L*'s.[55] And another odd misprint, *yet* for *ye* (probably *yee* in the copy) at II.iii.42, is presumably due to an *e/t* misreading; although such misreadings are not common elsewhere, they do crop up occasionally in Shakespearean texts, as in *stature* for *feature* at *Hamlet* III.i.167 (Q2) or in *bet* for *be(e)* at *Midsummer Night's Dream* II.ii.39 (Q1).

Although misprints due to the misreading of minim-letters (*m, n, u, i, c, r, w*) are common enough in early books, Shakespeare was, as Dover Wilson puts it, "more than ordinarily careless" in the formation of such letters, and it is therefore not surprising that an unusually high number of misprints appear in the Cotes Quarto which are probably due at least in part to minim-misreadings. In addition to the examples already cited—*Nenuan* for *Nemean, Creou* for *Creon, Anly* for *Aulis, ore* for *one, jave* for *jane,* possibly *misicall* for *musical* and *Nepture* for *Neptune*—minim-misreadings may have helped to produce *Artesuis* for *Artesius* at I.i.176, *Flavia* for *Flavina* at I.iii.63, *succard* for *smear'd* at I.iv.20,[56] *Strucke* for *Stuck* (?) at II.ii.55,[57] *path* for *patch* (?) at II.vi.33, *Beake* for *Brake* at III.ii.1, *bine* for *brine* at III.ii.28, *Baum* for *Bavian* at III.v.1, *taudem* for *tandem* at III.v.38, *aliijs* for *aliis* at III.v.139, *faire* for *fire* at IV.ii.91, *corect* for *court* at IV.ii.121, *armenypotent* for *armipotent* at V.i.60, *honour* for *humour* (?) at V.ii.54, *turne* for *tune* (?) at V.ii.73, and possibly *then* for

---

[54] "Loue" appears on the uncorrected sig. E4ᵛ of Q1, found in the Devonshire copy; other copies (collated by Greg in his 1957 Oxford facsimile) contain the corrected reading, "Ione."

[55] Cf. Pollard *et al., Shakespeare's Hand in the Play of Sir Thomas More* (1923), p. 107 and plates III, IV, and VII. The majescule *I*'s and *L*'s in the Fletcher verse-letter are quite dissimilar to one another.

[56] Corrected in some copies. Cf. n. 34 above.

[57] Four quarto readings on this list—*strucke, path, honour, turne*—are included only because nearly all editors have treated them as misprints; the accepted emendations are queried because in each case the original reading makes sense in its context and ought perhaps to be allowed to stand.

them at III.iii.30 and *fitst* for *first* at IV.ii.86 (although these last two may as easily have been mechanical slips).

Before citing further examples we must turn again to spellings—in particular to such old-fashioned spellings as *ar* and *wer* for *are* and *were*. That Shakespeare commonly dropped final mute *e* after *r* in this fashion is clear enough from his Addition to *More,* in which, for example, the word *are* appears a total of nine times but in eight of the nine instances is spelled *ar.* Similarly *More* gives us *ther, thers,* and *wer.* Not many such spellings, naturally, would be printed by the compositors of the early quartos, and in the few cases in which they do appear it is a reasonable assumption that they were carried over from the copy. Thus in *Hamlet* Q2 there are a number of examples of *thers,* one of *tha'r* (=*they are*), and two misprints which are explicable as misreadings of copy-spellings without *e*; at I.iii.74 the misprint *or* for *are* may be explained (as Dover Wilson points out) with reference to Shakespeare's spurred *a* (easily misread as *o*) and the copy-spelling *ar*; and at II.i.58 the reading *or tooke* (meaning *o'er-took* and printed *o're tooke* in the Folio) probably preserves Shakespeare's sometime spelling of the word usually then spelled *ore.* Related examples are scattered through other Shakespearean texts; *y'ar* (=*you are*) appears in *Lear* Q1 (IV.vi.8 & 10 and *yar* at IV.vii.49), another *or* for *are* occurs at *Macbeth* I.iv.1, another *or* meaning *o'er* occurs at *Midsummer Night's Dream* IV.i.76, *for* meaning *'fore* occurs at *All's Well* IV.iv.3, occasional examples of *wer* and *t'wer* survive in other texts, and so forth. Spellings of the same kind crop up at about a dozen points in *The Two Noble Kinsmen*—scattered throughout the text (e.g. at II.v.47 & 51, III.i.109, III.v.73 & 85, V.iii.24)—in such forms as *y'ar, t'wer,* and even *er* for *ere,* and the reading *for* at I.iv.54 which is emended to *'fore* in modern editions is another of the Shakespearean spellings that are sometimes treated as misprints. But the principal reason for introducing this class of spellings and apparent misprints is not so much to strengthen further the evidence for Shakespearean copy behind the Cotes Quarto as to prepare the way for a consideration of the first of the major cruxes in the text, to which we shall now proceed.

In Act I scene iv, after Theseus has defeated Creon and sent off the widowed Queens to do honor to their dead lords, he sees the gravely wounded Palamon and Arcite lying before him. He had been impressed by their valor in battle ("they were a mark/ Worth a god's view"), and he orders his best surgeons to attend them "and minister/ What man to man may do; for our sake, more . . ." The next lines of this speech in the quarto constitute what most editors have considered—and two editors, Skeat and Rolfe, have called—"the great crux" of the play:

> Since I have knowne frights, fury, friends, beheastes, [45
> Loves, provocations, zeale, a mistris Taske,
> Desire of liberty, a feavour, madnes,
> Hath set a marke which nature could not reach too
> Without some imposition, sicknes in will
> Or wrastling strength in reason, for our Love [50
> And great *Appollos* mercy, all our best,
> Their best skill tender.

"Theseus' meaning is plain enough," wrote Littledale; "the only difficulty is, how far should we *improve* on that meaning by altering the old punctuation or even the old reading." Despite the difficulty, most editors have admired this "cataloguing of circumstances altogether peculiar to Shakspeare" (Hickson), and although the customary number of "improvements" have been offered (e.g. Hudson's "zeal in misery's task" for line 46), many editors have been content merely to remove superfluous commas after *friends* and *loves*. The difficulty is more interpretive than textual, as may be suggested by Skeat's explanation of the lines (the one most often quoted by later editors):

'For I have known . . . the requisitions of friends, the provocations of love, . . . the desire of liberty, . . . a fever or a madness . . . [to have] proposed an aim (for endeavours) which the man's natural strength could not attain to, without at least some forcing, or some fainting of the will, or some severe struggle in the mind.' This is at least as good as any previous explanations, and further discussion of so difficult a passage would be useless.

Skeat takes *imposition, sickness,* and *strength* as grammatical objects of *without,* although he is evidently not wholly satisfied himself. Littledale put "which nature could not reach to/ Without some imposition" in parentheses, thus placing "sickness in will/ Or wrestling strength in reason" in apposition with *mark.* Most editors have simply avoided comment on lines 49–50. It seems surprising that no one has suggested that *o'er-wrestling* is what may have been intended—as it is in any case what one *hears.* The construction would be thoroughly Shakespearean (comparable for example with *o'er-wrested* at *Troilus* I.iii.157), and by placing "will" and "reason" in conflict with one another (as Skeat's and Littledale's glosses do not) it draws support from the several passages on reason pandering to will in the canonical plays. The following text is as conservative in its modernization as that of any editor, emending only by the removal of two superfluous commas and differing from previous versions only by treating *or* as a Shakespearean spelling of *ore:*

minister

What man to man may do; for our sake, more—
Since I have known frights, fury, friends' behests,   [45
Loves' provocations, zeal, a mistress' task,
Desire of liberty, a fever, madness,
Hath set a mark which nature could not reach to
Without some imposition, sickness in will
O'er-wrestling strength in reason; for our love   [50
And great Apollo's mercy, all our best,
Their best skill tender!

"These experiences have set us a mark which nature, left to itself, could never have set for us; without them, sickness in will would overcome strength in reason." There will be more to observe of this remarkable speech when, in Chapter VI, we consider its wider dramatic context. As for the manuscript, a text in which the greatest crux to disturb editors seems to be soluble merely by assuming that an *or* meaning *o'er* was taken over accurately from the copy is a very good text indeed.

In his analysis of dialogue Waller cites "a number of passages which can hardly represent the authors' final intentions" (p. 67); the preceding crux is among them, as is another major crux found at I.iii.89. In lines 64–88 of this scene Emilia delivers to Hippolyta a long and moving account of her childhood friendship with Flavina; she becomes more and more impassioned as she proceeds but at the climax breaks off abruptly and concludes thus:

This rehearsall   [88
(Which fury-innocent wots well) comes in
Like old importments bastard, has this end,
That the true love tweene Mayde, and mayde, may be
More then in sex individuall.

The accepted text includes Lamb's emendation for *fury-innocent* in line 89:

This rehearsal
(Which, ev'ry innocent wots well, comes in
Like old importment's bastard) has this end,
That the true love 'tween maid and maid may be
More than in sex dividual.

There is justice in Waller's objection that Lamb's *ev'ry* "does not satisfactorily answer all the questions which arise as to the origin of the error" (pp. 67–68). Perhaps *sorry innocence* (assuming *sory-innocenc* in the copy) would be better (*fury-* is an easier misreading of *sory-* than of *evry*). But

Waller, bent on treating the copy as disorderly foul papers, goes much further than previous critics in his objection to the passage; "comes in/ Like
old importments bastard," he says, "not only resists emendation but defies
sense"; it suggests to him, in fact, that "the author had not fully worked
out his meaning, nor [evidently regarding this as an alternative] found adequate expression for it."

   Importment or *emportment,* a cognate of the French *emportement,* means
a fit of passion, a surge of feeling, being "carried away." By *old importment*
Emilia refers to the intensity of her feelings for Flavina when they were
children. Her own long recital has re-created those feelings for her now,
and at line 88 she stops, embarrassed at having made too much a display
of herself, speaks apologetically of "old importment's bastard" (her present
agitation), and tries to sum up in lines 90-92. "Y'are out of breath . . ." is
Hippolyta's smiling reply. The passage requires only the emendation of
fury-innocent and to qualified readers has long made splendid sense.

   One other crux calls for attention before we sum up the extent of textual
corruption in the quarto as a whole. It occurs at III.iv.9, in the fourth soliloquy of the Jailor's Daughter. After Palamon had escaped from prison with
her help, he accidentally failed to meet her at the place in the forest she
had appointed; her fear that he has been devoured by wolves unsettles her
mind, and she wanders to the seashore where she thinks she sees a ship in
trouble:

> Yonder's the sea, and ther's a Ship; how't tumbles
> And ther's a Rocke lies watching under water;
> Now, now, it beates upon it; now, now, now,
> Ther's a leak sprung, a sound one, how they cry?
> Vpon her before the winde, you'l loose all els: [9
> Vp with a course or two, and take about Boyes.
> Good night, good night, y'ar gone . . .

Seward quoted the observation of his colleague Sympson that "Upon her
before the wind" is "not true Sea-Language"; editors have agreed but have
not found emendation easy. Seward read *Up with her* (eliding *before* to
'fore); he also recorded Theobald's conjecture, *Spoon her,* in his notes.
Weber read *Spoom her* and Skeat *Run her.* Somewhat surprisingly, *Spoom*
(or its variant *Spoon*) has had the most takers. An intransitive verb in all
its recorded uses, *spoom* means to move swiftly before the wind without
aid of sails; apart from the grammatical objection, *spoom* is not very apt
when applied to a ship striking a rock, and it also conflicts with the talk
of hauling up "a course or two" in the next line. *Run,* as Herford notes,
"is a simpler emendation, as well as a less dubious expression." None of

the suggested readings possesses much graphic plausibility, although it would no doubt be fanaticism to expect every emendation to satisfy this criterion. But if *Run* is the best proposal to date, it still seems a bit make-shift, and one is tempted to try to do better. Perhaps *Boom her* would serve. Except for the descender in the *p* it would satisfy graphic considerations fairly well, and its use in the present context—"push out the boom to make the sail catch the wind"—would be good nautical idiom in the earlier seventeenth century; the O.E.D. cites both transitive and intransitive uses of the verb *boom,* quoting (for example) a 1617 pamphlet in which a ship is said to be "booming by himself before the wind" (i.e. the ship is in full sail).

The passage in which *Or wrastling* occurs has been referred to as a "major crux" because it has been treated as such by most editors from Seward to the present day. *Fury-innocent* and *Vpon her* are perhaps the most problematical of all quarto misprints. The worst fault in the quarto is no doubt the omitted half-line at V.i.56 cited earlier (note 33), although Seward's emendation has satisfied nearly all editors. Yet the first of these four cases seems to contain only punctuational error, and it is fair to say that the quarto in general contains only minor misprints. All but *fury-innocent* and *Vpon her* are easily emended, and few emendations are subject even to minor dispute. There may, that is, be dispute as to whether *path* at II.vi.33 ought to be emended to *patch* or ought instead to be left alone, or as to whether "name; Opinion" at III.vi.291 should be emended to "name, opinion" or to "name's opinion"; but not even the most troublesome cases call for major surgery, and the excellent reputation the text enjoys among editors is fully justified. There are, to be sure, many more misprints than one finds, for example, in so clean a text as the Folio *Julius Caesar* (printed presumably from a very fair copy in the hand of a professional scribe), but several of the Shakespearean idiosyncrasies which would have been familiar to a King's company book-keeper would no doubt have taxed the wit of a Caroline compositor. The evidence points to an author's fair copy and is wholly consistent with the assumption of a prompt-book.

Waterson's Other Manuscripts

Since playwrights seem normally to have had little more commercial control over their manuscripts than a present-day movie scenarist has over his, the King's company plays acquired by John Waterson presumably came directly from the theatrical company. The evidence from these texts may be relevant, albeit indirectly, to the manuscript of *The Two Noble Kinsmen,* and it therefore deserves at least a brief summary.

In addition to *The Two Noble Kinsmen,* Waterson acquired eight plays belonging to the King's men. They were printed between 1623 and 1639. Waterson published Webster's *Duchess of Malfi* in 1623; the printer's copy is thought to have been a fair scribal copy.[58] Waterson acquired and registered the "booke" of Jonson's *The Staple of News* in April 1626, shortly after the play had failed on the stage; he did not publish it, however, but in 1631 transferred it to Robert Allot, for whom it was printed shortly thereafter; the text shows the usual unmistakeable signs of excellent Jonsonian autograph copy. The six other plays acquired (and published) by Waterson were Davenant's *The Cruel Brother* (1630) and *The Just Italian* (1630), Massinger's *The Emperor of the East* (1632) and *The Unnatural Combat* (1639), Fletcher's *The Elder Brother* (1637) and *Monsieur Thomas* (1639). Waller has observed that the texts of *The Cruel Brother, The Unnatural Combat,* and *Monsieur Thomas* show "signs of playhouse origin" (p. 65 n.). The manuscript of *The Emperor of the East* was entered in the Stationers' Register as a "play booke," and W. J. Lawrence has pointed out that both Massinger texts appear to have been printed from autograph promptbooks.[59] A fair transcript, according to Greg in his edition of the play, served as copy for *The Elder Brother.* And independent inspection of *The Just Italian* reveals a good text with numerous authorial directions, suggesting that the manuscript supplied to Waterson after the stage failure in 1630 was the author's fair copy.

All of these eight other texts, in short, give evidence of deriving from good or excellent manuscript copies. None of the eight shows evidence of having derived from foul papers or from that mysterious "more or less faithful copy of the foul papers" recently introduced by Fredson Bowers into bibliographical speculation. Yet not one of these eight other King's company plays shows quite such distinctive, ample, and varied evidence of having been printed from the company prompt-book—although probably at least half of them were so printed—as does *The Two Noble Kinsmen.*

Conclusion

The hypothesis advocated in the present chapter does not in itself conflict with the assumption of collaboration between Shakespeare and Fletcher, however sharply it conflicts with the customary assumption of a play distinctly divided into two separate compartments. Fair copies of collaborative plays were normally in the hand either of a professional scribe (as with *Sir John van Olden Barnavelt*) or of one of the authors (as with the original

[58] Cf. J. R. Brown, "The Printing of John Webster's Plays," *SB,* VI (1954), 134–137.
[59] Lawrence, *Those Nut-cracking Elizabethans* (1935), pp. 197–199.

book of *Sir Thomas More*). There is no evidence of transcription in *The Two Noble Kinsmen,* and the cumulative evidence from both the stage directions and dialogue is overwhelmingly in favor of authorial manuscript. There is no evidence of Fletcher's hand in the copy, and the evidence for Shakespeare's hand—in such misprints as *a eleven, Love,* and *Bravishd,* such anomalous spellings as *angle, were, sees, or,* and *aborne*—is spread throughout the text. The converging probabilities of spelling and misreading in the *wr*-words and *br*-misprints are collectively as rare an anomaly perhaps as the famous *scilens* which links the *More* Addition to the quarto of *2 Henry IV.* No solitary example is ever likely to be decisive, but the evidence for Shakespearean copy is a veritable network of cross-links between the quarto of 1634 and a group of quarto and Folio texts printed from eleven to more than thirty-five years earlier.

The present hypothesis, moreover, calls only for a single manuscript, while Waller's postulation of a transcript, in order to overcome the obstacle of a prompter's addition of actors' names in the 1620's (as well as the absence of evidence for Fletcher), requires the assumption of at least four different manuscripts (the foul papers, a near facsimile of the foul papers which reached the printer, a lost 1613 prompt-book, and a 1626 prompt-book which the company either lost or withheld from Waterson)—just as it requires some further hypothesis to explain why a supposed orthographic distinction in the manuscript was "almost hopelessly obscured" in the quarto. Any attempt to explain the complex mass of evidence in the quarto within the framework of received opinion on the authorship of the play is bound to produce an equally muddled theory. No doubt anything is "possible," but the assumption of a single manuscript in Shakespeare's hand which served as the prompt-book on more than one occasion provides a thoroughly satisfactory and unified explanation of all the bibliographical data, and there is no need to multiply extravagant *ad hoc* hypotheses. Setting the bibliographical data aside, moreover, one might add that the hypothesis of a Shakespearean manuscript does not require—as the Waller theory most definitely does require—that we ignore the question of verse-lineation treated in Chapter I, that we disregard most of the dating evidence (Appendix A), that we pay no attention to *Henry VIII* (Chapter III), or that we forget that Shakespeare himself was once intensely interested in *The Two Noble Kinsmen.*

The Folio Question

The usual explanation for the absence of *The Two Noble Kinsmen* from the 1623 Folio is that Heminge and Condell deliberately excluded it because it was only in part by Shakespeare. An alternative explanation might be that the manuscript had been lost at the time the Folio was printed. Although one's choice between these explanations (or one or another variation on them) will depend in part on literary considerations discussed in later chapters, to some extent it will also depend on our knowledge of the treatment of theatrical manuscripts, and that will perhaps justify its introduction at this point.

The King's men are known to have lost their prompt-book of *The Winter's Tale* some time between 1619 and 1623, and Jaggard's failure to include the play among the other comedies printed before work began on the histories is sometimes associated with this loss. Dover Wilson has suggested that if it were not for the accidental interruption in the printing of the Folio, *The Winter's Tale* might have been excluded; and Greg, in his summary of part of the evidence, describes its inclusion as an "afterthought" (*Folio*, pp. 415, 439).

As noted earlier in another connection, the King's men also lost their prompt-book of *Bonduca,* although they appear to have recovered it later. *The Honest Man's Fortune* is another recorded loss (most fully discussed by Gerritsen in his edition) which took place in the 1620's. Evidently the actors did not always keep their books under lock and key. The most widely advertised loss of a manuscript was that of *The Wild-Goose Chase,* and if Bald's interpretation of the preparations for the 1647 Folio is correct, it was from the King's company itself that the manuscript strayed; [60] in any case, it was apparently not recovered for Moseley until four or five years later. *The Mad Lover,* too, seems to have existed in but a single good manuscript copy which also went temporarily astray.[61] Even by the middle of the seventeenth century, it would appear, there might be no more than a single good manuscript suitable for printing available to a bookseller who was friendly to the actors and who was anxious to publish such popular and successful plays as *The Mad Lover* and *The Wild-Goose Chase.*

With these lost prompt-books in mind we might now return to the customary explanation for the absence of *The Two Noble Kinsmen* from the 1623 Folio. It is often asserted that Heminge and Condell included in the

---

[60] Bald, *Beaumont & Fletcher Folio,* pp. 1–6.

[61] *Ibid.,* pp. 6–9, 103–104. (Cf. also Bentley, *Jacobean and Caroline Stage,* III, 375–376. It may be possible, as Bentley suggests, that the manuscript that came into the hands of Sir Aston Cokayne was a private transcript, but if, as Bald assumes, it was the prompt-book and Cokayne returned it to Cotton to give to the printers, then the irregular late addition of *The Mad Lover* to the S.R. entry is accounted for; otherwise, Cokayne's testimony and the late entry of the prompt-book must be regarded as mere coincidence.)

Folio only those plays they knew to be substantially Shakespeare's and deliberately excluded all others. Their authority is immense, and rightfully so. There are nevertheless certain serious objections to assuming that the thirty-six Folio plays represent accurately their careful decision about the proper limits of the canon. Nor are these objections confined to the obvious cases of *The Two Noble Kinsmen* or *Pericles*.

Troilus and Cressida is in the Folio because Heminge and Condell knew it to be Shakespeare's. Yet it is now fairly clear that they would have been willing in the face of difficulties to allow the Folio to be published without the play. Both the prefatory catalogue of Shakespeare's plays which failed to list *Troilus,* and the address signed by Heminge and Condell which assured the reader that he had been provided with "all" of Shakespeare's plays, were printed, along with the other preliminaries, before "the eleventh hour" (as Greg puts it) at which *"Troilus* after all became available" (*Folio,* p. 447). We cannot tell how closely *The Winter's Tale* escaped omission, but the inclusion of *Troilus* was apparently a matter of last-minute luck.

A further objection to undue awe before authority, however, is actually prompted by a good deal more respect for the intelligent authority of Heminge and Condell than some students of *The Two Noble Kinsmen* have been willing to accord them; the objection is based, moreover, on something more solid than either bibliographical or historical evidence. It is this. If Heminge and Condell excluded *The Two Noble Kinsmen* from the Folio not because the manuscript was for some reason unavailable, but rather because they "knew" that Shakespeare was not substantially involved in the play, then they were wrong. The assumption that the play was not available when the Folio was printed is—it becomes clear with a little thought—a good deal easier to tolerate.

But it is time to turn more directly to the question of Shakespeare's alleged collaboration with Fletcher. It will be best to begin with *Henry VIII.*

III

Henry VIII: The Consequences of a Problem of Authorship

> Observations are made only because of some interest or expectation—
> however dim, unvoiced or unverbalised this may be—and expectations
> are such that if they were verbalised they would be expressions of
> hypotheses.
>
> *John Oulton Wisdom*

"Since Spedding dealt with *Henry the Eighth* the majority of critics attribute this play to Shakespeare and Fletcher." Spedding dealt with the play in 1850; A. C. Bradley made the comment in 1929; some scholars today would still regard it as valid. Nevertheless, title in the play evidently reverted to Shakespeare between 1931 and 1957. The next few pages present a brief chronicle of modern *Henry VIII* scholarship, in the course of which the choice of 1957 as a cut-off date for the dual attribution should appear, if not justifiable, at least explicable. A longer chronicle, going back to Spedding and his followers, will then develop the interconnections between study of *Henry VIII* and study of *The Two Noble Kinsmen*. The balance of the chapter will finally deal directly with more substantial questions of *Henry VIII*, and in particular will try to show the practical consequences for interpretive criticism of its "problem of authorship."

The Present Position

The same critical splinter-group that challenged the orthodox Hickson views on the authorship of *The Two Noble Kinsmen* (beginning with Boyle about 1880 and ending with Sykes about 1920) was active in promoting Massinger as co-author of *Henry VIII* as well. Their arguments, invariably taking Fletcher's presence for granted without discussion, need not concern us, but it is against the background of their activity that one must consider the more reputable modern scholarship on the play. Thus Willard Farnham's 1916 *PMLA* article on "colloquial contractions" was not designed to confirm the Spedding division of authorship in *Henry VIII* any more than it was designed to confirm the Hickson division of *The Two Noble Kinsmen;* its purpose was to repudiate the arguments for Massinger.

Against the same background Marjorie Nicolson in 1922 published her study of *Henry VIII*.[1] One of her principal conclusions, that Massinger was not co-author of the play, seems in retrospect little more significant than the proposition that Bacon did not write *Hamlet;* but her essay still retains its interest. Part of it consisted of a report on the use of sources in the play. Accepting Spedding's division, Miss Nicolson noted that "both authors have simply versified long passages from the chronicles"—i.e. as Shakespeare had "simply versified" North's Plutarch in such passages as Enobarbus' description of Cleopatra's barge—and she summed up, as no editor to that time had done, the extent of the debts:

In the Shakespearean portions there are fourteen direct borrowings from Holinshed; three from Foxe; one from Hall; two which may be from Cavendish or Holinshed. Fletcher has ten from Holinshed, two from Hall, four from Foxe, four which may be from Cavendish or Holinshed.

(pp. 487–488)

The only conclusion she drew from these findings, however, was that "a study of sources . . . throws little real light upon the problem of authorship."

A year later Baldwin Maxwell published another study of the problem of authorship.[2] More familiar with the plays of Fletcher than some earlier students of *Henry VIII*, Maxwell noticed that the scenes assigned to Fletcher in the play seemed quite dissimilar to his other work. He re-examined Spedding's original arguments and went further than Miss Nicolson into the matter of sources. Convinced of the general value of statistical tests in determining authorship, Maxwell nonetheless noted that Spedding, who had clinched his division with a set of metrical statistics purporting to illustrate Shakespeare's and Fletcher's versification, had actually worked without

[1] Nicolson, "The Authorship of *Henry the Eighth*," *PMLA*, XXXVII (1922), 484–502. One section of this article was concerned with the question, "What was it that Shakespeare had in mind when he set about the play which he never finished?" (p. 490); there followed a speculative reconstruction.

[2] Maxwell, "Fletcher and *Henry the Eighth*," *Manly Anniversary Studies in Language and Literature* (1923), pp. 104–112.

representative figures for any other plays but *Henry VIII* and that, in fact, Spedding "cannot be said to have made any tests whatsoever"; he also noted that Fletcher had made no close verbal borrowings from Holinshed when he wrote *Bonduca* (his one play deriving from this source) but had invented fresh speeches to replace what Holinshed offered, and that this was quite unlike the practice of whoever wrote *Henry VIII*. Maxwell did not then challenge the assumption of divided authorship, but he concluded that the "non-Shakespearean author" of part of the play, whoever he was, had not—for the reasons mentioned and several others—been accurately identified. When Sir Edmund Chambers in *William Shakespeare* gave his summary of research on *Henry VIII* up to 1930, he granted the force of Maxwell's arguments and agreed that *"Henry VIII* is not very characteristic Fletcher"; but he added he did not think the play very "characteristic" Shakespeare either, and said he saw "no reason to dissent" from the customary Spedding view.

The first substantial challenge to the assumption of dual authorship appeared in 1931. Peter Alexander, in a patient analysis of earlier work on the play, re-created for his readers a sufficiently comprehensive history of earlier opinion to make intelligible the unusual success of the Spedding theory in the absence of creditable evidence.[3] One response to Alexander is worth quoting at length—not only for its value as a concise summary of the narrative part of the essay but also because, although it represented what was still a minority reaction in 1939 when it appeared, it is quite representative of informed opinion today:

In a splendidly sane article . . . Mr. Peter Alexander has traced the history of the conjectures which led eventually to the almost universal acceptance of the view that *Henry VIII* was written . . . largely by John Fletcher. The belief in the play's dual authorship was first presented by Malone. Thoroughly sound had been Roderick's observation that the verse of *Henry VIII* differed from that of other Shakespearean plays; but, as Mr. Alexander points out, when Malone . . . combined Roderick's observation with Theobald's guess that the eulogy of Elizabeth showed that the play had been first written before 1603, he presented a remarkably "casual combination of conjecture and fact" in stating that the panegyric on James was "added in 1613, after Shakespeare had quitted the stage, by that hand which tampered with . . . the play so much, as to have rendered the versification of it of a different colour from all the other plays of Shakespeare." Later, after Spalding and Hickson had argued for the collaboration of Shakespeare and Fletcher in *The Two Noble Kinsmen,* Spedding, acting upon a chance suggestion of Tennyson, advanced the view that Fletcher was the second author in *Henry VIII*. Inevitable was the next step—

---

[3] Alexander, "Conjectural History, or Shakespeare's *Henry VIII*," *Essays and Studies,* XVI (1930), 85–120.

taken in defiance of all the external evidence—Boyle's denial of . . . Shakespeare and his assignment of the play to Fletcher and Massinger. . . . [But] it is Spedding's view which has for the past sixty years been generally accepted.

Mr. Alexander has done more than reveal the gradual growth in the conjectural history of *Henry VIII*. He has pointed out that characteristics which have been claimed to be peculiar to Fletcher are to be found in the later plays of Shakespeare. . . .

These comments were written by Baldwin Maxwell to introduce his chapter on *Henry VIII* in *Studies in Beaumont, Fletcher, and Massinger* (1939); the chapter reprints his earlier published work on the play—revised: "in the light of Mr. Alexander's paper," he writes, "[I] have abandoned the adjective 'non-Shakespearean' in referring to the scenes which had been generally assigned to Fletcher."

G. Wilson Knight's brief discussion of the play in *The Criterion* (January 1936) was revised and expanded for *The Crown of Life* (1947); the attention Knight gives to the authorship question makes his essay a valuable complement to the earlier discussions, and it has undoubtedly been instrumental in re-establishing belief in Shakespeare's sole authorship. On the other hand, it is probably also true—since Knight does not subscribe to the same totemic system to which many of his academic contemporaries belong—that his arguments had the initial effect of strengthening the position of Spedding among those scholars for whom metrical tests and the like still carried weight.

The Problem of "Henry VIII" Reopened, by the South African philologist A. C. Partridge, was published in 1949. The most ambitious defense of the Spedding division since C. Knox Pooler's Arden edition of the play in 1915, Partridge's brief (28-page) study cites a few earlier arguments on behalf of that division and offers as fresh corroborative evidence a tabulation of ten "little mannerisms of grammatical usage, easily passed over in the weightier aesthetic considerations" (p. 12)—specifically, it gives statistics on the frequency and distribution of *hath, has, doth, does, them, 'em, ye, y'*, "the expletive *do*," and "notional verbs inflected *-th.*" Consideration of this curious book must be reserved for a later point in the discussion.

Of the scholars whose work has been mentioned so far—Farnham, Nicolson, Maxwell, Alexander, Knight, and Partridge—the most markedly influential appears to have been Alexander; he reiterated his arguments at the 1948 Shakespeare Conference in Stratford before a large gathering of British and foreign scholars, and with enough success to be cast by Partridge soon after in the role of leading adversary. In any case, the great majority of the references to the play in the annual volumes of the *Shakespeare*

Survey since its founding in 1948 seem to take Shakespeare's single author-ship for granted, and not many of the scholars who in recent years have assumed the validity of the older theory seem to have been fully acquainted with the counter-evidence.

That evidence, however, has been brought together in the Introduction to the 1957 Arden edition of the play by R. A. Foakes. Other recent editors —notably C. J. Sisson and Hardin Craig in their editions of the complete works—had already rejected the collaboration theory, but the Arden text is the first important separate edition of the play since the Yale edition of 1925 and the old Arden edition of 1915, and its thoroughly documented sur-vey of both sides of the authorship question, favorably received by most reviewers, leads one to believe that the Spedding theory has about run its course. Nothing compelled a Mediterranean ship-captain in the early 1500's to abandon his belief that the earth was flat, of course, but the tenure of the collaboration theory is not very secure today.

It is true that hardly any evidence directly concerning the play has yet been mentioned, but the history of much scholarly opinion on the play has had so little to do with direct inspection of evidence that it has seemed best to begin this account with a frank imitation, perhaps a parody, of the more depressing conventions. Since, as Partridge conceded, there is as strong a *prima facie* case for attributing *Henry VIII* to Shakespeare as there is for any play in the Folio, it cannot be said that assuming the cor-rectness of current opinion begs the question of authorship, but of course the reader is quite justified if he feels that the "weight-of-opinion" argument implied in the preceding account is not very satisfying. The question that has indeed been begged is how Spedding's views came so long to prevail, and an explanation that proceeds along different lines from those followed by Alexander will suggest that the relevance of *The Two Noble Kinsmen* and *Henry VIII* to each other is quite different from what is still generally supposed.

Spedding and Hickson in 1850

A word first about the critical background of the Spedding theory. Since the action of the play deals with the public and private life of the King from the time he is still influenced by Wolsey until the time Elizabeth is born, the ways in which critics have regarded the character of the King have naturally affected their sense of the dramatic action. Not all critics, however, have distinguished between the King as defined by the play and the historical Henry VIII. Hazlitt, for example, failed to make any distinction whatever between the two, and although he admired the play, he praised Shakespeare for the "great truth" with which he had "represented in all the bloated deformity of mind and person" this "disgusting" man; Hazlitt even expressed surprise that Henry—with "his vulgarity, his arrogance, his sensuality, his cruelty"—was not "hooted from the English stage." [4] This representation was, of course, the popular nineteenth-century view of the historical Henry—the Holbein portrait (created in the King's last years) seen through the eyes of historians Shakespeare never knew. The King we encounter in the play (to speak merely of his physical image for a moment) is youthful and vigorous; even before we first set eyes on him, we hear reports that his chivalric accomplishments at the Field of the Cloth of Gold caused all beholders to marvel. The method by which the popular image of Henry obscured the dramatic image is interestingly suggested in a comment by the once influential Ulrici (1839), whose reading was at least a little more careful than Hazlitt's:

Shakspeare has . . . not spared Henry's character: he appears everywhere as the obstinate, capricious, selfish and heartless man that he was—a slave to his favourites and to his passions. That Shakspeare has not *expressly* described him as such, that he has rather characterised him tacitly through his own actions, and no doubt sedulously pushed his good points into the foreground, could not—without injustice—have been expected otherwise from a national poet who wrote in the reign of Henry's daughter.[5]

Critics who knew the truth about the historical King Henry—and there was apparently only one main truth about him to many of them—would naturally want Shakespeare to share in their perception.

Commentators who saw the King in this light were naturally disturbed by the outcome of the play. To Ulrici, for example, the conclusion of the play stood in "sharp contradiction with the beginning and the middle." And much of the essay Spedding wrote for the *Gentleman's Magazine* [6] was addressed to this subject:

The strongest sympathies which have been awakened in us run opposite to the course of the action. Our sympathy is for the grief and goodness of Queen Katharine, while the course of the action [after the divorce] requires us to entertain as a theme of joy and compensatory satisfaction the coronation of Anne Bullen and the birth of her daughter; which are in fact a part of Katharine's injury, and amount to little less than the ultimate triumph of wrong.

(p. 116)

[4] William Hazlitt, *Characters of Shakespear's Plays* (1817), pp. 240, 242.

[5] Hermann Ulrici, *Shakspeare's Dramatic Art,* trans. L. Dora Schmitz (1876), II, 300.

[6] J[ames] S[pedding], "Who Wrote Shakspere's Henry VIII.?" *Gentleman's Magazine,* August 1850, pp. 115–123. Subsequent references given in the text.

Spedding rivalled Hazlitt in his impatience with the King:

Throughout the play the king's cause is not only felt by us, but represented to us, as a bad one. We *hear,* indeed, of conscientious scruples as to the legality of his first marriage; but we are not made, nor indeed asked, to believe they are sincere, or to recognise in his new marriage either the hand of Providence, or the consummation of any worthy object, or the victory of any of those more common frailties of humanity with which we can sympathise. The mere caprice of passion drives the king . . .

Only an unusual critic would regard the caprice of passion as an uncommon frailty; but in any case Spedding said that he knew of

no other play in Shakspere which is chargeable with a fault like this, none in which the moral sympathy of the spectator is not carried along with the main current of action to the end. In all the historical tragedies a providence may be seen presiding, . . . as just and relentless as the fate in a Greek tragedy. Even in *Henry IV.,* . . . we are never allowed to exult in the success of the wrong-doer, or to forget the penalties which are due to guilt.

(p. 117)

Spedding's interpretation, according to which the actions of an evil King are "crowned with all felicity," in this way led him to feel that Shakespeare could not have been sole author. He then indicated the kind of play he would presumably have allowed Shakespeare to have written:

[Although] the incidents of the reign of Henry VIII. could not . . . be altered at pleasure to suit the purposes of the artist, . . . they admitted of many different combinations. . . . By . . . carrying the story on to the birth of Anne Bullen's still-born son and her own execution, [the play] would have yielded the argument of a great tragedy and tale of retributive justice. Or . . . by representing the question of the divorce as the battle-ground on which the question between Popery and Protestantism was tried out, . . . and by connecting with the birth of Elizabeth the ultimate triumph of the Reformed religion, . . . our sympathies might have been turned that way, and so reconciled to the prosperous consummation.

(pp. 116–117)

Spedding was quite convinced, in fact, that if Shakespeare had written the play, the "focus of poetic interest" would "naturally" have been upon "the final separation of the English from the Romish Church" (p. 123). Alexander's comment on this suggestion was that Shakespeare "did not write *King John* round the signing of Magna Carta." But Spedding did not come to his conclusion, of course, until he had conducted a close scene-by-scene analysis of the actual play:

If any of your readers care to follow me in this inquiry, I would ask him to do as I did,—that is, to read the whole play straight through, with an eye open to notice the larger differences of effect, but without staying to examine small points. The effect of my own experiment was as follows:—

The opening of the play . . . seemed to have the full stamp of Shakspere, . . . the same close-packed expression; the same life, and reality, and freshness; the same rapid and abrupt turnings of thought; . . . the same impatient activity of intellect and fancy, which having disclosed an idea cannot wait to work it orderly out; the same daring confidence . . . which plunges headlong into a sentence without knowing how it is to come forth; . . . the same entire freedom from book-language and common-place . . . which distinguish the magical hand which has never yet been successfully imitated.

In the scene in the council-chamber which follows (Act i. sc. 2), where the characters of Katharine and Wolsey are brought out, I found the same characteristics equally strong.

But the instant I entered upon the third scene, in which the Lord Chamberlain, Lord Sands, and Lord Lovel converse, I was conscious of a total change. I felt as if I had passed suddenly out of the language of nature into the language of the stage, or of some conventional mode of conversation. The structure of the verse was quite different and full of mannerism. The expression became suddenly diffuse and languid. The wit wanted mirth and character. And all this was equally true of the supper scene which closes the first act.

The second act brought me back to the tragic vein, but it was not the tragic vein of Shakspere. . . .

(p. 118)

And so forth. The dialogue that opens I.iii is about as "diffuse and languid" as steel, but there is no doubt that the wit is not of a sort which a nineteenth-century English critic would publicly approve. An average Victorian reader, one assumes, would be comfortably warmed by the language of Spedding's essay; yet it was not language of the sort quoted so far that made the essay a landmark in Shakespearean scholarship, and Spedding's distinction between the language of nature and of convention was based on something more precise than his moral feelings or his conception of history, whatever they were. His essay had begun by calling attention to comments from various critics which, he said, "betrayed a consciousness that there is something peculiar" about the play; Coleridge, for example, had described it as "a sort of historical masque or shew-play," and Ulrici, who found "a profound moral purpose" in each of the plays of Shakespeare, "is obliged to confess that he can make nothing of *Henry VIII*" (p. 115). Even more striking, added Spedding, "a peculiarity of another kind has also been detected, I forget by whom, namely, the unusual number of lines with a redundant syllable at the end." [7] And a little later Spedding remarked that he "had also heard it casually remarked by a man of first-rate judgment on such a point that many passages in *Henry VIII.* were very much in the manner of *Fletcher*" (p. 117). Stimulated by these suggestions, Spedding had counted the number of lines with "redundant syllables." He found that in some scenes the number of feminine lines came to more than fifty per cent, while in the remaining scenes the number came to less than fifty per cent; this discovery he described as "a distinction so broad and so uniform" that it "cannot have been accidental," and, he added, "the more closely it is examined the more clearly will it appear that the metre in these two sets of scenes . . . bears evidence of different workmen" (p. 122). [8] Shakespeare was identifiable by his preference for 10-syllable lines as well as his advocacy of right, Fletcher by his preference for 11-syllable lines as well as his permissive attitude toward "the ultimate triumph of wrong." Spedding did not put it that way, but that in substance is what his analysis amounted to. His conclusion was a model of objectivity in that he did not compromise with the results of his verse-test; if more than half the lines in a scene were afflicted with "redundant syllables," the scene was not by Shakespeare. Spedding did not actually discuss any genuine examples of Fletcher's verse in his essay; the quotations he offered to illustrate the work of Fletcher were all drawn from *Henry VIII* itself, and he made only the briefest reference in passing to a few scenes in plays of the Fletcher canon.

The verse-table that Spedding invented must have appeared to many Victorians as the equivalent for literature of the Kelvin mechanical model that would render scientific laws sensible to mortal eyes. Actually, his innovation did not gain wide publicity for another twenty-odd years. Its impact on later scholarship we shall observe in a moment, but the year 1850 saw the uneasy merger of two previously separate critical traditions concerning the theory of dual authorship, and this little-known event cannot pass without notice if the later development of that theory is to be fully understood.

---

[7] Criticizing Warburton's edition of Shakespeare in remarks published in the 6th edition (1758) of Thomas Edwards' *Canons of Criticism,* Richard Roderick cited the high incidence of feminine endings in the play in order to disparage "that heap of emendations founded upon the presumption" that Shakespeare was "unknowing or unsolicitous" about his meters; for to Roderick, "that all these peculiarities were done by him advertently, and not by chance, is . . . as plain to all sense . . . as that Virgil intended to write Metre, and not Prose, in his Aeneid."

[8] Spedding's division, recorded by nearly all editors since the 1870's, gives I.i–ii, II.iii–iv, III.ii.1–203, V.i to Shakespeare, the rest to Fletcher. His split assignment for III.ii was no doubt prompted by the non-mathematical perception that "Wolsey's farewell" fell into falling rhythms, and he was presumably guided by the scene-division that Pope had wrongly introduced at the exit of the King at line 203.

Spedding's essay concluded with a brief solitary reference to *The Two Noble Kinsmen,* "the condition and supposed history of which is in many respects analogous" to that of *Henry VIII.* At this point a footnote directed the reader to "see an excellent article" on the subject in the 1847 *Westminster Review,* but Spedding added little else. The author of that 1847 article was, of course, Samuel Hickson, who now felt impelled to publish some remarks on *Henry VIII.* The following letter by Hickson appeared in *Notes and Queries* for 24 August 1850:

I had no sooner read . . . "Who wrote Shakspeare's Henry VIII.?" than I became aware that I had been anticipated in at least the publication of a discovery I made three or four years ago, but for the making known of which a favourable opportunity had not occurred. . . . I was anxious to arrive at a more satisfactory conclusion than has yet presented itself to me; and a paper on the subject commenced more than two years ago, I, with this feeling, laid aside. My present object is to strengthen the argument of the writer . . . by recording the fact that I, having no communication with him, or knowledge of him, . . . should have arrived at exactly the same conclusion as his own . . . that Fletcher has at least an equal claim with Shakspeare to the authorship of *Henry VIII.*

In the unfinished paper to which I have alluded, . . . having stated it to be my intention to confine myself to the simple inquiry, *"What did Shakspeare really write?"* I continued:—

"To those who consider the text as having been settled 'by authority,' this question may seem superfluous; but, not to refer to plays of very early date, in connection with which we could bring forward facts that, we doubt not, would be considered sufficiently startling; we now state it as our belief that a great portion of the play of *Henry VIII.*—nay more than half, was *not* written by Shakspeare."

My intention now is, not to enter into any argument in support of this view, but to state the results . . . in the following extract from my note-book:—

Henry VIII

"Act I. Scene 1. Shakspeare.
  "   2. Ditto.
  "   3. Fletcher.
  "   4. Ditto.
Act II.   "   1. Ditto.
  "   2. Ditto. [etc.]"

Hickson gave no statistics as Spedding had done, but of course his text must have been similar to Spedding's, ditto his command of arithmetic, and no doubt he could have produced a fine test if he had wanted to. But he simply reported that his conviction about the accuracy of the division "is as complete as it is of my own identity," and the doubts that had led him to delay publication had to do only with the possible circumstances of dramatic composition—on which, in conclusion, he now offered a few speculations. As Alexander has noted, Theobald took Cranmer's final prophecy about Elizabeth to indicate that the play had been written during Elizabeth's lifetime, and this guess became the basis of much later conjecture about revision of the original play; such a theory would make Shakespeare responsible for Cranmer's lines on Elizabeth but not his lines on James. Hickson was unsure about the order of composition, but he was happy to note that the division of authorship proved that "the flatteries of James and Elizabeth may now go packing together" (i.e. may be assigned to Fletcher) and "the character of Shakspeare" may thus "shine out . . . brighter."

The great prestige attached to literary "discovery" in the age of Collier's forgeries, and the very slender acknowledgment Spedding had made to Hickson's article on *The Two Noble Kinsmen,* would go far towards accounting for this preposterous letter. There had been nothing in the 1847 article to suggest Hickson had connected Fletcher with *Henry VIII* or any other of the canonical plays.[9] His claim to have anticipated Spedding "three or four years ago," however, would probably not have disturbed anyone who found Spedding's analysis effective. Except, perhaps, Spedding himself. Spedding sent the following letter, dated 11 September 1850, to the *Gentleman's Magazine,* where it appeared in the October issue:

I was much gratified, though not at all surprised, to find, by a letter from Mr. Samuel Hickson to the editor of "Notes and Queries" . . . that the question "Who wrote Henry VIII.?" had already engaged that gentleman's attention, and that he had come to the same conclusion with myself as to the parts which were written by Fletcher. . . . The exactness of the coincidence should surprise those who doubt the correctness of the conclusion; for the inquiries were certainly quite independent and unknown to each other. The resemblance of the style, in some parts of the play, to Fletcher's, was pointed out to me several years ago by Alfred Tennyson (for I do not know why I should not mention his name); and long before that, the general distinctions between Shakspere's man-

---

[9] On the other hand, William Spalding once suggested (in his review of Dyce's Beaumont and Fletcher for the July 1847 *Edinburgh Review*) that if *The Winter's Tale* had been omitted from the 1623 Folio and if he and his contemporaries had to determine its authorship purely by internal evidence, then "Beaumont and Fletcher (as an eminent living critic has remarked to us) might be believed to have written all its serious parts, more especially the scenes of the jealousy of Leontes, and those beautiful ones which describe the rustic festival" (p. 31).

ner and Fletcher's had been admirably explained by Charles Lamb in his note on the Two Noble Kinsmen, and by Mr. Spalding in his Essay [i.e. the 1833 *Letter*]. And in respect to this I had myself derived additional light, more perhaps than I am aware of, from Mr. Hickson himself. . . . But, having been thus put upon the scent, and furnished with principles, I followed the inquiry out by myself, without help or communication. That two independent inquirers should thus have arrived at the same conclusions upon so many particulars, must certainly be considered very singular, except upon one supposition; viz. that the conclusions are according to reason. . . . I should have been more surprised if the coincidence had been less exact. . . .

The way in which the word "independent" is toyed with takes one's breath away, and there is wit in the final remark as well. The substance of the letter suggests that Spedding was interested in something more than further promotion of his thesis; that purpose would have been more effectively served if Spedding had induced some friend to write. The references to authorities offer a lead: when he had cited his authorities in the essay printed two months earlier, this respected scholar had been precise in identifying a few critics who had been struck with "peculiarities" in *Henry VIII*, but he had forgotten the name of Roderick and he had oddly failed to mention Malone's suggestion (designed, as Alexander noted, to harmonize the speculations of Theobald and Roderick) that a second writer had handled the play after Shakespeare had retired. He also neglected at that time to mention the opinions of either Lamb or Spalding on *The Two Noble Kinsmen*. Apparently his original brief note on *The Two Noble Kinsmen* had drawn more of a response than he had hoped for, and his letter, still silent on Roderick and Malone, calls attention to Hickson's predecessors on *The Two Noble Kinsmen* in a way that one suspects was designed to undercut Hickson after he had been so forward.[10] This is not to say, of course, that Lamb and Spalding did not influence him; one may suspect, indeed, that their influence had been quite as great as that of the "man of first-rate judgment" who had "casually remarked . . . that many passages . . . were very much in the manner of *Fletcher*." Presumably that man had been Tennyson, and it is not strange that Spedding no longer knew any reason for withholding the name of his eminent friend who, according to the later account, had "several years ago . . . pointed out . . . the re-

---

[10] Hickson, at least, seems to have placed some such construction on the Spedding letter, for he wrote another letter to *N&Q*, 16 Nov. 1850, in which he drew attention to as many pre-Spedding references as he could find that might cast suspicion on the integrity of *Henry VIII*.—Subsequent letters from Hickson, alleging small bits of stylistic evidence for Fletcher's presence in the play, appeared in *N&Q* on 18 Jan. 1851 and 26 Apr. 1851 (cf. pp. 142–143 below).

semblance of the style . . . to Fletcher's";[11] Spedding's lessened reticence may be put down to the confidence that accompanies success. In any case the great triumvirate of the Shakespeare-Fletcher collaboration theory consisted of Spalding, Hickson, and Spedding, and 1850 was the year in which *Henry VIII* and *The Two Noble Kinsmen* were first made to stand in a curious relationship to each other that was little analyzed by later scholarship. Twenty-four years later the theory came to be regarded as an established fact.

The Spedding Theory and the New Shakspere Society

Spedding outlived both Spalding and Hickson, and he became one of the better known members of Dr. Furnivall's Society. In the first volume of the Society *Transactions* (1874), about 370 of the 515 pages were devoted to six long metrical papers by Fleay, to discussions by Society members of these papers, and to John Ingram's short history of metrical tests in which the Spedding analysis of *Henry VIII* was held up as a "perfect model of Shaksperian criticism" (p. 444) and the Hickson essay on *The Two Noble Kinsmen,* although it had included no verse-table, came in for honorable mention. The Appendix to this volume of *Transactions* contained the following:

1. Reprint of Spedding's August 1850 essay on *Henry VIII.*   pp. 1*–18*
2. Reprint of Hickson's "confirmation of Mr Spedding's paper" (i.e. his letter to *Notes and Queries,* 24 August 1850).   18*–20*
3. Reprint of Spedding's reply to Hickson.   21*–22*
4. A "fresh confirmation of Mr Spedding's division" by Fleay; Fleay averaged Spedding's figures for lines with feminine endings (Sh: 1 in 3.0/ Fl: 1 in 1.7).   23*
5. "Another fresh confirmation" by Furnivall, who computed averages for run-on lines (Sh: 1 in 2.03/ Fl: 1 in 3.79).   24*
6. Reprint of Hickson's 1847 article on *The Two Noble Kinsmen.*   25*–61*
7. Hickson's division "confirmed by metrical tests": feminine endings as counted by Fleay (Sh: 1 in 3.5/ Fl: 1 in 1.8).   61*–64*
8. Hickson's division "confirmed by the stopt-line test": run-on lines as counted by Furnivall (Sh: 1 in 2.41/ Fl: 1 in 5.53).   64*–65*
9. Reprint of Roderick's comments on the meter of *Henry VIII.*   66*–68*

[11] Tennyson's only recorded comment is that "much of *Henry VIII* . . . is . . . by Fletcher, with passages unmistakably by Shakespeare. . . . I could swear to Shakespeare in the *Field of the Cloth of Gold* . . ." (*Alfred Lord Tennyson: A Memoir by his Son* [1897], II, 291). Made in 1883 after Shakespeare's presence in the play had evidently been questioned, these remarks sound defensive of Shakespeare; and Tennyson oddly fails to mention Spedding or to claim any share of credit for his theory.

Method and results, like the chicken and the egg, have the power to perpetuate one another. The tests supposedly validated the divisions of authorship, the divisions validated the tests for many Victorian students, the division of each play was alleged to support the other, and the geometry of mutual support made possible the failure of respectable scholars to note absurdities as remarkable in their way as Collier's more material fabrications of a generation earlier.[12] Although 1 in 1.39 pages of the *Transactions* proper (exclusive of the Appendix) was given over to metrical science, perhaps it would not be unscientific to suggest that the Appendix, although it occupied only 1 in 8.57 pages of the entire volume, must have had the greater effect in establishing standards and procedures for what Furnivall called "the second Victorian school of Shaksperians." The significance of the material in that Appendix, faded by time, will be easier to assess if we recall a few of the attitudes and purposes expressed in the activities of the New Shakspere Society.

In his "Founder's Prospectus" Furnivall compared the Victorian Shakespeare scholar to "our geniuses of Science [who] are so wresting her secrets from Nature as to make our days memorable for ever." Metrical tests first interested him for their possible value in determining the chronology of Shakespeare's plays—an overriding interest:

Unless a man's works are studied in the order in which he wrote them, you *cannot* get at a right understanding of his mind. . . . This has been specially brought home to me by my work at Chaucer. Until I saw that his *Pity* was his first original work, the key of his life was undiscovered; but that found, it at once opened his treasure-chest. . . .[13]

Such emphasis on chronology—often no doubt a valuable way of organizing attention—must seem absurdly exaggerated to most of us. But as long as

---

[12] It was not until more than fifty years later, for example, that Alexander (in his *Essays and Studies* article) pointed out this flaw in the assumption that each of the several verse-tests gave "independent" confirmation of the others: "Up to a certain point of course both weak endings and run-on lines may be found increasing with double endings; but it is also clear that a point must be reached when the others will fall away before the double endings, as a play with a double ending to every line could have no light or weak endings and would be largely end-stopped. The other differences, therefore, in 'Fletcher's' part . . . are related to the large increase in the double endings" (p. 105).

[13] "Founder's Prospectus" (bound into the volume of 1874 *Transactions* and separately paginated), pp. 6–7. Cf. Lord Kelvin: "The luminiferous ether . . . is the only substance we are confident of in dynamics. One thing we are sure of, and that is the reality and substantiality of the luminiferous ether." Perhaps it was the Victorian taste for certainty that once prompted Darwin to ask, "Who would trust the convictions of a monkey's mind?"

one assumes that there are "secrets" whose "right" interpretation may be "discovered" if only one can find a "key," perhaps as good a case can be made for the value of chronological study as for any other kind. Whether the assumption itself is anything more than a linguistic convenience is a question that need not now concern us. Certain derivative assumptions found in that "Prospectus" might, however, be observed. Furnivall considered "the gradual changes in [Shakespeare's] versification" to be "the most satisfactory . . . evidence" for scientific students of Shakespeare to examine, not only because they provided so sizeable a body of evidence but also because these changes were, as he put it, "undesigned." And Fleay was equally clear about his need to assume, for the purpose of solving the problems he wished to solve, that

if the peculiarities of a writer are regarded as matters of chance or arbitrary choice, it is absurd to take them as a basis of investigation: but they are not so: in every writer there are tricks of style and of metre which *unknown to himself* pervade all his work.

(1874 *Transactions,* p. 365)

The immodest assumption that a critic deals with factors of which he is conscious where the poet was not is probably still widely held (it seems to rest on the critic's unconscious identification of verbal formulation with "knowledge"), although not many critics today would be any more willing to apply it to a poet's choice of meters than was Roderick (cf. note 7 above).

The first metrical paper by Fleay was presented at the opening meeting of the Society in March of 1874. This was his famous "On Metrical Tests as Applied to Dramatic Poetry"; once regarded as "epoch-making" (as Willard Farnham called it in 1916), the paper does indeed appear to have ushered in a general fashion for statistical tests of literary style in all their multifoliolate variety. The influential Dr. Furnivall[14] supported and encouraged his fellow scholar at first, but by June of 1874 the two men had quarrelled bitterly; an ill-tempered but solidly documented attack by Furnivall on several of Fleay's many vulnerable arguments was followed by Fleay's departure from the Society. The differences between the two men may have been personal as well as intellectual, but a comment by Furnivall before the final break is suggestive of the form their arguments took; it is taken from the discussion on 8 May (in the *Transactions*) of a paper by Fleay dividing *Timon of Athens* between Shakespeare and Tourneur:

[14] Son of a doctor who amassed a fortune of £200,000 in the operation of a private insane asylum, Furnivall was active in organizing the Early English Text, Chaucer, Wyclif, Ballad, and Browning Societies.

To me this paper has been more satisfactory than any former one of Mr Fleay's; and for this reason: that it is drawn up on the model of Mr Spedding's examination of Shakspere's *Henry VIII.,* which I have more than once urgd on Mr Fleay as the pattern to follow, and which was really and truly in 1850 the pioneer of the work that we have now, twenty-four years after, begun to do; that is to say, the Paper first criticizes the play upon aesthetic grounds, and then verifies the results by metrical tests.

(p. 242)

Although this tribute to Spedding merely hints at the distinction, Fleay usually professed a commitment to metrical "science," while Furnivall sometimes spoke up against his prolific colleague on behalf of his own brand of "the higher criticism." [15] In practice the distinction between the two attitudes seems to have amounted to this: when Fleay found that for some reason he was required to alter one of his published judgments, he uncovered some error in his original verse-statistics which he could then correct to support his new position; [16] Furnivall was less skillful in cooking his figures, showed less patience with arithmetic, disliked Fleay, and was therefore prone to dismiss difficulties in the results of his own tests with some such comment as "counting can never be a better judge than real criticism." [17] The passage quoted above is notable too in foreshadowing Furnivall's later

[15] One example of this criticism in operation deserves preservation; Furnivall here explains (in his Foreword to the 1876 N.S.S. reprint of Spalding's *Letter,* p. vii) why upon reconsideration he has come to doubt Shakespeare's presence in any part of *TNK:* "When at one's reading-party one turns to the cleverest and most poetic-natured girl-friend, and says, 'This is assignd to Shakspere. Do you feel it's his?' She answers, 'Not a bit. And no one else does either. Look how people's eyes are all off their books. They don't care for it: you never see that when we're reading one of Shakspere's genuine plays.' "

[16] Characteristic reactions by Fleay (1874 *Transactions,* pp. 23* & 39) after learning he had overlooked some dating evidence:

I regret that a mis-reading of my table . . . led me to allow *Henry VIII.* to have the date 1603 [Malone's date] attached to it.

Cymbeline . . . was misplaced [= dated earlier than *Hamlet*] through another cause, a numerical blunder.

[17] The occasion for this statement is notable. Furnivall's count of run-on lines in *TNK* had been intended to support Hickson's division, but Furnivall was distressed to find that, according to his own figures, II.i should have been assigned to Fletcher, whereas he was sure it was by Shakespeare; hence he added this comment. As it happens, however, he had used a text in which II.i and II.ii were combined into a single scene; if he had used an accurately divided text, his figures would have supported Hickson. Ingram (*Transactions,* p. 455) noted the Director's error and took it as a piece of unconscious testimony to the value of metrical tests. Maybe; but it also means that Furnivall was persuaded (for a while) that II.ii had been written by Shakespeare.

need—after Fleay's departure—to rely on Spedding's and Hickson's essays, and on his own metrical tests, to lend pedigreed authority to the pronouncements of the Society on such matters as the spuriousness of various plays or parts of plays which he and his colleagues particularly disliked. In his report of July 1875 on the first year's work of the Society (printed with the 1874 *Transactions*) he spoke with pride of the fact that the Society had reprinted "that most able, but almost overlookt and disregarded" article by Spedding, and on this occasion he described it as containing "the most striking [N.B.:] confirmation of Mr Tennyson's view [!] of the play," adding that its conclusions had received further confirmation from Hickson (alluding to the letter of 24 August 1850) "on aesthetic grounds"! Spedding and the New Shakspere Society were much obliged to each other.

Interestingly enough, the metrical tests which have long been interpreted as verifications of dual authorship can, without any juggling, be shown to be fairly consistent with the assumption of single Shakespearean authorship not only of *Henry VIII* but of *The Two Noble Kinsmen* as well. When the figures on feminine endings, run-on lines, weak and light endings, midline speech-endings, and so forth—the phenomena represented in metrical tables as showing a chronological increase in Shakespeare's work—are recalculated for each of the two plays as a whole (rather than divided, as in the tables printed by Chambers, between the "two parts" of each play), the results are generally consistent with the figures for other late plays (the widest discrepancy being the figure for feminine endings in *Henry VIII*, 46% as against 35% in *The Tempest*); the inaccuracies in the figures based on mislined texts of *The Two Noble Kinsmen* (which show 41% feminine endings, whereas a corrected text would show a lower proportion) might even allow one to claim that there is greater "objectivity" in this reinterpretation than in the view the figures have long been alleged to support, since those figures were computed by adherents to the theory of dual authorship. A similar reinterpretation might be made of the non-metrical tests.[18] No inference about authorship is here being urged—else the matter would not be reviewed so cursorily—but it does seem fair to make these points against the claims of those who have preferred to draw their conclusions from pseudo-scientific statistical tables rather than from literary interpretation and analysis. Science is consciousness, not magic. Alexander

---

[18] The 1916 Farnham contraction-test discussed in Chapter I furnishes a conveniently brief example. Farnham noted a sharp chronological increase in Shakespeare's use of the contractions selected for his test (e.g. 9 in *Romeo*, 90 in *Othello*, 154 in *Winter's Tale*). In all of *Monsieur Thomas* (cited by Farnham as typical of Fletcher) there are 48—while in merely the 12 "Fletcher scenes" of *TNK* there are 61, and there are 141 in the play as a whole.

Bryan Johnson observed of metaphysics, as long ago as 1836, that "[although it] is fallen into disrepute, it is abandoned like a mine which will not repay the expense of working, rather than like a process of mining which we have discovered to be constitutionally incapable of producing gold." The same figure—suitably reduced in scale to match the triviality of the subject—might be applied to most of the "objective tests" for determining authorship, and perhaps should also be applied to the notion that there can be any such thing as an "objective test" in the popular sense of those words.

The New Shakspere Society in its later years, and Fleay in his independent writings, were among the progenitors of disintegrationist criticism in Shakespearean studies. The disintegrationist movement was perhaps more closely paralleled by the efforts of the Baconians than by any activities in Homeric scholarship, and the Baconian underplot reminds us, if any reminder is necessary, that this malaise had broader roots in late-Victorian culture than can be accounted for by the work of any single band of scholars. M. C. Bradbrook has remarked that the "work [of] the disintegrators . . . in the early years of this century forms one of the curiosities of critical history," and that the works of J. M. Robertson in particular, although "now hardly read at all, [were] once thought worthy of refutation by Chambers or Greg." [19] It is equally startling to recall that this Lucifer among disintegrators once impressed T. S. Eliot as well—that Eliot's 1919 essay on *Hamlet* was predicated in part on the assumption, taken over from Robertson, that in the most literal sense the play contains a good deal of unassimilated work by dramatists other than Shakespeare (cf. page 12). The recollection points up the sharp change in our thinking that has taken place during the intervening years. It might be suggested that the best efforts of the "new criticism" and the "new bibliography" have both proceeded from the same general change in attitudes toward knowledge, and that the various ways in which *Henry VIII* has been read, studied, and written about may eventually be seen to illustrate part of this change. But back to specifics.

At the beginning of 1885 Robert Boyle, tutor to Czar Nicholas II, sent from his residence in St. Petersburg to the New Shakspere Society in London a paper on the authorship of *Henry VIII*.[20] A companion-piece to his 1882 essay on *The Two Noble Kinsmen*, Boyle's paper attacked the play and sought to establish Massinger as its co-author. Although Furnivall in

[19] Bradbrook, "Fifty Years of the Criticism of Shakespeare's Style," *Shakespeare Survey* 7 (1954), p. 6.

[20] Boyle, "*Henry VIII*. An Investigation into the Origin and Authorship of the Play," 1880–86 *Transactions*, pp. 443–487. Comments on Boyle's views—by Furnivall, Robert Browning, and others—are printed in the Appendix to this volume of N.S.S. *Transactions*, pp. 118*–126*.

his report ten years earlier on the first year's work of the Society had asserted that Spedding had "assignd, once and for ever, to Shakspere his
part of the play," he now stated that he "welcomed Mr Boyle's paper as a
relief, having always found *Henry VIII.* so much *in the way* in dealing with
Shakspere's work." Furnivall then read a communication he had solicited
from Browning (whom he had by then made "President" of the Society)
in which Browning indorsed Boyle's views on the play—including even the
mediumistic view that an original play by Shakespeare about Henry VIII
had been lost in the burning of the Globe. The other scholars present at the
meeting at which Boyle's paper was presented—their views are recorded in
the *Transactions*—were unpersuaded and unimpressed with its arguments,
and not until 1919, in the work of H. Dugdale Sykes, did Boyle find another
champion with the ardor of Furnivall.[21] Parenthetically, one curious aspect
of the views of Boyle, Furnivall, and Sykes is that, while they had preserved
the main lines of Hickson's division of *The Two Noble Kinsmen* when
they argued for Massinger's presence in that play, they did not attempt to
preserve Spedding's division of *Henry VIII:* they redivided the play, finding "Massinger" in part or all of several scenes (Boyle four and Sykes seven)
given by Spedding to Fletcher. Although their views on *Henry VIII* never
gained many supporters, the principal result of their efforts was to keep
the distracting question of Massinger's partial authorship alive in the minds
of editors and scholars for about forty years. The question was still alive
when the next item to be considered was first published.

The Spedding Theory in the Twentieth Century

The 1915 Arden Shakespeare edition of *Henry VIII* by C. Knox Pooler
contains what is probably the most substantial defense of the theory of dual
authorship between Spedding's original essay and Partridge's *Problem of
"Henry VIII" Reopened,* for it assembles in one place nearly all the pieces
of "stylistic" evidence for Fletcher that had appeared in scattered sources
from the time of Hickson's later communications to *Notes and Queries*

---

[21] Sykes, *Sidelights on Shakespeare* (1919), pp. 18–47. A revealing sidelight on Sykes
may be found in the proposal on p. 28 to emend *notion* at *Henry VIII* I.ii.85 to
motion. "It is strange," Sykes wrote of *notion,* "that it has never been noticed that
there is here a corruption of the text." As Baldwin Maxwell pointed out in his 1926
review of this book for *MP* (reprinted in his 1939 *Studies in Beaumont, Fletcher, and
Massinger*), the suggested emendation to *motion* was excellent, for it not only made
sense as *notion* did not, but it was already the reading of the Folio and of nearly all
editions of the play; the edition owned by Sykes contained a misprint, and he evidently
consulted no other.

(cited in note 10 above) to the time Spedding's theory had won fairly general acceptance. Hickson had cited as characteristic of Fletcher such items
as the use of the word "thousand" without an article, the use of the phrase
"a long farewell," and so forth. Pooler's Introduction presents thirteen such
allegedly Fletcherian "mannerisms and affectations" found in the play, followed by similar examples from passages—not invariably by Fletcher—in
the Beaumont-Fletcher canon. The very first example is the phrase "to the
height," which occurs once in *Henry VIII* and is paralleled eight times by
Pooler in six plays of the Fletcher canon. But in *Henry VIII* the phrase occurs at I.ii.214, the last line of a scene usually assigned to Shakespeare;
hence Pooler adds this comment:

> In this list I have included the expression "to the height," chiefly because it
> illustrates the difficulty of the subject. It does not occur in Shakespeare and it
> does occur in plays written wholly by Fletcher. On the other hand it is not un-
> common in Massinger, and its presence in Scene ii., which is not Fletcher's, may
> be a sign that this scene was written or altered by Massinger.
>
> (p. xxviii)

The absence of the phrase "to the height" in other plays by Shakespeare
would hardly suffice to justify Pooler's inference, but (as noted in the new
Arden edition) the phrase occurs also at *Troilus* V.i.3.

Pooler's most ambitious example is not a single phrase but a general
class of "mannerisms" involving the use of *one* as a substantive—"new legs
and lame ones" (I.iii.11), "a supper and a great one" (I.iii.52), "a wife, a
true one" (III.i.126), and so forth. (The others occur at II.i.119, III.ii.102
[a passage given to Shakespeare], III.ii.438, IV.i.55, IV.ii.51, V.iii.7.) These
are followed by twenty examples from fourteen texts in the Fletcher canon,
no more than two per play in thirteen cases, three from *The Woman's Prize*
(e.g. "sausages, and smoked ones"). But Pooler might just as easily have
turned to plays of Shakespeare and found, for example, "lungs and rotten
ones" at *The Tempest* II.i.47, "a humming, and that a strange one too" at
line 318 of the same scene, "yond same black cloud, yond huge one" at line
21 of the next scene, and so forth. The "stylistic" evidence for Fletcher
that had been accumulated during the sixty-five years between the Spedding
essay and the Pooler edition, in short, is not very substantial.

The principal scholarly and critical writings devoted to *Henry VIII* since
1915 have already been sketched in brief. By the time Alexander addressed
the 1948 conference at Stratford, it would appear that the Spedding theory
was already on the wane. We might therefore now turn to what is perhaps
the most important essay of this century to go against the grain. A. C.

Partridge put forward in 1949 "the fullest and most compelling argument yet" (Foakes) on behalf of the Spedding division of authorship, and his argument is interesting for its technique of persuasion as well as for the direct evidence it brings to bear on the play.

Since every scholar must to some extent create as well as anticipate the context within which his arguments and evidence are to be considered, it may be best to illustrate part of the context Partridge creates in *The Problem of "Henry VIII" Reopened*. This is hardly to suggest, of course, that his readers approached his book in a state of blank ignorance, but it seems advisable nevertheless to show just how widely he "reopens" the "problem" of *Henry VIII*. He begins as follows:

> The disintegration of Shakespeare, which the eighteenth century began, was advanced by scholars of the later nineteenth century, among them Spedding, Hickson, Fleay and Boyle. The climax of speculative dismemberment was reached in the works of J. M. Robertson on the Shakespeare canon. But the methods of all, except the first two, have been seriously discredited, and there has been in the last twenty-five years a progressive reinstatement of Shakespeare, based upon the authority of the First Folio.
>
> (p. 7)

Partridge then ascribes to "modern textual science and bibliography" most of the credit for this "reinstatement":

> For the first time a fairly coherent explanation has begun to emerge for anomalies of the First Folio and its relation to the quartos. It has thus been made possible for traditionalists, like Professor P. Alexander (one among many honoured names), to cling to the momentous document of 1623 as a proof of their faith in Shakespeare.

Yet, Partridge adds, modern bibliographers

> have only theorized about collaboration among playwrights. The determination of many of the so-called spurious parts of the Shakespeare canon is, therefore, still a vexed question. No approach to Shakespeare short of bardolatry . . . can escape the accumulated force of the arguments . . . that some parts of the doubtful plays can hardly be by Shakespeare's hand. Perhaps the most objective and plausible of the theses is that of Spedding and Hickson with regard to *Henry VIII*.
>
> (p. 8)

Assuming, perhaps, that his audience is well acquainted with the arguments of Spedding, Partridge does not discuss them. The only opponent of the Spedding theory whom he mentions is Alexander. He says Alexander "assumed" that "the metrical tests used by Spedding and Hickson are unreliable criteria of poetic style" and that "the results of the tests, upon which Fletcher's claims to part authorship are based, are insufficient evidence by themselves of his hand in *Henry VIII*" (p. 10). Partridge handles such objections with considerable ingenuity:

On the validity of the evidence of metrical tests *alone*, . . . Professor Alexander . . . has rightly pointed out the possibility of their fallaciousness. But in this he was anticipated by one of the contributors to the metrical apparatus, F. J. Furnivall, who said that 'Counting can never be a better judge than real criticism.' [Cf. note 17 above.] It is impossible to apply the tests to isolated individual lines, as Boyle would do. But the arguments of Spedding and Hickson are on broader and more tenable principles. I do not propose, however, to re-traverse the ground of the metrical evidence, because it seems to me that comparable results can be obtained by an entirely different method of scrutiny.

(pp. 11–12)

Partridge does not, then, re-traverse any of Spedding's or Hickson's "principles," nor does he discuss the verse-rhythms of the play, although he does make repeated references to the "objectivity" of Spedding and Hickson.[22]

The direct evidence from which Partridge's different method of scrutiny is constructed consists of a tabulation of *ye*'s, "expletive *do*'s," and so forth. His figures are reproduced in the table below. The parts of the play assigned to Fletcher are indicated by italic type; III.ii is divided at line 203; the left-hand column records instances of "the periphrastic auxiliary verb *do*, used as a mere expletive, in affirmative statements"; the right-hand column tabulates "notional verbs inflected in *-th*" (of which all four examples occur in stage directions):

	do	hath	has	doth	does	them	'em	ye	y'	-th
Prologue						1		2		
I.i	10	5	4		1	5	2	1		1
I.ii	3	3	1	1	1	5	2			2
I.iii			2				7			

[22] Partridge identifies the contribution by Hickson he has in mind as the letter of 24 August 1850 which we examined earlier, and many editorial references to the same letter down to the present day speak solemnly of its "independent" confirmation of Spedding's thesis. Perhaps the present writer is blinded by prejudice, but he fails to see why Hickson's collection of ditto-marks should have been allowed to pass as scholarly evidence for so many years.

	do	hath	has	doth	does	them	'em	ye	y'	-th
I.iv						1	12	4	4	
II.i	1		4		1		4	4		
II.ii		1	9		1	1	2	3		
II.iii	3	1			1				1	
II.iv	12	3	2		1	7				2
III.i	1		4				4	20		
III.ii.a	12	7	6	1	4	2	1			
III.ii.b	1	1	7		1	1	2	6		
IV.i			2			1	3	3	1	
IV.ii					1	2	3	5		1
V.i	5	3	1		2	4			1	
V.ii	1		2		1		6	12	1	
V.iii	1						13	7	2	
V.iv			3		1		1	6	1	
Epilogue							2			

Many of the *'em*'s and *ye*'s, of course, appear as the "redundant syllables" at the ends of feminine lines. Partridge's control texts appear to have been the *Shakespeare-Grammatik* of Franz and Fletcher's *Bonduca* (version unspecified), but he offers no complete set of figures on his ten forms for any play but *Henry VIII*. The inferences he would desire to draw from these statistics may be expressed as follows: since there are two *ye*'s in the Prologue, Fletcher wrote it; since there are seven *'em*'s in I.iii, Fletcher wrote it; and so forth. The slender essay designed to make inferences of this sort credible is remarkable both for what it includes and what it leaves out. It includes many observations on the language and style of seventeenth-century drama:

If language was, as T. S. Eliot says, 'at the tips of the senses,' logical development of ideas could not have been regarded as one of its highest functions. Verbal magic and power were fascinations not confined to Marlowe, and on the analytical side subtle distinctions of meaning were a by-product of both. Elizabethan English shows language in a highly fluid state. . . .

(p. 27)

Sometimes its generalizations are more precise:

Notional verbs with sibilant or affricative stem-finals continued, with the stricter grammarians like Jonson, to take the *-th* ending, though generally this phonetic habit was falling into disuse too.

(p. 19)

Occasionally it seeks to describe the actual language of the play:

[Shakespeare] tends to lose track of his relative clauses, especially in continuative function and in proximity to participial phrases, or adverbial clauses, of time. . . .

(pp. 29–30)

More significantly perhaps, the essay makes repeated references to critics who are said or implied to have agreed with Spedding or Hickson. Some of the critics Partridge cites—Farnham for example—may be said to have supported the Spedding position in much the same way that American college teachers may be said to have supported the use of the loyalty oaths they have sometimes been required to sign. Other of these critics—Emerson for example—are quoted in such a way as to obscure the fact that their views on the play have been quite irreconcilable with those of Spedding and Partridge.[23] Yet despite Partridge's skill in drawing just the testimony he wants from the witnesses he selects, his case for Fletcher, finally, is left curiously incomplete in one respect. He makes three references to *The Two Noble Kinsmen*:

The contention of the traditionalists that Shakespeare may have written the whole [of *Henry VIII* is strengthened by] . . . the absence of evidence (apart

---

[23] Partridge says he was struck, on re-reading the play, by "fairly sharp transitions from one grammatical idiom to another," one being "involved, though poetically pregnant" and the other "fluent and lucid in syntactical pattern" (p. 15); he then says "Emerson in *Representative Men* noted a cognate difference" between two styles in the play; he quotes from Emerson to support this point but suppresses the context in which Emerson spoke of "unmistakeable" evidence of Shakespeare in the play— "through all its length."

from the doubtful authority of his name on a title page) that Shakespeare was ever a collaborator with other dramatists.

(p. 9)

While Sykes produces from *The Two Noble Kinsmen* a convincing list of parallel phrases in Massinger's work to prove his partnership with Fletcher, Lit[t]ledale outdoes him with a much more imposing list from Shakespeare.

(p. 32)

The inclusion of *Henry VIII* in the folio by Heminge and Condell may have been based on real knowledge of how much Shakespeare did write, and the exclusion of *The Two Noble Kinsmen* on the fact that their colleague wrote little of it, if anything at all.

(p. 34)

Whatever opinion Partridge may hold, if any, about the authorship of *The Two Noble Kinsmen,* it is surely curious that he makes no further use than this of the Waterson-Cotes title-page, the *solitary* external link between Shakespeare and Fletcher and—would it be going too far to suppose?— the cornerstone over which the whole Spedding theory was built.

Perhaps Partridge wished to confine his argument to what was *directly* relevant to *Henry VIII*—like the "metrical evidence" of Samuel Hickson! One recent editorial champion of the Spedding metrical test and the Spedding division, the late John Munro (a one-time protégé of Furnivall), in his 1957 London Shakespeare, has outdone Partridge by offering a review of evidence on the authorship of *Henry VIII* that omits (along with much else) any mention of *The Two Noble Kinsmen* whatever. Some who have read and been affected by such discussions, however—good scholars for whom questions of authorship are often, understandably enough, of rather marginal interest—seem to have held less stringent views of what is relevant, and have, perhaps from laxity or perhaps because they have normally agile minds, been influenced by that title-page. A concrete instance of how this influence has expressed itself in recent years may be seen in the following typical example. Here is an excerpt from the *Shakespeare Quarterly* review by T. M. Parrott of Peter Alexander's *Shakespeare Primer* (1951):

Alexander makes . . . positive statements on matters which are still controversial. . . . He makes Shakespeare the sole author of *Henry VIII*. . . . This has been a favorite thesis of his since . . . 1931. . . . He lays great stress on Cranmer's closing speech, "a prophetic vision of England's greatness," as expressing "what Shakespeare felt to be the truth." He neglects to add that the speech closes with a fulsome flattery of James I [as one] . . . who would give future generations cause to bless heaven for him. The very next generation of Englishmen, however, saw civil war, the fall of the monarchy, and the death on the scaffold of the son of James. If it was Shakespeare who prophesied here, he was singularly ill-inspired; a Shakespeare lover would be happier in ascribing the whole speech to the courtly playwright, John Fletcher. The repeated assertions of Alexander . . . do not seem to have carried much weight with modern scholars; Kittredge, for example, as late as 1936 states flatly that Shakespeare's share in the play is limited to a few scenes. . . . Mention might also be made here of Partridge's recent *Problem of Henry VIII.* In view of the fact, ignored by Alexander, that the names of Shakespeare and Fletcher appear as joint-authors on the title-page of the *Two Noble Kinsmen,* 1634, it would seem that the whole question of their collaboration calls for further investigation. Certainly [!] a Primer should not contain one scholar's positive assertion as to the play's authorship.

The review recalls some of the complexities of determining "relevance." Perhaps Alexander should have mentioned the Spedding theory in his *Primer,* and perhaps he should have said that Cranmer's speech closes with "fulsome flattery" of James; but perhaps his fully recorded and documented views on *Henry VIII* leave him blameless on this score, somewhat as Shakespeare must be considered blameless with respect to Charles's blood even without our having to impute ill inspiration to poor Fletcher. It is true that "the whole question of . . . collaboration calls for further investigation," and it is good to have a generally well-informed Shakespearean like Parrott grant some puzzlement on the subject, although it is possible he is mistaken about the sources of most of the confusion, just as one hopes his reference to Kittredge is based on a misconception.[24]

It is also true, however, that Alexander has almost totally avoided reference to *The Two Noble Kinsmen* throughout his career, and so—by a fairly remarkable coincidence—have Craig, Knight, Sisson, and most of the other defenders of *Henry VIII.* In many respects it seems unfortunate that Alexander, when he traced the origins of Spedding's theory, pursued Spedding's inspiration back only to Malone, Roderick, and Theobald, and for the most part ignored the equally important line going back through Hickson to Spalding and beyond. Considering the accumulation of misleading and false assumptions he had to overcome, however (to say nothing of the burdensome obligation in 1931 of speaking with some politeness about the arguments of a Spedding and a Furnivall), it is hardly surprising that he should

---

[24] Kittredge, indorsing the Spedding division, stated that it is "certain" that "the greater part" of *Henry VIII* is "not Shakespeare's," and he neither referred nor alluded to any dissenting view. Parrott assumes that Kittredge had become familiar with and rejected Alexander's challenge. It is also possible that Kittredge's introductory comment to one play among the thirty-eight in his 1936 edition was written before he encountered the Alexander essay. The alternative assumption of Parrott's does less credit to Kittredge.

choose to avoid the added complications of *The Two Noble Kinsmen* or that he should place a good deal of stress upon the authority of the Folio.

Reliance on the authority of the Folio has been described as a reliance on "faith." Perhaps the insult is better deserved by those disintegrators whose techniques of counting *'em*'s and "redundant syllables"—along with their hazel-rod methods of "higher criticism"—tell them what is and what is not authentic in the Folio. The authority of the Folio is quite consistent with evidence and coherent thinking; unlike the 1647 Folio published by Moseley—or for that matter the Waterson-Cotes Quarto of 1634—the authority of the Shakespeare Folio is not based merely on a title-page; it is supported by everything we know of the intelligent interest of Heminge and Condell and the origins of that interest in a long and intimate friendship with Shakespeare.

The most seriously disturbing problem of Shakespearean attribution—if one allows oneself to be disturbed by such problems—remains *The Two Noble Kinsmen*. Many scholars still appear to believe that the inevitable concomitants of admitting Shakespearean responsibility for *The Two Noble Kinsmen* are to undercut the authority of Heminge and Condell and to open the door to arguments for divided authorship in *Henry VIII*. It takes very little effort to see how this belief has come about, but it may be worth considering whether it does not in fact defeat the very purposes that have caused it to be held (since it hardly protects Heminge and Condell's reputation to assume they "knew" *The Two Noble Kinsmen* was not by Shakespeare), and whether it is not itself predicated on further assumptions about *The Two Noble Kinsmen*—such as the metrical proofs of divided authorship— which derive most of their strength from the circumstance that scarcely anyone has looked into them.

What is notable about the positions taken in modern criticism of *The Two Noble Kinsmen* (in the essays cited in Chapter I) is that they represent the converse of the majority position on *Henry VIII*. The better critics such as Spencer and Muir have usually either ignored *Henry VIII* or (with little or no discussion of the grounds for their views) have cited it as a known example of collaboration in order to strengthen their cases for Shakespeare's participation in *The Two Noble Kinsmen*. Muir is among the most recent to capitalize on *Henry VIII* for this purpose, although—evidently in deference to changing opinion—he has been notably more diffident than his predecessors in doing so. Muir's essay is traditional in another respect, however; it shows traces of the usual rage many advocates for Shakespeare's hand in *The Two Noble Kinsmen* have come to feel after they have become moderately familiar with the play and with parts of its bizarre critical fortunes. Even more impassioned was the study that preceded Muir's—the essay by Marco Mincoff published in 1952. Mincoff's introductory paragraphs made much of the "overwhelming coincidence" of collaboration between Shakespeare and Fletcher on three plays (the third of course being *Cardenio*), and the accurately phrased notice given to this essay by Harold Jenkins in the 1954 *Shakespeare Survey* may suggest how the better discussions of the "Shakespearean part" of *The Two Noble Kinsmen* have sometimes produced results which must disturb those who have found the arguments for single authorship in *Henry VIII* attractive:

At the . . . end of Shakespeare's career the case for his collaboration with Fletcher is strengthened by M. Mincoff's powerful argument for his part-authorship of *The Two Noble Kinsmen*.

(p. 140)

In a more recent essay defending the Spedding division of *Henry VIII*, Mincoff has stressed the same point about the "Fletcher scenes" that we saw him make earlier with respect to *The Two Noble Kinsmen*, namely that Fletcher's style is so "considerably modified" in his parts of *both* plays that, "even if the name of Shakespeare was not so closely and definitely connected with them already, one might almost deduce his [Shakespeare's] presence from his effect on his partner alone"! [25] Mincoff is not the only critic to have made this thought-provoking observation, but perhaps more than enough has already been said about the surfaces of critical opinion. The remainder of this chapter will deal with several of the connections between the problem of authorship and the critical fate of the play, then with the design of the play itself and with interrelations between the "two parts" which most critics of the Spedding camp seem to have overlooked.

The Effects of the Problem of Authorship

There is an obvious although rather peculiar relation between the problem of authorship and critical response to the play itself. Perhaps the word "relation" should read "obstruction." The assumption of dual authorship, according to one critic writing in 1948, "underlies the dearth of critical comment on the play itself; it is assumed to be of interest only in that it was a collaboration of such a kind that no unity of conception and design ought to be expected of it." [26] The assertion of neglect is all too easily verifiable;

[25] Mincoff, *"Henry VIII and Fletcher," SQ*, XII (1961), 239, 244.
[26] Frank Kermode, *"What Is Shakespeare's Henry VIII About?"*, *Durham Univ. Jour.*, New Ser., IX (1948), 48. Reprinted in E. M. Waith, ed. *Shakespeare: The Histories* (1965).

the play is omitted from many comprehensive studies of Shakespeare that might reasonably be expected to consider it.[27] Possibly the neglect ought to seem more surprising than it does; certainly it can bring to mind embarrassing questions about the courage and independence of critics.

The direct connection between the Spedding theory and later attacks on the design of the play is best seen by going back to one part of that theory barely touched on earlier—the speculations about what kind of a play Shakspere might have written. Since, according to Spedding, in the extant play the King is "crowned with all felicity," the conclusion shows that "passion has its way"—a conclusion "in which we can have no interest." Analysis of the play, moreover, showed that V.i and an (unspecified) part of V.ii "seemed . . . strangely out of place":

Though full of life and vigour, and . . . not unworthy of Shakspere, [they] are utterly irrelevant to the business of the play; for what have we to do with the quarrel between Gardiner and Cranmer? Nothing in the play is explained by it, nothing depends upon it.

(It also appears that there are only sixty-eight "redundant syllables" in the 176 lines of V.i.) The words "strangely out of place" created the necessary puzzle, and Spedding proceeded to explain. Shakespeare must have written three acts of a play when some emergency arose for which the actors needed a complete manuscript in a hurry (Spedding suggested the occasion would have been the festivities that followed the wedding of Princess Elizabeth in February 1613); Shakespeare "thought that his half-finished work might help" his fellows, and he gave it to them "to make what they could of it." And although "it was not unusual in those days, when a play was wanted in a hurry, to set two or three or even four hands at work upon it," the company ended by putting the incomplete manuscript

into the hands of Fletcher . . . who finding the original design . . . utterly beyond his capacity, expanded the three acts into five, by interspersing scenes of show and magnificence; . . . [he] dropped all allusion to the great ecclesiastical revolution, which he could not manage and for which he had no materials supplied him. . . .

The irrelevant Shakespearean material in Act V, then, had originally been intended to serve as a prelude to "the establishment of Cranmer in the seat

[27] E.g. Tillyard's and Traversi's books on the late plays, Tillyard's and L. B. Campbell's books on the histories, Clemen's and Stauffer's books on Shakespeare's imagery, and so forth. Both Miss Campbell and Tillyard acknowledge that their omission was due to the problem of authorship. (It must be added that Tillyard has since, after coming to accept Shakespeare as sole author, written an interesting note on the play, *Critical Quarterly*, III [1961], 22–27.)

of highest ecclesiastical authority," after which would inevitably follow a dramatization of the great "revolution" which Fletcher was unequipped to handle. Such a scheme would even have allowed Shakespeare to make dramatic use of "such reason and religion as there were in Henry's scruples."

One is almost bound to admire so ambitious an effort to produce a coherent theory, and to regret that so few of Spedding's latter-day admirers have felt an equal obligation. The details are as masterfully worked out as in the theory offered by Swinburne in his mock "Report" on the "Newest Shakespeare Society," according to which the Nurse in *Romeo and Juliet* represented the widow of Sir Thomas More, and Romeo and Paris at Juliet's tomb stood for Burghley and Essex contending before the tomb of "their common mistress" Elizabeth—

who towards the close of her reign may fitly have been regarded as one already buried with her fathers, though yet living in a state of suspended animation under the influence of a deadly narcotic potion administered by the friends of Romeo—by the partisans, that is, of the Cecilian policy. The Nurse was not less evidently designed to represent the Established Church. Allusions to the marriage of the clergy are profusely scattered through her speeches. . . .[28]

Spedding, however, carried conviction, and it was evidently not only his invention of the numbers game, but the genuine skill with which he removed from Shakespeare the suspicion of having indorsed an unfashionable view of history, which prevented many learned readers from noting anything in the play that might upset the theory. After the gyroscope that Spedding designed had been set spinning by the New Shakspere Society, however, the well-cluttered mind of the disintegrator forgot most of the more complicated supporting arguments in the essay, retaining only the essential points of a hastily-written, ill-constructed play.

The editors of the Yale text of 1925 were able to report, from their own study of *Henry VIII,* that "the drama is not a drama at all," but rather a "series of almost unrelated scenes" without any sort of coherence; that "the characters neither develop, nor are they consistent"; and so forth. This failure they sought to account for as follows:

The play apparently was thrown together hurriedly, without much planning, to meet some emergency. . . . The emergency may . . . have been purely theatrical: that the manager was disappointed in a play for which he had contracted, or that the play he had intended to produce was unavailable for one of a hundred reasons, and a new play had to be substituted.

(pp. 151–152)

[28] Swinburne, *A Study of Shakespeare* (1880), pp. 312–313.

The "manager" who might dictate to Shakespeare is not identified, and one wonders whether the editors (John Berdan and Tucker Brooke) had in mind his intimate friends Burbadge, Heminge, Condell, or some other of his fellow-sharers. Wasting no time on such conjecture, however, they pressed their charge of slipshod construction by asserting that "the authors" must have "read their Holinshed rapidly" because (for example) they "put the coronation banquet in Whitehall" whereas in Holinshed "the banquet . . . is plainly stated to have been held in Westminster Hall"; feeling that "the authors . . . must be held responsible" for such "obvious errors," the Yale editors devoted most of their commentary to disparaging the play in like fashion. Perhaps in 1925 it seemed there was little else to do. Once the division of the play had been established, verified with metrical evidence both scientific and comprehensive (it covered every line in the text), and defended with both aesthetic and historical argument by expert authority, it became clear that the work of discovering truth had largely been done and that all one could hope to add to the great agglutinative Body of Knowledge would be a few humble bits of further confirmation—even if it involved the unpleasant pedagogical duty of spanking the authors for failing to master their history lessons.

One final example of hostile criticism, more recent, ought to be cited. The author of an academic study of Fletcher, avoiding any excursion into the problem of authorship except for a brief acknowledgment that he accepts the Spedding division on Kittredge's authority, summarizes the most common charge against the structure of the play:

> Among Shakespeare's history plays *Henry VIII* is conspicuous for its disunity. As the crowd of notable historical personages parades before us, our attention is drawn first to Buckingham, then to Queen Katherine and Wolsey, and finally to Cranmer. No theme unites their successive stories except that most general of tragic themes: how are the mighty fallen! And even this unifying principle does not apply to Cranmer, who narrowly escapes the dismal fate of the other three and ends the play with the triumphant prophecy of the Elizabethan glories to come.[29]

Although an objection of this sort is not unusual, its particular expression in this case is instructive. The critic formulates a "unifying principle"—the process is neither simple nor passive—and then goes on to damn the play for failing to live up to it.

"Opinion, however, seems at last to be changing," as more than one reviewer of the Foakes edition has remarked about the authorship question.

[29] Eugene M. Waith, *The Pattern of Tragicomedy in Beaumont and Fletcher* (1952), p. 119.

Insofar as one may speak intelligibly of "general" opinion, the change in attitudes toward the play evidently began about the time of the Alexander essay. Much of that essay, to be sure, had nothing directly to do with the character of the play. The sections that traced the provenance of the Spedding theory, for example, would hardly seem to be related to questions of dramatic structure. Alexander suggested that when J. M. Robertson found 2% feminine endings in one scene of *The Comedy of Errors* and 24% in the next and then proceeded to line up further distinctions to verify the authorship assignments for which these statistics were claimed as presumptive evidence, he was doing nothing more outrageous than Spedding had done; but this point, too, obviously had no literary bearing on *Henry VIII*. A context is that which surrounds, and these more or less peripheral arguments created for many readers a new context within which the play itself might be considered. A further argument, although still addressed to the question of authorship, did make a simple, clear, and important point about the dramatic design. Spedding had found it "inconceivable that a judgment like [Shakespeare's] . . . could have been content with a conclusion so little in harmony with the prevailing spirit and purpose of the piece"; but in two passages that Spedding gave without hesitation to Shakespeare, Alexander pointed out, the birth of Elizabeth and the benedictory tone at the end of the play had been carefully prepared for. As early as II.iii.75 the Lord Chamberlain says of Anne:

> I have perus'd her well;
> Beauty and honour in her are so mingled
> That they have caught the king: and who knows yet
> But from this lady may proceed a gem
> To lighten all this isle.

And at III.ii.49 Suffolk says of Anne:

> She is a gallant creature, and complete
> In mind and feature. I persuade me, from her
> Will fall some blessing to this land, which shall
> In it be memoriz'd.

These and other examples were cited by Alexander to confute Spedding's assertion of divided minds on subject matter. Probably some of Alexander's readers had not considered these lines carefully before he drew attention to them. But of course it might not matter even if they had: for if a reader, brought up to believe in a division of authorship, wished to accommodate these dramatic anticipations into his own privately revised, perhaps never fully articulated, version of that theory, it might have been possible for him to do so. Once a theory is widely held it can be rationalized almost indefinitely.

Consider the subtler example of an older reader of the play who did *not* know that Spedding had described Buckingham's language in I.i as "impetuous and fiery" and his language in II.i as "languid." Spedding had insisted that "the difference was too great to be accounted for by the mere change of situation, without supposing also a change of writers." A reader, knowing only of the division, would not need Spedding to guide him, for the division would have alerted him to seek out differences, and of course they are there. Buckingham speaks thus of Wolsey in the former scene:

> This butcher's cur is venom-mouth'd, and I
> Have not the power to muzzle him, therefore best
> Not wake him in his slumber. A beggar's book
> Outworths a noble's blood.
>
> (I.i.120–123)

But after he comes from his arraignment in the later scene, his words fall into the famous "pronominal rhythms" (as Wilson Knight calls them):

> All good people,
> You that thus far have come to pity me,
> Hear what I say, and then go home and lose me.
> I have this day receiv'd a traitor's judgment,
> And by that name must die. . . .
>
> (II.i.55–59)

Having seen the large differences, and looking perhaps for a convenient means of articulating it to himself, the reader might well take the line of least resistance and use the ready-made labels "Shakespeare" and "Fletcher" —around which he would then continue to polarize his responses. The play was evidently not attentively read, for (to continue with the same example, one of many suggested by Knight) it was much earlier, in the opening scene itself, that Buckingham's voice—the instant after Brandon ordered his arrest—lost all of its "impetuous and fiery" qualities and fell suddenly into the rhythm and tone of a man who (like Wolsey and Katherine later) was bitterly sensible of having been betrayed:

> Loe you, my lord,
> The net has fall'n upon me; I shall perish . . .
>
> It will help me nothing
> To plead mine innocence, for that dye is on me
> Which makes my whit'st part black. The will of heav'n
> Be done in this and all things . . .
>
> (I.i.202–203, 207–210)

Presumably the given source-material would prompt Shakespeare to explore specifically Christian attitudes in the play, and the frequent tricks of rhythm that accompany devotional speech and common Christian set-phrases (*God's peace be with him, God forgive me,* and so forth) must have caught his ear; they crop up in every scene in which, given the character and situation, they might be dramatically relevant; they are strongest in the great final speech of Buckingham and in parts of Wolsey's final scene, and in both instances they are often derived (as Richmond Noble has shown) from scriptural literature. Wolsey's "Vain pomp and glory of this world, I hate ye," for example, is taken over from the baptismal service—appropriately, for it leads directly to the line "I feel my heart new open'd." And his closing speeches in the later parts of III.ii are of course shot through with the phrasing of sermons: "Mark but my fall . . . ," "cherish those hearts that hate thee . . . ," "then, if thou fall'st, O Cromwell,/ Thou fall'st a blessed martyr." Buckingham's didacticism is rather different, although a few fragmentary phrases cannot suggest the actual inflections of a dramatic voice. The longer speeches of Buckingham, Wolsey, and Katherine probably furnished models for some of the declamations in later plays by Fletcher, but the most common application of the phrase "Fletcherian style" to these speeches, when it is supposed to suggest what they have in common with those in Fletcher's plays, evidently means little more than this: a style of dramatic speech in which someone laments something in lines that often run into falling rhythms and sometimes end in a pronoun. That is not a very good definition of anyone's style. Whenever the phrase has been made to apply more generally to *all* of the parts assigned to Fletcher, it has meant something else: dramatic verse showing a preponderance of feminine endings *per se*. The latter application naturally fits every scene Spedding assigned to Fletcher—how could it fail?—but it is perhaps as thin a definition of style as the human mind can construct. There are many passages in those scenes for which even the term "falling rhythm" is quite inappropriate and which are so distinctly unlike anything ever attempted by Fletcher that their long ascription to him is downright astonishing; Emerson once singled out the breathless account of the coronation by the Third Gentleman at IV.i.62 as an example of verse-structure and movement so Shakespearean as to be "like [an] autograph":

> The rich stream
> Of lords and ladies, having brought the queen
> To a prepar'd place in the choir, fell off
> A distance from her; while her grace sat down
> To rest a while, some half an hour or so,

In a rich chair of state, opposing freely
The beauty of her person to the people.
Believe me sir, she is the goodliest woman
That ever lay by man: which when the people
Had the full view of, such a noise arose
As the shrouds make at sea in a stiff tempest,
As loud, and to as many tunes. Hats, cloaks
(Doublets, I think) flew up, and had their faces
Been loose, this day they had been lost. Such joy
I never saw before. Great-bellied women,
That had not half a week to go, like rams
In the old time of war, would shake the press
And make 'em reel before 'em. No man living
Could say 'This is my wife' there, all were woven
So strangely in one piece.

The passage is interesting for much more than its versification, of course, and we shall later return to it.

The most satisfying defenses of the authenticity of the play have been based principally on evidence of its dramatic integrity and the Shakespearean character of its design. The defenders have naturally had to meet objections that were not knowingly based on the assumption of dual authorship; and some of these objections might indeed have arisen even without the authorship controversy. Evidently the history play has always been subject to a certain doubleness of judgment, and *Henry VIII* has suffered unusually in this respect. If a critic were confident that he possessed a firm objective grasp of the truth of history, it would not be surprising if he made that truth a standard by which a dramatization of historical events might be judged; if the critic disregarded the circumstance that his historical King Henry would be almost as much a verbal re-creation as the dramatic King Henry, his grasp of truth would be that much firmer; negative capability would stand little chance against positive thinking. A characteristic set of cliché judgments on the historical Henry VIII some years ago would have been that he was a weakling under Wolsey, a tyrant toward Katherine, a debauchee with respect to Anne Bullen, and in sum a capricious bully whose main redemption lay in the mysterious historical force by which he was destined to release England from papal servitude and establish her national identity; as the comments of Hazlitt, Ulrici, and Spedding should suggest, the play was sometimes condemned for failing to make such judgments, and when at other times such judgments were read into it—silently imported without explicit reference to history—it was often condemned for failing to make them emphatic enough. It followed that *Henry VIII* showed poor character-development. Similarly, the lines in the Prologue telling the audience they will see "mightiness" come to meet "misery" have been read as if they were a literal summary of the principal action of the play—as if, for example, the play were mainly about Wolsey or Katherine—and they have accordingly been cited to document a bill of complaints against the workmanship—including, for example, the charge that Act V is irrelevant to the main action. The reply to such attacks coincides with the defense of Shakespeare's authorship.

The Design of the Play

The play is often described as if it were a dramatic *Monk's Tale* in which "our attention is drawn first to Buckingham, then to Queen Katherine and Wolsey" (Waith); but in actual fact the King is the central figure. It is true that the dramatic King Henry undergoes no such spectacular change as the dramatic Cardinal. The plot takes us from the time that the King is overshadowed by Wolsey to a time in which he has become master in his own land and Cranmer has become his faithful instrument; the separation from Katherine and the marriage with Anne move almost in parallel with the Wolsey-to-Cranmer line of development. As the discussion that follows seeks to show, the play is as political in its concerns as any of Shakespeare's English histories, and the importance of each major character depends—as usual in the histories—on the relation between that character and the King.

The King in Act I is a monarch whose reign is marked both by the opulence of his court and the dissatisfaction of his subjects. The opening dialogues describe the state visit to France whose hoped-for outcome had been enduring peace and a prosperous England. Norfolk had been present at the Field of the Cloth of Gold, and he describes to Buckingham the almost too splendid pageantry that had been contrived as entertainment:

> you lost
> The view of earthly glory: men might say
> Till this time pomp was single, but now married
> To one above itself. Each following day
> Became the next day's master, till the last
> Made former wonders, its. To-day the French,
> All clinquant all in gold, like heathen gods
> Shone down the English; and to-morrow they
> Made Britain India: every man that stood
> Show'd like a mine.
>
> (I.i.13–22)

Buckingham asks who it was who "set the body and the limbs/ Of this great sport together," and when he learns that Wolsey had arranged it all, the "earthly glory" suddenly seems to him nothing but "fierce vanities" and he is astonished that Wolsey, "such a keech" (lump of congealed fat), "can with his very bulk/ Take up the rays o'th'beneficial sun,/ And keep it from the earth." Norfolk agrees that Wolsey is an upstart, "not propp'd by ancestry," who has arrogantly pushed himself into a "place next to the king." Since Wolsey was responsible for burdening the nobility with the extravagance of the French meeting, he is to blame for many of them having

> so sicken'd their estates that never
> They shall abound as formerly
>
> (I.i.82–83)

and for others having sold their lands, "broke their backs with laying manors on 'em," and beggared their children.

Wolsey is first portrayed, then, as a solemn lord of misrule, fat on the body politic, an uncomic Falstaff come to power. His taste for opulence is later to be given as much a personal as a political emphasis—as in I.iv, where he plays the generous host and entertainer—but our first view of him stresses his relation to the land, his bulky interposition between sun and earth or King and people. The alliance he has arranged with the "heathen" French ("their clothes are after such a pagan cut," the Lord Chamberlain is to comment in I.iii) is a particular sore point with the nobility; the conference in the vale of Andren had been nothing but waste and "vanity," since the French are not going to keep faith; even before the meetings had been concluded, there had been a great storm which those assembled had taken as "a general prophecy":

> this tempest
> Dashing the garment of this peace, aboded
> The sudden breach on't.
>
> (I.i.92–94)

And much of the following scene develops Wolsey's effect on the social fabric at home, dramatized in the taxation issue:

> upon these taxations,
> The clothiers all not able to maintain
> The many to them longing, have put off
> The spinsters, carders, fullers, weavers, who
> Unfit for other life, compell'd by hunger
> And lack of other means, in desperate manner
> Daring th'event to th'teeth, are all in uproar . . .
>
> (I.ii.30–36)

The desperation of the nobility is matched by the suffering of the lesser classes, and the blame is again placed on Wolsey. The conflicts have been clearly embodied for the audience in a series of striking theatrical climaxes: Wolsey's strange procession across the stage (directed at I.i.114), highlighting the clash between Wolsey and Buckingham around which most of the dialogue in the first scene is built; the destruction of Buckingham with his arrest near the end of the scene, confirming the view of the nobles that Wolsey is at the highest point of his power; and the confrontation in the next scene between Wolsey and Katherine—his proud arrogance opposed to her proud righteousness—with the King as yet a mere arbiter, not deeply interested in the taxation issue, not yet deeply involved in his responsibilities.

Wolsey's role is too wide in its range of implications to be defined wholly by its political aspect. Abergavenny tells us that the Cardinal's pride is from hell, or,

> If not from hell the devil is a niggard,
> Or has given all before, and he begins
> A new hell in himself.

(I.i.70–72)

Abergavenny and his friends see Wolsey as a satanic torturer; their language draws explicitly from the conception of England as Jerusalem that pervades every scene of this play, it looks forward to Wolsey's own later comparisons of himself to Lucifer in III.ii, and the last phrase in the passage cited hints at the pathos in Wolsey's personal drama which is to become apparent even before Wolsey expresses it directly in his final soliloquy or his address to Cromwell.

Our first encounter with the King and our first direct experience of his relation to Wolsey come in the second scene. If the opening scene had not sufficed to warn critics that "Shakespeare's original intention" had been to dramatize Wolsey's decline rapidly,[30] this scene should have done so. The King makes his appearance "leaning on the Cardinal's shoulder" and thanking him for apprehending Buckingham's treason, but at once Norfolk and Katherine mount their attack on Wolsey's commissions and the King challenges Wolsey to defend himself; in the Cardinal's slow reply we hear the accomplished confidence of a still powerful old man, his injured voice

---

[30] Miss Nicolson, conjecturally reconstructing the play Shakespeare "never finished" (cf. n. 1 above), supposed that the *rise* of Wolsey would have accompanied the fall of Katherine and that Wolsey would have been overthrown "in the last part" of the play. Of the extant conclusion many post-Spedding critics felt that (as Dowden put it in the Renaissance Shakespeare) "the fifth act, for one who has been deeply interested in the story of the Cardinal, is an artistic impertinence."

starched with dignity and rising (at "we") to a deliberate regality never assumed by the King, and never again to be attempted by Wolsey himself:

> if I am
> Traduc'd by ignorant tongues, which neither know
> My faculties nor person, yet will be
> The chronicles of my doing, let me say
> 'Tis but the fate of place, and the rough brake
> That virtue must go through: we must not stint
> Our necessary actions in the fear
> To cope malicious censurers . . .
>   If we shall stand still,
> In fear our motion will be mock'd or carp'd at,
> We should take root here, where we sit;
> Or sit state-statues only.
>
> (I.ii.71–78, 85–88)

It is not so much the King's revocation of Wolsey's tax as it is the curtly instructive tone of his response that suggests his dependence upon the Cardinal has been exaggerated by commentators:

> Things done well
> And with a care exempt themselves from fear;
> Things done without example, in their issue
> Are to be fear'd. Have you a precedent
> Of this commission? I believe, not any.
>
> (I.ii.88–92)

A moment later the King is speaking to Katherine:

> The gentleman is learn'd, and a most rare speaker,
> To nature none more bound; his training such
> That he may furnish and instruct great teachers,
> And never seek for aid out of himself. . . .
>   This man so complete,
> Who was enroll'd 'mongst wonders (and when we,
> Almost with ravish'd list'ning, could not find
> His hour of speech a minute) he, my lady,
> Hath into monstrous habits put the graces
> That once were his, and is become as black
> As if besmear'd in hell. . . .
>
> (I.ii.111–114, 118–124)

These lines follow Katherine's "I am sorry that the Duke of Buckingham/ Is run in your displeasure," and of course they sum up the King's attitudes toward Buckingham. But Katherine's two lines would not blot out most of the action and dialogue which precede them, and the audience, which at this point knows more than the King, would probably note the ironic appropriateness of the speech to the relationship between the King and Wolsey. The opening lines of the scene had already made clear that Buckingham's condemnation was a foregone conclusion, and the whole focus of the scene—even, indeed especially, during the interrogation of Buckingham's Surveyor—is on the King himself. As one critic has pointed out, "the pretended threat both to his own life and to the Tudor succession is what brings him into the arena to deal with his own affairs."[31] The question of Buckingham's innocence or guilt is, in the eyes not of the King but of the audience, left ambiguous—a point which sometimes troubled critics preoccupied with "character":

Buckingham . . . is a contradiction. . . . Was he innocent or guilty? It cannot be told from anything in the drama, yet this must be the central point of his character. There is left only the uncertain inference that Wolsey bribed his servants to commit perjury.[32]

There is left *also* the "uncertain inference" that Buckingham might seize the throne "if the king/ Should without issue die" (lines 133–134), and the "contradiction" is dramatically useful: Buckingham is made to appear sufficiently the innocent victim for Wolsey to appear his cruel tormentor, while he is made to appear sufficiently guilty to keep the audience from blaming the King, or even from regarding him simply as Wolsey's dupe. The actual trial of Buckingham is reduced to a mere offstage report by the walking Gentlemen in II.i, and even in his moving speech of farewell Buckingham himself (at II.i.88–94) is made to identify the health of the land with the success of the King. The action of the play shows us a King who reigns becoming a King who rules, and the principal episodes are made to serve this development.

The portraits of Wolsey and Katherine which have so dominated the imagination of most commentators are brought into surprisingly close association throughout the play. Both Katherine and Wolsey are older than the King, and before Act II is concluded the fortunes of each have become associated with the past. Since responsibility for bringing about the divorce is at first attached almost entirely to Wolsey, and since his later opposition to the divorce is one of the principal causes of his downfall, he and Kath-

[31] Muriel St. Clare Byrne, "A Stratford Production: *Henry VIII*," *Shakespeare Survey 3* (1950), p. 123. A "descriptive analysis" of Tyrone Guthrie's 1949 production, this essay also constitutes one of the finest interpretive commentaries on the text yet to appear.

[32] Denton J. Snider, *The Shakespearian Drama: The Histories* (1889), p. 488.

erine become instruments, so to speak, of each other's destruction. And it is during Katherine's final scene that (by still another of Shakespeare's many drastic and purposeful rearrangements of historical chronology and event) our last view of Wolsey—Griffith's report in IV.ii—associates his end with Katherine's. The Cardinal and Queen whom Henry inherited are undoubtedly larger and more complex figures than their later counterparts Cranmer and Anne; this is due in part to the broadening of the social vision in the later acts—after the conflicts in which Wolsey and Katherine have played leading parts are resolved and both the new Queen and Archbishop are described and seen against the celebrating crowds of the coronation and christening scenes. Acts II and III dramatize the separation from Wolsey and the divorce from Katherine, and they create a new image of the King.

The divorce from Katherine, first rumored at II.i.147, is all but settled by the end of Act II, and it is in connection with the divorce that the question of "conscience" is first raised. (Parenthetically, the word itself is used much more frequently in this than in any other of Shakespeare's plays—although its significance is hardly a function of its mere statistical frequency.) The reasons for the divorce are not at first made clear. At one point the dialogue makes explicit what may already have been a suspicion in the minds of the audience since the King met Anne at Wolsey's banquet:

> *Chamberlain.* It seems the marriage with his brother's wife
>   Has crept too near his conscience.
> *Suffolk.*   No, his conscience
>   Has crept too near another lady.
>
> (II.ii.16–18)

But throughout this scene (as in the one preceding) the major share of credit for the divorce is emphatically assigned to Wolsey:

> He dives into the king's soul, and there scatters
> Dangers, doubts, wringing of the conscience,
> Fears and despairs, and all these for his marriage. . . .
>
> (II.ii.26–28)

And the sharp contrasts drawn between Henry and Wolsey in the speeches of Norfolk and the Lord Chamberlain (for example, "Heaven will one day open/ The king's eyes . . .") are calculated to make Henry appear simply naive when, shortly later, he welcomes Wolsey as "the quiet of my wounded conscience" (II.ii.74). This last point is mentioned because it is reportedly still common for directors and actors (following the lead of older editors) to treat Henry's closing words to Wolsey about Katherine—

> But conscience, conscience;
> O 'tis a tender place, and I must leave her.   *Exeunt.*

—as if they must be spoken with some sort of lusty hypocritical leer.[33] The scene as a whole implies that Henry speaks them earnestly, and the transition to the next scene again implies that Henry's failing is a lack of self-knowledge, that he may be guilty of dull-wittedness but not of conscious malice:

> O my lord,
> Would it not grieve an able man to leave
> So sweet a bedfellow? But conscience, conscience;
> O 'tis a tender place, and I must leave her.   *Exeunt.*
> *Scene III—Enter* Anne Bullen *and an* Old Lady.
> *Anne.* Not for that neither; here's the pang that pinches:
> His highness having liv'd so long with her, and she
> So good a lady . . .

Whether or not Henry throws away his last line as he and Wolsey go off, the first phrase which Anne speaks is probably to be understood by the audience—if it is to be understood at all!—as a comment on Henry's "But conscience, conscience . . ." The moral issue of the divorce from Katherine, so rapidly developed in the first three scenes of Act II, remains ambiguous throughout these scenes while the other characters speculate on the King's motives and reasons; it is resolved in an unexpected way during the fourth scene, after Katherine's appearance at the trial in Black-Friars.

The trial is ostensibly the trial of Katherine. Yet the dialogues in the preceding scenes have fully apprised the audience of Katherine's fate (even to the accurate prediction, at II.ii.34–36, of her final attitude toward the King), and the outcome of the trial with respect to Katherine is no longer in itself a live dramatic issue. Near the beginning of the trial, moreover, Katherine addresses herself directly to the King rather than to the court ("Sir, I desire you do me right and justice . . ."), and from the outset of the scene it is upon the trial of Henry, not of Katherine, that the attention of the audience is mainly focussed. Each time Katherine and Wolsey contradict each other (II.iv.73 ff.) they raise questions which the audience must look to the King to answer. After Katherine delivers her final challenge to Wolsey and departs, Henry's warm praise of her (lines 131–141) establishes him in the sympathy of the audience. Then follows his great "conscience" speech, the turning-point of the action and (incidentally) the longest speech in the play.

[33] Cf. Roy Walker, "Theatre Royal," *Twentieth Century*, CLIII (1953), 465.

Henry begins by clearing Wolsey of any responsibility for the divorce (lines 153–165). Since the "inducement" of a "scruple" about his marriage with Arthur's widow had been attributed by others to Wolsey in the earlier scenes, this exoneration of Wolsey comes as a dramatic surprise. The consequence of Henry's taking responsibility, ironically, is to reinforce the effect of Katherine's attacks on Wolsey by diminishing his power in our eyes; we are being prepared to see Wolsey's role reduced to that of the mere ineffectual servant he is to play in III.i. And by removing the blame from Wolsey, Henry's introductory lines also reduce us to a state of ignorance about the causes of the divorce itself, and therefore (unless we hasten to fetch our explanation from the irrelevant historical sources adduced by Victorian editors) they prepare us to absorb the explanation which Henry himself proceeds to supply.

The dramatic importance of Henry's explanation is heavily underscored by the first two lines:

> I will be bold with time and your attention:
> Then mark th'inducement: thus it came; give heed to't:
> My conscience first receiv'd a tenderness,
> Scruple and prick, on certain speeches utter'd
> By th'Bishop of Bayonne, then French ambassador,
> Who had been hither sent on the debating
> A marriage 'twixt the Duke of Orleans and
> Our daughter Mary: i'th' progress of this business,
> Ere a determinate resolution, he
> (I mean the Bishop) did require a respite,
> Wherein he might the king his lord advertise
> Whether our daughter were legitimate
> Respecting this our marriage with the dowager,
> Sometimes our brother's wife.
>
> (II.iv.166–179)

As a piece of necessary exposition on the origin of the King's "prick" of "conscience," this passage may be merely the Shakespearean equivalent of an historical program note, but its sequel, as Henry goes on to justify the divorce, is a powerful expression of royal concern—a speech in which any distinction between private and public feelings has become imperceptible:

> This respite shook
> The bosom of my conscience, enter'd me,
> Yea, with a spitting power, and made to tremble
> The region of my breast, which forc'd such way
> That many maz'd considerings did throng

And press'd in with this caution. First, methought
I stood not in the smile of heaven, who had
Commanded nature, that my lady's womb
If it conceiv'd a male-child by me, should
Do no more offices of life to't than
The grave does to th'dead: for her male issue
Or died where they were made, or shortly after
This world had air'd them. Hence I took a thought
This was a judgment on me, that my kingdom
(Well worthy the best heir o'th'world) should not
Be gladded in't by me. Then follows that
I weigh'd the danger which my realms stood in
By this my issue's fail, and that gave to me
Many a groaning throe: thus hulling in
The wild sea of my conscience, I did steer
Toward this remedy whereupon we are
Now present here together: that's to say,
I meant to rectify my conscience, which
I then did feel full sick, and yet not well,
By all the reverend fathers of the land
And doctors learn'd. . . .

(II.iv.179–204)

181 *spitting* = stabbing

Eliminated in most stage productions, this speech is nevertheless "the key passage in the play." [34] The substance of the King's defense—the stillbirths or deaths of his sons and the danger to the succession—is new; yet the language of his defense recalls much of the language and action we have been observing in the two preceding acts (language and action not explicitly concerned with the succession): the conflicts of the opening scenes had been portrayed against the external kingdom; the prophetic tempest of the opening scene had been accompanied by images of a "sicken'd" land, its inhabitants tormented or hungry or fearful of "most poor issue." Wolsey—to cite but one contrasting image—had imagined himself as a "new trimm'd . . . vessel" sailing confidently and unharmed through a sea filled with "malicious censurers" who were "rav'nous" in their lust to destroy him (I.ii. 78–81). One line of dramatic development in Act II shows the disorders of the state gradually internalized, as it were, until they become the distemper of the King: "the danger which my realms stood in/ By this my issue's

[34] Byrne (cf. n. 31), p. 125. The speech may have been cut because it could not be forced to yield the "vicious hypocrisy" that directors and actors were assured by many editors it must contain; in a note on II.iv.170, for example, D. Nichol Smith's edition cites the *DNB* comment on Henry VIII: "All that was said . . . officially as to the origins of the king's scruples . . . is unworthy of serious refutation."

fail" has pierced the conscience of the King, the sickness of the land has "press'd" into "the region of my breast." After "hulling" aimlessly in a "wild sea," the King—independent of Wolsey—now attempts to "steer."

Through a remarkable piece of Shakespearean sleight-of-hand, never in the play are we made aware of Henry rejecting Katherine; indeed, he usually speaks as her advocate. By the introduction of the succession issue in particular, the action of the divorce has been made dramatically indistinguishable from the separation from Wolsey and the King's movement toward full control over his own affairs. Speaking in soliloquy near the end of the trial scene, Henry shows impatience with the "dilatory sloth and tricks of Rome" and he apostrophizes the absent Cranmer (II.iv.236–238). This is the earliest and most notable of the many anticipatory references to his "well-beloved servant Cranmer" before Cranmer finally enters as the King's loyal aide in Act V. (A certain rough progression may be observed in the tone of these references—from Norfolk's condescension at III.ii.72 and Wolsey's mixture of fear and contempt at III.ii.102 through the straight reports at III.ii.401 and IV.i.24 to "the virtuous Cranmer" at IV.i.105 and the Cranmer of whom Lovell speaks with awe at V.i.38.) Already in Act II, however, the King's supremacy has been asserted. In the next act it is established—partly through a scene which provides the emotional surrogate of a final confrontation between Henry and Katherine.

The relationship between the King and Wolsey is perhaps most richly explored in the scene in which that relationship is finally dissolved: Act III scene ii. This is the scene in which Wolsey makes his final appearance—and in which Spedding claimed to distinguish sharply between two styles, Shakespeare's ending with line 203a, Fletcher's beginning with line 203b. The division made it all but inevitable that critics would find Fletcher "contradicting" Shakespeare—finding, for example, that the Wolsey who appears after line 203 is "a very different Wolsey from Shakespeare's" (Nicolson). The facts are otherwise. After the not very successful interview with Katherine, Wolsey arrives at court "moody" and "discontented" (lines 75, 91). His political navigations have begun to "founder" (lines 37–40). He sounds edgy and erratic long before the King (at line 201) hands him the two papers revealing that his surreptitious accumulation of wealth and his intervention in the divorce case have been discovered. Wolsey had earlier been unwilling to remain a "state-statue" (I.ii.88), and here we find him "in most strange postures" (III.ii.118). In two strange asides he makes clear the sources of the "mutiny in's mind":

> Anne Bullen? no; I'll no Anne Bullens for him,
> There's more in't than fair visage. Bullen?

> No, we'll no Bullens. . . .
>   I know her for
> A spleeny Lutheran, and not wholesome to
> Our cause, that she should lie i'th'bosom of
> Our hard-rul'd king. Again there is sprung up
> An heretic, an arch-one, Cranmer, one
> Hath crawl'd into the favour of the king . . .
>   (III.ii.87–89, 98–103)

"Crawl'd" recalls the use of "crept" in both moral and sexual senses in the passage at II.ii.16–18 cited earlier. Although Henry and Katherine do not face each other after the divorce, Wolsey's behavior throughout III.ii is rather like that of a jealous lover, and the dialogues between Wolsey and the King, as the excerpts below may suggest, amount to a rejection-scene (i.e. in much the way that *Othello* III.iii parodies a scene of sexual seduction). Wolsey is only half-ignorant that the King is reproaching him in these lines:

>   My father lov'd you,
> He said he did, and with his deed did crown
> His word upon you. Since I had my office
> I have kept you next my heart . . .
>   as my hand has open'd bounty to you,
> My heart dropp'd love, my power rain'd honour, more
> On you than any; so your hand and heart,
> Your brain and every function of your power,
> Should, notwithstanding that your bond of duty,
> As 'twere in love's particular, be more
> To me your friend, than any.
>   (III.ii.154–157, 184–190)

Wolsey's flattering replies are similarly impressive in their warmth and weight of feeling:

>   I do profess
> That for your highness' good I ever labour'd
> More than mine own: that am, have, and will be
> (Though all the world should crack their duty to you
> And throw it from their soul, though perils did
> Abound as thick as thought could make 'em, and
> Appear in forms more horrid) yet my duty,
> As doth a rock against the chiding flood,
> Should the approach of this wild river break,
> And stand unshaken yours.
>   (III.ii.190–199)

To this, the ordinary courtly lover is but a kitten. When the unapprecia-
tive King hands Wolsey the papers, dryly wishes him good appetite, and
departs, we hear a different tone of voice, but the imagery is still Petrarchan:

> What should this mean?
> What sudden anger's this? How have I reap'd it?
> He parted frowning from me, as if ruin
> Leap'd from his eyes. So looks the chafed lion
> Upon the daring huntsman that has gall'd him . . .
>
> (III.ii.203–207)

When he discovers the inventory of "all that world of wealth I have drawn
together/ For mine own ends," he hesitates a moment, then starts on a new
round of nervous calculations aimed at restoring himself in favor (lines
210–220). But with the discovery of the second paper he realizes he is finished, and it is here that one detects, along with the echo of Marlowe, the
first touch of "Fletcherian languor":

> What's this? 'To th'Pope'?
> The letter, as I live, with all the business
> I writ to's holiness. Nay then, farewell:
> I have touch'd the highest point of all my greatness,
> And from that full meridian of my glory
> I haste now to my setting. I shall fall
> Like a bright exhalation in the evening,
> And no man see me more.
>
> (III.ii.220–227)

The figure created by these lines is pitiable—and self-pitying—but he has
not yet settled down in the bed critics have made for him. A moment later
he refuses to surrender the great seal which the King "with his own hand"
gave him (lines 236–250); his jealous reproaches as he is forced to yield
are ironically reminiscent of Katherine's reproaches to him during the interview scene (III.i.98 ff.). And Wolsey seems angrily unmindful, even later
in the scene, that he is supposed to suffer from a Fletcherian melancholia:

> *Surrey.* Thou art a proud traitor, priest.
> *Wolsey.*   Proud lord, thou liest. . . .
> *Surrey.*   Thy ambition,
>   Thou scarlet sin, robb'd this bewailing land
>   Of noble Buckingham, my father-in-law;
>   The heads of all thy brother-cardinals
>   (With thee and all thy best parts bound together)
>   Weigh'd not a hair of his. . . .

Wolsey.　　　　　This, and all else
　This talking lord can lay upon my credit,
　I answer, is most false. The duke by law
　Found his deserts. How innocent I was
　From any private malice in his end,
　His noble jury, and foul cause can witness. . . .

(III.ii.252, 254–259, 264–269)

The two hundred remaining lines of the scene give us a writhing, tortured figure, by turns self-righteous, weak, hectic, worldly-wise, fatuously self-deluding, nobly forgiving, coolly sarcastic, and occasionally resigned. His final soliloquy gives us his own late image of himself—not now the "new trimm'd . . . vessel" of Act I but a lonely figure "swimming" in a "sea of glory" who has gone "far beyond my depth" and whose "high-blown pride" has "at length broke under me" so that he is left to drown in that same "rude stream" of "rav'nous . . . censurers" he had feared from the beginning might prevent his devoted service to the King.

The choric Gentlemen who reported in Act II that the commons wished Wolsey "ten faddom deep" (II.i.51) return in Act IV to describe the new political climate—a time of "general joy" in which "the citizens . . . have shown at full their royal minds" (IV.i.7–8). The coronation parade (whose "rich stream" of lords and ladies is described in the most elaborate stage direction in the Folio) superficially recalls the festivities at the Field of the Cloth of Gold; Wolsey ran that show, at which "madams . . . Not us'd to toil, did almost sweat to bear/ The pride upon them" and "dwarfish pages" were artificially "all gilt" (I.i.22–25); the new celebration contrasts with Wolsey's pageantry in its unforced naturalness—expressed, for example, in the images of teeming fertility and vigor we saw in the report by the Third Gentleman (pages 157–158 above) with its concluding vision of the crowds all "woven . . . strangely in one piece." And if "every man show'd like a mine" at the Field of the Cloth of Gold, now that "the old time of war" is past,

　　　Our king has all the Indies in his arms,
　　　And more, and richer, when he strains that lady;
　　　I cannot blame his conscience.

(IV.i.45–47)

The light humor of the Gentleman's comment is appropriate to the altered—less constricted—atmosphere of the coronation scene. In sharp contrast to this kind of rejoicing comes the following scene—"tender and pathetick . . . above any other part of *Shakespeare's* tragedies, and perhaps above any scene of any other poet" (Dr. Johnson)—in which Griffith describes the rejected and dying Wolsey begging "a little earth for charity" (IV.ii.23) to the calm figure of the ill and more quietly rejected Katherine. Katherine's apparent weakness is here poised against so many contrasting elements that "resignation" is little more appropriate a term for her attitude than it is for Wolsey's. With the solemn music of the choreographed Vision still playing, she tells Griffith and Patience of the angels who brought her garlands "which I feel/ I am not worthy yet to wear"—but then concludes, "I shall assuredly" (lines 91–92); the same tensile strength is evident in her magisterial treatment of the rude Messenger (lines 100–108); and she is given the same closing line as Laertes and Antony. It is Wolsey who had been forced to "play the woman" (III.ii.430). But in IV.ii both Wolsey and Katherine are seen as private and lonely figures; it was in Act III that Katherine was retired, and Wolsey destroyed, as creatures of history.

Juxtaposed to the tragic events of the play is a sequence of counter-movements clustered mainly about Anne. It can be traced, as Wilson Knight has pointed out, in the "sexual freedom [of] . . . the lords' conversation on the way to Wolsey's feast, through that feast, its merriment and gay talk," in the dialogues with "the Old Lady and her willingness to 'venture maidenhead' for a crown," in the "seething fertility and enthusiastic crowds" of the coronation scene, in the mixture of "religious reference with a bawdy broad-talk" throughout the Porter's scene ("what a fry of fornication is at door! On my Christian conscience this one christening will beget a thousand . . ."); it is reflected in the rich sexual punning that occurs even in the soberer scenes of the play; and it culminates, of course, in the final prophecies of national glory spoken above the newborn royal child.[35]

The King is kept offstage throughout Act IV (a device of Shakespearean construction, used in maybe a dozen plays, enhancing the stature of the protagonist on his return), and when we encounter him again in Act V he is being drawn into the Gardiner-Cranmer dispute. Without his intervention Cranmer would presumably have been condemned for heresy. This episode—which Spedding thought "strangely out of place," which directors usually butcher or wholly remove, which even sympathetic interpreters of the play have sometimes glossed over—comprises almost two-thirds of Act V (scenes i and ii in the Folio and in the Foakes edition, scenes i–iii in misdivided texts), and it calls for close consideration. According to the traditional view of the structure of the play—"a chronicle-history with three and a half catastrophes" (Hertzberg), "a collection of falls" (Frank Kermode)—the episode is merely an incomplete and not very purposeful

---

[35] Cf. Knight, *The Crown of Life*, pp. 297–306.

parallel to the "catastrophes" of Buckingham, Katherine, and Wolsey. Miss Byrne and R. A. Foakes, however, both lay stress on the role of the King in this episode; his active participation in the dispute—first by testing Cranmer, then by good-naturedly reassuring him, finally by intervening against Gardiner—exemplifies the virtuous exercise of royal authority and dramatizes the final commitment of the King. Again, the structure of the play seems a good deal more coherent once it is allowed that *Henry VIII* is somehow mainly about Henry VIII. But of course wise audiences are not very deeply interested in anything as abstract as "structure"; they are attracted, if at all, by the experience of the play, and there is more to attract them in the Gardiner-Cranmer episode than any schematic diagram can show.

Gardiner had made one appearance before Act V. He had been nominated by Wolsey as the King's secretary, and he entered briefly at II.ii.116 where, in his aside to Wolsey ("But to be commanded/ For ever by your grace, whose hand has rais'd me"), he was established as Wolsey's creature in the minds of the audience. The association is strengthened in Act V; his first substantial speech (V.i.2–5) unmistakably echoes one of Wolsey's major speeches earlier in the play (III.ii.144–149), his subsequent flattery of the King (V.ii.148–155) resembles—in a thinned-out fashion—Wolsey's magnificent flatteries in III.ii (although it is even more peremptorily dismissed), and at one later point he is even given his little repentance bit (V.ii.205). But if he is a miniature Wolsey, he is a peculiarly ineffectual one. Long before Henry enters the council-chamber in V.ii we had been made aware that Gardiner's actions against Cranmer would fail; the dialogues between Henry and Dr. Butts implied as much (V.ii.19–34), and even before the end of the preceding scene—at about the same time that Anne's child was delivered—Cranmer had been comforted by the King's words and reassured by the gift of his ring (V.i.150). Much earlier still in V.i, there had been yet another augury that Gardiner would not succeed. Lovell is a sort of dramatic weathercock who had spoken of Wolsey with awe in Act I, and when Gardiner solicits his support against Cranmer near the beginning of V.i, his reluctance to go along with the attack hints pretty strongly that Cranmer will be perfectly safe:

> Th'archbishop
> Is the king's hand and tongue, and who dare speak
> One syllable against him?

> (V.i.37–39)

Of course this reply of Lovell's is rather comic within its context, since Gardiner has just finished uttering quite a number of subversive syllables.

And comedy is the point to which these solemn remarks have been leading.

There is, as we have just seen, little suspense over the outcome of the Gardiner-Cranmer episode. And while both of the scenes embodying that episode do offer a fascinating Shakespearean sketch of political maneuverings, the older critics who read these scenes as if they were seriously concerned with ideology (for example, as if they were intended to introduce a "great ecclesiastical revolution" of which Cranmer was spokesman) completely overlooked the tone of the dialogues:

> *Lovell.*　　　　　　The queen's in labour,
> They say in great extremity, and fear'd
> She'll with the labour end.
> *Gardiner.*　　　　　　The fruit she goes with
> I pray for heartily, that it may find
> Good time, and live: but for the stock, Sir Thomas,
> I wish it grubb'd up now.
> *Lovell.*　　　　　　Methinks I could
> Cry the amen, and yet my conscience says
> She's a good creature, and sweet lady, does
> Deserve our better wishes.
> *Gardiner.*　　　　　　But sir, sir,
> Hear me Sir Thomas, y'are a gentleman
> Of mine own way: I know you wise, religious,
> And let me tell you, it will ne'er be well,
> 'Twill not Sir Thomas Lovell, take't of me,
> Till Cranmer, Cromwell, her two hands, and she
> Sleep in their graves.
> *Lovell.*　　　　　　Now sir, you speak of two
> The most remark'd i'th'kingdom: as for Cromwell,
> Beside that of the jewel-house, is made master
> O'th'rolls, and the king's secretary; further sir,
> Stands in the gap and trade of moe preferments,
> With which the time will load him. Th'archbishop
> Is the king's hand and tongue, and who dare speak
> One syllable against him?
> *Gardiner.*　　　　　　Yes, yes, Sir Thomas,
> There are that dare, and I myself have ventur'd
> To speak my mind of him: and indeed this day
> Sir (I may tell it you) I think I have
> Incens'd the lords o'th'council that he is
> (For so I know he is, they know he is)
> A most arch-heretic . . .

(V.i.18–45)

The irascible Gardiner combines the wisdom of Polonius with the modesty of Glendower, and the actor who plays this pint-sized Wolsey needs a tongue as thick as the character's wit: "Hear me Sir Thomas . . . Let me tell you . . . Take't of me . . . Yes, yes, Sir Thomas,/ There are that dare, and I myself. . . ." The height and weight of this teller-off can be measured against his crony Lovell, whose will to be agreeable to whomever he's with (audible also in his earlier scenes) is bridled only by his will to be agreeable to the whole crowd at once ("Now sir . . . two/ The most remark'd i'th'kingdom . . ."). Gardiner pushes his village zealotry to its suicidal limit in the next scene, where he continues to speak as diplomatically in public as he had in private ("That's the plain truth; your painted gloss discovers/ To men that understand you, words and weakness") and where, his hands already full with Cranmer, he takes on Cromwell too (V.ii.104–120). Perhaps his finest moment, however, comes when the King enters the council-chamber "frowning," and this self-proclaimed master of blunt open-dealing suddenly does his city-mouse act:

> Dread sovereign, how much are we bound to heaven
> In daily thanks, that gave us such a prince,
> Not only good and wise, but most religious:
> One that in all obedience, makes the church
> The chief aim of his honour, and to strengthen
> That holy duty out of dear respect,
> His royal self in judgement comes to hear
> The cause betwixt her and this great offender.
>
> (V.ii.148–155)

A few moments earlier we had seen the King literally standing above the councillors and observing them critically—playing Prospero—and the councillors themselves, chastened by Cranmer's display of Henry's ring, had just taken a friendlier tack toward "this great offender"; the cantankerous Gardiner is utterly powerless, and he cuts an almost pitiably comic figure. For in Act V we entered a new dramatic kingdom—the first scene had even begun with a clock striking the hour of one—in which everything is so under control that petty malice and sinister conspiracy, however realistically they are dramatized, have taken on the air of an Illyrian charade.

The entire last act, in the highly original economy of this play, is a celebration of the new order—first in the political comedy at court, then among the festive crowds for whom the christening is a people's holiday which the Porter's Man can compare to "may-day morning," and finally in Cranmer's utopian "oracle of comfort." The palmy but frustrated hopes of the earlier meeting at Andren, suddenly asserted and as quickly withdrawn in the imagery of the opening scene of the play, now emerge enlarged and transformed in the swelling prophecies of "a thousand thousand blessings,/ Which time shall bring to ripeness":

> In her days every man shall eat in safety
> Under his own vine what he plants, and sing
> The merry songs of peace to all his neighbours. . . .
>   Peace, plenty, love, truth, terror,
> That were the servants to this chosen infant,
> Shall then be his, and like a vine grow to him . . .
>   (V.iv.33–35, 47–49)

The "chosen infant" who will "lighten all this isle" (II.iii.79), although she is at the center of the ceremony, is merely the occasion—not the cause—of the "Holy-day" toward which the action of the play has been moving, and the particular identities of the three royal figures in Cranmer's lines coalesce in these final images of ritual communion between King and people. "King Henry is the one king in Shakespeare in whom you cannot dissociate man from office" (Knight), and the dénouement of *Henry VIII* invests that office with a breadth and fullness of social and human meaning which transcend the private tragedies of Katherine and Wolsey. The unity of the play should manifest itself to the reader who does not allow "the crowd of notable historical personages" who inhabit it to obscure the role of the King in their midst.

Concluding Observations

Early stage tradition, interestingly, draws particular attention to the role of the King. Langbaine, referring to the production first mounted by Sir William Davenant in 1663–64, wrote in 1691 that the play "frequently appears on the present Stage; the part of *Henry* being extreamly well acted by Mr. *Betterton*." [36] According to Downes, who had been the prompter at the Davenant production, Betterton's performance was an authoritative one:

The part of the King was so right and justly done by Mr. *Betterton,* he being Instructed in it by Sir *William,* who had it from Old Mr. *Lowen,* that had his Instructions from Mr. *Shakespear* himself, that I dare and will aver, none can, or will come near him in this Age, in the performance of that part. [37]

Shakespeare was present in London in the spring of 1613 when Lowin would have been rehearsing the part, and Davenant had known Lowin since

[36] Gerard Langbaine, *An Account of the English Dramatick Poets* (1691), p. 457.
[37] John Downes, *Roscius Anglicanus* (1708), p. 24.

the late 1620's (when both *Henry VIII* and Davenant's own early plays were being performed by the King's company), so that the testimony of Downes in this matter carries some weight. But of course it is the text itself which warrants emphasis on the part of the King, just as it is a careful study of the text itself—whether in combination with external evidence such as that derived from sources [38] or in exclusive concentration on the internal organization of the drama—which best confutes the theory of divided authorship.

Some of the critical writings on *Henry VIII* in recent years have played down the authorship controversy, possibly in the hope that it will fade from living memory as soon as an older generation of scholars, raised in the belief that the play was the result of divided authorship, is replaced by a younger generation unburdened by the worn-out assumptions of the past. But dead, in effect, as the "problem" of *Henry VIII* now is, and unpleasant as it therefore is to say more about the arguments concerning it, it is still germane to the larger subject of this book; it is still worth considering how nearly a century of scholarship could be so thoroughly and without qualification stupid and wrong. Perhaps it had something to do with certain older habits of interpretation, since no new documentary discoveries have brought about the change in opinion. There are still a few points that call for explanation.

Comparisons between the work of Shakespeare and Fletcher have been curiously sparse in the accumulated writings on the authorship controversy —especially among the contributions of Spedding partisans. It was response beyond the call of duty that led Wilson Knight in *The Crown of Life* to offer what may be the only direct and detailed comparative analysis, with quotation, between passages from Fletcher's work and from *Henry VIII* (pp. 263-272). Spedding himself offered only brief references to three scenes from the Fletcher canon—Act III scene i of *The Captain*, Act V of *The Honest Man's Fortune*, and those parts of Act IV in *Thierry and Theodoret* that Lamb printed in his *Specimens*—which interested readers might look into if they wished. Apparently he considered his choices carefully, for he assured his readers that all three were genuine specimens of Fletcher's work, that all three dated from about 1612-1613, and that if any of these scenes were placed beside any "Fletcher scene" in *Henry VIII*,

---

[38] In this connection it may be noted that the most exhaustive study of sources to date is to be found in the Introduction, notes, and Appendix of the 1957 Arden edition. Foakes draws attention to the ways in which widely scattered extracts from at least four different sources are intricately dovetailed, altered, and elaborated in the shaping of the play—a complicated adaptation "not easily fitted into a theory of collaborative writing" (p. xxiii).

"the identity [of authorship] . . . will be felt at once." With respect to the authenticity and contemporaneity of the passages, one may assume that Spedding proceeded on the best knowledge available to him when he wrote. Actually, the scene from *The Captain* and part perhaps of the last act of *The Honest Man's Fortune* may not be authentic Fletcher, and *Thierry and Theodoret* may be a later play. These considerations do not matter, however, if one merely wishes to gauge Spedding's notions of the "identity" of styles and metrical workmanship. One might go, then, to the last act of *The Honest Man's Fortune;* parts of this act, as it turns out, are in prose and were mislined as verse in the nineteenth-century editions employed by Spedding—mislined as such loose verse, moreover, that with regard to "metre" they could be said to resemble *Henry VIII* with about as much justice as *Evangeline* could be said to resemble *The Aeneid*. And if one extends the scope of one's comparison beyond the "structure . . . of [the] metre" on which Spedding laid so much emphasis, the results are even more surprising. One must assume that Spedding's readers, if they actually turned to the last act of *The Honest Man's Fortune,* followed the same procedure their critic had recommended for *Henry VIII:* "do as I did, . . . read . . . with an eye open to notice the larger differences of effect . . . without staying to examine small points"—because it is *very* difficult, assuming otherwise, to credit their trust in him when they reached the point at which Veramour's breeches and codpiece were inspected on stage. They must not have noticed.

Readers of an older generation, if they had been shown that Spedding's ideas of style were not adequate to support his thesis about the authorship of *Henry VIII,* would perhaps have retorted that Spedding's literary taste was not directly relevant, that raising such a question implied an *ad hominem* argument, and that all that was important was the "objective truth" of the question of authorship which Spedding had raised; if Spedding's examples were faulty, other examples and other arguments had also to be considered. There is a verbal issue involved here; readers of an older generation would normally assume that "Fletcher" was "Fletcher," whether they or Spedding were using the word, and that the printed texts ascribed to Fletcher were identical for all readers simply because the letters on the pages fell into almost identical configurations. That would be an epistemological blunder, not merely a semantic one, and it would be rather similar to the blunder by which it was once commonly assumed that a good "test of authorship" consisted, statistically speaking, of screening out 99.99% of the text of *Henry VIII* and deciding the issue on the basis of what was left, even when the .01% that was left had been carefully selected by someone who had decided the issue in his own mind before he applied himself to making that selection.

It is of course a little absurd to think that many of the Shakespearean scholars who considered *Henry VIII* ever felt the need to make elaborate formal comparisons. They simply read the play and as long as the Spedding theory was current they readily saw "two hands" in it. In addition they usually agreed that, questions of authorship aside, it was in any case "a very broken-backed affair" (as it was called by Marco Mincoff *despite* his observation of "Shakespearean" characteristics in the so-called "Fletcher part"). The question then is where these scholars—and all their students and readers who looked at the play and agreed—found the evidence that convinced them. The answer must be that they made it up themselves; they would make it up in part out of the materials in the play, to be sure, but out of the most dishearteningly small bits of evidence that the crippling assumptions and expectations they brought to their reading would permit them to notice. The readers who do and will continue to find the play wholly Shakespeare's, and who will go on to point out the complexity of its expressive vision and the unity of design they will also observe in it, will also be making up their evidence. They will also be making it up in part out of the materials of the play, but out of the much wider range of materials that their different expectations will permit *them* to notice.

IV

Cardenio and Theobald

> The composing of chess problems . . . is a beautiful, complex and
> sterile art related to the ordinary form of the game only insofar as,
> say, the properties of a sphere are made use of both by a juggler in
> weaving a new act and by a tennis player in winning a tournament.
> Most chess players . . . are only mildly interested in these highly
> specialized, fanciful and elegant riddles.
>
> *Vladimir Nabokov*

No discussion of the assumed collaboration between Shakespeare and
Fletcher would be complete without an account of the lost play known as
Cardenio. In *The Shakespeare First Folio* (1955) Sir Walter Greg has provided a concise and authoritative statement of current information and opinion on this subject:

To the collaboration-plays should perhaps be added *Cardenio,* a dramatization, presumably, of the story of Cardenio and Luscinda from *Don Quixote*
(available in Shelton's translation of the first part in 1612). This play was acted
at court in the winter of 1612–13 (as 'Cardenno') and again on 8 June (as
'Cardenna'), and a manuscript of 'The History of Cardenio' was registered for
publication by Humphrey Moseley on 9 September 1653 as by Fletcher and
Shakespeare. Moseley's attributions, though most likely derived from the manuscripts, do not always carry weight. However, Cervantes's tale, with altered names,
supplies the plot of a play called *Double Falsehood, or the Distressed Lovers,*
printed in 1728 as 'Written Originally by W. Shakespeare; and now Revised
and Adapted to the Stage by Mr. Theobald, the Author of Shakespeare Restor'd'.
In spite of some improbabilities in Lewis Theobald's account, there seems no
sufficient reason to doubt that he based his version on an early manuscript,
perhaps bearing an ascription to Shakespeare, or to believe that he was perpe-
trating 'so agreeable a Cheat' as that of which, even at the time, he was accused.
His indignant repudiation of the suggestion that the original might have been

by Fletcher precludes our supposing that he had somehow acquired Moseley's manuscript or even knew of his entrance.

(pp. 98–99)

Apparently Moseley never published either *Cardenio* or these two other plays he registered in the same entry: "Henry y^e. first, & Hen: ye 2^d. by Shakespeare, & Dauenport." In the same year that he recorded these manuscripts, Moseley, who had taken over *The Two Noble Kinsmen* from Waterson, advertised that play, despite the title-page, as by Beaumont and Fletcher, and this circumstance, along with his failure to publish the three 1653 manuscripts, would tend to support Greg's supposition that he did not invent the Shakespearean attributions but was merely following the manuscripts.[1] These guesses concerning Moseley are, however, of little consequence, although the two Shakespeare-Davenport attributions may provide a convenient standard of reference for the degree of attention that might have been paid to *Cardenio* had it not been for the observation, by Gamaliel Bradford in 1909, of the likely connection between that play and Theobald's *Double Falsehood*.[2] An inquiry into *Cardenio* calls for consideration both of Theobald's play and of the theories that have been proposed since 1909 to account for its relation to the play registered by Moseley. The problems involved are unusual, and many peculiarities in Theobald's behavior have led some investigators to find the existing play rather more of a puzzle than the missing one.

Theobald's Play

Double Falsehood was first staged on 13 December 1727. Newspaper advertisements preceding the actual performances claimed that the play was based on a hitherto unknown Shakespearean original; the public was invited to judge for itself the merits of the claim. Evidently the play was a success; its initial run lasted through ten performances and it was twice revived later in the same season.[3] The text was printed by John Watts early in 1728, and on the title-page Theobald repeated his claim in the words quoted above by Greg. But despite the fact that Theobald's reputation as an authority on Shakespeare had already been established, none of his contem-

---

[1] Moseley's 1653 advertisement, as well as his 1654 list with *TNK* offered among various "Beaumont and Fletcher" plays printed in quarto, may be found in Greg, *Bibliography*, III, 1175–1177.

[2] It should perhaps be mentioned that Sir Henry Herbert licensed the lost *Henry the First* as by Davenport in 1624. Bradford: cf. n. 9 below.

[3] Cf. John Geneste, *Some Account of the English Stage* (1832), III, 203–204, and T. R. Lounsbury, *The Text of Shakespeare* (1906), pp. 145–152.

poraries seems to have accepted the title-page assertion. Nor has anyone since. From Theobald's day until the present, however, the great majority of critics—even including Pope[4]—have agreed that Theobald probably did obtain an authentic Jacobean manuscript; although speculation on its authorship has occasionally run to Massinger (Malone) and Shirley (Farmer), the name most frequently suggested during the past two centuries has been that of Fletcher. For what it is worth—merely to satisfy curiosity—here is a characteristic passage that has reminded some critics of Fletcher:

> *Violante.*   How his Eyes shake Fire,
>   And measure ev'ry Piece of Youth about me!   [*Aside*
>   The Ewes want Water, Sir: Shall I go drive 'em
>   Down to the Cisterns? Shall I make haste, Sir?
>   'Would I were five Miles from him—How he gripes me! [*Aside*
> *Master.* Come, come, all this is not sufficient, Child,
>   To make a Fool of me.—This is a fine Hand,
>   A delicate fine Hand,—Never change Colour;
>   You understand me,—and a Woman's Hand.
>
>   (IV.i)

Before 1909 there had been a few dissenters from majority opinion (such as Isaac Reed) who felt that *Double Falsehood* was entirely Theobald's invention. Since 1909 there have been a few critics who have argued that the original play was probably a Shakespeare-Fletcher collaboration; we shall come to their arguments a little later.

Theobald's own testimony about the earlier play appears in the preliminaries to the published text. Theobald had been granted a copyright license on 5 December 1727, and the text of the license (reprinted with the play) indicates that Theobald had stated in his application

That He ha[d], at a considerable Expense, Purchased the Manuscript Copy of an Original Play of WILLIAM SHAKESPEARE . . . and, with great Labour and Pains, Revised, and Adapted the same to the stage . . .

                                                      (sig. A1ᵛ)

Theobald's "Preface of the Editor" begins as follows:

The Success, which this Play has met with from the Town in the Representation, (to say nothing of the Reception it found from those Great Judges, to

----

[4] In a letter of 9 June 1738 to Aaron Hill, Pope said of Theobald: "I never supposed [the play] to be his: He gave it as *Shakespear's,* and I take it to be of that Age"; *Correspondence of Alexander Pope,* ed. George Sherburn (1956), IV, 102. Cf. James Sutherland, ed. *The Dunciad* (1943), pp. 180–182.

whom I have had the Honour of communicating it in Manuscript;) has almost made the Purpose of a Preface unnecessary . . .

(sig. A5)

In a letter dated 10 December 1727 (first brought to light in 1940), Theobald offered the Countess of Oxford tickets to a performance of *Double False-hood,* adding in a postscript, "If your Honour has any mind to read the play in manuscript, upon the earliest intimation of your pleasure you shall command it." [5] Since this letter antedates the opening performance by only three days, perhaps Theobald's promise referred to the manuscript of his revision. In any case there is no record of his communicating the original manuscript to any judge at all. In this connection we may note an interesting feature of the published dedicatory epistle; Theobald dedicated the play to Bubb Dodington, promising him that if he would take it into his protection, future ages would remember Dodington as the same friend to Shakespeare's "remains" as "his own SOUTHAMPTON was to his *living Merit":*

I flatter Myself, that if You shall think fit to pronounce this Piece genuine, it will silence the Censures of those *Unbelievers,* who think it impossible a Manu-script of *Shakespeare* could so long have lain dormant. . . . Permit me . . . to convert *Panegyrick* into a most ardent Wish, that You would look with a Tender Eye on this *dear Relick* . . .

(sigs. A3^v–A4^v)

Dodington's reaction is not recorded, but this printed dedication (dated 21 December 1727) makes it fairly clear that Theobald had shown him no original manuscript; more important, Theobald evidently implies that his own text is a sufficient reflection of the original play to satisfy any "Great Judges." There may, of course, be conscious irony in this last phrase, since by 1727 Theobald might have been justified in regarding himself as the most knowledgeable of all living scholars of earlier English drama.

As the "Preface of the Editor" continued, however, Theobald referred to no less than three manuscript copies of the original play. The theatrical success of the play, he had begun,

has almost made the Purpose of a Preface unnecessary: And therefore what I have to say, is design'd rather to wipe out a flying Objection [or] two, than to labour at proving it the Production of *Shakespeare.* It has been alledg'd as incredible, that such a Curiosity should be stifled and lost to the World for above a Century. To This my Answer is short; that tho' it never till now made its Appearance on the Stage, yet one of the Manuscript Copies, which I have,

[5] Cf. John Cadwalader, "Theobald's Alleged Shakespeare Manuscript," *MLN,* LV (1940), 108–109.

is of above Sixty Years Standing, in the Handwriting of Mr. *Downes,* the famous Old Prompter [active from 1661 to 1706]; and, as I am credibly inform'd, was early in the Possession of the celebrated Mr. *Betterton,* and by Him design'd to have been usher'd into the World. What Accident prevented This . . . I do not pretend to know: Or thro' what hands it had successively pass'd before that Period of Time. There is a Tradition (which I have from the Noble Person, who supply'd me with One of my Copies) that it was given by our Author . . . to a Natural Daughter of his . . . in the Time of his Retirement from the Stage. Two other Copies I have, (one of which I was glad to purchase at a very good Rate,) which may not, perhaps, be quite so Old as the Former; but One of Them . . . has fewer Flaws and Interruptions in the Sense.

(sigs. A5–A5^v)

Having dealt in this fashion with the question of provenance, Theobald proceeded to wipe out a quite different kind of flying objection:

> Others again, to depreciate the Affair, . . . have been pleased to urge, that tho' the Play may have some Resemblances of *Shakespeare,* yet the *Colouring, Diction,* and *Characters,* come nearer to the Style and Manner of FLETCHER. This, I think, is far from deserving any Answer; I submit it to the Determination of better Judgments; tho' my Partiality for *Shakespeare* makes me wish, that Every Thing which is good, or pleasing, in our Tongue, had been owing to his Pen.

(sig. A5^v)

In a second edition, also published in 1728, Theobald made a few changes in the preface. A curious addition asserts that, although he had once intended to prove the play Shakespeare's by the peculiarity of the language, he finally decided no proof was necessary; and at the end of the passage just quoted he made a remarkable alteration of the phrase "in our Tongue" into a direct reference to Fletcher, "in that other great Poet"—i.e. his partiality for Shakespeare made him wish that everything good or pleasing in Fletcher had been owing to Shakespeare. Theobald's only other recorded comment on the entire affair is a defense of one line in the play against a sally by Pope that it was too bathetic to be by Shakespeare.[6] Beyond what has been mentioned, silence. Theobald never published the original text; his preserved correspondence nowhere refers to it; there is no further record of his alleged manuscripts during his life or since his death in 1744. The sale catalogue of his possessions after his death reveals no trace of anything that might be identified as a source manuscript for *Double Falsehood.*[7]

---

[6] First published in Mist's *Weekly Journal* of 27 April 1728, then partly reprinted in his 1733 edition of Shakespeare (IV, 187–188), his defense rebutted Pope by citing classical parallels to the line Pope had ridiculed (given below in the quotation from Oliphant) but is otherwise uninformative.

[7] Cf. Chambers, *William Shakespeare,* I, 542.

But it is recorded that the printer Watts paid him one hundred guineas for the publishing rights,[8] and it was evidently not for lack of public success that Theobald chose, after 1728, to remain quiet about the affair in which, as he said in his epistle to Dodington, he might be suspected of "so *agreeable a Cheat.*"

Theobald's preface mentioned Shelton's translation of *Don Quixote* as the source of *Double Falsehood,* and a few Victorian critics—e.g. Sidney Lee in his 1898 biography of Shakespeare—guessed at some kind of association between that play and *Cardenio.* Gamaliel Bradford, however, was the first to argue that two hands could (partly through metrical analysis) be sharply distinguished through Theobald's text and to imply that one of these was Shakespeare's.[9] Bradford's thesis was soon attacked on the grounds that the link between *Double Falsehood* and Cervantes was spurious,[10] but Walter Graham in 1916 proved the connection with detailed evidence that left subsequent scholarship with no further doubts on this point.[11] Observing also that the language and versification of *Double Falsehood* were unlike Theobald's original dramatic writings, Graham then produced a verse-table to show a division in the surmised source-play between "parts possibly by Fletcher" and "by another." Parts of Acts II and IV and all of Act V, he thought, might be assigned to Fletcher, mainly on the basis of feminine endings in 44% of the lines—as against 32% in the remainder of the play. Graham acknowledged that "the wholesale leveling which Theobald may have effected" would mean that "evidence obtained by verse tests must be relative and approximate indeed," but despite the fact that Theobald's generation was notoriously prone to metrical regularization, and despite the fact that he found nothing in the text that he was willing to cite as evidence of Shakespeare's hand, he found significance in his 32%–44% distinction. This argument was published in the same era in which J. M. Robertson cited twelve feminine endings in *Hamlet* II.i.1-19 (63%) as evidence against Shakespeare's authorship of the scene;[12] perhaps it would be well to recognize that many professional literary scholars used to be afflicted, in their reverent attitude toward metrical statistics, with

---

[8] The payment is listed among various similar records preserved by "Eu. Hood" (Joseph Haslewood) in *Gentleman's Magazine,* XCIV (Pt. I, 1824), 223.

[9] Bradford announced his thesis in a letter to *The Nation* (New York), LXXXVIII (1909), 328, and developed his arguments more fully in "The History of Cardenio," *MLN,* XXV (1910), 51–56.

[10] R. Schevill, "Theobald's *Double Falsehood,*" *MP,* IX (1911), 269–285.

[11] Graham, "The *Cardenio–Double Falsehood* Problem," *MP,* XIV (1916), 269–280, 568. Graham edited *Double Falsehood* in 1920 (Western Reserve Studies, Vol. I, no. 6); the Introduction to his edition incorporates the material of the 1916 article.

[12] Robertson, *The Problem of "Hamlet"* (1919), p. 58 n.

what amounted to a mild form of collective insanity. Graham, it should be added, also proffered the useful suggestion that Theobald may have acquired Moseley's manuscript, and he remarked that Moseley's entry probably "assigned the lost play correctly to Fletcher, at least, if not to Shakespeare."

In 1919 Richard F. Jones, author of the most thorough and sympathetic study of Theobald's life and work, was led by his study of the *Double Falsehood* affair to the conclusion that Theobald

did not himself really believe Shakespeare was the author. It is entirely probable that he obtained manuscripts bearing Shakespeare's name, . . . but a man of Theobald's thoroughgoing scholarly nature, who insisted that all conclusions should be supported by proof and authority, would not have rested content with the feeble reasons, justly satirized by Pope, which were given in the preface. He would have continued in the design, he said he once had [i.e. in the second version of the preface], of proving Shakespeare's authorship by the peculiarity of the language, a task he was entirely competent for. . . . Had he believed the work Shakespeare's, he would certainly have made some mention of it in his edition . . . [and] drawn on it for illustrative or evidential material in his notes. Nowhere does he allude to the play, and even in his correspondence with Warburton, where many of his personal affairs find a place, he is . . . silent on the matter. As has been stated, he probably felt that Fletcher was concerned in the authorship of the play, though we have no evidence that he had ever heard of *The History of Cardenio.* The whole affair is the most faint-hearted undertaking with which Theobald has favored us.[18]

Since Jones's conclusions were not accepted by several later scholars who dealt with *Cardenio,* it will be necessary at this point to go back over some of the ground we have already covered and examine it more closely.

An Explanation

The earliest mention in print of Fletcher's possible connection with *Double Falsehood* was made by Theobald himself. If we were to take his words at face value, we would evidently be required to believe that certain theatergoers in December 1727 attended his play, were well enough disposed towards Theobald to accept his claim to have been following an older manuscript, remained sufficiently skeptical to dismiss his claim for Shakespeare, and at the same time were sufficiently perceptive to hit upon the notion that the original was by Fletcher. If Theobald's ignorance of the Moseley ascription is to be credited, his critics ought presumably to be credited with the

---

[18] Jones, *Lewis Theobald* (1919), pp. 105–106.

same ignorance. Their perception, in that case, would be perhaps the most extraordinary element in the entire mystery. It is in fact quite probable that neither Theobald nor his critics—if there actually were such critics before the play appeared in print—knew of the Moseley entry, since Theobald would hardly have risked his claim for Shakespeare it he were aware of a contradictory record, and anyone else who knew of such a record would almost certainly have published the information at once—or turned it over to Pope, who would have known what to do with it. Only in the later eighteenth century did scholars such as Steevens and Capell begin to examine the Stationers' Register. But Theobald would not have had to know of the Moseley entry if he had acquired a manuscript with Fletcher's as well as Shakespeare's name on it. Whether it would have been the same manuscript as Moseley possessed or not is immaterial, for manuscript attributions were likely enough to be copied. Alternatively, the first manuscript Theobald acquired may have attributed the play to Shakespeare and another copy, acquired later, may have given the dual attribution. Still another possibility is that Theobald acquired a manuscript with Shakespeare's name on it but, as he grew familiar with the play, was led by his own considerable experience with earlier drama to attribute the play rather to Fletcher. If we assume, in whatever way we choose to imagine, that Theobald "probably felt that Fletcher was concerned in the authorship of the play," the entire episode begins to make some sort of sense. The reader may be puzzled that so obvious an assumption is being pressed at such length; subsequent discussion of the later scholarship will make clear enough the need for this procedure. A highly conjectural explanation, then, might be constructed along some such lines as these:

Theobald at some time was offered, perhaps at considerable expense, a manuscript bearing an attribution to both Shakespeare and Fletcher. He acquired it in the natural enough hope that there was some basis for the Shakespeare attribution. As he grew familiar with the play, he himself began to doubt Shakespeare's responsibility for much, if any, of the text. If opportunity arose, he might acquire additional manuscript copies in order to secure his copyright, to secure his exclusive knowledge of the Fletcher attribution, or both.

If he actually believed in Shakespeare's authorship when he came to prepare his adaptation, it is unlikely he would take pains to remove whatever seemed most Shakespearean while still retaining whatever seemed most like Fletcher. The decision to lay public claim to possession of an exclusively Shakespearean original might have proceeded from such considerations as the following. Perhaps, if the manuscript had been costly, he wished to recoup his original losses. Perhaps he still hoped that traces of Shakespeare might be discerned, in which case it would probably have been clear to him that to publish Fletcher's name as co-author would merely facilitate the instant repudiation by his audience of his claim for Shakespeare—a repudiation which, in any event, seems to have followed despite the precaution. A similar repudiation would presumably follow his revelation or publication of the original manuscript, and to announce Fletcher's name would likewise have increased whatever pressure he may have felt—if only in his own mind—to disclose the original. In short, his only hope for even the slightest success with any claim for Shakespeare's presence would have been to make precisely the sweeping claim he did make. That he could not have believed in that claim himself is suggested by virtually every other act of commission or omission of which we have knowledge.

The financial expectations of the course he took—expectations fully realized —would by themselves suffice to make his behavior understandable. Venal as such behavior must seem, it might be noted that unless we assume Theobald thought there was little in the original text worth revealing apart from what he actually did transcribe, it is impossible to account for his behavior without imputing to him incomparably more reprehensible actions and motives than those suggested here—i.e. total fraud on the one hand, or total suppression of genuinely Shakespearean text on the other.

The newspaper advertising—unusual at the time—would no doubt be good business policy; it would also serve as a useful precaution in the event Theobald had overlooked, say, some other manuscript copy with a Fletcher attribution, for the invitation to the public to judge the Shakespeare claim for itself would constitute a virtual challenge to anyone who might possess other information to come forward. Similarly with the disclaimer of Fletcher in the preface—a precaution against being totally discredited if information connecting the play positively with Fletcher were ever independently brought forward. His alteration of the phrase "in our Tongue" in the first edition to "in that other great Poet" in the second, accompanied by his forswearing any intention to argue his claim for Shakespeare, comes close to an admission that he recognized his claim to be untenable and implies he had abandoned any hope of having his story fully credited; meanwhile it saved him from embarrassment or exposure by letting the issue continue to be joined merely on the lesser question of a Jacobean source— on which he evidently knew full well he could be believed without the need for further explanation. It would not be surprising if he then said no more about the matter and perhaps liquidated his manuscripts.

Motives, of course, are something we invent to explain puzzling behavior. This excursion into the mind of Lewis Theobald may well be regarded as fantastic; hardly any of the details are separately defensible. Yet his behavior can be explained along lines at least similar to those suggested, and the alternative possibilities lead to sheer confusion with respect both to Theobald and to *Cardenio*. On the one hand, to assume that Theobald cooked the whole thing up is virtually impossible.[14] But the opposite line of explanation, which involves giving Theobald's story even more credit than the account just offered treats as acceptable, was once argued in the 1920's, and some of its premises survive—perhaps unwittingly—in present-day scholarship.

Alternative Arguments

In 1927 E. H. C. Oliphant advanced an ingenious defense of Theobald's veracity and fair-dealing on all matters connected with his *Double False-hood*. The most telling point in Oliphant's account links together two independent items—Theobald's repudiation of Fletcher in his preface and his probable ignorance of the Moseley entry:

Moseley help[s] to make plain to us the honesty of Theobald. The latter . . . was ignorant that the names of Fletcher and Shakespeare had ever been connected in a play on the subject of Cervantes' story. How can it be supposed that he would otherwise have failed to make much of the fact, or that, when his enemies and critics pointed out that "the coloring, diction, and characters" were "nearer to the style and manner of Fletcher" than to those of Shakespeare, he should have so indignantly denied the correctness of their view? What a feast for those who see nothing but irony in life to note how Theobald's enemies, in attacking his honesty, have helped to prove it, and how Theobald, equally ignorant of the facts, violently repudiated these proofs! To us the admission of Fletcher's presence in *Double Falsehood* is a long step toward its identification with *Cardenio,* and consequently toward Shakespeare's connection with it.[15]

Whether or not they bear in mind Theobald's assertion that his revised text would suffice to make of Dodington another Southampton, lovers of irony may find themselves hard put to it to accept the view that Theobald was a respectable and honest nincompoop who was fully persuaded that he possessed a Shakespearean original, and at the same time an unwitting scoundrel who throughout his distinguished career disdained to reveal a single passage from it. Irony too requires coherence, and we might credit Theobald with more intelligence than his single whole-hearted advocate finds in his

---

[14] The issue seems to have been closed when Graham confirmed Bradford's source argument, but if anyone should wish to excogitate the theory that Theobald invented the play without reference to a *Cardenio* manuscript, he would presumably have to begin by assuming that Theobald learned in some fashion that Shakespeare's name had been associated with a play on the Cardenio story, go on to argue that Theobald then worked up an original play from the Shelton translation and that in it he imitated Fletcher, etc.

[15] Oliphant, *The Plays of Beaumont and Fletcher* (1927), p. 289.

behavior. Nor is Oliphant plausible when he gives credit to metrical distinctions in a text he is forced to describe as so "badly mangled" that only "a few odd lines bearing some resemblance" to Shakespeare are to be found in it:

Printed as prose [in *Double Falsehood*] is a sentence more like Shakespeare than any one else:

> Not love, but brutal violence prevail'd,
> To which the time and place and opportunity
> Were accessories most dishonorable.
>
> (II.i)

The use of "heirs" as a verb (I.i) also seems to point to Shakespeare. And, finally, let me quote a passage from III.i which it requires some boldness to quote, since it contains the famous line denounced by Pope as being too bathetical to be by any possibility Shakespeare's:

> Is there a treachery like this in baseness
> Recorded anywhere? It is the deepest;
> None but itself can be its parallel.
> And from a friend professed! Friendship? Why, 'tis
> A word for ever maimed: in human nature
> It was a thing the noblest, and 'mong beasts
> It stood not in mean place: things of fierce nature
> Hold amity and concordance. Such a villainy
> A writer could not put down in his scene
> Without taxation of his auditory
> For fiction most enormous.

I have not at hand, for quotation, Theobald's defense of the line which Pope ridiculed ["None . . . parallel"]; but he is stated by Lounsbury to have shown conclusively "that this particular line selected for animadversion was not different in character from several others to be found" in Shakespeare.

(p. 297)

Oliphant's quotations are ludicrous, but his argument (that Theobald's ignorance of the Moseley entry validated his repudiation of Fletcher) was taken seriously by later scholars—among them Sir Edmund Chambers.

When Chambers summarized his findings on the *Cardenio* question in *William Shakespeare,* he made clear that the feeble writing throughout *Double Falsehood* rendered the claim to detect Shakespearean survivals exceptionally difficult to credit: "while I can see traces that may well be Fletcher's, I cannot find a single passage which compels a belief in Shakespeare" (I, 542). Chambers was nevertheless reluctant to trust his own literary judgment in this matter. Three considerations seem to have kept open for him the possibility of Shakespeare's participation in *Cardenio*. One, of course, was his assumption of dual authorship in *The Two Noble Kinsmen* and *Henry VIII*. A second seems to have been the Oliphant argument about the Moseley entry:

It is, of course, most unlikely that Theobald knew anything of the *Cardenio* record [of performances at court in 1612–13], and to some extent, therefore, that supports his story. Similarly, he cannot have known of Moseley's entry, since he repudiates Fletcher.

That Theobald's denial of the presence of Fletcher in the play was to be regarded as perfectly sincere, despite the fact that virtually no one believed it to be true, naturally led Chambers to find the entire record of Theobald's behavior a sheer "mystification"; the unnecessary link between Theobald's denial and his probable ignorance of the Moseley entry is perhaps the principal cause that the subject has not yet been closed—as might be inferred from the final sentence (q.v.) in the Greg summary quoted earlier (pages 180–181). There is, however, an important third consideration. Bradford, Graham, and Oliphant had argued that Theobald's revising and adapting would satisfactorily explain the paucity of evidence for Shakespeare. Chambers, dismayed by the metrical statistics as well as by the Theobald play, nevertheless felt constrained, presumably because he had accepted the repudiation-of-Fletcher argument, to accept this invisible-evidence argument as well—although, ironically, his acceptance is phrased as a somewhat despairing admonition against such procedures as those followed by Oliphant:

But what possible criterion can distinguish, through the veil of adaptation, second- or third-rate work of Shakespeare from that of a contemporary disciple, or even from what Theobald himself, with his mind steeped in Shakespeare, might write.

Perhaps both Chambers and Greg, however, might have come to different conclusions regarding *Cardenio* if they, or any of the previous scholars who studied *Cardenio,* had brought to bear on this question some serious consideration of what is actually to be found in genuine adaptations of Shakespeare.

No doubt most readers are to some extent aware of the butcheries that took place in most Restoration and eighteenth-century adaptations of Shakespeare, although perhaps the only widely familiar passage from the text of these plays (since it is reprinted in Brooks and Warren's *Understanding Poetry*) is the passage in *Macbeth* beginning "Tomorrow and tomorrow and tomorrow" as revised by Davenant. The reader may recall that even in that mangled rationalization Davenant preserves a great deal of the original, and that the closing lines (from "Life's but a walking shadow" through "signifying nothing") are in fact retained without change. Most of the dramatic adaptations, for all their absurdities, likewise preserve a substantial share of the dialogue from the originals on which they are based. And scholars who have examined Theobald's one adaptation from Shakespeare, *Richard II,* have almost invariably noted (but without reference to the *Cardenio* question) its unusual fidelity to the original.[16] Theobald's alterations are considerable—most of Shakespeare's first two acts, for example, are scrapped—but Theobald preserves more than most adapters, and well over half of his text, in fact, consists of dialogue taken over virtually unaltered from Shakespeare. If Shakespeare's play had been lost, one would still be able to identify the slightly altered deposition scene in Theobald's version, for example, as his.[17] With regard to the point at issue, one cannot insist that much Shakespeare would inevitably survive a process of revision, but one might at least distinguish between probabilities: after the Paris première of *Apollon Musagète,* a Russian aristocrat protested to Balanchine, "Where did you ever see Apollo on his knees?" and to this Balanchine rejoined, "Where did *you* ever see Apollo?" No matter how much revision by Theobald we may choose to assume took place, no matter how vapid we may choose to assume a late piece of writing by Shakespeare to have been—and the improbability of each assumption increases in direct proportion to the weight we allow it—there ought to be something better than the Oliphant conjecture, which serves only to make Theobald's behavior inexplicable, and something better than the inverted reading of the textual evidence in *Double Falsehood,* to justify the still prevalent assumption that Shakespeare collaborated with Fletcher on *Cardenio.* But to

---

[16] Performed in 1719, *Richard II* "Alter'd from Shakespear, by Mr. Theobald" was printed in 1720. A good description of the adaptation appears in George C. D. Odell, *Shakespeare from Betterton to Irving* (1920), I, 241–243. Critics since Geneste have regularly mentioned that over half of the play consists of unaltered Shakespearean dialogue; the point is made, for example, by Odell, p. 243; by Jones, *Lewis Theobald,* p. 22; by E. B. Koster, "Lewis Theobald," *English Studies,* IV (1922), 23. When Jones came to discuss *Cardenio* on a later page in his study of Theobald, he censured Graham for omitting "what should not be omitted in any discussion" of *Double Falsehood,* "namely, the . . . adaptation of *Richard II*" (p. 105 n.), but Jones was simply ignored by Oliphant and his brief note failed to attract the attention it deserved. But cf. pp. 194–195 below.

[17] From Richard's "To do what service am I sent for hither?" at IV.i.176 until his exit at l. 318, Theobald (1720 text, pp. 32–36) cuts about fifteen lines and, in the remaining 130, makes a dozen or so minor changes (e.g. 203 *Now* becomes *Yet*) and about half a dozen slightly larger ones (e.g. 302 *I'll beg one boon* becomes *I've but one suit*); one speech is reassigned (ll. 177–180 are given to Northumberland).

expect opinions on disputes concerning Shakespeare to be rationally grounded may be to expect miracles.

One article on our present subject has appeared since the publication of the Greg summary.[18] Kenneth Muir has defended the accepted view of *Cardenio* with such consummate skill that he has led at least one careful and unbiased reader—a typically uninformed reader, however—to his "tentative conclusion of Shakespeare's responsibility for the first three acts, the last two being given to Fletcher." [19] Having read *Double Falsehood,* Muir must naturally suppose "it would be vain to expect any certain traces of Shakespeare" (p. 206). Hence he begins as follows:

> A play entitled *Cardenio* was acted at Court by the King's Men in 1613; and this was ascribed by Humphrey Moseley, when he entered it . . . in 1653, to 'Mr. Fletcher and Shakespeare'. The assumption was a reasonable one since Shakespeare and Fletcher had collaborated about the same time in *The Two Noble Kinsmen,* and (many critics believe) in *Henry VIII.*

It must be to Moseley that Muir's careful prose ascribes "the" assumption. Since Moseley was a notoriously careless busy man, and known to have been dishonest as well, his advertisements in 1653 and 1654 attributing *The Two Noble Kinsmen* to Beaumont and Fletcher—despite the title-page— are not perhaps of much significance, but they do make the ascription to him of Muir's own "reasonable . . . assumption" seem rather daring. So does the absence of any indication that Fletcher collaborated with Shakespeare on *Henry VIII* or that anyone thought so before the Spedding attack on that play in 1850; neither Spedding nor most of his followers, for that matter, have thought *Henry VIII* an active collaboration—they have insisted that Fletcher worked up Shakespearean left-overs—and the "many critics" referred to by Muir comprise the multitude of unconcerned scholars upon whom Spedding and Furnivall imposed.

Muir goes on to construct—out of a detailed comparison between *Double Falsehood* and Shelton's Cervantes, out of a Fletcher-like passage in Theobald's play, and so forth—an impressive and lengthy argument (pp. 202– 205) for the generally conceded point that Theobald was following an older manuscript. In the course of his exposition Muir introduces, but does not discuss, the point given currency by Oliphant: "if he [Theobald] had known of Moseley's entry he would have used it to support the play's authenticity,

[18] Muir, "Cardenio," *Études anglaises,* XI (1958), 202–209. Reprinted in Muir, *Shakespeare as Collaborator* (1960).

[19] *Abstracts of English Studies,* I (1958), 381. Points left by Muir in the form of strong implication are accurately translated by the anonymous abstracter into direct statement.

rather than have denied that Fletcher had had a hand in it" (p. 205). This confident assertion is welded to the early-manuscript argument in the final summary; Muir's last paragraph, although it opens with the useful concession that "it is clearly impossible to come to any definite conclusions about *Double Falsehood*," moves at once to conclusions that seem reasonably definite:

. . . but it seems more likely that Theobald was working on an old manuscript than that he knew of Moseley's entry of *Cardenio*. . . . If indeed he had one or more manuscripts, there would be strong reason to believe that *Double Falsehood* was a debased version of *Cardenio*, and equally strong reasons for believing that the original authors were Shakespeare and Fletcher. With few exceptions, critics have endeavoured to escape from this conclusion.

Muir must be referring to endeavors left unpublished; his own view has prevailed, if not since Bradford, at least since Oliphant.

Muir's arguments include the metrical statistics compiled by Graham—given without indicating Graham's lines of division between authors (different from Muir's) but looking very precise nonetheless. They also include the citation of one passage from the text which strikes Muir as "genuinely Elizabethan, . . . definitely not Fletcherian, . . . [and] either Shakespearian or a remarkably clever imitation" (p. 208)—the first ten lines of this speech in I.ii:

> I do not see that Fervour in the Maid,
> Which Youth and Love should kindle. She consents,
> As 'twere to feed without an Appetite;
> Tells me, She is content; and plays the Coy one,
> Like Those that subtly make their Words their Ward,
> Keeping Address at Distance. This Affection
> Is such a feign'd One, as will break untouch'd;
> Dye frosty, e'er it can be thaw'd; while mine,
> Like to a Clime beneath *Hyperion*'s Eye,
> Burns with one constant Heat. I'll strait go to her;
> Pray her to regard my Honour: but She greets me. . . .
> I was about to seek thee, *Leonora*,
> And chide thy Coldness, Love.

Perhaps more important, Muir's arguments include incidental reference to one new item. The first to mention Theobald's adaptation of *Richard II* in an essay designed to show that Shakespeare was involved in *Cardenio*, Muir makes a rather curious use of it. At one point in his discussion he says of Theobald—

It is a calamity, if he really possessed an authentic Shakespearian manuscript, that he should have published only a version which was avowedly altered, and which was probably as much a perversion as his revisions of other Elizabethan plays . . .

(p. 204)

—and Muir then inserts the following footnote:

Theobald claimed that he had written the passage [*DF* I.iii]:

> *Strike up, my Masters;*
> *But touch the Strings with a religious Softness:*
> *Teach sound to languish on thro' Night's dull Ear,*
> *Till Melancholy start from her lazy Couch,*
> *And Carelessness grow Convert to Attention.*

There are some passages as good as this in Theobald's adaptation of *Richard II*. In this version he eliminates the first two acts of Shakespeare's play, though he salvages some of the more famous lines [i.e. from Acts I and II] and gives them to other characters. He adds a love interest—Aumerle loves Lady Piercy and is executed for conspiracy against Bolingbroke. The speech at the end of Act I gives a favourable idea of Theobald's talents as a poet:

> *Thou chid'st me well,*
> *For setting up my Rest in giddy State,*
> *And Ostentation of despised Empire.*
> *By Heav'n, I want no kingdom, having thee. . . .*
>   [Eight more lines are given by Muir, as good as the nine
>   already quoted; the note then concludes as follows:]

But *Richard II* contains no passages added by Theobald as good as the best in *Double Falsehood*, and none which strike the reader as effectively Shakespearian.

In the unlikely event that Muir's reader were to wonder, as he read this tricky note, how much Shakespeare survived in Theobald's *Richard II*, he would probably guess, wrongly, that if it had amounted to anything significant, Muir would surely have mentioned it.

Conclusion

Since the arguments presented by Oliphant and Muir have not been subjected to proper scrutiny, *Cardenio* has persisted as a live issue to the present day. The lingering belief in Shakespeare's co-authorship, as we have observed, is based primarily upon four assumptions:

(1) That Shakespeare and Fletcher collaborated on *Henry VIII* and *The Two Noble Kinsmen* near the time *Cardenio* was first acted. (This assumption is dealt with in other chapters.)

(2) That Theobald's *Double Falsehood* was based on *Cardenio*. (This assumption is very probably correct.)

(3) That the absence of dialogue in *Double Falsehood* that can seriously be claimed for Shakespeare is due to a sweeping revision of *Cardenio* by Theobald. (This rationalization for the absence of evidence is not only a flagrant instance of *petitio principii;* it also goes against the evidence of Theobald's behavior elsewhere, and it requires the further supposition that Theobald would purge his manuscript of precisely that evidence he most needed to support his public claims about the play.)

(4) That Theobald's denial of Fletcher's connection with *Double Falsehood* tends to validate the 1653 Moseley attribution of *Cardenio* to Shakespeare and Fletcher. (Instead of proving that Theobald was ignorant of any connection between Fletcher and *Cardenio,* this illogical argument serves only to inhibit any satisfactory explanation of the entire *Double Falsehood* affair.)

The persistency with which *Cardenio* survives in serious studies of Shakespeare does little credit to Shakespearean scholarship. Theobald's behavior is easily intelligible on the hypothesis of Jones and others that his repudiation of Fletcher was insincere, and the most reasonable position with respect to the authorship of *Cardenio* is that, whoever wrote the play, Shakespeare had nothing to do with it.

V

The Readers of
The Two Noble Kinsmen

> Criticism cannot be appreciated without some understanding of the
> time and of the place in which it is written. . . . What we have to
> study is the whole pattern formed by Shakespeare criticism from his
> own time to ours.
>
> *Eliot*

One who reads *Hamlet* or *King Lear* does not normally proceed through
the play asking himself "Who wrote this speech?" or "Could Shakespeare
have written this scene?" When critics in the Robertson era did read plays
in this fashion, the results were often grimly destructive of dramatic values.
Since the eighteenth century most readers of *The Two Noble Kinsmen*
have, unfortunately, felt the pressure of such questions. Yet their recorded
responses *seen as a whole* can help to remove the distraction these questions
invariably cause. The present chapter deals with what many readers in the
past have observed in the play and with how they related what they observed
to the question of authorship. Among their observations were many verbal
resemblances between the text of the "Fletcher scenes" and the texts of
other plays, and we shall look at some of these resemblances in detail. By
the end of the chapter, hopefully, the reader should feel that he has been
given a reasonable picture of the entire critical history of the play—along
with a fresh opportunity to consider the dramatic workmanship of at least
a few of the scenes commonly ascribed to Fletcher.

Eighteenth-century Views

The views of eighteenth-century critics were excluded from Chapter I
since (apart from Seward's lineation) they had little effect on the division

of authorship. It may be noticed as we proceed that these critics did not, as later critics generally did, pass quickly over nearly all of the twelve scenes that came eventually to be assigned to Fletcher. Of the eight critics prior to Lamb who expressed views on the question of authorship, four require only brief mention. Pope's comments of 1725, including his intriguing reference to a "tradition" of Shakespeare's authorship, have already been recorded elsewhere (page 17); but his ascription of the entire play to Shakespeare seems to have been rather casual and was, in any case, left undefended. Six years later Theobald referred to the play (privately in a letter to Warburton) [1] as "Fletcher's Two Noble Kinsmen . . . , in the writing which Play Shakespeare assisted; and indeed his workmanship is very discoverable in a number of places." In 1747 Warburton himself remarked that the first act was written by Shakespeare, "but in his worst manner." [2] And in 1773 Richard Farmer, advocating a textual emendation for *Cymbeline* I.iii.37, brought into his discussion a parallel passage from the rose dialogue between Emilia and her Woman at II.ii.163–169 and referred to the passage as "those beautiful lines . . . which I have no doubt were written by *Shakespeare*." [3]

The other eighteenth-century critics—Seward, George Colman, Isaac Reed, George Steevens—deserve more space. Their chronology may be noted briefly. The comments of Seward in his 1750 edition provoked a cursory reply from Colman in the next Beaumont and Fletcher of 1778. To this latter edition Reed added a few footnotes. The most ambitious commentary of the period—in fact the most elaborate discussion of authorship prior to Spalding's *Letter* of 1833—was produced by Steevens, who offered it, not with a text of the play, but in company with his 1780 essay on *Pericles;* although frequently reprinted down to 1821, Steevens' analysis was generally disregarded by Spalding and later critics, but as we shall see it is not negligible.

Seward did not try to identify the authorship of every scene in the play, but he did defend several of his ascriptions with reasons and evidence of a genuinely literary character (as many of the metrical testers, for example, did not), and this circumstance, along with the fact that he was virtually the first to explore the problem, lends some interest to his observations. In order to make his more bizarre statements intelligible, we should first recall the widespread eighteenth-century belief in what Rowe called

---

[1] Letter of 18 Nov. 1731, printed in John Nichols, *Illustrations of the Literary History of the Eighteenth Century* (1817), II, 623.

[2] Warburton's edition of Shakespeare (1747), Vol. I, sig. e1.

[3] Steevens' Shakespeare (1773), Vol. X, sig. Qq3ᵛ.

the "almost universal . . . ignorance" of Shakespeare's age and, especially, in Shakespeare's own "ignorance of the ancients"; this parochial belief,[4] already explicit in Rowe's 1709 biography of Shakespeare and reaching its high-water mark in Farmer's 1767 *Essay on the Learning of Shakespeare,* evidently exerted considerable influence upon Seward. Thus when Seward saw in the offstage report of the combat between Palamon and Arcite in V.iii an example of the technique of Greek tragedy, it was normal for him, even though the scene recalled to him no particular passages in Shakespeare or Fletcher, to remember that Fletcher had attended a university and to reason therefrom that "as *Fletcher* was a Scholar and *Shakespear* not one in *Greek* the former was probably the Author here." [5] Similarly, as noted elsewhere (page 28), the sprinkling of Latin quotations in III.v, although to us they seem merely an obvious dramatic manifestation of Gerrold's pedantries, led Seward to suggest that Fletcher had "the greatest Share" of this scene too—even though he saw that the "Schoolmaster and his Fellow-Comedians seem very like the Farcical Clowns in *Midsummer-Night's Dream,* and other Plays of *Shakespear."* The remainder of Seward's scene-ascriptions and comments, however, were based more directly on what he knew of the text of Shakespeare and Fletcher.

The scene to which he gave most attention was II.ii; the dialogue of the kinsmen in prison recalled to him no less than five passages from other plays—including Mowbray's banishment speech (I.iii.159 ff.) and Richard's prison soliloquy (V.v.19 ff.) from *Richard II,* the Spartan hounds passage in *A Midsummer Night's Dream* (IV.i.107–131), and the dialogue from *Cymbeline* III.iii in which Guiderius and Arviragus "make . . . our cage . . . a quire, as doth the prison'd bird,/ And sing our bondage freely." These four passages inclined him to assign the scene to Shakespeare, but he hesitated because of a resemblance he saw between the prison dialogue and a speech in *The Lover's Progress,*[6] a play he had some reason to believe was by Fletcher. Malone and Chalmers had not yet published excerpts from Sir Henry Herbert's office book, and G. E. Bentley had not yet set that evidence in order; if they had, Seward might have been reassured to know that *The Lover's Progress* had undergone—in Bentley's

---

[4] On which cf. Peter Alexander, *Shakespeare's "Henry VI" and "Richard III"* (1929), pp. 120 ff.

[5] Seward's Beaumont & Fletcher (1750), X, 108. Seward's comments, scattered throughout his notes, are conveniently brought together in Colman's edition (1778), X, 118–121, and again in Weber's (1812), XIII, 151–155.

[6] Seward cited the 4th-act speech in which Lidian "describes the Happiness of Solitude" (beginning at "these wild fields are my gardens . . ."), Cambridge Beaumont & Fletcher, V (1907), 133.

words—a "thorough rewriting" by Massinger, and even that Massinger was probably at work on his new version during the month after *The Two Noble Kinsmen* was published.[7]

Seward's remaining comments on the scenes later credited to Fletcher were on the whole less precise than his citations of textual parallels to the prison dialogue. He thought that *"Shakespear* had a very great Hand in all the Acts of this Play, particularly in the whole charming Character of the *Jailor's Daughter,* or else that *Fletcher* more closely imitated him in this than in any other part of his Works," and in connection with Act IV he noted in the part of the Daughter "such characterising Strokes, and such strong Features of both *Ophelia* and *Lear* in their Phrensies, that one cannot but believe that the same Pencil drew them all." He also suggested, on the strength of the Prologue and Epilogue (for example, the modest promise of "many a better" play at Epilogue 16), that the play had been performed when Shakespeare was still alive, because "had *Fletcher* finish'd a Work of *Shakespear*'s, he would probably have spoke in a different Stile." Supportive evidence appears in several posthumous prologues to other King's company plays, such as those to *The Elder Brother* and *The Lover's Progress,* in which explicit tribute is paid to Fletcher's memory. One final comment of Seward's might be added—his opinion of the play:

The Play almost every where abounds with such sublimity of . . . Sentiment and Diction . . . that were the Beauties to be mark'd with Asterisms, after Mr. *Pope* and Mr. *Warburton*'s Manner, scarce a Page would be left uncover'd with them.

By the later nineteenth century this evaluation would be regarded as ludicrous; it was, nevertheless, representative of critical opinion for a long period of time, similar assessments of the play being expressed by editors and critics into the first half of the nineteenth century.

Since Colman held the play in almost as high esteem as Seward, his ascription of it to Beaumont and Fletcher is at first sight surprising, although his treatment of the authorship question was generally perfunctory. He could not ascribe the play to Fletcher alone because it seemed to him quite unlike those plays he held to be Fletcher's unaided work. Despite his

---

[7] Cf. Bentley, *Jacobean and Caroline Stage,* III (1956), 359–363. Bentley's detailed explanation of the complex evidence may be outlined briefly: *The Lover's Progress,* based on a 1623 play of Fletcher, was written by Massinger in the spring of 1634 and paid for at the rate of a new play; Massinger's prompt-book (apparently the copy for the printed text) was licensed by Herbert on 7 May. (Waterson had registered *TNK* on 8 April, presumably—like the Shakespeare Folio plays registered in November 1623—after printing was completed.) Cf. pp. 234–236 below.

general superiority to contemporary prejudice (he dismissed "Shakespeare's supposed want of erudition," for example, with appropriately casual contempt), he shared with most critics of his time an almost superstitious reverence for external authority in preference to internal literary evidence; he noted that the play had not been included in any of the Shakespeare Folios, and its presence in the 1679 Beaumont and Fletcher Folio was for him the strongest possible ground for ascribing it to "the same Authors." Shakespeare's name on the title-page of the 1634 quarto he put down to "the craft of a publisher," apparently in the conviction that a Caroline bookseller would inevitably appraise Shakespeare's name more highly than Fletcher's. The actual indications, although slight, are different; there is the matter of majority taste in the 1630's, when Fletcher was much more fashionable than Shakespeare; and there is the record of Waterson's transfer of the play to Moseley in 1646 attributing it, along with two other plays, to Fletcher alone (cf. page 15), suggesting that neither Waterson nor Moseley cared to make any special fuss over Shakespeare's name. Colman's treatment of the absence of the play from the 1623 Folio is interestingly expressed:

Had Shakespeare been considered as one of the joint Authors, is it not natural to suppose, that a play of so much excellence would have found a place in the Collection of his Dramas published by Hemings and Condell?

When in Victorian years facts came to speak for themselves, and in very firm voices too, critics who rejected or repudiated the play naturally regarded it as a self-evident fact that it had been "rejected" or "repudiated" by Heminge and Condell. The absence of the play from the Folio may eventually be considered along the lines of recent attempts to work out an improved explanation of the absence of *Pericles*,[8] but Colman's question offers the occasion to raise a related question. If it should become clear that the absence of the play from the Folio is not adequately accounted for merely by assuming collaboration—if, that is, in order to reconcile the distinct presence of Shakespeare in a good deal of the play with our respect

---

[8] Cf. Greg, *The Shakespeare First Folio* (1955), p. 98. The quarto of *Pericles* printed for Gosson in 1609 was apparently a "stolne and surreptitious" text derived from heterogeneous copy (part of which, as Sisson has shown, probably consisted of Shakespeare's foul papers) rather than from the prompt-book registered by Blount in 1608. Heminge and Condell, in view of their promise to provide true copies "perfect of their limbes" in the 1623 Folio, were presumably unwilling or unable to reprint this "maimed and deformed" text of 1609, and Greg suggests that the company prompt-book "may have gone astray after the performance at Whitehall in 1619, like that of the slightly later *Winter's Tale,* and have never [or at least not by 1623] been recovered."

for Heminge and Condell, we were forced to seek some other explanation than that they "knew" the play was not his—would its absence from the Folio not then appear to testify against, rather than to support, the Waterson title-page attribution to Fletcher? This purely speculative question is raised at this time merely to call attention to the point that many eighteenth-century critics saw no way in which an attribution of such long standing might be challenged; they were not prepared, for example, to recognize that after Waterson had secured his copyright the later transmission of the text would be determined quite without reference to literary evidence. Traditions grow in prestige merely by enduring.

Isaac Reed may have agreed with Colman's views on the authorship of the play, but one suspects otherwise. A few of Colman's notes to the 1778 edition drew quotations from other plays, usually Shakespeare's, for the ordinary purposes of glossing odd words or illustrating this or that unusual passage. The same edition, however, included a few other notes, initialed by Reed, in which the sole apparent purpose was to call attention to somewhat similar passages in plays of the Shakespeare canon. The two longest of these notes were attached to speeches concerning the Jailor's Daughter. Concerning the Wooer's narrative account of how he prevented the Daughter from drowning herself (IV.i.71–125), Reed's note remarked that "this description bears a striking resemblance" to Gertrude's lines on Ophelia's death (*Hamlet* IV.vii.167–184), and it quoted most of the passage to demonstrate his point. His other long note was appended to the Daughter's first soliloquy (II.iv.1–33) and cited part of Helena's first soliloquy in *All's Well that Ends Well* (I.i.90–109) for comparison. The resemblances to which Reed called attention impressed many later editors sufficiently to retain these notes even when they dropped most of Colman's. Later we shall return to these passages and make the comparisons Reed suggested. But this account must now turn to George Steevens and the highly unusual contributions he made to the authorship question.

The Steevens Theory

Steevens gave long and careful attention to the text of the play and came to the conclusion that it had been written entirely by Fletcher. His explanaion is a respectable piece of work, and if the reader has not encountered it before he may find it rewarding to examine despite its strange conclusion.[9]

[9] Steevens' essay first appeared in Malone's *Supplement to the Edition of Shakspeare . . . Published in 1778* (1780), II, 168–175, and was reprinted in Steevens' 1793 Shakespeare (XIII, 621–627), in Reed's 1803 and 1813 editions (XXI, 401–404 in both), in the

"An alert, shrewd and skittish scholar, enlivening his later editions with obscene annotations fathered facetiously on two respectable clergymen who had incurred his enmity" (J. Isaacs), Steevens could be depended upon for a cunningly constructed argument. His opening remarks on *The Two Noble Kinsmen* stressed external considerations:

This play . . . was not printed till eighteen years after the death of Shakspeare; and its title-page carries all the air of a canting bookseller's imposition. Would any one else have thought it necessary to tell the world, that Fletcher and his pretended coadjutor, were *"memorable worthies?"* The piece too was printed for one *John Waterson,* a man who had no copyright in any of our author's other dramas. It was equally unknown to the editors in 1623, and 1632; and was rejected by those in 1664, and 1685.—In 1661, *Kirkman,* another knight of *the rubrick post,* issued out *The Birth of Merlin,* by Rowley and *Shakspeare.* Are we to receive a part of this also as a genuine work of the latter? for the authority of *Kirkman* is as respectable as that of *Waterson.* . . . [Both cases exemplify] the craft or ignorance of these ancient *Curls* . . .

This spirited attack on Waterson, as we shall see, is later to be drastically modified by Steevens. His need to introduce his discussion with so vehement a repudiation of the title-page should then appear to have been forced upon him by the peculiarity of his principal argument:

The language and images of this piece coincide perpetually with those in the dramas of Shakspeare.

That the play is entirely by Fletcher because it seems so Shakespearean in language may seem a strange argument indeed, but a number of points about Steevens' explanation show him to be a skillful reasoner. "The same frequency of coincidence" with the language and images of Shakespeare, Steevens goes on,

occurs in no other individual of Fletcher's works; and how is so material a distinction to be accounted for? Did Shakspeare assist the survivor of Beaumont in his tragedy? Surely no; for if he had, he would . . . more studiously have abstained from the use of marked expressions in this than in any other of his pieces written without assistance. . . . It was his business to coalesce with Fletcher, and not to withdraw from him. But . . . let me ask where we are to look for any single dialogue in which these lines of separation are not drawn.

This last remark is strange and rather chilling; Steevens evidently assumes a unified play, wholly by Fletcher, with little bits and phrases of Shake-

Malone-Boswell Shakespeare of 1821 (XXI, 233–241), and in Weber's 1812 Beaumont & Fletcher (XIII, 157–165). Steevens' final revisions were incorporated in Reed's 1803 edition, the copy followed here.

spearean writing marked off by "lines of separation" in every dialogue. A little later it should be clear that Steevens is not cooking his argument but is reporting with perfect honesty his experience in reading the play. He goes on to say that if the examples of Shakespearean language and imagery

are to be regarded as landmarks to ascertain our author's property, they stand so constantly in our way, that we must adjudge the whole literary estate to him. [Note how suddenly this unthinkable thought vanishes.] I hope no one will be found who supposes our duumvirate sat down to correct what each other wrote. To such an indignity Fletcher could not well have submitted; and such a drudgery Shakspeare would as hardly have endured. . . .

But, that my assertions relative to coincidence may not appear without some support, I proceed to insert *a few of many instances* that might be brought in aid of an opinion which I am ready to subjoin. . . .

There follows a list of thirty-eight parallels (i.e. seventy-six passages, half from *The Two Noble Kinsmen*) with examples drawn from fifteen canonical plays. Fourteen of the parallels come from the twelve scenes assigned by the Victorians to Fletcher, and these are drawn from ten different canonical plays. Steevens gave only brief references to the passages—in connection with Arcite's speech on his banishment (II.iii.1–23), for example, he said merely "see the speech of *Romeo* on the same occasion" (*Romeo* III.iii.29 ff.)—but when "viewed in their natural situations" as he recommended, his parallels showed a degree of taste and sensitivity to style far superior to the kinds that went into the compilations of "Alas, sir's" and "to the height's" with which Victorian cranks brought the use of parallel-passage evidence into disrepute. The speeches of Arcite and Romeo will be reproduced later in our discussion; it is not Steevens' list of Shakespearean parallels itself, however, but the further inferences Steevens derived from the list that call for consideration at this time. Seldom before or since has anyone cited an elaborate list of Shakespearean parallels for the purpose of proving that Shakespeare had nothing to do with the work under investigation.

As an historical scholar Steevens had presumably thought more about the conditions of the Caroline period than Seward or Colman; it may have occurred to him that Fletcher's name would be a more likely candidate for a Caroline publisher's imposture than would Shakespeare's, and that this possibility might undercut his opening attack on Waterson's credibility. In any case, as his discussion continued he worked up an odd excuse for Waterson as an alternative to the earlier suggestion of deliberate fraud—namely, that the play was like enough to Shakespeare perhaps to have deluded some of the King's players themselves and that the players in turn may have thereby misinformed Waterson. A summary of Steevens' main arguments had best be given in his own words:

Let the criticks . . . who suppose [Shakespeare] . . . to have been so poor in language as well as ideas, that he was constrained to borrow . . . from above a dozen entire plays of his own composition, advance some hypothesis more plausible than the following; and yet I flatter myself that readers may be found who will concur with me in believing this tragedy to have been written by Fletcher in silent *imitation* of our author's manner. No other circumstance could well have occasioned such a frequent occurrence of corresponding phrases, &c.; nor . . . could any particular, but this, have induced the players to propagate the report, that our author was Fletcher's coadjutor in the piece.—There is nothing unusual in these attempts at imitation. Dryden, in his preface to *All for Love,* professes to copy the style of Shakspeare. Rowe, in his *Jane Shore,* arrogates to himself the merit of having pursued the same plan. How far these poets have succeeded, it is not my present business to examine; but Fletcher's imitation . . . is chiefly *verbal;* and . . . was perfect enough to have misled the judgment of the players . . . who . . . must have had much of Shakspeare's language recent in their memories. . . .

Noting that Theseus, Gerrold, the Countrymen, the Daughter, and the Doctor resembled other characters by Shakespeare, Steevens added that these resemblances constituted another factor leading the actors to

conclude that the play . . . was in part the production of the same writer. Over this line, the criticks behind the scenes were unable to proceed. Their sagacity was insufficient to observe that the general current of the style was even throughout the whole, and bore no marks of a divided hand.

Presumably the pressures of argument led Steevens to forget that by the time the play was published Heminge and Condell had been dead for several years and that the leading players in the King's company were those of a younger generation whose esteem for Fletcher would not easily have permitted such an error. As Lowin and Taylor testified in the preliminaries to *The Wild-Goose Chase* (1652), they looked back upon Fletcher as their "lost Friend, . . . th' *Grand Wheel* that set *Us* smaller Motions in Action! . . . the Pride and Life o'th'Stage! . . . *He* that gave us being [and] is no more."

All but one of the remaining points in Steevens' theory may simply be listed briefly. He rejected Colman's suggestion that Beaumont was connected with the play. He cited a dramatic contradiction in the Dryden-Lee *Oedipus* (1679) that escaped the attention of the collaborators in order to illustrate what he had looked for and been quite unable to find in *The Two Noble Kinsmen.* He said, although he knew no dating evidence, that he thought Fletcher must have written his imitation after the death of Shakespeare. He also remarked that it was "peculiarly apparent" that the quarto text had been printed from "a prompter's copy, as it exhibits such stage-directions as I do not remember to have seen in any other drama of the same period"; it might be added that, despite the relatively cursory attention Steevens must have given to such evidence (in comparison with that which now appears to be obligatory in professional scholarship), it is doubtful whether this remark would require any qualification today.

Before we look at the one remaining point in Steevens' theory, we might note of the theory as a whole that it does not insist upon manuscript interpolations, it does not demand that we imagine two actors declaiming hundreds of lines from an upper stage in the prison scene, it attaches no mystical significance to the number of syllables that Seward allotted to the line, and it entails no pledge of allegiance to Mrs. Grundy. Steevens also seems to have understood that knowledge is organic, that it is in one mind at a time or it is nowhere, and he tried to deal directly and rather comprehensively with a large body of very difficult evidence. One of his basic assumptions, however, was the plain impossibility that a complete play by Shakespeare had been visible to all eyes since 1634 with all eyes somehow blind to it. The notion still does, admittedly, seem rather strange. We might note in this connection how slowly professional students found themselves able to accept any part of the play as Shakespeare's. After Lamb and Coleridge had indorsed Shakespeare's partial authorship, one Shakespearean editor, forty years after Steevens' death, finally admitted the play to a volume of "doubtfully" Shakespearean works and made clear that he himself could accept none of it. Two centuries were required for the play to gain even partial acceptance from more than a very small number of able minds.

Steevens' final point involves a comparison with *Pericles,* which most eighteenth-century editors had rejected as non-Shakespearean. Malone in 1780 had readmitted *Pericles* to the canon and was willing at first to regard it wholly as Shakespeare's. In the essay on *Pericles* to which his analysis of *The Two Noble Kinsmen* was appended, Steevens dissuaded Malone from this view, arguing that only parts of the play (scattered through all five acts) had been written by Shakespeare. His final point about *The Two Noble Kinsmen* makes a distinction, ·puzzling but not inexplicable, between the language of that play and the language of *Pericles.* The language of both plays, Steevens says, "coincides" frequently with Shakespeare, but

Pericles . . . will not be found on examination to comprize a fifth part of the coincidences which may be detected in [*The Two Noble Kinsmen*] . . . ;

neither will a tenth division of the same relations be discovered in any one of his thirty-five dramas which have hitherto been published together.

In other words Steevens thought he saw only one-fifth as many verbal "co-incidences" or "relations" to canonical plays in *Pericles* as in *The Two Noble Kinsmen,* and ten times as many such relations in *The Two Noble Kinsmen* as in any single canonical play to the rest. That these were his actual observations may be believable if we take into account that he was highly suspicious of *Pericles* and perhaps (to borrow his arithmetic) five times as suspicious of *The Two Noble Kinsmen.* Probably neither play has much more or less Shakespearean reminiscence about it than might be found—if one were looking—in any other but the earliest of Shakespeare's plays. But again it is not Steevens' observations so much as the inferences he drew from them that concern us.

The paradoxical use to which Steevens put his own selection of evidence suggests it is not merely evidence or the lack of it that lies at the heart of the problem of authorship. His interpretations of the evidence he gathered from *Pericles* and *The Two Noble Kinsmen* were colored by his attitudes toward each play. Steevens was a notoriously severe critic who loathed what he professed to loathe (the Sonnets, for example) in language exhibiting much verbal coincidence with his reflections on booksellers. His feeling about *Pericles,* briefly, was that it was much too patchy and poor to be more than partly the work of Shakespeare, but he was willing to grant this much and to allow the play its place in editions of Shakespeare. It had a certain authority deriving from the 1609 title-page and from its inclusion in the Third and Fourth Folios; only one name, Shakespeare's, was attached to it; Malone, a friend, had held that it was entirely by Shakespeare; it was being read and talked about by scholars known to Steevens, a circumstance which reflection suggests is probably worth a dozen title-pages. In other words, Steevens observed the evidence for Shakespeare's hand in *Pericles* within what might be termed a frame of familiarity, and he therefore found this evidence, as he put it, "irresistible." He looked harder and closer to observe what he reported to be five times the same kinds of evidence in *The Two Noble Kinsmen,* but to this Shakespearean authority the play was an alien object to which title resided in the Fletcher estate. What is especially notable in his behavior toward the two plays is that, in rejecting *The Two Noble Kinsmen,* he found no specific fault with it; he even in-dorsed the reputation which, as he said, it "has so long and so indisputably maintained." But while he must have become intimately familiar with the play in order to produce his long list of parallels, and while he was a more intelligent and sensitive reader than most of the little foxes of the New Shakspere Society, he must have become acquainted with it in some strange way which alienated him from it—much as Eliot was put off by *Hamlet* when he was led to worry about its authorship. Steevens' praise of the play was consequently rather cool. To search through and beyond a text for the identity of its author inhibits one's search for its internal interrelationships. Steevens' theory provides a clear model of what happens when a critic recognizes strikingly Shakespearean language in a play he "knows" is not by Shakespeare, and it provides a more general model of the curious inhibitions of response to any text which for one reason or another is approached as suspect. A reader's attitude is surely as important as his knowledge.

The Psychological Problem

The most open-minded reader who encounters some Shakespearean turn of phrase in a supposedly non-Shakespearean scene of *The Two Noble Kinsmen* is apt to be highly suspicious of it. For instance, when he encounters the phrase "thereby hangs a tale" at III.iii.54 (to cite a trivial example for the sake of simplicity), he may be startled into recalling the same phrase from his reading of Shakespeare, and his reaction might be to interpret the repetition much as Steevens and many later critics interpreted more numerous and more complex examples—i.e. as a deliberate imitation or borrowing (or perhaps as an unconscious echo) on the ground that Shakespeare seldom repeats himself. So astute a critic as Clifford Leech has recently argued that "the echoing of Shakespeare is so evident in many passages" of *The Two Noble Kinsmen* "that we cannot possibly credit him with their authorship."[10] The reader referred to a moment ago may or may not be aware that "thereby hangs a tale" occurs in no less than four plays of the canon and that the same pun occurs in all five instances; for he is not ordinarily alerted by a problem of authorship to pay attention to Shakespeare's fairly extensive repetitions or near-repetitions, and whenever he does momentarily notice them he probably fits each example silently into its immediate dramatic context and forgets about it.

At some point, however, a reader may become aware of such pervasively Shakespearean language in one or another scene of the play that a theory of Fletcher imitating or echoing Shakespeare will no longer satisfy him. Hart-

---

[10] Leech, *The John Fletcher Plays* (1962), p. 146. Leech reluctantly concedes Shakespeare's authorship of only two scenes in the play—I.i and V.i—and describes them as "easily detachable" from the rest (p. 153)!

ley Coleridge is one reader who started out with such a theory and then modified it. Coleridge noted that Emilia's dialogue with Hippolyta about her childhood friendship with Flavina (I.iii.57–96) was so like the "dialogue of maiden friendship" between Helena and Hermia in *A Midsummer Night's Dream* (III.ii.192–221) as to have led some readers to believe it was by Shakespeare; in a marginal note in his copy of Stockdale's Shakespeare he called the passage from *The Two Noble Kinsmen* "a better piece of writing" than Helena's speech, but he added that "it was not Shakspeare's way to emulate himself" and he called the resemblance *"primâ facie* evidence that it is not Shakspeare's." [11] His long note concluded, however, with these words:

Still it must be confessed that if Fletcher did write the speech of Emilia, he has imitated Shakspeare's diction and versification very closely.

And later, after further reading and reflection, he added the following:

P.S. I am now convinced that the scene in the *Two Noble Kinsmen* is Shakspeare's.

A process of thought much like that recorded in Coleridge's informal note must be supposed to lie behind many of the more formal critical statements on the problem of authorship. A case very much in point is that of Charles Lamb, whose reaction to the Steevens theory helped directly or indirectly to shape the responses of most subsequent critics of the play. Lamb comes next.

Lamb and His Influence

Lamb's celebrated comparisons of Shakespeare and Fletcher appeared among the notes which he subjoined to the dramatic extracts included in his popular and often reprinted *Specimens of English Dramatic Poets, Who Lived about the Time of Shakspeare* (1808). The note to *The Maid's Tragedy,* for example, contained his famous dictum that "Beaumont and Fletcher were but an inferior sort of Shakspeares and Sidneys." One of his two more elaborate comparisons appeared in his comment on *The Two Noble Kinsmen.* The play was described in *Specimens* as "a tragedy by John Fletcher" (this was the first appearance of the play since 1634 outside a collection of Fletcher's work), and a note added that "Fletcher is said to have been assisted in this Play by Shakspeare." Lamb excerpted three passages—part of the opening scene (I.i.25–243), the speech by Emilia that

[11] Hartley Coleridge, *Essays and Marginalia* (1851), II, 137–138.

later attracted Hartley Coleridge (I.iii.57–92), part of the prison dialogue between the kinsmen (II.ii.1–118)—and his comment, stimulated in part by his reading of Steevens, came after the third:

This scene [II.ii] bears indubitable marks of Fletcher: the two which precede it [I.i and I.iii] give strong countenance to the tradition that Shakspeare had a hand in this play. The same judgment may be formed of the death of Arcite [Pirithous' speech in V.iv], and some other passages, not here given. They have a luxuriance in them which strongly resembles Shakspeare's manner in those parts of his plays where, the progress of the interest being subordinate, the poet was at leisure for description. I might fetch instances from Troilus and Timon. That Fletcher should have copied Shakspeare's manner through so many entire scenes (which is the theory of Mr. Steevens) is not very probable, that he could have done it with such facility is to me not certain. His ideas moved slow; his versification, though sweet, is tedious, it stops every moment; he lays line upon line, . . . adding image to image so deliberately that we see where they join: Shakspeare mingles every thing, he runs line into line . . . ; before one idea has burst its shell, another is hatched and clamorous for disclosure. . . .

Weber reprinted this note in 1812, Spalding and Hickson drew upon it later, and Spedding also referred to it (in his October 1850 reply to Hickson's letter) as one of two guides—the other being Spalding's essay—which "admirably explained" the distinctions requisite for a stylistic analysis of the two hands he had counted in *Henry VIII*. In his original essay on that play (in August 1850), Spedding had already cited Lamb's other extended comparison between Shakespeare and Fletcher, the note on *Thierry and Theodoret,* concerned with morals as well as metrics:

I have always considered this [IV.i] to be the finest scene in Fletcher, and Ordella the most perfect idea of the female heroic character, next to Calantha in the Broken Heart of Ford, that has been embodied in fiction. She is a piece of sainted nature. Yet noble as the whole scene is, it must be confessed that the manner of it, compared with Shakspeare's finest scenes, is slow and languid. Its motion is circular, not progressive. Each line revolves on itself in a sort of separate orbit. . . . Another striking difference perceivable between Fletcher and Shakspeare, is the fondness of the former for unnatural and violent situations. . . . He seems to have thought that nothing great could be produced in an ordinary way. . . . Shakspeare had nothing of this contortion in his mind, none of that craving after romantic incidents, and flights of strained and improbable virtue, which I think always betrays an imperfect moral sensibility.

Lamb himself is a piece of sainted nature in his way, and however antidramatic his attempt to approach the personalities of the dramatists through their work, it is easy to see the appeal his distinctions must have made to nineteenth-century interest in individual character and nineteenth-century concern for pattern only insofar as it related to inner moral growth. It is less easy to see, however, that Fletcher ever tried to produce "nature" or develop characters "naturally" in his plays,[12] and if we were to retain Lamb's Shakespearean criterion and to abandon only a little of his gravity we should probably find the scene from *Thierry and Theodoret* quite as "strained and improbable" as anything in Fletcher's tragicomedies (it is the scene in which Thierry unknowingly selects his own wife Ordella for sacrifice). We are not at the moment as concerned, however, with nineteenth-century misreadings of Fletcher as we are with the treatment meted out to *The Two Noble Kinsmen*.

Coleridge added little to what Lamb had already said, but his views were complementary to Lamb's, they naturally carried weight with many readers, and they ought perhaps to be recorded at this point. His first comment, written after 1811, appeared in his "Notes on Beaumont and Fletcher":

> On comparing the prison scene of Palamon and Arcite, Act ii. sc. 2, with the dialogue between the same speakers, Act i. sc. 2, I can scarcely retain a doubt as to the first act's having been written by Shakspeare. Assuredly it was not written by B. & F. . . .
>
> The main presumption . . . for Shakspeare's share in this play rests on a point, to which the sturdy critics of this [Colman] edition (and indeed all before them) were blind,—that is, the construction of the blank verse, which proves beyond all doubt an intentional imitation, if not the proper hand, of Shakspeare. Now, whatever improbability there is in the former, (which supposes Fletcher conscious of the inferiority . . . of his versification, and of which there is neither proof, nor likelihood,) adds so much to the probability of the latter. . . .[13]

And a later remark by Coleridge in the *Table Talk*—"I have no doubt whatever that the first act and the first scene of the second act of the Two Noble Kinsmen are Shakspeare's"[14]—gave encouragement to Hickson when he revised Spalding's division and assigned II.i to Shakespeare.

Lamb and Coleridge were thus instrumental in gaining general acceptance of Shakespeare's presence in the play. That would seem to have been their purpose. At the same time, of course, they were in effect sanctioning the establishment of a division between authors and they were selecting the prison dialogue as a prime example of Fletcher's style. From Spalding to

[12] For an illuminating discussion of the deliberate "artificiality" in Fletcher's plays, cf. Arthur Mizener, "The High Design of *A King and No King*," *MP*, XXXVIII (1940), 133–154.

[13] *Literary Remains of Samuel Taylor Coleridge,* ed. Henry Nelson Coleridge, II (1836), 320–321.

[14] *Specimens of the Table Talk,* ed. H. N. Coleridge (1835), II, 119.

Hickson to Littledale to Theodore Spencer, critics seeking to illustrate Fletcher's style in the play have usually drawn their principal (usually their only) examples from this scene. But at this point we shall have to give further and final notice to James Spedding, since it was he who brought about what once appeared to be a genuine simplification in the task of identifying the work of Fletcher.

Spedding is in many respects the pivotal figure in this history; his essay links the discussions of versification by his predecessors with the metrical apparatus developed by his followers. His own tendency to derive particular facts of style from previously established general principles may be exemplified by his bizarre description of the language in *Henry VIII* I.iii as "diffuse and languid"—a description owing more to Lamb's remark about the "slow and languid" versification of Fletcher than to anything in the scene itself. In his scientific pursuit of the noumena of style Spedding resembles the curious chap who wanted to distinguish between a head of lettuce and a head of cabbage and, rejecting sight and taste as too subjective, proceeded to take measurements of their diameters. By tacitly identifying rhythm with meter Spedding was able to divorce discussion of style from discussion of meaning, and his rule that a certain proportion of double-ended lines indicated the hand of Fletcher made it possible for the New Shakspere Society to freeze all inquiry into the twelve scenes of *The Two Noble Kinsmen* that its metrical statistics were thought to have proved "certainly Fletcher's"—although they did not prevent Boyle and Furnivall from reassigning the "Shakespeare scenes" in both this play and *Henry VIII* to Massinger. Ironically, the application of Spedding's principle to the text (the traditionally mislined text) of *The Two Noble Kinsmen,* if it had been carried out accurately by Fleay or Littledale after they collected their scene-by-scene statistics, would have called for the reassignment of four or five of the twelve "Fletcher scenes" to Shakespeare; with a more accurately edited text the same principle would have required the reassignment of another four scenes to Shakespeare; even on the most mindless metrical grounds alone, that is, there are no more than three or four scenes in *The Two Noble Kinsmen* that satisfy Spedding's mechanical criterion of double endings in over half the lines. By way of writing a final epitaph on the Spedding-Fleay-Furnivall operation, it should be added that the incidence of double or triple endings in Fletcher's plays seldom seems to fall as low as a mere fifty percent.[15] But such points would hold sig-

---

[15] Although accurate statistics have never been published, Tucker Brooke's observation seems to correspond roughly with what one usually encounters in Fletcher's work: "Fletcher early developed an individual type of blank verse, marked by an enormous

nificance only to a Victorian. Spedding's influence on studies of *The Two Noble Kinsmen,* however, goes far beyond metrical matters; for critics from Littledale to Theodore Spencer, wanting to confirm Fletcher's presence through textual comparisons between this play and "known" work of Fletcher, have regularly drawn upon passages from *Henry VIII,* rather than from plays genuinely by Fletcher, to supply their illustrations.[16] The circularity of the argument owes its life to Spedding.

Lamb was the first to point to metrical criteria as a means of establishing divided authorship, and he was also the first to point to moral criteria for this purpose. The Victorian critics, as we have seen, were no less skillful in constructing their moral apparatus than in producing their metrical tests. Perhaps the subtlest of all the moralist critics was Boyle, and this recapitulation of nineteenth-century developments might well conclude with a brief and fascinating example of the arguments with which Boyle (in the New Shakspere Society *Transactions* of 1882) tried to establish Massinger as co-author of *The Two Noble Kinsmen.* In the opening scene the First Queen begs Theseus to proceed at once against Creon, because if he first goes through with his marriage to Hippolyta,

> Our suit shall be neglected; when her arms,
> Able to lock Jove from a synod, shall
> By warranting moonlight corslet thee—oh, when
> Her twinning cherries shall their sweetness fall
> Upon thy tasteful lips, what wilt thou think
> Of rotten kings or blubber'd queens? what care
> For what thou feel'st not? what thou feel'st being able
> To make Mars spurn his drum. Oh, if thou couch
> But one night with her, every hour in't will
> Take hostage of thee for a hundred . . .

> (I.i.196–205)

Boyle argued that Shakespeare could not have written this passage because, he said, it shows the First Queen "gloating over her unclean reminiscences" (p. 383).

A short summary might be in order. The play began its critical career firmly rooted in the Fletcher canon. As it came in for formal professional

---

proportion (*c.*90 percent) of end-stopped lines and an unprecedented number (*c.*70 percent) of double or treble endings" (Baugh *et al., A Literary History of England* [1948], p. 574).

[16] Spencer, for example, although he had examined several genuine plays of Fletcher in his 1936 *Death and Elizabethan Tragedy,* seized upon Wolsey's address to Cromwell in *Henry VIII* for a passage to compare with the cousins' prison dialogue in *TNK* (*MP,* XXXVI [1939], 264–265).

study, critics noted various Shakespearean features about it which led them first to regard it as an instance of Fletcher deliberately imitating Shakespeare. As critics became more familiar and at ease with the play, they abandoned the imitation theory and felt more confidence in ascribing certain scenes to Shakespeare outright. By 1847 Hickson had claimed for Shakespeare twelve rather widely distributed scenes. After Spedding introduced the issue of *Henry VIII* Furnivall's industrialization of scholarship seems to have overtaken the study of the play. The reader is already familiar with the principal later developments. By the time of the Littledale edition there was widespread agreement that "the only valid hypothesis" was that Fletcher had completed a fragmentary play left behind by Shakespeare. Then followed the scholarly era during which critics debated whether Massinger or Shakespeare had written the "non-Fletcherian" scenes. By 1930 Chambers was able to dismiss both the Victorian theory of dramatic construction and the Massinger arguments, regarding the play rather as a simultaneous collaboration between Fletcher in London and Shakespeare possibly "at a distance" (meaning perhaps that Shakespeare sent his share from retirement in Stratford).[17] Chambers and most present-day critics, however, have been somewhat vague about the precise kind of collaboration they imagine to have taken place.

The assumption of Fletcher's presence in the text, whatever its origins, has of course been many times defended on literary grounds. The remainder of this chapter will be concerned mainly with several of the underplot scenes in the play and with the non-metrical observations on these scenes by various representative critics. The observations of the nineteenth- and twentieth-century critics should eventually be seen to connect surprisingly well with the comments of Lamb's predecessors reviewed earlier.

The Wooer's Narrative

We might consider first the resemblances urged by Isaac Reed between the Wooer's account of the Daughter's attempted suicide and Gertrude's description of Ophelia's death. Comparisons of one kind or another between

---

[17] Chambers, *William Shakespeare*, I, 532. On the related but mysterious subject of Shakespeare's "retirement" it might be remembered that there is no evidence that Shakespeare *did* retire from writing (the evidence concerns his retirement from acting, and Ward's testimony that he lived at Stratford "in his elder days" specifies that he continued to supply the stage with plays "every year"). And although New Place became his home as early as 1597, during the last few years of his life he still spent a good deal of time in London (cf. Edgar I. Fripp, *Shakespeare: Man and Artist* [1938], II, 768–769, 806, 814–817).

the Daughter and Ophelia have in fact been a commonplace since the time of Seward—largely perhaps because of this speech by the Wooer.

> *Queen.* . . . Your sister's drown'd, Laertes.
> *Laertes.* Drown'd! Oh, where?
> *Queen.* There is a willow grows aslant a brook,
>   That shows his hoar leaves in the glassy stream.
>   There with fantastic garlands did she come
>   Of crowflowers, nettles, daisies, and long purples,
>   That liberal shepherds give a grosser name,
>   But our cold maids do dead-men's-fingers call them.
>   There on the pendant boughs her coronet weeds
>   Clamb'ring to hang, an envious sliver broke,
>   When down her weedy trophies and herself
>   Fell in the weeping brook. Her clothes spread wide
>   And, mermaid-like, awhile they bore her up;
>   Which time she chanted snatches of old tunes,
>   As one incapable of her own distress,
>   Or like a creature native and induced
>   Unto that element; but long it could not be
>   Till that her garments, heavy with their drink,
>   Pull'd the poor wretch from her melodious lay
>   To muddy death.
>   (*Hamlet* IV.vii.165–184)

> *Jailor.* . . . Why all this haste, sir?
> *Wooer.* I'll tell you quickly. As I late was angling
>   In the great lake that lies behind the palace,
>   From the far shore, thick set with reeds and sedges,
>   As patiently I was attending sport,
>   I heard a voice, a shrill one; and attentive
>   I gave my ear; when I might well perceive
>   'Twas one that sung, and by the smallness of it,
>   A boy or woman. I then left my angle
>   To his own skill, came near, but yet perceiv'd not
>   Who made the sound, the rushes and the reeds
>   Had so encompass'd it. I laid me down
>   And listen'd to the words she sung; for then,
>   Through a small glade cut by the fishermen,
>   I saw it was your daughter.
> *Jailor.* Pray go on, sir.
> *Wooer.* She sung much, but no sense; only I heard her
>   Repeat this often, 'Palamon is gone,
>   Is gone to th'wood to gather mulberries.

I'll find him out tomorrow.'

1ˢᵗ Friend. Pretty soul!

Wooer. 'His shackles will betray him, he'll be taken;
And what shall I do then? I'll bring a bevy,
A hundred black-eyed maids that love as I do,
With chaplets on their heads of daffadillies,
With cherry lips and cheeks of damask roses,
And all we'll dance an antic 'fore the Duke
And beg his pardon.' Then she talk'd of you, sir—
That you must lose your head tomorrow morning,
And she must gather flowers to bury you
And see the house made handsome. Then she sung
Nothing but 'willow, willow willow'; and between
Ever was 'Palamon, fair Palamon,'
And 'Palamon was a tall young man.' The place
Was knee-deep where she sat; her careless tresses
A wreath of bulrush rounded; about her stuck
Thousand fresh water-flowers of several colors,
That methought she appear'd like the fair nymph
That feeds the lake with waters, or as Iris
Newly dropp'd down from heaven. Rings she made
Of rushes that grew by, and to 'em spoke
The prettiest posies—'Thus our true love's tied,'
'This you may lose, not me,' and many a one;
And then she wept, and sung again, and sigh'd,
And with the same breath smil'd and kiss'd her hand.

2ⁿᵈ Friend. Alas, what pity it is!

Wooer. I made in to her.
She saw me and straight sought the flood. I sav'd her
And set her safe to land; when presently
She slipp'd away, and to the city made
With such a cry and swiftness that, believe me,
She left me far behind her. Three or four
I saw from far off cross her—one of 'em
I knew to be your brother; where she stay'd,
And fell, scarce to be got away. I left them with her
And hither came to tell you. . . .

(IV.i.70–125)

Neither Reed nor any of the later editors who retained his reference to
Hamlet specified the resemblances that had struck them, perhaps because
they were so strong and so obvious (more than sufficient, in fact, to supply
material for an "image-cluster test"). No doubt the editors noted that each
passage has to do with the grief of a lovesick girl, that the "careless tresses"

which "a wreath of bulrush rounded" recall Ophelia's "coronet weeds," and that there are further similarities in the speech rhythms and syntax and in the references to flowers, rushes, leaves, reeds, willows, tears, death, burial, the watery setting, the comparison of one girl to a mermaid and the other to a rainbow, the far-off quality of the setting lent by the opening lines of each description, the tenderness of the speaker, the tie between the girl and the listener (brother or father), snatches of old tunes, and so forth.

Reed would probably have seen little point in detailing the resemblances, since they are much more pervasive than any collection of factors that can be discriminated in a list. Such a list, moreover, probably has little direct relevance to whether or not one believes the two passages were written by the same writer. One might suppose that the fortuitous resemblances within two dissimilar dramatic situations imply an identical writer rather than an imitator. But to pursue this line of reasoning might soon bring us into the realm of authorship tests with their implicit claims to penetrate the mysteries of the Shakespearean unconscious. Perhaps as we come gradually to observe the marks of conscious dramatic purpose within the play, we shall find that the identification of the unconscious mind from which various scenes may be thought to have emerged will somehow quietly take care of itself. It seems a little presumptuous to speak solemnly about uncovering secret aspects of the mind of the writer who has done most to educate—and to a large extent create—the English consciousness.

On the other hand, we might consider Shakespeare's equally strong impression on the unconscious minds of critics and scholars who have written about *The Two Noble Kinsmen.* For example, Steevens' theory of authorship is unworkable in view of Shakespeare's obvious presence in the play, but his evidence, reinterpreted, may make sense; despite his avowal to the contrary, Steevens may be said to have testified to Shakespeare's sole authorship. Later critics too, consciously certain that Shakespeare had nothing to do with the "Fletcher scenes," seem unwittingly to have left a surprising volume of testimony implying otherwise. No consistency should be expected from the later commentators who will from time to time be quoted, but the ways in which they deny Shakespeare's authorship of this or that scene should sometimes prove interesting to analyze.

We might begin, for example, in the scene with the Wooer's narrative that we just examined; a panoramic view of nineteenth-century opinion appears in the headnote to IV.i in Littledale's 1876 Text:

A certain resemblance between the descriptive passages in this scene and the Queen's picture of Ophelia's death, has been the chief agent in misleading critics to suppose that the Jailor's Daughter is a copy of Ophelia. No view, Hickson points out, can be more erroneous, for "not only the circumstances, but the springs of action, are different from those of Ophelia; and we beg to assure such as may not have examined the question for themselves, that the language and sentiments are still more unlike. But the description in this scene has a certain resemblance to the circumstances of the death of Ophelia, and was probably written with that scene in view. It has no reference whatever to the *character* of the jailor's daughter, and it is the only circumstance in the whole play common to her and to Ophelia". . . .

   The following . . . illustrates the diversity of critical opinion:—"The Jailor's Daughter . . . has been long admired as an extremely well-wrought copy of Ophelia" [Weber]. . . . Here is the other extreme:—"a wretched interpolation in the story, and a fantastic copy of Ophelia" [Hazlitt]. . . .

Both Littledale and Skeat were struck by a few other recollections of *Hamlet* in passages concerned with the Daughter—both in III.ii, which they assigned to Shakespeare, and in III.v, which they did not.[18] But the prevailing view in the nineteenth century seems to have been that the Wooer's narrative bore "a certain resemblance" to Shakespeare, while (a) it was unrelated to the *"character"* of the Daughter whom it helps to characterize, and (b) it had no relation to either the motives or the dramatic circumstances of Ophelia. With respect to (a) it would be difficult to answer Hickson directly, since he failed to specify which character of the Daughter he had in mind—the Shakespearean Odette he found in II.i, III.ii, and IV.iii, or the Fletcherian Odile he found in II.iv, II.vi, III.iv, and the rest. But no doubt we must eventually look into the matter of the Daughter's character, for it does seem to be crucial to a full understanding of the problem of authorship; if Hickson had, for example, been impressed enough with the flavor of the Wooer's speech to have thought for a moment of including this scene among those he transferred from Spalding's Fletcher column to his own Shakespeare column, he would almost certainly have been dissuaded by the fact that the Daughter, when she enters a little later in this scene, speaks lines which acknowledge that Palamon is sexually attractive to her; for Hickson and his contemporaries, meanings were magically encapsulated within words, and sexual words were unambiguously impure; impure words, impure meanings; impure meanings, impure character; impure character, impure dramatist; Fletcher; and who at that time would have dared to say no? When Victorian readers were forced to accept such language in familiar Shakespeare plays—when they did not either ignore it or insist that it had been

---

[18] Littledale cited Hamlet's "you are a fishmonger" in his note on the Daughter's "I know you; y'are a tinker . . ." (III.v.85), finding one meaningful and the other not; Skeat's note on "How stand I then?" (III.ii.20) comments that "the very phrase is in *Hamlet*"; and so forth.

interpolated—they were in effect allowing themselves to be educated about language, drama, and meaning. But we must pass on to (b), and on this point Hickson and Littledale were perfectly right; the Daughter is unquestionably not Ophelia; we are not reading *Hamlet*. *The Two Noble Kinsmen* is something more than a parcel of Shakespearean reminiscences.

If we consider the Wooer's speech merely by itself, we should find it difficult—impossible, in fact—to find anything in all of Fletcher's work which would look as good beside it—although this is hard to show directly, since there is nothing in Fletcher that either resembles it or has, indeed, ever tempted anyone to offer such a comparison. As a description evoking pity, it is remarkable in sustaining for so long its dramatic transparency: the speaker never tells us how to feel, or even, directly, how he himself feels, although when he comes to the lines—

> methought she appear'd like the fair nymph
> That feeds the lake with waters, or as Iris
> Newly dropp'd down from heaven

—he is no longer describing a sight, but a vision, and we are forced to recognize that his speech dramatizes much more powerful emotions than we are led to believe lie behind Gertrude's "poor wretch." This recognition might therefore lead us to consider what kind of a speaker is imagined here, and accordingly we must take into account some part at least of the dramatic context. For just as "our cold maids," the comment on the long purples, and phrases like "an envious sliver" help to create or express Gertrude's matronly self-awareness and to decorate her pity with a certain regal formality, the fullness of detail that the Wooer presents to his audience, together with his own lack of explicit self-expression, seem to have a great deal to do with the underlying conception of his entire role. The Wooer appears in a total of four scenes, of which only one, II.i (normally credited to Shakespeare), comes before the present scene, and in that earlier scene we find the same characterization.

The Wooer is given only a few lines in II.i, which had begun with a dialogue about the Daughter's dowry:

Jailor. . . . Marry, what I have (be it what it will) I will assure upon my daughter at the day of my death.
Wooer. Sir, I demand no more than your own offer, and I will estate your daughter in what I have promis'd.
Jailor. Well, we will talk more of this when the solemnity [Theseus' wedding] is past. But have you a full promise of her? When that shall be seen, I tender my consent.

Wooer. I have, sir. Here she comes.

Enter Daughter.

Jailor. Your friend and I have chanc'd to name you here upon the old business; but no more of that now. . . .

(II.i.8–20)

The conversation turns immediately to the prisoners, and the Daughter talks of nothing in this scene but Palamon and Arcite. The Wooer has only a single other line to speak, but—taken together with his mannerly replies to the surly Jailor (whose respectfulness in both II.i and II.ii is reserved for the moneyed classes)—it suggests a good deal about his role; it too is a reply, this time to his fiancée:

Daughter. It seems to me they have no more sense of their captivity than I of ruling Athens. . . . Yet sometime a divided sigh, martyr'd as 'twere i'th'deliverance, will break from one of them; when the other presently gives it so sweet a rebuke that I could wish myself a sigh to be so chid, or at least a sigher to be comforted.

Wooer. I never saw 'em.

(II.i.38–47)

He is equally reticent and self-effacing in IV.iii and V.ii. And when he enters in IV.i with his anxious questions about the Daughter, and prefaces his unhappy news with these words to her father—

> you must know it, and as good by me as by another that less loves her

—the fact that it is the girl's cast-off lover who goes on to describe her singing of Palamon makes his lines more affecting.

His speech is the third report of the scene. The composition of the entire scene gives us a variety of dramatic voices startlingly greater than one is accustomed to find in Fletcher. It had opened with the Jailor asking a friend if he had heard how the Duke felt about the escape of Palamon from prison. Of this the friend knew nothing, but he had been present when (in III.vi) Emilia and Hippolyta had pleaded with Theseus for the lives of Palamon and Arcite,

> Begg'd with such handsome pity that the Duke
> Methought stood staggering whether he should follow
> His rash oath or the sweet compassion
> Of those two ladies . . .

(IV.i.10–13)

Then a second friend rushed in—

Be of good comfort, man; I bring you news, good news. . . . Palamon has clear'd you, and got your pardon, and discover'd how and by whose means he escap'd, which was your daughter's, whose pardon is procur'd too . . .

(IV.i.19–25)

And as he gets his breath back, he completes the first friend's report:

They that never begg'd but they prevail'd had their suits fairly granted: the prisoners have their lives . . .

Both bits of news, naturally, become ironically relevant to our reception of the Wooer's narrative later in the scene—where we saw the Daughter convinced that Palamon will be executed and that her father too, because of her, will be beheaded. In the final episodes of the scene the Daughter is brought home; she talks distractedly of "maids that love as I do," asks about her wedding-gown, sings broken fragments of love-ballads, and is patiently humored by her father and his guests; during all this the Wooer stands silently aside.

We shall have to pause here, even though it has not yet been possible to show that the Wooer's narrative is something more than that celebrated "lingering over an emotional effect" which is half-rightly said to be a hallmark of Fletcher. To do that, we should have to examine the precise relevance of this scene to the larger dramatic pattern; whereas our present purpose is merely to consider another facet of the problem of authorship, and this requires that we deal with this scene more or less in isolation.

Suppose that someone wished to argue that Fletcher had written IV.i, and wished to do it without devising another sleight-of-hand "test." He might appropriately decide to read carefully through the text of Fletcher's works to see if he could come up with examples of dialogue to show to his audience in which he, or they, would be able to discriminate a sufficient number of factors—diction, grammar, imagery, "thought," or whatever else one may notice—to demonstrate some genuine resemblances to the language of this scene. In preparing his massive edition of the play Littledale seems actually to have made such an attempt; witness his 1876 note on the "posies" (lines 111–112) of this scene:

Fletcher is full of allusions to these mottoes, e.g. *Knight of B. P.* [Beaumont], V.iii; *Loyal Subject,* II.ii ("the jewel's set within."); *Pilgrim,* I.ii ("Be constant, fair, still?" 'Tis the posy here, and here without, "Be good."); *ib.* IV.i ("Prick me, and heal me."); *Woman Hater,* IV.i ("poesies for chimneys."); *Rule a Wife,* IV.i. . . . [etc.]

(Knowing Fletcher to be the author, Littledale was able to ignore all Shakespearean examples.) This is the only sort of verbal evidence that has been collected to support the ascription of this scene to Fletcher, and there is no other sort. Hence the need for those who believed in Fletcher's authorship to account for the language of the scene by saying that Fletcher wrote with Shakespeare "in view." With respect to the style of one "Fletcher scene," at least, what Steevens reported in 1780 has merely been confirmed by later criticism.

The Daughter's Scenes

We might turn next to a group of related scenes. The Daughter speaks four soliloquies in the play, each of which comprises a single brief scene (II.iv, II.vi, III.ii, III.iv), and all of which are very different in style from the Wooer's narrative. We shall take up the first three of these. The first two (II.iv and II.vi) are usually ascribed to Fletcher; the third (III.ii) is usually ascribed to Shakespeare by authorities whose skepticism is so great as well as so one-sided that perhaps they may be trusted on this point. Most of the three soliloquies will be reproduced as we proceed, and it is the authorship of the first two, in any case, which it will be assumed is in dispute.

The three soliloquies are threaded into the plot as follows:

II.iii] Arcite, released from prison but reluctant to be separated from Emilia, disguises himself to avoid going into banishment. He decides to seek honors in the athletic contests being held before Theseus.

II.iv] The first soliloquy. The Daughter has become infatuated with Palamon and plans to help him escape from prison.

II.v] Having won a victor's garland, Arcite is taken up by Theseus and introduced into the service of Emilia.

II.vi] The second soliloquy. The escape of Palamon has been accomplished; the Daughter tells of having sent him to a hiding-place where she will later join him.

III.i] Arcite, accidentally separated from Theseus' hunting-party, comes upon Palamon and promises to return later with food and files.

III.ii] The third soliloquy. Night. The Daughter cannot find Palamon and fears he has been killed by wolves.

The first soliloquy marks the Daughter's second appearance in the play. In II.i she had been attracted by both Palamon and Arcite; now her choice has settled on Palamon. She had been seen with others in II.i; she is seen

alone here in II.iv; she spoke prose in II.i, and she speaks verse, a rhyth-
mically incisive and vigorous verse, in this scene:

> Scene 4. *Enter Jailor's Daughter alone.*
> *Daughter.* Why should I love this gentleman? 'Tis odds
> He never will affect me. I am base,
> My father the mean keeper of his prison,
> And he a prince. To marry him is hopeless,
> To be his whore is witless. Out upon't!
> What pushes are we wenches driven to
> When fifteen once has found us! . . .

(II.iv.1–7)

Possibly some notion of the late Shakespeare standing aloft on Dowden
Heights would still lead a few readers to decide that in these lines it is impossible to hear "Shakespeare's voice," and this reflection might cause them
to miss the characteristic voice of the Daughter as well as the compactness
of the exposition. It is essential to the progress of the action both in the main
plot and the underplot for the girl to be infatuated with Palamon, for her to
know clearly from the start what her chances are, and for the audience to
know that when Palamon is out of prison he will be free to pursue Emilia
without having incurred an obligation to the Daughter that would require
him to reject her and thus seem guilty of deliberately hurting her. The girl
goes on to say that "first I saw him" and "thought he was a goodly man" . . .

> Next I pitied him—
> And so would any young wench, o'my conscience,
> That ever dream'd, or vow'd her maidenhead
> To a young handsome man. Then I lov'd him—
> Extremely lov'd him— infinitely lov'd him.
> And yet he had a cousin, fair as he too.
> But in my heart was Palamon, and there—
> Lord, what a coil he keeps! To hear him
> Sing in an evening, what a heaven it is!
> And yet his songs are sad ones. Fairer spoken
> Was never gentleman. When I come in
> To bring him water in a morning, first
> He bows his noble body, then salutes me thus:
> 'Fair gentle maid, good morrow, may thy goodness
> Get thee a happy husband!' Once he kiss'd me;
> I lov'd my lips the better ten days after.
> Would he would do so every day! He grieves much,
> And me as much to see his misery.

What should I do to make him know I love him?
For I would fain enjoy him. Say I ventur'd
To set him free? What says the law then? Thus much
For law or kindred! I will do it,
And this night, or tomorrow, he shall love me.   *Exit.*

(II.iv.11–33)

During the intervening scene (II.v), she presumably helps him to escape.

Scene 6. *Enter Jailor's Daughter alone.*
Daughter. Let all the Dukes and all the devils roar,
He is at liberty! I have ventur'd for him;
And out I have brought him to a little wood
A mile hence. I have sent him where a cedar,
Higher than all the rest, spreads like a plane
Fast by a brook; and there he shall keep close
Till I provide him files and food, for yet
His iron bracelets are not off. Oh Love,
What a stout-hearted child thou art! My father
Durst better have endur'd cold iron than done it.
I love him beyond love and beyond reason
Or wit or safety. I have made him know it.
I care not. I am desperate. If the law
Find me, and then condemn me for't, some wenches,
Some honest-hearted maids, will sing my dirge
And tell to memory my death was noble,
Dying almost a martyr. That way he takes
I purpose is my way too. Sure he cannot
Be so unmanly as to leave me here. . . .
                         And yet he has not thank'd me
For what I have done; no, not so much as kiss'd me;
And that, methinks, is not so well; nor scarcely
Could I persuade him to become a freeman,
He made such scruples of the wrong he did
To me and to my father. Yet I hope,
When he considers more, this love of mine
Will take more root within him. Let him do
What he will with me, so he use me kindly;
For use me so he shall, or I'll proclaim him,
And to his face, no man. I'll presently
Provide him necessaries and pack my clothes up,
And where there is a path of ground I'll venture,
So he be with me. By him, like a shadow,
I'll ever dwell. . . .

(II.vi.1–19, 21–35)

Since there is universal agreement that both speeches are by the same writer, it might seem profitless to seek out the confirmatory features of style. Yet if we were forced to satisfy ourselves on this point, it would probably require little more than a careful reading aloud of the girl's lines. She has a fairly extensive repertory of mannerisms which provide good evidence that the same mind imagined the very distinctive voice we hear in both soliloquies. Her lyrical self-confidence in the first gives way to a more nervous willfulness in the second, but in both she exclaims, she questions, she narrates, she speculates, she rhapsodizes, she is by sudden turns thoughtful, impudent, wistful, exuberant, matter-of-fact. Both speeches proceed in short sentences, and almost every pause signals some distinct shift in tone. We ought to be able to recognize this fitful young voice if we meet it again.

We might also, returning to the narrative, note how skillfully each soliloquy carries forward the action; how the dramatist arranges matters so that nothing will "sully" Palamon's "gloss of youth" (I.ii.5) during the escape episode; how he prepares to keep the girl, albeit reluctantly, as innocent as Ophelia. The Daughter's comments on Palamon in both speeches serve these purposes as surely as the lines in which she identifies the events that are taking place, and in the second soliloquy she shows some signs of uneasiness about her own future as well. Her third soliloquy in III.ii will be seen to develop naturally and inevitably out of what she has said and done in these earlier scenes. There may be a temptation in reading it to look for the details that Hickson and Littledale selected for attention in order to prove that it had been written by Shakespeare. It might be more useful instead to observe how the speech again carries forward the plot the separation from Palamon and the development of the girl's madness out of her earlier obsessiveness—and, especially, how it is again imagined through many of the same mannerisms of speech we observed in the earlier soliloquies:

> Scene 2. *Enter Jailor's Daughter alone.*
> *Daughter.* He has mistook the brake I meant, is gone
>   After his fancy. 'Tis now well-nigh morning.
>   No matter. Would it were perpetual night,
>   And darkness Lord o'th'world! Hark. 'Tis a wolf.
>   In me hath grief slain fear, and but for one thing
>   I care for nothing, and that's Palamon.
>   I reck not if the wolves would jaw me, so
>   He had this file. What if I halloa'd for him?
>   I cannot halloa. If I whoop'd, what then?
>   If he not answer'd, I should call a wolf,
>   And do him but that service. I have heard
>   Strange howls this livelong night. Why may't not be

> They have made prey of him? He has no weapons;
> He cannot run; the jingling of his gyves
> Might call fell things to listen, who have in them
> A sense to know a man unarm'd, and can
> Smell where resistance is. I'll set it down
> He's torn to pieces. They howl'd many together,
> And then they fed on him. So much for that!
> Be bold to ring the bell; how stand I then?
> All's char'd when he is gone. No, no, I lie.
> My father's to be hang'd for his escape,
> Myself to beg, if I priz'd life so much
> As to deny my act; but that I would not,
> Should I try death by dozens. I am mop'd.
> Food took I none these two days.
> Sipp'd some water. I have not clos'd mine eyes
> Save when my lids scour'd off their brine. Alas,
> Dissolve my life! Let not my sense unsettle,
> Lest I should drown or stab or hang myself!
> Oh state of nature, fail together in me,
> Since thy best props are warp'd. So, which way now?
> The best way is, the next way to a grave.
> Each errant step beside is torment. Lo,
> The moon is down, the crickets chirp, the screech-owl
> Calls in the dawn. All offices are done
> Save what I fail in. But the point is this—
> An end, and that is all.   *Exit.*

She names her fears, then shrugs them off, then resigns herself to them; her unsteadiness is far different from the saucy assurance with which her first soliloquy began, but the brittle rhythms—her nervous way of cate-chizing herself and speculating on the gambling odds for every event—are consistent throughout the three scenes. The constructive design by which Palamon is made simply to pass beyond her reach will perhaps recall the skill that produced the gradual and theatrically invisible rejection of Kather-ine in *Henry VIII*. And—in the language of no more than the brief span of narrative we have gone over—the space from

> What pushes are we wenches driven to
> When fifteen once has found us!

to the line

> Each errant step beside is torment

is a considerable imaginative distance—although this circumstance is hardly likely to be used as an argument for divided authorship by anyone who has travelled that distance. One wonders how many *have;* Hickson, who was deeply impressed by most of what he encountered in twelve scenes of the play, was able to say of the two "Fletcher" soliloquies in II.iv and II.vi nothing at all except that they were "injurious to the action." *What* action he and so many others have affected to protect against Fletcher's depredations is something they have left not the slightest record of having perceived— although the action of the play was probably immediately apprehensible to the porter who sold refreshments at Blackfriars in 1613. The Daughter's first three soliloquies, authorship question or no, show a purposeful singleness of design.

Although in his 1885 Introduction Littledale devoted three pages of analysis (with citation of Shakespearean parallels) to III.ii, his presentation of the evidence for Fletcher's authorship of II.iv and II.vi was quite brief; it is nevertheless complete:

[II.iv] Now comes the Gaoler's Daughter, moralizing on her love for Palamon, in Fletcher's peculiarly prurient way. Observe the phrase "young handsome man," which we find also in IV.ii.3, "young handsome men," and Epil. l. 6, "young handsome wench."

[II.vi] This soliloquy is Fletcher's, but it is Fletcher in his better frame of mind. He has, however, gone on the wrong track, having made her passion extravagantly sensual, mere frenzy of lust, and therefore totally unlike that disinterested [!] solicitude of true love which she displays in III.ii.

In other words, both soliloquies offend against nineteenth-century decorum, and although there is nothing like them in Fletcher they must be assigned to him.

Is there anything like them in Shakespeare? Although other and perhaps better examples might be cited, the comparison proposed by Reed may be worth looking into. In their notes to the Daughter's first soliloquy, most editors (excluding Littledale, who felt obliged to drop all references to Shakespeare in his notes to this scene) [19] retained Reed's reference to "the speech of Helena in *All's Well,* I.i.90, especially the lines—'Twas pretty, though a plague . . . &c" (Skeat's note):

[19] Where earlier editors glossed unusual words or phrases by citing examples from Shakespeare (comparing e.g. "what a coil he keeps" at II.iv.18 to *All's Well* II.i.27 or *Timon* I.ii.236, or citing Shakespearean parallels for the sense of *affect* at II.iv.2), Littledale, when—as usually happened—he was unable to replace them with examples from the Fletcher canon, either removed the Shakespearean references in his glosses (as with *affect*) or eliminated the gloss entirely (as with *coil*), preferring instead to supply such notes as that which asserts (without reference to any other text) that *thus much* (II.iv.31) is "one of Fletcher's *heavy* monosyllabic double-endings."

> *Lafew.* Farewell, pretty lady, you must hold the credit of your father.
> *Exeunt Bertram and Lafew.*
> *Helena.* Oh were that all! I think not on my father,
> And these great tears grace his remembrance more
> Than those I shed for him. What was he like?
> I have forgot him. My imagination
> Carries no favor in't but Bertram's.
> I am undone: there is no living, none,
> If Bertram be away. 'Twere all one
> That I should love a bright particular star
> And think to wed it, he is so above me:
> In his bright radiance and collateral light
> Must I be comforted, not in his sphere.
> Th'ambition in my love thus plagues itself:
> The hind that would be mated by the lion
> Must die for love. 'Twas pretty, though a plague,
> To see him every hour, to sit and draw
> His arched brows, his hawking eye, his curls,
> In our heart's table: heart too capable
> Of every line and trick of his sweet favor.
> But now he's gone, and my idolatrous fancy
> Must sanctify his relics. . . .
>
> (*All's Well* I.i.89–109)

Comparison with the Daughter's first soliloquy reveals certain similarities and several more interesting differences. In each case we are made aware of the disparity in social status between the heroine and the man she wants; each sets aside the thought or memory of her father as her mind turns eagerly to a lover she thinks unattainable; each is tortured by "th'ambition in [her] love," and the rhythmic and verbal similarities in which both speakers express this feeling could be explained, among other ways, by identical authorship. At the same time, the Shakespearean Latinisms of Helena's speech are almost totally missing from the Daughter's; but then this is true of the Daughter's other soliloquies—including III.ii—as well, and diction such as "our heart's table" might sound peculiar in her mouth, for there is wide social disparity between Helena and the young girl. Helena is upper middle-class, and she will get her unwilling count; the Daughter does not even have a name, and her very kind knight is out of the question for her.

Comparisons crossing between plays are seldom very illuminating, however, and it would perhaps be more helpful, since the role of the Daughter has created difficulties for so many readers, to look more generally at the characterization of the Daughter in the underplot as a whole.

One point about the construction of the play emerges from any comparison of passages selected at random from the first and last of the three underplot scenes usually assigned to Shakespeare:

Jailor. They are fam'd to be a pair of absolute men.
Daughter. By my troth, I think fame but stammers 'em; they stand a grise above the reach of report.
Jailor. I heard them reported in the battle to be the only doers.
Daughter. Nay, most likely, for they are noble suff'rers. I marvel how they would have look'd had they been victors, that with such a constant nobility enforce a freedom out of bondage, making misery their mirth and affliction a toy to jest at.

(II.i.28–36)

Jailor. Look where she comes. You shall perceive her behavior . . .
Daughter. Now for this charm that I told you of. You must bring a piece of silver on the tip of your tongue, or no ferry. Then if it be your chance to come where the blessed spirits—as there's a sight now! We maids that have our livers perish'd, crack'd to pieces with love, we shall come there, and do nothing all day long but pick flowers with Proserpine. Then will I make Palamon a nosegay—then let him mark me—then—

(IV.iii.8–9, 18–25)

These passages clearly span so wide a range of dramatic development (even with regard to plot alone) that if we accept them as Shakespeare's we are forced to assume that the shape and direction of the underplot are wholly his,[20] and that he did not, for example, leave a few well written fragments which Fletcher somehow made use of in an underplot of his own later fashioning. Some critics have held this other view because they could accept as Shakespeare's only those underplot scenes in which they saw no impropriety; others, like Spalding, have of course rejected the underplot as a whole. In connection with the latter view, the theory maintained by Hazlitt in 1820—a blend of Steevens and Colman—is worth noting; Hazlitt thought that the first act of the play had been written by Beaumont and Fletcher

in imitation of Shakespear's manner; but I see no reason to suppose that it was his. . . . The subsequent acts are confessedly Fletcher's, and the imitations

---

[20] The same point might in fact be urged on the strength of II.i alone. As Kittredge observed in his 1936 edition, "If Shakespeare, as seems likely, wrote the first scene of Act ii, he must have had the main point of the underplot in mind—that is, the love of the jailer's daughter for Palamon."

of Shakespear which occur there . . . (of Shakespear's manner . . . as it was congenial to his own spirit and feeling of nature) are glorious in themselves, and exalt our idea of the great original which could give birth to such magnificent conceptions in another. The conversation of Palamon and Arcite in prison is of this description—the outline is evidently taken from that of Guiderius, Arviragus, and Belarius in Cymbeline, but filled up with a rich profusion of graces that make it his own again. . . .

The jailor's daughter . . . is a wretched interpolation in the story, and a fantastic copy of Ophelia.[21]

Perhaps the too facile separation of conception from language made by Hazlitt led him to postulate this wonderful theory of Shakespeare's mind and Fletcher's hand somehow going together; but what is even more noteworthy about this version of the imitation theory is that the story of the Daugher still offends Hazlitt as a "wretched interpolation" even though in his view it has been "interpolated" by Fletcher into his own play.

Mysteries are often most easily explained by attending carefully to whatever is most obvious and visible: the social class of the Daughter is lower than that of Shakespeare's other heroines. Nineteenth-century critics evidently thought about this point too, although the following comment on it (by an obscure member of the New Shakspere Society) probably expresses their thinking in a crudely exaggerated way:

Love between persons of very different rank has been held by many dramatists to be a fine subject for the stage. Shakspere never introduces it. *Ophelia* loves a Prince, and *Violet* a duke, and Rosalind a Squire's son; but gentlehood unites all. Helena in *All's Well* is a gentlewoman. With anything like levelling aspirations Shakspere had clearly no sympathy . . .
Fletcher . . . is answerable for . . . all the underplot.[22]

If critics sometimes dramatize their own characters, the character emerging from these comments recalls a description in Raymond Chandler of somebody so low he'd steal the straw from his own mother's kennel.

What evidently happened was that many readers were choosing not so much between Shakespeare and Fletcher as between Shakespeare and not-Shakespeare, and that (as in Hazlitt's case) their likes and dislikes derived more from their feelings about social decorum than from any inferences about dramatic purpose. That would to some extent explain their distress

[21] William Hazlitt, *Lectures Chiefly on the Dramatic Literature of the Age of Elizabeth* (1820), pp. 158–159, 163.
[22] To the 1876 N.S.S. edition of Spalding's *Letter* Furnivall appended "the Paper with which Mr J. Herbert Stack opend the discussion at our Reading of the *Two Noble Kinsmen*" (pp. 113–116); the quotations are from this paper.

over the character of the Daughter. Yet nineteenth-century critics were, as we have already seen, of more than one mind about the Daughter. Hickson and his fellows attended to the pathos in her role in the three scenes they ascribed to Shakespeare, seeing her in these scenes as a blood relative of Mrs. Jameson, while in the remaining scenes they attended to the other aspects of her role which in their minds related her to Chloë, that urbane nymph in *The Faithful Shepherdess*. Against this black-and-white view, meanwhile, stood the all-black view of such critics as Hazlitt and Spalding. Actually, in refusing to be overcome by the girl's pathos and purity in II.i, III.ii, and IV.iii, this latter group was in some respects more sensitive than the former. Their dislike of the Daughter at least signified the recognition—missed by Hickson and others in the case of three scenes—that the girl is in no way the simple artless innocent which Hazlitt and Hickson alike demanded of their Shakespearean heroines.

A moment ago we looked at this line from one of her mad speeches in IV.iii:

> Then will I make Palamon a nosegay—then let him mark me—then—

The pauses in her speech as just given follow the quarto, but most editors since Seward have inserted another stop:

> Then will I make Palamon a nosegay—then let him—mark me—then—

The contrast is small but telling; in the Seward version the added incoherence makes the girl more pathetic; but it is wrong dramatically as well as textually; in the original ("then let him mark me") there is a touch of petulance—and it is essential. The sharp edges in the characterization of the Daughter begin with her unconscious callousness toward her lover in II.i (as she praises the prisoners to his face) and they reappear in every scene, whether she is supposed to be sane or mad. There is, for example, the brash impudence with which her second soliloquy closes:

> Farewell, father!
> Get many more such prisoners and such daughters,
> And shortly you may keep yourself. Now to him!
> (II.vi.37–39)

There is the curiously wan, ineffectual didacticism of her mad scenes:

> . . . there th'offending part burns, and the deceiving part freezes: in troth, a very grievous punishment, as one would think, for such a trifle. Believe me, one would marry a leprous witch to be rid on't, I'll assure you.
> (IV.iii.40–44)

(The single passage in which the Daughter is made to seem almost wholly passive and unqualifiedly pitiable is, appropriately, the narrative in IV.i in which we see her through the eyes of her lover.) Each time she appears the particular qualities of tone and energy that her voice expresses are conditioned by her lack of status. In her first scene she says of the prisoners and of herself—

It seems to me they have no more sense of their captivity than I of ruling Athens . . .

(II.i.38–39)

—and as the play proceeds we see her gradually rejecting her initially clear awareness that she has no chance with Palamon; not wanting to believe it, she won't believe it, and her madness grows out of the attendant anxiety and frustration. The monitory tone of "then let him mark me," the put-on condescension of "Believe me . . . I'll assure you," the will to see herself above her station—these are most elaborately developed in her final scene:

Jailor. Come, your love Palamon stays for you, child, and has done this long hour, to visit you.
Daughter. I thank him for his gentle patience. He's a kind gentleman, and I am much bound to him. Did you ne'er see the horse he gave me?
Jailor. Yes.
Daughter. How do you like him?
Jailor. He's a very fair one.
Daughter. You never saw him dance?
Jailor. No.
Daughter. I have often. He dances very finely . . . He'll dance the morris twenty mile an hour, and that will founder the best hobby-horse (if I have any skill) in all the parish . . . You know the chestnut mare the Duke has?
Jailor. Very well.
Daughter. She is horribly in love with him, poor beast, but he is like his master coy and scornful.
Jailor. What dowry has she?
Daughter. Some two hundred bottles, and twenty strike of oats; but he'll ne'er have her; he lisps in's neighing able to entice a miller's mare; he'll be the death of her.
Doctor. What stuff she utters!
Jailor. Make curtsey, here your love comes.
Wooer [disguised as Palamon]. Pretty soul, how do ye? That's a fine maid! There's a curtsey!
Daughter. Yours to command i'th'way of honesty. How far is't now to th'end o'th'world, my masters?
Doctor. Why, a day's journey, wench.

Daughter. Will you go with me?

Wooer. What shall we do there, wench?

Daughter. Why, play at stoolball; what is there else to do?

Wooer. I am content if we shall keep our wedding there.

Daughter. 'Tis true. For there, I will assure you, we shall find some blind priest for the purpose that will venture to marry us, for here they are nice and foolish. Besides, my father must be hang'd tomorrow, and that would be a blot i'th'business. Are not you Palamon?

Wooer. Do not you know me?

Daughter. Yes, but you care not for me. I have nothing but this poor petticoat and two coarse smocks.

Wooer. That's all one; I will have you.

(V.ii.55–66, 70–72, 81–115)

She tries to put on airs, although playing the role of a great lady is hard for her to sustain. After haughtily dismissing her father's execution as "a blot i'th'business," she finally breaks down tearfully over her lack of a dowry— the subject with which the underplot began in II.i and with which it ends in V.iv. The underlying conception of her role throughout the play is coherent, and if it had not been for the assumption of dual authorship the fundamental point about her social condition would probably have seemed obvious to most critics.

The Gathered Evidence of Style

In his scene-by-scene review of the question of authorship, Littledale wrote of the Daughter's first two soliloquies only what was quoted earlier (page 227), and of her fourth soliloquy (III.iv) he wrote only that "the ridiculous chatter in this scene gives us Fletcher's idea of mad talk." Elsewhere in his Introduction, however, he added another comment; in his summary of earlier critical opinion he quoted Schlegel's view that the Daughter was "certainly not Shakspeare's" because she was an "imitation" of Ophelia, and to one phrase from the Schlegel quotation—"the daughter . . . whose insanity is artlessly conducted in pure monologues"—he attached the following footnote:

Every reader of the play must have been struck by the frequency of monologues, above mentioned by Schlegel. Of these, Shakspere wrote but one, Act III. sc. ii.; the others are imitations of this scene. In *Cymbeline*, Posthumus soliloquises in a scene of the same kind, Act II. sc. v.

The point toward which so much of the discussion in the present chapter has been moving, no doubt already obvious, perhaps had better be stated explicitly. Wherever adherents to the theory of dual authorship have sought to explain one or another of their "Fletcher scenes" by reference to other writing in which they could detect some sort of verbal resemblance, their references have usually been to the work of Shakespeare. This has been true of critic after critic, dealing with scene after scene. Arcite's soliloquy on his banishment in II.iii, which had reminded Steevens of Romeo's banishment speech, led Skeat (in the notes to his 1875 edition) to recall in addition Valentine's similar soliloquy at *Two Gentlemen of Verona* III.i.170. Spalding and Hickson both regarded Gerrold as a "copy" of Holofernes, and Skeat's note on Gerrold's prologue to the morris dance in III.v remarked, typically, that "the whole scene is copied" from *A Midsummer Night's Dream* V.i. The angry interchanges between Palamon and Arcite in four scenes of Acts II and III led George Brandes to assert another verbal imitation of Shakespeare, "echoes from . . . *Julius Caesar* (the quarrel between Brutus and Cassi[us])." [23] Hickson regarded Emilia's soliloquy before the pictures in IV.ii as an "elaborate imitation" of the portrait scene in *Hamlet* ("See what a grace was seated on this brow . . ."). The same soliloquy led Littledale to cite passages from *The Rape of Lucrece* and *Timon of Athens* ("Admirable!" says the Poet of the Painter's picture at I.i.30, "How this grace/ Speaks his own standing! What a mental power/ This eye shoots forth! How big imagination/ Moves in this lip!"). These examples are representative, not exhaustive. Nor did any of these critics find in Fletcher's work a comparable record of parallels.

One critic, Littledale, did attempt however to cite Fletcherian parallels for a few of these scenes in his 1885 Introduction. He appears to have read and re-read carefully all of the work attributed to Fletcher in a conscious search for parallels to *The Two Noble Kinsmen,* to have cited the lesser items in his 1876 textual notes (such as the note on "posies" quoted earlier), and to have presented the more substantial examples in his later Introduction. The results are instructive. He cited only two plays more than once. One of the two was, of all plays, *Henry VIII* (cited three times, once in connection with the Prologue to *The Two Noble Kinsmen* and twice in connection with II.ii). The other was *The Lover's Progress,* and in this play he referred to no less than eight speeches which resembled passages in *The Two Noble Kinsmen* (both in "Fletcher scenes" and "Shakespeare scenes"). One of the eight (the only one he quoted at length) is the first speech by Olinda in *The Lover's Progress* I.i; Olinda, like Emilia in her picture scene, finds it

[23] George Brandes, *William Shakespeare: A Critical Study,* trans. William Archer *et al.* (1898), II, 312.

difficult to choose between rival lovers, and her lines do show some resemblances to Emilia's soliloquy in IV.ii:

> . . . turning this way
> To brave *Clarange,* in his face appears
> A kind of Majesty which should command,
> Not sue for favour. If the fairest Lady
> Of *France,* set forth with natures best endowments . . .
> Did now lay claim to either for a husband,
> So vehement my affection is to both,
> My envie at her happiness would kill me . . .

"Natures best endowments" (like Emilia's "If wise nature,/With all her
best endowments . . ." at IV.ii.7–8) is but one slight instance of many, and
a check of Littledale's other references—or simply a reading of *The Lover's
Progress*—will indeed reveal a number of verbal resemblances to passages
from *The Two Noble Kinsmen.* However superficial they may be, they
are possibly more than can be put down to pure coincidence. But *The
Lover's Progress* in its present form was written not by Fletcher but by
Massinger; Massinger's habitual and frequent direct borrowings from
Shakespeare have been liberally documented; [24] and (as mentioned earlier)
when Massinger was at work on *The Lover's Progress* he very likely had a
printed copy of *The Two Noble Kinsmen* before him.[25] In any case, it is

[24] C. M. Ingleby *et al., The Shakespeare Allusion Book* (rev. edn., 1932), I, 296–304,
340; A. H. Cruickshank, *Philip Massinger* (1920), pp. 163–168; Baldwin Maxwell,
Studies in Beaumont, Fletcher, and Massinger (1939), pp. 65–73; T. A. Dunn, *Philip
Massinger* (1957), pp. 207–210. Cruickshank points out that although Massinger's
borrowings from Shakespeare may be found in plays written before 1623, their
incidence so increases in his later plays that "we may infer that Massinger studied
the Folio of 1623 carefully" (p. 168).

[25] To account for the echoes of *TNK* it is not strictly necessary to assume that
Massinger had a printed text, but the combination of circumstances—the fact that
more such echoes have been found in *Lover's Progress* than in any other "Fletcher"
play, the increase in Massinger's other Shakespearean borrowings after the 1623 Folio
appeared, the licensing of Massinger's prompt-book a month after Waterson registered
TNK—surely points strongly to this conclusion. Even without reference to these circumstances, however, it is odd that Littledale should have treated *Lover's Progress*
as a source of "Fletcherian" evidence; for even though he did not possess all the
evidence available to Bentley (cf. n. 7 above), he might easily have observed the
same points noted by Bentley in the Prologue and Epilogue: "These verses are
much more informative than most such. They tell us that *The Lover's Progress* is an
old play *'long since writ'* by Fletcher, that the company is today presenting it *'for a
new',* that the *'profest Writer'* (presumably the one advertised on the playbills) *'sits
within',* *'Still doubtfull, and perplex'd too, whether he/ Hath done* Fletcher *right',*
that the play is so completely revised that this *'profest Writer'* felt justified in *'De-
manding, and receiving too the pay/ For a new Poem'.*"

surely noteworthy that the most elaborate record of supposed parallels to *The Two Noble Kinsmen* from the work of Fletcher gathered by an advocate of dual authorship should be drawn from a play written by Massinger in 1634 and from another play genuinely by Shakespeare.

Advocates of dual authorship have unwittingly gathered evidence for Shakespeare's hand in "Fletcher scenes" with astonishing persistency. Another example of a kind not previously cited may be furnished from Littledale. After Palamon and Arcite have both seen Emilia and begun to quarrel, Palamon warns Arcite, "you must not love her," and Arcite replies:

> I will not as you do, to worship her,
> As she is heavenly and a blessed goddess;
> I love her as a woman, to enjoy her.
> So both may love.
>
> (II.ii.201–204)

Since Littledale acknowledged that the choice of a subject for the play must have been Shakespeare's, he apparently saw nothing odd—even though he gave II.ii to Fletcher—in commenting on these lines as follows in his 1876 notes:

Cf. *Knightes Tale,* 294 [Robinson text, 1152] seqq. It is worth noting that Shakspere shows his early acquaintance with this sophism of Arcite's, in the sonnet in *L.L.Lost* . . . IV.iii.64–7:—

> "A woman I forswore; but I will prove,
> Thou being a goddess, I forswore not thee:
> My vow was earthly, thou a heavenly love;
> Thy grace being gained cures all disgrace in me."

The passage forms a suggestive link between *L.L.Lost, M.N.D.,* and Chaucer's Theseus.

The suggestive link is not consciously allowed to extend, however, to the lines of Arcite which actually suggested it to Littledale!

Quite apart from longer passages in the play that have been described as elaborate imitations of Shakespeare's style, Shakespearean characteristics have been recognized throughout the whole of the scenes ascribed to Fletcher. Detailed lists identifying the minutiae of Shakespeare's style in those scenes have, with the usual irony, been compiled and published by Victorian scholars who accepted the ascriptions to Fletcher on metrical and moral grounds and failed to see the implications of the linguistic evidence they had themselves collected. These lists consist of the majority of editorial notes in a few Victorian editions of the play, and they deserve at least a few words of explanation and description. Only three editions of the play can be said to be heavily annotated—Skeat's (1875), Rolfe's (1883), and, of course, Littledale's. The notes in the Skeat and Rolfe editions, in glossing unusual expressions in the text of the supposed Fletcher scenes, cite or refer to parallel usages in the text of Shakespeare's canonical plays at least ten times as often as they cite or refer to the text of Fletcher; the apparent implication of this raw statistic is misleading only in its possible suggestion that the few references to Fletcher are significant, for it is almost invariably the most commonplace of archaic expressions (e.g. *innocent* meaning *idiot*), which might be illustrated from either author, for which references are given to Fletcher.[26] Littledale, as indicated earlier, studiously eliminated as many references to Shakespeare as he could for these scenes;[27] when passages required illustrative explanation and examples could not be furnished from Fletcher or some other contributor to the Fletcher Folio, he preferred to cite from obscure authors rather than from Shakespeare;[28] in short, he assiduously multiplied insignificant references to non-Shakespearean texts—and he still ended up, in his notes on these scenes, with more explanatory references to Shakespeare than to Fletcher and others. The graded weight of the evidence in Littledale's notes may be illustrated by a comparison. His note on *narcissus* at II.ii.132, informing us that in *"Faithful Shepherdess,* II.i, the plant is mentioned, as 'for swellings best',," exemplifies the general pointlessness of most of his references to Fletcher. In contrast, Gerrold's instructions to his crew at III.v.90—"Go take her [the Daughter], and fluently persuade her to a peace"—had puzzled a number of previous editors, and to knock down their unjustified proposals to emend (e.g. *peace* to *place*), Littledale found it helpful to note,

Somewhat similarly the Duke says of Malvolio, "Pursue him, and entreat him to a peace" (*Twelfth Night,* V.i.[389]) = pacify him.

[26] This happens in Skeat with *innocent* at IV.i.54, *trace* at III.v.15, etc.

[27] Cf. n. 19. Fuller illustration may be found in the notes to V.ii. Skeat's notes to this scene gave no references to Fletcher, seven to Shakespeare (e.g. his note on l. 22 cited the similar remark at *As You Like It* IV.ii.9). For most of these seven references Littledale made inappropriate substitutions; for instance, Skeat had cited *Merry Wives* III.iv.47 to amplify his explanation of the identical phrase "come cut-and-long-tail" at *TNK* V.ii.67, whereas Littledale, after explaining the phrase, referred to *Wit at Several Weapons* II.iii (Cambridge text, IX, 93), in which a reader would find the words "with cut and long tail" but would be unable to see their relevance either to V.ii.67 or to Littledale's explanation.

[28] It is something of an accomplishment for Littledale to have found in the dancing horse of V.ii.59 ff. another allusion to Banks's much-alluded-to performing horse of the 1590's, to have referred his readers to five other places in which they might find similar allusions made over a sixty-year period, but to have avoided any mention of *Love's Labor's Lost* I.ii.57.

The evidence contained in the editorial notes of these three texts (and the lesser quantity of similar evidence in other editions) is too trivial, detail by detail, to dwell on at length, but a reader who consults these editions and observes it in the mass will find that its variety and cumulative weight make it somewhat more substantial than the evidence of *ye*'s and the like for which such ambitious claims have been made.

One final witness remains to be heard from in this review of critical testimony on the language of the play. During the years in which Massinger was considered a possible co-author, there appeared Tucker Brooke's edition of the play in *The Shakespeare Apocrypha* (1908). The only "critical edition" of the text published in our century, this volume also contained a highly influential Introduction. Brooke began his discussion of the question of authorship by listing the usual breakdown of scenes between "the Fletcher part" and "the non-Fletcher part" of the play; below that list he printed a short table of metrical statistics for the two "parts" (citing Littledale's figures on feminine endings and run-on lines), and underneath this table he wrote:

The utter dissimilarity [between the parts] is obvious at a glance [at the table]. In fact there is not the least difficulty in distinguishing the parts, except in one or two prose scenes . . .

(p. xli)

Brooke then proceeded to discuss "the non-Fletcher part," remarking that the "answer" to its question of authorship "depends on the balancing of the undeniably Shakespearian tone of the style against the quite un-Shakespearian characterization." His own view in 1908 was that "the quite un-Shakespearian characterization" was decisive:

On the utter absurdity of associating Emilia, as she appears in any scene of the play, with Imogen or Miranda, or indeed with any other reputable dramatic heroine, Dr. Furnivall appears to have spoken the final word. Nor can her coarseness be explained, as critics have attempted to explain the spinelessness of Palamon and Arcite, by the theory that Fletcher has marred the promise of Shakespeare's plan. In the most distinctly un-Fletcherian scenes of all she is what Dr. Furnivall has called her, 'a silly lady's-maid or shop girl, not knowing her own mind . . .'

And at this point Brooke provided specific references:

Note, for instance, her really revolting wishy-washiness and ingrained sensuality in what are perhaps her best scenes, IV.ii (the portrait scene) and V.iii.

(p. xliii)

Once we get over the mincing silliness of the prose and begin to observe more closely what Brooke has done, we may note that when he had looked at a table of metrical statistics he had found "not the least difficulty" in identifying IV.ii as one of Fletcher's scenes, but when, two pages later, he wrote with the language of the scene itself in mind, he described it as among "the most distinctly un-Fletcherian scenes of all." [29] Even during the confusions of the disintegrationist era there was further unintentional testimony against dual authorship and, albeit indirectly, for Shakespeare.

Perhaps the final part of this discussion ought simply to present, for comparisons such as might have been made by the critics whom we have been reviewing, a passage from the play along with passages from Shakespeare and Fletcher. The selection of the first three passages below has been dictated by Steevens and Skeat (cf. pages 204 and 234). No one has suggested a comparable passage from Fletcher, but perhaps the speech below from *The Humorous Lieutenant* will do as well as any; the play is one of Fletcher's best, and Demetrius is a prince—as well as a grief-stricken lover at the time he speaks the lines.

> *Arcite.* Banish'd the kingdom? 'Tis a benefit,
>   A mercy I must thank 'em for; but banish'd
>   The free enjoying of that face I die for,
>   Oh, 'twas a studied punishment, a death
>   Beyond imagination! such a vengeance
>   That, were I old and wicked, all my sins
>   Could never pluck upon me. Palamon,
>   Thou hast the start now; thou shalt stay and see
>   Her bright eyes break each morning 'gainst thy window
>   And let in life into thee; thou shalt feed
>   Upon the sweetness of a noble beauty
>   That nature ne'er exceeded nor ne'er shall. . . .
>
>   (*TNK* II.iii.1–12)

> *Valentine.* And why not death rather than living torment?
>   To die is to be banish'd from myself,
>   And Silvia is myself. Banish'd from her
>   Is self from self—a deadly banishment!
>   What light is light, if Silvia be not seen?
>   What joy is joy, if Silvia be not by?
>   Unless it be to think that she is by
>   And feed upon the shadow of perfection. . . .
>
>   (*Two Gentlemen* III.i.170–177)

[29] Many years later (as noted in Chap. I) Brooke abandoned his assumption of Massinger's partial authorship in favor of Shakespeare's, but he then refrained from any further comment on IV.ii or on the other issues he had discussed in 1908.

Romeo. Hence banished is banish'd from the world,
And world's exile is death. Then 'banished'
Is death misterm'd. Calling death 'banished,'
Thou cut'st my head off with a golden axe
And smilest upon the stroke that murders me.
Friar. Oh deadly sin, oh rude unthankfulness!
Thy fault our law calls death; but the kind Prince,
Taking thy part, hath rush'd aside the law,
And turn'd that black word death to banishment.
This is dear mercy, and thou see'st it not.
Romeo. 'Tis torture, and not mercy. Heaven is here
Where Juliet lives; and every cat and dog,
And little mouse, every unworthy thing,
Live here in heaven, and may look on her;
But Romeo may not . . .

(*Romeo* III.iii.19–33)

Demetrius.   . . . Art thou dead, Celia?
Dead, my poor wench? my joy, pluck'd green with violence?
Oh, fair sweet flower, farewell! Come, thou destroyer,
Sorrow, thou melter of the soul, dwell with me!
Dwell with me, solitary thoughts, tears, cryings!
Nothing, that loves the day, love me or seek me!
Nothing, that loves his own life, haunt about me!
And, Love, I charge thee, never charm mine eyes more,
Nor ne'er betray a beauty to my curses;
For I shall curse all now, hate all, forswear all,
And all the brood of fruitful Nature vex at;
For she is gone that was all, and I nothing!

(*Humorous Lieutenant* [Bond text] IV.ii.76–87)

Demetrius' speech no doubt makes Arcite's look the more Shakespearean by contrast, and so would any other selection from Fletcher. Difference in dramatic situation alone would not explain the contrast. Since Celia has not really been "pluck'd green with violence," Demetrius' lines could appropriately be set against some speech of Romeo in Act V rather than the three banishment speeches—and the contrast in idiom and movement would be just as great. To search in Fletcher's work for passages whose language seriously resembles that of passages assigned him in *The Two Noble Kinsmen* is to come to appreciate the fact that the traditional scholarship on the play has failed to bring them forward because there aren't any; critics who have casually referred to "the well known style of Fletcher" in parts of the play have been whistling in the dark. No single speech can of course be asserted to be "typical" of a dramatist's style, but the contrast between Arcite's and Demetrius' language is typical of the contrast any other comparative observation would reveal.

As for the possible assertion that Arcite's lines represent Fletcher's imitation of Shakespeare, two answers may be made. With regard to logic, to argue this conclusion from the verbal resemblances to Romeo's and Valentine's speeches would be no better warranted than to argue that Romeo's speech was an imitation of Valentine's. And with regard to evidence, such a conclusion might be considered as part of the whole complex of imitation theories from the eighteenth century onwards; to test them, all one need do is inspect the wide variety of Shakespearean styles in the so-called Fletcher scenes—the banishment speech, the Daughter's soliloquies, the Countrymen's comic prose, the arguments between Palamon and Arcite, Gerrold's doggerel address to Theseus, the flower dialogue in the garden, Emilia's soliloquy before the pictures, the Wooer's narrative; Fletcher has been credited with the most astonishing virtuosity as an imitator! No other writer in our language has made so many critics recall so many different passages in Shakespeare, and the imitations that have been loosely talked about all seem, like Arcite's speech, to be much more deeply pervaded with Shakespearean language than could be accounted for by any theory of imitation. No theory of imitation has yet been extended to the bibliographical evidence —no one has yet argued that Fletcher imitated Shakespeare's handwriting and spelling as well as his literary habits—but such an argument would be no more or less unreasonable or perverse or muddle-headed than the argument used by critic after critic that (as Clifford Leech puts it) "the echoing of Shakespeare is so evident in many passages . . . that we cannot possibly credit him with their authorship." After two centuries it is time that this kind of odd ingenuity be at last subordinated to common sense.

Conclusions

Certain general issues implicit in the history of earlier scholarship on the play might be given attention in our summing-up. The assumption that, according to Kenneth Muir, "every modern critic" would adopt is the same assumption that nearly every critic since Lamb has adopted, namely "that two authors are discernible in the play" and "that Fletcher is one of them." Fletcher's presence, moreover, is invariably described as "certain," and the description signifies, among other things, that he who uses the term not merely feels that certainty is attainable but that seeking for certainty is desirable. There is, however, an alternative view according to which certainty is not merely unattainable (which probably sounds old-hat), but that seeking for it is wholly undesirable (which is by no means old-hat). Most men try to work out reasonable assumptions to account for the data they observe; if after they succeed they go on to christen their conclusions "certainties," the consequence (if only as a matter of verbal feedback) is likely to be that they become blind to any contradictory evidence that would require them to revise or improve their assumptions. It is a philosophical commonplace that the general assumptions one holds lay down limits for what one is able to see, and to treat any belief as "certain" virtually guarantees that, in the unlikely event that one is forced by circumstances to observe contradictory evidence, one must either distort and misinterpret that evidence—or else label it "inexplicable"—as a means of protecting that original belief. On the other hand, one is seldom likely to miss whatever evidence would support one's beliefs. The Waller essay on the printer's copy is a case in point, and indeed the entire history of professional scholarship on *The Two Noble Kinsmen,* from the time of Seward and Farmer to the time of Waller and Muir, may be seen to illustrate the dangers of proceeding on the still generally unquestioned assumption that "certainty" is a desirable condition. Our beliefs must always be provisional hypotheses subject to amendment as experience demands, and perhaps it will be greatly to our advantage if we think of them as such.

The assumption of dual authorship in *The Two Noble Kinsmen* has usually been maintained by critics who, in general, did not say very much about the language of the scenes they ascribed to Fletcher. When they did observe and comment on the language of these scenes, however, they were usually forced to acknowledge that it resembled the language of Shakespeare, but they dismissed these resemblances as instances of "elaborate imitation," apparently on the assumption that other kinds of evidence for authorship, less visible to the naked eye, must carry more weight; the language they found in the play did not influence them as much as did the words of earlier scholars, and as evidence they found it less admissible than the numerical abstractions of the metrical testers and the moral abstractions of the critics of character. As a consequence most of them were persuaded that they had found not only two authors, but two Daughters, two Emilias, two Wooers, two mutually opposed dramatic purposes, and two of everything else their metalinguistic antennae could pick up. The failure of most critics to exercise their normally respectable talents for skepticism on the Fletcher attribution, and simply to check that attribution with reasonable care against the language of Fletcher's own work, is in some respects the most puzzling feature in the entire critical history of this play. Possibly this failure has some connection with traditional notions of the proper use of skepticism; once we abandon the view that skepticism is an instrument for the communal accumulation of "certainties" and come to see it instead merely as a device for developing workable assumptions, we may find that more than one traditionally insoluble problem has seemed so only because it has been wrongly approached; once we come to question what the word "knowledge" has been used to refer to, for example, we may find that many a solemn reference to "a gap in our knowledge" looks like a decorous academic metaphor for a hole in the head.

If Critic A were to state that he is convinced the entire play is by Shakespeare, and Critic E were to state that he is convinced the entire play is by Fletcher, we would naturally interpret their statements as expressions of distinctly contradictory beliefs. The meanings of the statements would appear to be irreconcilable. But of course meanings are events in the minds of men; they are not something magically encapsulated in the marks men make on paper. Suppose we were to substitute Pope or De Quincey for Critic A and Steevens or Hazlitt for Critic E. We would then be able to inquire into the meanings intended by these men, and we would be able to see that their meanings were by no means irreconcilable; for the criteria which lay behind their final verdicts evidently included the observation, common to all four critics, that the language of the play resembled the language of Shakespeare and not Fletcher. Steevens' or Hazlitt's views on the play may be readily accommodated to the final verdicts of Pope and De Quincey, while Pope's and De Quincey's views cannot be honestly accommodated to the verdicts of Steevens or Hazlitt. Similarly with virtually every other critic who has left us testimony regarding his reading of the text. Critics as far removed from one another in time and in point-of-view as Seward and Halliwell-Phillipps or as Brandes and Marco Mincoff, each of whom arrived at very different verdicts regarding authorship, have been at one in describing the language as Shakespearean. If the testimony of these many critics and scholars deserves more respectful attention than we are able to allow to the metrical tests, or even if the apparent discrepancies in the verdicts of these many critics are merely thought to require rational explanation, then there is but one hypothesis of authorship which will allow their testimony to be reconciled, and which that testimony may therefore be said strongly to support.

VI

The Composition of the Play

The expectation of ignorance is indefinite, and that of knowledge is often tyrannical. It is hard to satisfy those who know not what to demand, or those who demand by design what they think impossible to be done. I have indeed disappointed no opinion more than my own.

Dr. Johnson

The Two Noble Kinsmen was probably completed by the autumn of 1613. In the summer of that year Fletcher was at work in collaboration with Daborne, Field, and Massinger on a play for the Lady Elizabeth's company,[1] and this fact constitutes an obstacle to the common view that he must also have somehow collaborated with Shakespeare at about this time on *The Two Noble Kinsmen*. The argument of this chapter is that Shakespeare must have written the entire play alone.

In the process of adapting *The Knight's Tale* to the stage, two authors would presumably have had to agree on certain ways of treating their source, and our discussion will begin by comparing Chaucer's tale with a connected group of dramatic scenes based upon it; the comparison reveals certain obstacles to collaboration—not insuperable in themselves, but not negligible either—which the advocates of dual authorship have not considered. Certain items of historical evidence to be presented following the treatment of sources—for example, the neglected testimony of Leonard Digges that Shakespeare did not collaborate—raise further obstacles to the assumption of dual authorship. The remainder of the chapter is given over to the examination of elements of design in the language and structure of the play; the purpose is of course to demonstrate the integrity of the play and—taken together with such evidence and argument as have been offered in the preceding five chapters—to prove the case for Shakespeare.

[1] Cf. Art. 68, *Henslowe Papers,* ed. Greg (1907), pp. 65–66.

The Relationship to Chaucer

The following parallel passages from Chaucer and the play illustrate one important aspect of the adaptation:

(1) From the description of Palamoun and Arcite after the defeat of Creon:

> Nat fully quyke, ne fully dede they were . . .
>
> *(Knight's Tale* 1015)

> They are not dead?—Nor in a state of life.
>
> (I.iv.28–29)

(2) From the description of the knights accompanying the cousins:

> The cercles of his eyen in his heed,
> They gloweden bitwixen yelow and reed . . .
> His shuldres brode, his armes rounde and longe . . .
>
> (2131–2132, 2136)

> The circles of his eyes show fire within him . . .
> . . . his shoulders broad and strong;
> Arm'd long and round . . .
>
> (IV.ii.91, 94–95)

(3) From Egeus' lines in the last part of the *Tale* and the proverb-like closing of Act I:

> This world nys but a thurghfare ful of wo,
> And we been pilgrymes, passynge to and fro.
> Deeth is an ende of every worldly soore.
>
> (2847–2850)

> Heavens lend
> A thousand differing ways to one sure end.—
> This world's a city full of straying streets,
> And death's the market place, where each one meets.
>
> (I.v.13–16)

This minute sample of verbal parallels is representative. (A substantial number of longer examples may be found in the editorial notes of Knight, Skeat, and Littledale.) The detailed correspondences show clearly that the scenes in the play based on Chaucer were written with Chaucer's words, and not merely with some abstract of his plot, firmly in the mind of the author or authors. This point itself has been widely recognized by students of the play, but its bearing on the problem of authorship has not been recognized. The close *verbal* relationship between the texts will be worth keeping in mind throughout our analysis of the adaptation.

The close verbal relationships between many passages in Shakespeare's text and his sources, Holinshed and North for example, are too familiar to need illustration. Many other dramatists of course borrowed from or echoed their sources in similar ways. Yet the major contributors to the Fletcher *Quellenforschungen* (Weber, Dyce, Greg, Chambers, and others) do not find such evidence in Fletcher's plays; as Baldwin Maxwell says in his essay on *Henry VIII,* close verbal borrowing is "most emphatically . . . not characteristic" of Fletcher. If these scholars are right, the parallels with *The Knight's Tale* in the six "Fletcher scenes" of *The Two Noble Kinsmen* based upon it amount to presumptive evidence against Fletcher's authorship of those scenes. It might be argued that Fletcher could have modified his usual practice on a single occasion, although to assume again that he adopted a practice like Shakespeare's would be to add one more item to the rather longish list of *ad hoc* hypotheses which any theory of dual authorship must seek to accommodate. To this argument about Fletcher's normal working habits, on the other hand, one might raise the legitimate objection that it is too negative and too general; it leads nowhere, and it is also possible that further study of Fletcher's sources will someday disclose evidence of direct borrowings. The verbal parallelism between Chaucer and the play is nevertheless worth our attention; for if we begin to examine in specific detail the precise relationships between the two texts, a few further facts emerge which do bear on the question of authorship and which depend wholly upon visible evidence that no presently unknown knowledge of Fletcher could be imagined seriously to affect. We might proceed, then, to take up a representative group of dramatic scenes and to consider the elements they borrow from or add to their counterpart episodes in Chaucer.

We shall consider a sequence of four scenes—II.v, III.i, III.iii, and III.vi —which incorporate material from one continuous episode in Part II of *The Knight's Tale,* beginning with Arcite's efforts to approach Emilia and ending with Theseus' interruption of the duel between the two knights (lines 1418–1825). The events in the play include Arcite's encounter with Theseus and his introduction into the service of Emilia (II.v), his accidental encounter with the fugitive Palamon (III.i), the scene in which Arcite brings his cousin meat and drink (III.iii), and the scene of the duel (III.vi). These dramatic scenes have the advantage for our purpose of straddling the conventional division between authors; nearly all critics assign II.v, III.iii, and III.vi to Fletcher and agree with Middleton Murry that

III.i "belongs, wholly and indubitably, to Shakespeare."[2] But now that the lines have again been drawn, we must set the question of authorship aside for a while and look to see how the scenes are plotted in relation to their source.

All of the events involving Theseus in Acts II and III are imagined to occur during the three-day festival of May. Arcite makes his first impression on Theseus by winning the May-game contests he had learned about from the Countrymen in II.iii. Still in his "poor disguise," he stands before Theseus:

> *Theseus.* What country bred you?
> *Arcite.* This; but far off, prince.
> *Theseus.* Are you a gentleman?
> *Arcite.* My father said so—
>   And to those gentle uses gave me life.
> *Theseus.* Are you his heir?
> *Arcite.* His youngest, sir.
> *Theseus.* Your father
>   Sure is a happy sire then. What proves you?
> *Arcite.* A little of all noble qualities:
>   I could have kept a hawk, and well have holloa'd
>   To a deep cry of dogs. I dare not praise
>   My feat in horsemanship; yet they that knew me
>   Would say it was my best piece. Last and greatest,
>   I would be thought a soldier.
>
> (II.v.6–20)

This circumstantial detail is invented for the play, as is Arcite's assignment to the service of Emilia:

> *Pirithous.*   I shall give you
>   To a most noble service—to this lady,
>   This bright young virgin; pray observe her goodness;
>   You have honor'd her fair birthday with your virtues,
>   And as your due y'are hers . . .
>
> (II.v.47–51)

In Chaucer Arcite is first employed as a laborer by Emelye's chamberlain and later raised to the service of Theseus. That May Day is Emilia's birthday is, more interestingly, another invented detail in the play.

Here we must turn for a moment to a brief episode in Chaucer. Arcite, now a squire in the service of Theseus, rises early one bright morning,

---

[2] John Middleton Murry, *Shakespeare* (1936), p. 385.

mounts his "courser startlynge as the fir" (1502), and goes forth "to doon his observaunce to May" (1500). He rides toward a grove where he hopes to find woodbine or hawthorn to make himself a garland of branches,

> And loude he song ayeyn the sonne shene:
> "May, with alle thy floures and thy grene,
> Welcome be thou, faire, fresshe May,
> In hope that I som grene gete may."
>
> (1509–1512)

A moment later in the poem Arcite comes upon Palamoun, but at this point we shall return to the play, where a few details from these dozen lines reappear in two separate scenes.

A later passage in the scene we were looking at picks up hints from the passage in Chaucer, echoing the phrase "to doon his observaunce to May" (also found at *A Midsummer Night's Dream* I.i.167 within a context showing other echoes of *The Knight's Tale*), and permitting us also to learn where Arcite's "courser startlynge as the fir" comes from:

> *Theseus* [to Hippolyta]. Sweet, you must be ready—
> And you, Emilia—and you, friend—and all—
> Tomorrow by the sun, to do observance
> To flow'ry May, in Dian's wood. Wait well, sir,
> Upon your mistress. Emily, I hope
> He shall not go afoot.
> *Emilia.* That were a shame, sir,
> While I have horses.—Take your choice, and what
> You want at any time, let me but know it . . .
>
> (II.v.64–72)

Emilia's present of the horses is also original to the play.

It is the next day as III.i opens to "noise and halloaing, as people a-Maying." Arcite, separated from Theseus and his party, enters alone. His three-line song to May in Chaucer is here transmuted into a visionary prayer to Emilia (and in language that anticipates that of the Wooer's later vision of the Daughter):

> *Arcite.* The Duke has lost Hippolyta; each took
> A several laund. This is a solemn rite
> They owe bloom'd May, and the Athenians pay it
> To th'heart of ceremony. Oh queen Emilia,
> Fresher than May, sweeter
> Than her gold buttons on the boughs, or all
> Th'enamell'd knacks o'th'mead or garden! Yea,

> We challenge too the bank of any nymph
> That makes the stream seem flowers! Thou, oh jewel
> O'th'wood, o'th'world, hast likewise bless'd a place
> With thy sole presence . . .

(III.i.1–11)

Emilia has kept the promise she made in the earlier scene:

> She takes strong note of me,
> Hath made me near her, and this beauteous morn,
> The prim'st of all the year, presents me with
> A brace of horses . . .

(III.i.17–20)

The gift is referred to once more in the play, for after the final tournament in Act V Pirithous describes how Arcite has been thrown and crushed by a "hot horse, hot as fire," the very "steed that Emily/ Did first bestow on him" (V.iv.62 & 78).

The three third-act scenes with Palamon and Arcite (III.i, III.iii, III.vi) follow Chaucer's narrative fairly closely, departing mainly by way of amplification. Palamon's grove, first referred to in the play by the Daughter in II.vi, is supposed to be the site of the action in all three scenes. Both in the poem (1574 ff.) and the play (III.i.31 ff.), Palamon starts out of his hiding-place in fury when he hears Arcite praise Emilia. Weak and hungry, he nevertheless challenges Arcite to a duel. In Chaucer, Arcite promises to bring "mete and drynke this nyght" (1615) and "tomorwe" (1610) to bring "harneys" for the duel. The distinction is evidently rather casual in the poem and is there left undeveloped, so that six lines after we hear of Arcite's departure we hear of his return with swords and armor and the duelling episode begins. The knights arm each other (1649 ff.). Then we are told—for the first time in the poem—that Theseus and his companions are out hunting (1673 ff.). Theseus at once comes upon the knights (1697) and interrupts the duel.

Shakespeare does more with Arcite's promises. First, Arcite tells Palamon he will return

> With wholesome viands. These impediments
> Will I file off; you shall have garments, and
> Perfumes to kill the smell o'th'prison. . . .

(III.i.92–94)

These details form the narrative base for III.iii, the strange brief scene in which Arcite (throughout dependent on Palamon) tries to conciliate his cousin:

> Sit down and, good now,
> No more of these vain parleys. Let us not,
> Having our ancient reputation with us,
> Make talk for fools and cowards . . .
>
> (III.iii.12–15)

This entire episode is framed by the two night-soliloquies of the Daughter, and the young men's dialogue about the wenches they have known also acts as a foil to Palamon's closing outburst about Emilia and the renewal of their quarrel.

After offering to bring Palamon food and files and garments, Arcite's promises in III.i had gone on—

> After,
> When you shall stretch yourself, and say but 'Arcite,
> I am in plight,' there shall be at your choice
> Both sword and armor.
>
> (III.i.94–97)

He repeats this second promise (matching the promise of "harneys" in the poem) more bitterly at the end of III.iii:

> I'll come again some two hours hence, and bring
> That that shall quiet all—
> *Palamon.* A sword and armor.
> *Arcite.* Fear me not. You are now too foul. Farewell . . .
>
> (III.iii.64–67)

And the second meeting comes in III.vi—after the opening soliloquy of Palamon (another uncanny "Fletcher imitation" of Shakespeare):

> *Palamon.* About this hour my cousin gave his faith
> To visit me again and with him bring
> Two swords and two good armors. If he fail,
> He's neither man nor soldier. When he left me,
> I did not think a week could have restor'd
> My lost strength to me, I was grown so low
> And crestfall'n with my wants. I thank thee, Arcite,
> Thou art yet a fair foe; and I feel myself,
> With this refreshing, able once again
> To outdure danger. To delay it longer
> Would make the world think, when it comes to hearing,
> That I lay fatting like a swine, to fight,
> And not a soldier. Therefore this blest morning

Shall be the last; and that sword he refuses,
If it but hold, I kill him with. 'Tis justice.
So, love and fortune for me!

(III.vi.1–16)

Before we proceed further into so long and complex a scene as III.vi, it might be advisable to pause and see what conclusions can be drawn from such material as we have already observed.

Every theory of dramatic construction proposed by the principal advocates of dual authorship has presumed a play divided into two incompatible halves. The recent Waller theory, for example, assumes that the two authors wrote their respective shares at the same time while they were both in London, that they never consulted each other, and that Fletcher fitted the parts together so carelessly as to leave glaring inconsistencies visible in the received text. It is wonderful to note how little there is in the standard scholarship on the play that would inhibit the formulation of so absurd a theory. It is a fair guess that many normally intelligent readers, assuming divided authorship, have often missed the host of perfectly obvious and simple details of plot of the sort we have been observing, details beyond interpretive controversy, which show—on an extremely low level of literary significance, to be sure—a careful job of dramatic construction. If, for example, we note that Arcite's promise in III.i to bring Palamon "perfumes to kill the smell o'th'prison"—a detail not found in Chaucer—is carried out in III.iii, we are noting the kind of detail within which the wheels of the plot revolve— details which any schoolboy should be able to see without unusual effort, but which sober scholars have often either overlooked or else perhaps felt beneath their dignity to think about. When Dyce first invented the argument that, since the underplot was "of a nature not to be tolerated in any work" with which Shakespeare was concerned, the Shakespearean "portions" must have "existed before Fletcher contributed anything to the play," Ulrici was prompted to reply:

how does Dyce, with such a supposition, conceive the whole to have come into its present shape? Can he have thought that Shakspeare worked piecemeal in the manner of a joiner, who first makes the legs and then the top of a table, &c. Or, in the case before us, are we to suppose that Shakspeare wrote the first and the fifth acts—which stand in no sort of connection—and of the intermediate part nothing but the first scene of the third act [as Dyce on Spalding's auhority had maintained], in which the . . . kinsmen dispute about their passion for Emilia, without having previously described the origin of this passion . . . ? [3]

[3] Hermann Ulrici, *Shakspeare's Dramatic Art,* trans. L. Dora Schmitz (1876), II, 405.

Those who, like Ulrici, have solved the constructional problem by absolving Shakespeare of all responsibility for any part of the play seem in retrospect to have been curiously cold judges of dramatic poetry, but they have usually shown themselves capable, on their assumption of single authorship, to observe evidence that their opponents have, so to speak, willed out of sight. Most of the theories of dual authorship are, in short, hopelessly incapable of accounting for the plotting of the play. Jacobean dramatic collaboration did of course take place, usually—we assume on what little evidence we have—with writers working on separate scenes or dramatic sequences with the aid of an author's plot, or else with one writer making use of the work of another in producing his final manuscript. Whatever method of collaboration we might try to imagine, the play as it stands forces us to conclude that one or both writers took pains to maintain consistency over the most minute details of plot. And it is at this point that the question of sources comes most importantly into the problem of authorship before us.

It is the further complications of the details borrowed, adapted, or altered from *The Knight's Tale* which—taken along with the normal intricacies of plot-construction—stand as obstacles to any theory of collaboration that might be freshly attempted. If two collaborators worked from a common source such as *The Knight's Tale* (with or without the aid of an agreed-upon dramatic outline) and if they both felt free to draw so many minute details and scattered phrases directly from it, they would have to have been extraordinarily careful not to step on each other's toes in their redistribution of those details and phrases in the dialogue of the play. We might at this point go back to III.vi, then, for further comparisons.

Following Palamon's soliloquy, Arcite's entrance, and a powerful speech by Arcite (lines 29–46) which is not based on Chaucer, the events of III.vi keep to the order of the poem. After the memorable episode in which Palamon and Arcite arm each other (lines 47–137, elaborately expanded from *The Knight's Tale* 1649–1652), Theseus interrupts their duel and orders that both shall die; Theseus' companions intercede for the cousins, and the scene ends as Theseus alters his decree, releasing the knights on their oath to return for the final contest at the appointed time. A number of speeches in this scene follow Chaucer closely, particularly during the episode in which Theseus interrupts the duel (1706–1741 in the poem, lines 169–220 in the play). From this episode the two corresponding speeches in which Palamon asks for death illustrate the kind of adjustments that took place:

> "Sire, what nedeth wordes mo?
> We have the deeth disserved bothe two. . . .

And as thou art a rightful lord and juge,
Ne yif us neither mercy ne refuge,
But sle me first, for seinte charitee!
But sle my felawe eek as wel as me;
Or sle hym first, for though thow knowest it lite,
This is thy mortal foo, this is Arcite,
That fro thy lond is banysshed . . ."

(1715–1716, 1719–1725)

In the play Palamon's exposure of the disguised Arcite is placed earlier (at III.vi.180 ff.), and the change wittily shifts the emphasis in his plea:

Palamon. Thou shalt have pity of us both, oh Theseus,
If unto neither thou show mercy. Stop,
As thou art just, thy noble ear against us;
As thou are valiant, for thy cousin's soul,
Whose twelve strong labors crown his memory,
Let's die together, at one instant, Duke—
Only a little let him fall before me,
That I may tell my soul he shall not have her.

(III.vi.213–220)

The joke and the other parallel features indicate the closeness of the adaptation, and this in turn points up the deliberateness with which the allusion to Hercules is introduced; the allusion recalls Theseus' first reference to "Hercules our kinsman" at I.i.70,[4] and it adds one more to the various close pairings of friends, relations, and lovers that are multiplied and stressed throughout the play almost like an iterative image.

Although in the poem Theseus' hunting-party is not mentioned before the duelling episode (1673 ff.), in the play Theseus and his companions appear also in II.v, the hunting-party is referred to in III.i, the proximity of Theseus which constitutes a danger to Palamon is referred to in III.iii, and the morris dance in III.v is performed before Theseus only when he is accosted by Gerrold and agrees to suspend the hunt (III.v.101 & 160). A generally accepted textual emendation provides a conveniently brief indicator of the way in which details from the source—analogous to those cited in our earliest comparisons—are taken over and redistributed among the several scenes in the play. Editors used to be puzzled by the quarto reading at III.i.2, "a severall land" (cf. page 248), until Skeat confirmed the reading Shakespeare must have meant by observing Chaucer's use of "launde"—at

---

[4] The notion of kinship between Theseus and Hercules (referred or alluded to at *TNK* I.i.70, II.v.2, III.vi.216, and *MND* V.i.47) was presumably derived by Shakespeare, as editors note, from the Plutarch-North *Life of Theseus.*

two points (lines 1691 and 1696) in the midst of the passage which constitutes the source not for III.i but for III.vi. Aspirin goes back only to the nineteenth century; any new theory of simultaneous collaboration ought perhaps to propose some Jacobean medicine, for the necessary adjustments of petty details would probably have been as painful a bother to two dramatists as spending time over them is to us. But we might now pass on to larger issues in the dramatic adaptation of Chaucer, and our next and final comparisons should suggest that the larger rearrangements of material from the source are even more difficult to square with the assumption of two hands in the text.

The passages to be examined are concerned mainly with the characterization of Theseus. One point having to do with another Shakespearean character, very much like him, might be presented first. In the essay which he has described as his solitary attempt at a "comprehensive statement" on Shakespeare's "total impact," Wilson Knight offers a comment on Shakespearean heroes which seems relevant to our subject even though Knight did not write with *The Two Noble Kinsmen* in mind. In his essay on "The Shakespearian Integrity," after remarking on the "coincidence of the human with the archetypal and the Christian" in several Shakespearean roles (e.g. Richard II), Knight introduces a transitional qualification and then proceeds into his final summation of the Shakespearean ruler:

But Shakespeare is too truly a dramatist and a Renaissance artist . . . to place his sole trust in poetry or religious meditation. His studious princes, as in *Measure for Measure* and *The Tempest,* must take up their burdens again; Fortinbras brings his name and army to cure Denmark of its mentally insoluble disease; and the last play of the whole sequence is *Henry VIII.* Perhaps Theseus comes nearest to Shakespeare's ideal of manhood, slight sketch though it be. See how, after the moonlit night of fears and fancies, he enters with the rising sun, to wake the lovers from their dreams.[5]

Parenthetically it may be remarked that *Henry VIII* is not only likely to be an earlier play than *The Two Noble Kinsmen,* but that—if and when the belief that Shakespeare collaborated with Fletcher is abandoned—it may come to be assumed, even on rather slight evidence, that *Timon of Athens* is Shakespeare's last play.[6] Nevertheless, if authority derives from broad

[5] G. Wilson Knight, *The Sovereign Flower* (1958), pp. 8, 226–227. The essay first appeared in *The Burning Oracle* (1939).

[6] That assumption might help explain the presence of a few scenes which look like "hurried and unrevised work" (Wilson Knight) in a play so fully formed as to make the still common supposition that Shakespeare deliberately abandoned it hard to accept. Probably such a suggestion about the date of *Timon* would have been made long ago had it not been for the obstruction of an assumed collaboration

and thorough experience of one's subject, not many critics have spoken on
Shakespeare with more authority than Wilson Knight, and his comment
on the earlier Theseus may eventually seem to apply with at least equal force
to the later.

After Chaucer's Theseus condemns the two knights to death,

> The queene anon, for verray wommanhede,
> Gan for to wepe, and so dide Emelye,
> And alle the ladyes in the compaignye.
> Greet pitee was it, as it thoughte hem alle,
> That evere swich a chaunce sholde falle;
> For gentil men they were of greet estaat,
> And no thyng but for love was this debaat . . .
>
> (1748–1754)

Out of these and several more lines of weeping by the almost supernumerary
women of the *Tale,* the dramatist—in dialogue that is freer in movement
and more impassioned than the formal appeals for aid against Creon in I.i
which it recalls—develops the eighty-line episode (III.vi.226–307) in which
Hippolyta, Emilia, and Pirithous persuade the reluctant Theseus to call
back his oath. Chaucer's Theseus, on the other hand, persuades himself;
reflecting that

> every man
> Wol helpe hymself in love, if that he kan,
> And eek delivere himself out of prisoun. . . .
>
> (1767–1769)

he comes, in the passage on "the god of love," to see that both knights have
already suffered unconscionably and that his earlier sentence of death had
therefore been part of "an heigh folye" (1798); he then digresses to amuse
himself at Emelye's expense (a passage which incidentally suggests the
disparity in stature between the roles of Emelye and Emilia):

> But this is yet the beste game of alle,
> That she for whom they han this jolitee
> Kan hem therfore as muche thank as me.
> She woot namoore of al this hoote fare,
> By God, than woot a cokkow or an hare!
>
> (1806–1810)

with Fletcher about 1613; the suggestion is raised here, not to urge its very slight
merits, but merely to indicate one of the reasons that *TNK* cannot yet, if ever, be confidently regarded as Shakespeare's last play.

But his thoughts then turn back to his own youth, he reflects on his own experience, and his recollection leads him finally to forgive the cousins:

> I woot it by myself ful yore agon,
> For in my tyme a servant was I oon.
> And therfore, syn I knowe of loves peyne,
> And woot how soore it kan a man distreyne,
> As he that hath ben caught ofte in his laas,
> I yow foryeve al hoolly this trespaas,
> At requeste of the queene, that kneleth heere,
> And eek of Emelye, my suster deere. . . .
>
> (1813–1820)

There is nothing quite like this speech in the corresponding scene of the play. Not that the dramatic Theseus of this episode is not very knowing; in place of the affectionate pat on the head, he offers Emilia a testy wisdom:

> *Theseus.* . . . Say I felt
> Compassion to 'em both, how would you place it?
> *Emilia.* Upon their lives; but with their banishments.
> *Theseus.* You are a right woman, sister; you have pity,
> But want the understanding where to use it.
> If you desire their lives, invent a way
> Safer than banishment. Can these two live,
> And have the agony of love about 'em,
> And not kill one another? Every day
> They'd fight about you; hourly bring your honor
> In public question with their swords. Be wise then
> And here forget 'em. It concerns your credit
> And my oath equally. I have said they die.
> Better they fall by th'law than one another.
> Bow not my honor.
> *Emilia.* Oh my noble brother,
> That oath was rashly made, and in your anger;
> Your reason will not hold it. If such vows
> Stand for express will, all the world must perish. . . .
>
> (III.vi.261–279)

Emilia's last words here recall an earlier speech in the play—the same speech the reader may have recalled a moment ago as he read the "experience" speech of Chaucer's Theseus—when Theseus had commanded "our richest balms" to save the lives of the two fallen knights:

> minister
> What man to man may do; for our sake, more—
> Since I have known frights, fury, friends' behests,

> Love's provocations, zeal, a mistress' task,
> Desire of liberty, a fever, madness,
> Hath set a mark which nature could not reach to
> Without some imposition, sickness in will
> O'er-wrestling strength in reason . . .
>
> (I.iv.43–50)

To show Theseus in III.vi arguing himself out of the death sentence he had passed on the knights (and at their own request) would be a dramatic anomaly, and if there is any speech in the play that forms the counterpart to the inner monologue of Chaucer's Theseus cited above (1813–1820) it would appear to be this first-act speech about the origin of ideals. In the corresponding early episode in the poem the captured knights were simply dispatched to prison (1022–1024) and there were no words from Chaucer's Theseus corresponding to the lines in I.iv. Palamon and Arcite are saved once in the poem, in the later episode, through Theseus' charity; they are saved twice in the play, first in I.iv through Theseus' charity, then in III.vi through Emilia's intercession. The speech of Theseus in I.iv sets some of the conditions, as it were, for Emilia's victory over him in III.vi; there, just before the final contest for her is to be arranged, she adopts the language he had used earlier, emerging as a spokesman for his own finest values.

Alterations of plot are of course inseparable from alterations of character. As part of his campaign to throw Shakespeare out of the play, Furnivall, entrepreneur of Chaucer as well as Shakspere, drew a contrast (in his 1876 Foreword to Spalding) between Emelye, whom he called a "daring huntress, virgin free, seeking no marriage-bed," and Emilia, whom he called "a silly lady's-maid or shop-girl." Shopgirl?

> Shall anything that loves me perish for me?
> That were a cruel wisdom! Do men proin
> The straight young boughs that blush with thousand blossoms
> Because they may be rotten?
>
> (III.vi.292–295)

On the contrary, the Emelye of the *Tale,* as one recent critic accurately observes, is a "shadowily insignificant" figure in comparison with the "far more sensitive" and "much more prominent" Emilia of the play.[7]

The several alterations we have been looking at appear to have been guided by intelligent purpose, and they required the adjustment of so many larger and smaller variables in the source as to have obscured that evidence of divided authorship which too many careless critics have declared to be

---

[7] E. C. Pettet, *Shakespeare and the Romance Tradition* (1949), pp. 173–174.

mathematically self-evident. The episodes we have looked at are representative, and almost any other sequence we might choose in comparing the two texts would reveal similar consistency of purpose. The role of Pirithous, for example, is much expanded in the play, and neither his part as advocate for the suppliant Queens in I.i nor his similar advocacy on behalf of the kinsmen in III.vi owes anything of consequence to Chaucer. But such points about internal dramatic relationships, finally, can best be made without distracting cross-references to sources.[8]

The Author's Tribute to Chaucer

The writer of the Prologue to *The Two Noble Kinsmen* makes an interesting acknowledgment of his debt to Chaucer. It may be mentioned first that the bibliographical evidence connecting the manuscript of the Prologue with the manuscript of the play [9] strengthens the already considerable documentary interest of this speech. Many of the Jacobean prologues which give evidence concerning dramatic dates and authorship (and which are lucidly interpreted by Bentley at more or less face value) provide far less information than does that of *The Two Noble Kinsmen*. The reference to "losses" at the end of the Prologue (discussed in Appendix A) reminds us that such speeches are distinctly occasional and that this Prologue is no exception; although it serves a dramatic purpose by translating the audience from the Blackfriars environment into the world of the play, it can be useful to think

---

[8] As a matter of record the known sources other than Chaucer (none of them very consequential) might be noted. Plutarch has already been mentioned (n. 4). Paul A. Jorgensen (*Shakespeare's Military World* [1956], pp. 187–188) has pointed out that Arcite's prayer to Mars in V.i echoes a passage in Barnabe Barnes's *Foure Bookes of Offices* (1606). Not previously noted is the fact that some of Gerrold's speeches in III.v echo speeches by the pedant Rombus in Sidney's untitled masque known as *The Lady of May* (cf. Sidney, *Complete Works,* ed. Feuillerat, II [1922], 331–336); the masque, performed in 1578 and published in 1598, also has a heroine pursued by two love-struck young men. Otherwise, Collier and later editors have speculated on a possible connection between *TNK* and an anonymous "palamon and arsett" mentioned in Henslowe's Diary, of which all it would seem possible to say is that it is lost, and that it is hard to imagine how a play written for Henslowe in 1594 could have any direct relevance to a King's company play by Shakespeare in 1613—especially one so palpably based on a direct and intimate acquaintance with Chaucer. Some editors have also thought fit to mention another lost play, *Palæmon and Arcyte* by Richard Edwards, reportedly performed before Queen Elizabeth at Oxford in 1566.

[9] E.g. in spellings such as *take* (=*tack*) at Prol. 26 and again at III.iv.10 and IV.i.196, and *travell* (=*travail*) at Prol. 29 and II.v.43 (where some editors, perhaps wrongly, print *travel;* on Shakespearean usage, cf. *Troilus* I.i.70, II.ii.4, and III.iii.154, in both Q and F texts, and Onions' *Shakespeare Glossary*). On the stage directions in the *TNK* Prologue, cf. pp. 94–95 above.

about that Blackfriars environment for a moment. The speaker tells us unambiguously that he is introducing a new play; this information appears partly in the opening lines, but mainly in the lines having to do with Chaucer, with which we are here more directly concerned. The dramatist seems so willing to share honors with Chaucer—he is so emphatic on the subject—that it becomes difficult to see how, if he had had a collaborator, the mere question of a rhyme would prompt him so ungenerously to refer to himself, in the singular, as the "writer":

> It [the play] has a noble breeder, and a pure,
> A learned, and a poet never went
> More famous yet 'twixt Po and silver Trent.
> Chaucer (of all admir'd) the story gives—
> There constant to eternity it lives;
> If we let fall the nobleness of this,
> And the first sound this child hear be a hiss,
> How will it shake the bones of that good man
> And make him cry from under ground, 'Oh fan
> From me the witless chaff of such a writer
> That blasts my bays and my fam'd works makes lighter
> Than Robin Hood!' This is the fear we bring—
> For to say truth, it were an endless thing,
> And too ambitious, to aspire to him,
> Weak as we are, and almost breathless swim
> In this deep water . . .
>
> $\qquad\qquad\qquad\qquad\qquad\qquad\qquad$ (10–25)

It may or may not be fanciful to see in the varying movement of the rhymed couplets signs of a renewed close acquaintance with Chaucer, but as one takes in the stylistic sophistications (the grammar of lines 10–12 and 24–25, for example) together with the unconventionality of the tribute, it is hardly possible to resist identifying the writer of the Prologue with the writer who had absorbed Chaucer so thoroughly in his compositional labors on the play. And if Fletcher had put his efforts into studying and adapting *The Knight's Tale* in partnership with Shakespeare, it is more than a little surprising that no record appears in either Prologue or Epilogue. Such speeches, especially in plays written for the King's company after the acquisition of Blackfriars, were frequently used to acknowledge collaboration or revision,[10] and the authorship of plays by established dramatists was ordinarily known to the audience[11]—perhaps through the announcements made from the

---

[10] Cf. Bentley, *The Jacobean and Caroline Stage*, III, 327, 334, 342, 358, 362, 365, etc., for citation and analysis of examples (one of which is reproduced on p. 235 above).

[11] Leaving aside such purely literary evidence as Meres's long list of dramatic ascrip-

stage at the end of performances or through the playbills circularized and posted about London [12]—so that a reference to a single writer in a prologue to a play of dual authorship (particularly a King's play of so late a date) would be an especially puzzling piece of deception, unlikely to be attempted and unlikely if attempted to succeed. But the simple and literal reading of the Prologue suggested here can hardly be called inescapable, since it is the one reading scholars have regularly refused to consider. The alternative readings—some examples are given in Appendix A—invariably raise more problems than they solve, while the literal reading fits all of the evidence except the attribution on the 1634 title-page.

Waterson's Title-page and the Testimony of Leonard Digges

The circumstances surrounding the publication of the 1623 First Folio and the preliminary matter in the Folio lend massive authority, of course, to the attribution of the Folio plays to Shakespeare. Other title-page attributions, as noted at the beginning of this study, may under certain circumstances carry no weight at all. As Greg has pointed out, early publishers did not provide information on their title-pages primarily for the convenience of future scholars:

> . . . only such information was given as might be thought to concern a prospective purchaser. And in this connection we may recall the habit of displaying the title-pages of new books about the city in the hope of attracting the notice of passers-by—
>
> > [I'll] have the copies of it pasted on posts
> > Like pamphlet title that sue to be sold,
>
> says a character in *The Honest Man's Fortune,* intending the widest publicity. . . . Most important was the name and address of the stationer from whom copies of the work could be obtained.[13]

Waterson's title-page of 1634, we may recall, is the earliest historical testimony of any connection between Shakespeare and Fletcher. But along with this title-page we might consider another document of earlier date.

---

tions in 1598, there is the theatrical evidence in several of the prologues and epilogues alluded to in the preceding note and there are such references as Henry Moody's dedicatory poem to Massinger printed with *A New Way to Pay Old Debts,* "The thronged audience that was hither brought/ Invited by your fame . . ."—all of which presuppose that audiences knew the identities of the dramatists.

[12] Cf. Chambers, *The Elizabethan Stage,* II, 547–548.

[13] Greg, *Some Aspects and Problems of London Publishing between 1550 and 1650* (1956), p. 82.

Leonard Digges (1588–1635) is the only known witness prior to Waterson to have left a comment on Shakespeare relevant to the subject of dramatic collaboration. Digges, the stepson of Shakespeare's friend and executor Thomas Russell, was a respected Oxford scholar remembered for his translation of Claudian (William Heminge called him "the Famous Digges, or Leonard Claudian"); [14] a lifelong member of both the London and Stratford circles in which Shakespeare moved, he was probably a friend of Shakespeare himself.[15] In 1623 he composed two dedicatory poems for a volume of Shakespeare's plays, the shorter of which appeared among the preliminaries to the 1623 Folio and the longer of which appeared in the 1640 Benson edition of Shakespeare's *Poems*.[16] In the longer version he wrote of Shakespeare:

> Nor begges he from each witty friend a Scene
> To peece his Acts with, all that he doth write,
> Is pure his owne, plot, language exquisite . . .

It is hard to believe (except perhaps in anti-Stratfordian circles) that a partnership between Shakespeare and Fletcher could have remained a closely guarded secret until the young bookseller Waterson chose to reveal it in 1634; that Digges could have written these lines (if there *had* been collaboration) under any other circumstances—or under any circumstances at all if he were honest—is equally hard to believe. Document for document, the poem by Digges would surely seem to outweigh the authority of a title-page written to be displayed as an advertisement on posts about the city;

[14] *William Hemminge's Elegy on Randolph's Finger*, ed. G. C. Moore Smith (1923), l. 72; William, a student at Oxford, was the son of Shakespeare's John Heminge.

[15] More informative than the *DNB* life of Digges is the chapter devoted to him by Leslie Hotson in *I, William Shakespeare* (1938), pp. 237–259. Cf. also Peter Alexander, *Shakespeare's Life and Art* (1939), pp. 131, 226.

[16] Both poems are reprinted in Chambers, *William Shakespeare*, II, 231–234. Hotson suggests, plausibly, that it was Edward Blount, his friend as well as his publisher, who probably arranged for Digges to contribute a poem to the Folio. That the poem printed in 1640 was written in 1623 is made clear not only by the fact that it applies to a collection of plays but also by its reference, in a passage naming the London theaters, to "new Fortunes younger brethren," an allusion to the rebuilt Fortune which opened in the spring of 1623. Hotson and Alexander suggest that the 1640 poem was rejected for the Folio because of its length, but a better reason has been advanced by Edgar I. Fripp (*Shakespeare: Man and Artist*, II, 868): in the poem Digges refers to an audience that "would not brooke a line/ Of tedious . . . *Catilines*," that found *Sejanus* "irkesome" after Shakespeare, and so forth; Fripp suggests that the poem was "declined by the Editors as severe on Jonson and somewhat slighting to the King's men"; Jonson, after all, had been associated with the publication of the Folio (cf. Greg, *The Shakespeare First Folio*, pp. 17–21), and Heminge or Condell or Blount might well have thought it undiplomatic to use the poem.

it has nevertheless been ignored by literary historians who still refer to three plays on which, they say, Shakespeare collaborated with Fletcher. The Digges poem appears to have been given serious attention only once in discussions by prominent scholars of the Shakespeare-Fletcher issue; Halliwell-Phillipps called attention to it more than eighty years ago, using it to support his argument that Shakespeare alone had written *Henry VIII* and that Fletcher alone had written *The Two Noble Kinsmen;* and it might be added that the latter half of this argument was based also on

the extreme improbability of a dramatist of Shakespeare's unrivalled power and rapidity of composition entering, at the maturest period of his reputation, into the joint-authorship of a play with a much younger writer, and of the latter having in such a case the assurance to be palpably imitating him, both characterially and verbally, in [what the N.S.S. critics had called] his portion of the work.[17]

And this same consideration appears to survive in the minds of many scholars and readers of the present day.[18]

If it were possible to read the Waterson title-page without reference to any other evidence, it would obviously be easier to interpret it as accurate than to reject the Fletcher attribution and postulate a lost manuscript to account for the absence of the play from the 1623 Folio. But if we gauge the value of a hypothesis by tracing out its consequences and by observing whether or not it illuminates the relevant data, the latter hypothesis possesses far greater relative simplicity. Characteristic of the attempts to verify the Waterson ascription are the reports of critics who claim to see "two utterly dissimilar styles" in the play or who find "filthy nymphomania" in the character of the Jailor's Daughter. One typical consequence of crediting the Fletcher ascription has been the disintegration of one of Shakespeare's finest history-plays. And typical of the dumbfounding logic that follows from defending the Waterson ascription is the recent argument by Kenneth Muir that "the use of *heirs* as a verb" in Theobald's *Double Falsehood,* since it "would appear to be beyond [Theobald's] . . . powers," helps to show that Shakespeare wrote three acts of the lost *Cardenio.* That Shakespeare wrote

[17] J. O. Halliwell-Phillipps, *Outlines of the Life of Shakespeare,* 3rd edn. (1883), p. 734.

[18] James G. McManaway, writing in the 1959 issue of *Shakespeare Survey,* observes that "popular reluctance to admit that Shakespeare ever had a collaborator is the chief obstacle to the inclusion of *The Two Noble Kinsmen* [in the canon], despite its [partial] acceptance by Coleridge, Bradley, Chambers, and Greg, to name only a few" (p. 149). If such reluctance really *is* the "chief" obstacle, the thesis of this book may encounter less resistance than its not too sanguine author anticipates.

all of *The Two Noble Kinsmen* is a more stable hypothesis. To verify it we may turn to almost any one of the hundreds of subjects of inquiry that have grown in confusion about the play for above two hundred years. It seems to make nearly every one of them, taken singly or in combination, more intelligible, and it is confirmed by careful analysis of the play.

De Quincey

De Quincey once held that the entire play was "beyond all doubt" by Shakespeare, and his assertion was unique in nineteenth-century criticism. The critics and scholars who came after De Quincey as a rule either ignored or misrepresented his opinion.[19] They were able to do so, presumably, because his remarks were buried in a footnote to an essay on another subject. But it would be wrong to assume that his opinion, however diffidently made public, was merely casual, for he added that he thought the play to be, "in point of composition, perhaps the most superb work in the language." A commitment of this sort must be remarkably rare in the history of English criticism. There is of course no need to try to determine the exact position of *The Two Noble Kinsmen* on any ideal literary hit parade, but De Quincey's high estimate is less far-fetched than many other recorded judgments on the value of the play.

[19] De Quincey's fullest comment on the play first appeared in a long note to an essay printed in *Blackwood's* for December 1828 (XXIV, 896–897):

> Shakspeare is no doubt a rhetorician, *majorum gentium;* but he is so much more, that scarcely an instance is to be found of his rhetoric which does not pass by fits into a higher element of eloquence or poetry. The first and last acts, for instance, of *the Two Noble Kinsmen,* [—] which, in point of composition, is perhaps the most superb work in the language, and beyond all doubt from the loom of Shakspeare, [—] would have been the most gorgeous rhetoric, had they not happened to be something far better. The supplications of the widowed Queens to Theseus, the invocations of their tutelar divinities by Palamon and Arcite, the death of Arcite, &c. are finished in a more elaborate style of excellence than any other almost of Shakspeare's most felicitous scenes. In their first intention, they were perhaps merely rhetorical; but the furnace of composition has transmuted their substance . . . into the pure gold of poetry.

De Quincey retained the note when in 1859 he reprinted the essay (newly titled "Rhetoric") in his own edition of his *Works* (X, 49). The dashes shown here in brackets were added by Masson in his 1890 edition of De Quincey (X, 108)—and wisely added, for they would help to prevent such misreadings as Littledale's: Littledale printed De Quincey's comment in the notes to his 1876 edition of *TNK* (p. 157), but in his 1885 Introduction (p. 74*), after giving a cross-reference back to the notes, he said that De Quincey "gives Acts I. and V. to Shakspere, but apparently without intending to include Act V. sc. ii"!

The Arrangement of the Story

The story itself has evidently given trouble to some critics, Theodore Spencer for example:

> The story of Palamon and Arcite, whether told by Boccaccio, Chaucer, or Shakespeare and Fletcher, is intrinsically feeble, superficial, and undramatic. For there is no real difference between Palamon and Arcite; they are both noble individuals, and the only reasons Palamon, rather than Arcite, wins the lady whom they both love are (*a*) that he saw her first and (*b*) that he had the sense to pray for success to Venus rather than to Mars.[20]

Spencer goes on to suggest that "these reasons . . . may have been more forceful in Chaucer's day . . . than they were in Shakespeare's," but a reply to his objections had better not fuss over history: an audience in Chaucer's, Shakespeare's, or our own day might well be less interested in the final score than in the progress of the game. Two young men, equally gifted with every aristocratic grace, fall in love with the same woman—beautiful as a goddess in the poem, but in the play possessing also "Those best affections that the heavens infuse/ In their best-temper'd pieces" (I.iii.11)—and during the ensuing conflict one of the lovers must die. One would think that this set of circumstances, which requires that we never be allowed to sympathize much more strongly with one protagonist than with the other, would be "intrinsically" capable of development into more poignant drama than, say, the story of a young man who plans to avenge the murder of his father; in any case, unless we are willing to try out the dramatic hypothesis that attracted Chaucer and Shakespeare, we are not likely to be able to see whatever virtues occur in its realization, and this is perhaps sufficient reason for giving it at least a provisional assent.

As far as the reasons for Palamon's final victory are concerned, for the moment it will have to suffice to say that he wins Emilia because Arcite is killed in an accident. Other reasons, if reasons are necessary, may appear as we continue with the play. No reasons that we might construct are any more readily found, supinely waiting for us in the text, than are the reasons constructed by Spencer. It seems strange that, given a rich variety of available alternatives, men should choose to construct reasons that restrict rather than enlarge their experience; probably they do so in the traditional belief that they are somehow engaged in a search for "ultimate" reasons—a prob-

---

[20] *MP*, XXXVI, 256. Spencer adds, however, that Chaucer makes the story "very appealing," and he observes that "the extension of . . . [the cousins'] personal quarrel into a quarrel that involves the gods" must have looked to Shakespeare "like good dramatic material" (p. 257).

lem with which the story of Palamon and Arcite is itself quite explicitly concerned.

The action of the play may be seen as falling into three movements—the war against Creon (Act I), the May Day contests (Acts II and III), and the final tournament (Acts IV and V).[21] The predominantly solemn first act, framed within the ceremonial formality of two processions, establishes Theseus as the arbiter of his subjects' destinies and introduces us to the heroism of Palamon and Arcite. The kinsmen appear almost to have lost their lives in their loyal service to Thebes:

> Had they been taken
> When their last hurts were given, 'twas possible
> They might have been recover'd . . .
>
> (I.iv.29–31)

Theseus orders his best surgeons to tend them, but the closing of Act I is funereally dark: "Death's the market-place, where each one meets."

The second movement is a curious blend of festive and romantic comedy; its postwar world is warmer and more human than that of Act I. The two cousins, as if reborn, treat their prison as an Arcadian retreat; both of them, to the Daughter, are a "holiday" to look upon; the garden by the prison, to Emilia, "has a world of pleasures in't." The foolishness of May runs through all the episodes, although it is seldom left untouched by apprehensiveness or foreboding. Even the stiff-necked Gerrold has evidently been a creature of impulse ("the matter's too far driven between him and the tanner's daughter to let slip now"). But the natural vitality that finds its expression in the country sports, the Daughter's infatuation, Palamon's escape, the pursuit of Emilia, the cousins' drinking scene, the episode of the staghunt, leads more often to conflict and pain than it does to order and fulfillment: the Daughter abandons father and lover, Arcite flouts Theseus' decree of banishment and must disguise his identity, the hunting party is separated, the quarrelling cousins are always in peril of discovery, Palamon fails the Daughter and "is gone after his fancy," and Cicely—"that scornful piece, that scurvy hilding"—breaks the oath she had sworn (III.v.48:) "by wine and bread" (!), and the Daughter must therefore be made to take her place in the morris dance. Comic or serious, promises and oaths and appointments, broken or kept, pervade the dialogue and action of all twelve

---

[21] Several Jacobean plays written for presentation at Blackfriars seem to have been designed with some such three-movement structure in mind, and there is historical evidence (e.g. in Knight's specification of longer intervals after Acts I and III than after Acts II and IV in the prompt-book of *Believe as You List*) that they were performed accordingly.

scenes. Only one minor action is fully resolved in this part of the play—the episode of the Countrymen:

> Duke, if we have pleas'd thee too,
> And have done as good boys should do,
> Give us but a tree or twain
> For a Maypole, and again,
> Ere another year run out,
> We'll make thee laugh, and all this rout.
>
> (III.v.148–153)

(This clumsy verse will later be memorably echoed in Theseus' own Epilogue to *his* play.) Gerrold and the Countrymen, after they are generously rewarded, are never to appear again, and only a few later lines (IV.iii.10–13) refer directly to any of them. Their final scene also gives us our last glimpse in Act III of the Jailor's Daughter. ("And are you mad, good woman?" Gerrold asks her; "I would be sorry else," she replies.) But after the dance she merely disappears, left as usual to go her own way, alone. The other episodes of Acts II and III are brought to a tentative and precarious resolution by Theseus' arrangements for the final tournament and by the conditions and oaths he imposes on the contestant knights.

The third movement is more complex in its internal structure than those which preceded. The final two acts progress through ever more sharply contrasted scenes and cross-rhythms. Poised against the intensification of conflict in IV.ii, V.i, and V.iii, the story of the Daughter is gradually resolved in IV.i, IV.iii, and V.ii (although the plots are so interlinked that the Jailor is called to the field of combat in V.ii and Palamon's knights on their way to execution give their purses to piece out the Daughter's dowry in V.iv). The cast of the play is augmented in these acts by the Jailor's Brother and two Friends, the Doctor, the Executioner, Palamon's and Arcite's Knights, Emilia's Servant, the Daughter's Maid, and a stream of Messengers and Attendants. Not every one of them is vital to the action, and there are other minor characters (such as the fishermen referred to by the Wooer in IV.i) kept wholly out of the action, but this crowding contributes to what Sir Edmund Chambers in another connection has called "the effect of solidity, as if life were passing on all the time behind the stage."

Palamon and Arcite are kept offstage for a long interval prior to the dénouement,[22] returning in Act V, as if from far away and long ago, grown in dramatic weight and stature; virtually all the *dramatis personae* in Act

---

[22] The same point was noted earlier of Henry VIII and is true also of Romeo, Hamlet, Pericles, and many other Shakespearean heroes; on this constructional peculiarity of Shakespeare's, cf. W. J. Lawrence, *Speeding up Shakespeare* (1937), pp. 39–51.

IV meanwhile comment upon or describe them. Act IV develops what Moulton would call the "passion-strain" of the play, juxtaposing as it does the crises of Emilia and the Daughter.

The latent eroticism of the original tale is made explicit in the central scene of Act IV, in which Emilia, to her own growing distraction, praises both of the knights as she tries to decide between them. She had once been certain that she would "never . . . love any that's called man" (I.iii.97); and although her attitude had softened by the time of the garden dialogue (II.ii.130–184), when Arcite entered her service she still thought herself "too wise" to fall in love (II.v.84); now she feels compelled at last to follow the advice of Theseus (III.vi.327–343) and make a choice, but in the warm comparisons of her soliloquy before their portraits, and in rhythms and accents strongly reminiscent of the lovesick Daughter's earlier soliloquies, she learns only that she is hopelessly in love with both:

> I am sotted,
> Utterly lost. My virgin's faith has fled me,
> For if my brother but even now had ask'd me
> Whether I lov'd, I had run mad for Arcite;
> Now if my sister, more for Palamon. . . .
>   What a mere child is fancy,
> That having two fair gauds of equal sweetness,
> Cannot distinguish, but must cry for both!
>
>   (IV.ii.45–49, 52–54)

She is deprived of the power of choice from without as well as from within when she is brought news that the knights have arrived for the tournament:

> *Emilia.* To end the quarrel?
> *Gentleman.* Yes.
> *Emilia.* Would I might end first!
>   What sins have I committed, chaste Diana,
>   That my unspotted youth must now be soil'd
>   With blood of princes?
>
>   (IV.ii.58–63)

As Theseus and his companions enter, they and Emilia are treated by Pirithous and a Messenger to a gallery of verbal portraits of the princes and other "sons of honor" who "must . . . die too" (lines 83–159)—an episode contributing to the action as much momentum as dramatic cunning can derive from the idea of human sacrifice. This scene as a whole is transitional between III.vi and V.ii; the vows sworn in the former give rise to the prayers delivered in the latter, but the religious character of the tournament (expressed in the opening speeches of V.i) is already emergent in the language of IV.ii, appearing even in casual oaths (as at line 160) as well as the language of Emilia as she contemplates "the loves and fights/ Of gods and such men near 'em."

Act IV had begun with the Jailor fearful he would be punished for allowing Palamon to escape; his fears are set to rest when he is told of the pardon that Palamon has secured for him from Theseus, and his anger at his Daughter is softened by the Wooer's account of her attempt at suicide. A fully "rounded" character, the Jailor in his later scenes behaves with less and less of his initial surliness toward the Wooer and with continuously more conspicuous kindness toward his Daughter. After the girl is brought home by her uncle, the Jailor joins his friends in humoring her by taking part in her sea-fantasy. Her earlier vision of a ship wrecked in a tempest started her on an imaginary journey whose destinations include the land of Pygmies (III.iv.15), the domains reached by Charon's ferry (IV.iii.20), and the end of the world (V.ii.97). The Doctor is brought in to cure her in IV.iii, and his plan for the Wooer to disguise himself as Palamon is put into motion before the opening of V.ii, where we learn that it has begun to take effect—to "reduce what's now out of square in her into their former law and regiment" (IV.iii.89). The marriage to which her Wooer looked forward in Act II came to appear less and less likely as the action unfolded (cf. IV.iii.56–63), but in the last scene of the play, as Palamon is being led to execution, we hear that she has been cured and is to be married shortly. Which is to say, the underplot has a shape, and it is more or less round.

The rough sketch of the action drawn in these pages is still incomplete, and parts of it no doubt more closely resemble a hymarx synopsis than Aristotle's chalk outline. Yet perhaps it is sufficient to refute the common assumption that the play lacks any controlling organization or consistent development—that some scenes are "easily detachable" from the rest. We might now look more closely at particular features of the play that indicate a single imagination at work.

The Wedding Symbolism

Among the members of the bridal procession who appear at the very beginning of the play, we encounter

a Nymph, encompass'd in her tresses, bearing a wheaten garland; . . . two other Nymphs with wheaten chaplets on their heads; then Hippolyta, the bride, . . . and another holding a garland over her head (her tresses likewise hanging); after her, Emilia . . .

Later in the first scene Theseus speaks to Capaneus' widow:

> I met your groom
> By Mars's altar. You were that time fair;
> Not Juno's mantle fairer than your tresses,
> Nor in more bounty spread her. Your wheaten wreath
> Was then nor thresh'd nor blasted; Fortune at you
> Dimpled her cheek with smiles . . .

(I.i.65–70)

The marriage symbolism is conventional. The flowing tresses are associated with virginity; the wheaten wreath (which the bridegroom lifts from the bride's head during the wedding ceremony) is a symbol of fertility.

As the wedding procession entered at the beginning of the scene, a boy robed in white sang *Roses their sharp spines being gone,* the first two stanzas of which made emblems of the wedding flowers strewn by the boy. The rose, for example, is (as Emilia says at II.ii.163) "the very emblem of a maid."

The final episode in the opening scene of Act V takes place at the altar of Diana. Attended by nymphs more colorful than Hippolyta's, Emilia enters

in white, her hair about her shoulders, a wheaten wreath; one in white, . . . her hair stuck with flowers; one before her carrying a silver hind, in which is convey'd incense and sweet odors . . .

> Emilia. . . .   Most modest queen,
> He of the two pretenders that best loves me
> And has the truest title in't, let him
> Take off my wheaten garland; or else grant
> The file and quality I hold I may
> Continue in thy band.

Here the hind vanishes under the altar, and in the place ascends a rose tree, having one rose upon it.

> See what our general of ebbs and flows . . .
> With sacred act advances: but one rose!
> If well inspir'd, this battle shall confound
> Both these brave knights, and I, a virgin flow'r,
> Must grow alone, unpluck'd.

Here is heard a sudden twang of instruments, and the rose falls from the tree.

> The flow'r is fall'n, the tree descends. Oh mistress,
> Thou here dischargest me. I shall be gather'd . . .

In explaining the expressive significance of the flowers or the flowing tresses or the wheaten garland, many editorial notes give cross-references between

I.i and V.i (though not to Emilia's garden dialogue in II.ii). Both of these widely separated scenes are accepted as Shakespeare's (even by Clifford Leech), and the closely similar symbolism in their stage directions and dialogue has apparently been recognized as an element of conscious design.

Although no editor or critic has suggested a connection, the passages just cited also recall several details from the Wooer's narrative in IV.i which we examined in the preceding chapter. The boy spoke of the Daughter's love for Palamon:

> Rings she made
> Of rushes that grew by, and to 'em spoke
> The prettiest posies—'Thus our true love's tied,'
> 'This you may lose, not me,' and many a one . . .

These lines allude, as Skeat's note says,

to a common practice, especially among the lower orders, of celebrating mock-marriages. The ring used in such ceremonies was a rush ring, or one made of some equally common and fragile material.

As the Daughter imagines her own rude wedding-arrangements, she is described in images that contrast fittingly with the symbolism of the formal processions and dialogues of Act I and Act V:

> Her careless tresses
> A wreath of bulrush rounded . . .

As the girl dreamed of saving Palamon from the wrath of Theseus, she thought of herself attended by

> 'a bevy,
> A hundred black-eyed maids that love as I do,
> With chaplets on their heads of daffadillies,
> With cherry lips and cheeks of damask roses . . .'

As we saw earlier (pages 214–219), the Wooer's narrative has been widely regarded as an imitation by Fletcher of the description of Ophelia's death. But *that* description did not envision flowing tresses, or a mock wedding-wreath, or a virgin rose, or a procession of attendant nymphs whose hair was "stuck with flowers." If Fletcher wrote IV.i, his ability to "imitate" the descriptions of Ophelia in language which is at the same time so precisely relevant to the other scenes in *The Two Noble Kinsmen*—to produce *those* verbal resemblances to *Hamlet* while establishing *these* relationships to the imagery of his collaborator—would certainly be a prodigious achievement. The conclusion that all these scenes were written by Shakespeare is surely more reasonable.

The Doctor's Scenes

The Doctor appears in only two scenes of the play, IV.iii and V.ii. These are the two scenes of which Hickson said, "the tone and moral effect . . . are so different . . . that the case of anyone who can . . . believe them to be by the same writer, we must give over as hopeless." Littledale singled out the characterization of the Doctor as particularly strong evidence of divided authorship. The kindly Doctor who tells the Wooer to approach the Daughter "stuck in as sweet flowers as the season is mistress of" (IV.iii.77–78) was observed by Littledale to resemble Cornelius, Cerimon, and the Doctors in *Macbeth* and *King Lear;* but the "despicable pandar" who urged the Wooer to lie with the Daughter and "please her appetite" (V.ii.50) no more resembled the Doctor of the earlier scene than Boult resembled Marina. To most of the critics who believe in dual authorship, these two scenes still seem to provide razor-sharp contrasts; and of all the inconsistencies of characterization these critics allege to occur in the play, none has been held to be more obvious than those in the role of the Doctor. But the allegations are as usual wholly inaccurate. In neither scene is the Doctor either a ministering angel or a pimp.

Littledale himself noted a curious point about the "good" Doctor of the earlier scene. As the Daughter says she will "come where the blessed spirits . . . pick flowers with Proserpine" and "make Palamon a nosegay," the Doctor observes: "How prettily she's amiss! Note her a little further" (IV.iii.26). Littledale remarked on this "small outbreak of professional enthusiasm with a good 'case' " and compared it to "that 'professional habit of mind,' which characterizes Shakspere's medical men; or, as Dr. Bucknill . . . defines it further: that 'sidelong growth of mind which special training impresses.' " Littledale stopped with the example cited, but other manifestations of that "sidelong growth of mind" occur in the speeches of the Doctor:

Do it home; it cures her *ipso facto* the melancholy humor that infects her . . .

(V.ii.51–52)

They may return and settle again to execute their preordain'd faculties, but they are now in a most extravagant vagary . . .

(IV.iii.65–67)

Here and elsewhere in both scenes this cool professional lapses into a jargon that, if considered apart from its dramatic context, would make of him a satiric figure. He is of course more than that, and his jargon is simply a part of his professional equipment—his means of intimidating his clients into accepting his prescriptions. His plan for curing the Daughter, moreover, is no different in the earlier scene—even if it is necessarily less explicitly expressed—than it is in the later; he tells the Wooer to disguise himself as Palamon, slip into the darkened room where the girl is to be confined,

crave her, drink to her, and still among, intermingle your petition of grace and acceptance into her favor . . .

(IV.iii.82-84)

It is hard to tell what sense Littledale made of these lines, since it is clear that he refused to allow them any sexual overtones.[23] As for the more explicit advice of the Doctor in the later scene, one need hardly appeal to the Jacobean attitudes towards permissible behavior between an engaged couple (or cite the early birthdate of Susanna Shakespeare) to clear it of the Victorian imputation of prurience; one has only to read it:

Doctor. . . . You should observe her every way. . . . If she entreat again, do anything; lie with her if she ask you.
Jailor. Hoa there, Doctor!
Doctor. Yes, in the way of cure.
Jailor. But first, by your leave, i'th'way of honesty.
Doctor. That's but a niceness. Ne'er cast your child away for honesty. Cure her first this way; then if she will be honest she has the path before her. . . . Pray bring her in and let's see how she is.
Jailor. I will, and tell her her Palamon stays for her, but Doctor, methinks you are i'th'wrong still.
Doctor. Go, go! You fathers are fine fools. Her honesty? And we should give her physic till we find that—
Wooer. Why, do you think she is not honest, sir? . . .
Doctor. She may be; but that's all one, 'tis nothing to our purpose . . .

(V.ii.19, 23-32, 34-41, 44-45)

Matter-of-fact wisdom is usually coarse; the blunt Doctor is a good foil to the worrisome father and the worried fiancé, and his peculiar blend of cynicism and practicality is consistent throughout both his scenes.

The part of the Daughter in these scenes is also alleged, naturally, to show inconsistency—and worse. A typical critic is Kenneth Muir, who complains of "the artificiality and unreality of the mad speeches" in the scenes he gives to Fletcher, as well as "the way in which the madness is used to arouse laughter."[24] A non-academic critic with a wider knowledge of Jacobean

---

[23] His adoption of the 1679 Folio misprint *carve* for the Quarto *crave* hardly made things better.
[24] Muir, *Shakespeare as Collaborator* (1960), p. 132.

drama and greater critical perception, on the other hand, reads these scenes as they have seldom been read since the play was divided a century ago; Kenneth Tynan observes that "her mad scenes are exquisite, and better written, I think, than Ophelia's"; the passage beginning "How far is't now to th'end o'th'world, my masters?" (V.ii.97), he adds, "is one of the tenderest in any language, and must go to disprove the legend that for the Elizabethans madness was a comic thing." [25] If the play is read with the kinds of intelligent respect readers normally bring to Shakespeare, these judgments will hardly cause surprise.

"The two bold Titlers"

Shortly after the cousins begin to quarrel over Emilia, this interchange takes place:

> *Palamon.* You shall not love at all.
> *Arcite.* . . . Who shall deny me?
> *Palamon.* I that first saw her; I that took possession
> First with mine eye of all those beauties
> In her reveal'd to mankind! If thou lov'st her,
> Or entertain'st a hope to blast my wishes,
> Thou art a traitor, Arcite, and a fellow
> False as thy title to her! . . .
>
> (II.ii.205, 207–213)

Arcite then swears, "if the lives of all my name lay on it," he has "as just a title to her beauty" as any "that is a man's son." This simple metaphor from law is elaborated in most of the later scenes of the quarrel—for example, as Arcite is called to Theseus' banquet:

> *Palamon.* Sir, your attendance
> Cannot please heaven, and I know your office
> Unjustly is achiev'd.
> *Arcite.* I've a good title;
> I am persuaded this question sick between's
> By bleeding must be cur'd. I am a suitor
> That to your sword you will bequeath this plea
> And talk of it no more.
>
> (III.i.124–131)

Or as Palamon reveals to Theseus that the banished Arcite "follows thy sister, . . . the fair Emilia,"

[25] Tynan, *He That Plays the King* (1950), p. 223. Cf. also pp. 222 & 251; Tynan calls *TNK* "the last of the great plays of the time," but says nothing of its authorship.

> Whose servant (if there be a right in seeing
> And first bequeathing of the soul to) justly
> I am . . .
>
> (III.vi.185–187)

And it reappears several times in Act V—for example, when Emilia, "the victor's meed" who must "crown the question's title" (V.iii.19–20), prays that the knight who "has the truest title in't" may "take off my wheaten garland" (V.i.165–166).

If there is significance in these recurrences, part of it derives from two passages spoken by Theseus in Act I. When Theseus agreed to delay his wedding and attack Creon at once, the grateful Queens flattered him:

> *First Queen.* Thus dost thou still make good the tongue o'th'world.
> *Second Queen.* And earn'st a deity equal with Mars—
> *Third Queen.* If not above him, for
>   Thou being but mortal makest affections bend
>   To godlike honors; they themselves, some say,
>   Groan under such a mast'ry.
> *Theseus.* As we are men
>   Thus should we do. Being sensually subdued
>   We lose our human title. . . .
>
> (I.i.253–261)

"They themselves" are the gods, hence "men" is emphatic; Theseus prefers "our human title." And in his victory scene, after describing Palamon and Arcite in battle as "a mark/ Worth a god's view," Theseus is told by his Herald that their wounds were almost fatal—

>   Yet they breathe
> And have the name of men.
> *Theseus.* Then like men use 'em.
> The very lees of such, millions of rates,
> Exceed the wine of others. . . .
>
> (I.iv.31–35)

—which is to say that he again moves past a comparison between men and gods to place a singularly high valuation on "the name of men," "our human title." (The most frequent noun in this play is *man*, but then *man* is the most frequent noun in Shakespeare.) The major tournament in the final act is to be a contest over this title.

The solemn sport of that tournament is rehearsed more than once earlier in the play. The wedding festivities and the war against Creon in Act I are both "sports . . . craving seriousness and skill." A profusion of references to chivalric contests and to lovers' games contributes to the texture of virtually every scene. In Act II Palamon and Arcite in prison describe nostalgically the various "games of honor" in which they can no longer engage. Arcite departs for the May "pastimes" to the Countryman's skeptical "He wrestle? He roast eggs!" and returns soon after, cubits taller, to Theseus' "I have not seen/ Since Hercules, a man of tougher sinews,/ . . . the best . . . that these times can allow." Theseus' own hunting expedition is a "solemn rite," a "ceremony" continuing throughout Act III ("May the stag thou hunt'st stand long/ And thy dogs be swift and strong").

Even the morris entertainment in III.v is a contest for the exhibition of intellectual judgment, athletic prowess, and courtly grace—a funhouse mirror held up to nature and art. It will begin, Gerrold tells us, when the Duke appears:

I meet him, and unto him I utter learned things, and many figures. He hears, and nods, and hums, and then cries 'Rare!' . . . Then do you, as once did Meleager and the boar, break comely out before him like true lovers, cast yourselves in a body decently, and sweetly, by a figure, trace and turn, boys.

And he advises the Bavian:

Be sure you tumble with audacity and manhood.

The actor Gerrold addresses is probably carrying his baboon-head under his arm, but he must already be wearing the costume "with long tail, and eke long tool":

My friend, carry your tail without offense or scandal to the ladies . . .

And in Gerrold's brief moment alone as the dancers go off to prepare, we find that he is reflective and, indeed, religious:

Give me some meditation. . . . Pallas inspire me!

Gerrold, "the rectifier of all" (III.v.115) who presents the morris dance, is in more than one respect like Theseus, the "purger of the earth" (I.i.51) and "the true decider of all injuries" (III.vi.191) who arranges the final tournament. The "dainty Duke, whose doughty dismal fame" (III.v.120) is praised by the "dainty Domine" (II.iii.43), admirably incorporates in himself, by parody as well as parallelism, the attributes of his subjects.

The games continue beyond the May Day scenes. In Act IV we meet the Wooer for the first time after he has been deserted by the Daughter. Alone, he has been "patiently . . . attending sport, . . . angling/ In the great lake that lies behind the palace"; hearing the girl nearby, "I then left my angle/ To his own skill. . . ." The Daughter herself later imagines that she will "go to barley-break"; this game is also known as "last couple in hell" (because those who are "it" are said to be "in hell"), and it is this lovers' game that presumably leads her to imagine herself being placed in a lovers' hell ("I were a beast and I'd call it good sport"). So too in Act V. The final scene with the Daughter gives us (among other games) the Wooer's invitation to the girl to come to dinner, "and then we'll play at cards." At the same time, the Jailor is summoned to the field of combat; the Doctor eagerly hastens to join him because he "will not lose the fight." The spectators expect a magnificent show; "Nature now/ Shall make and act the story," says Theseus, "the belief/ Both seal'd with eye and ear."

The anthropologist who studies the most venerable cultures (as Huizinga has shown) often finds it difficult to draw the line between the permanent social order and the province of play. Shakespeare's acute sense of the analogies between these two realms is no doubt responsible for the frequent stage/world metaphors we find in most of his plays. Nowhere else, however, are these analogies more central to the dramatic design than in the play of Palamon and Arcite. The final tournament gathers together the values associated with the games that precede it. Perhaps this can best be seen by tracing the development of the two heroes.

The stage-by-stage development of the contest between the cousins is humanly the most interesting part of the play and (but this is a tautology) thematically the most important. Angry outbursts between the cousins diminish in frequency as the play progresses, "gods" are brought increasingly to the fore, the conflict itself is gradually elevated and generalized. The nature of the transformations may be measured in the large differences in tone between episodes which occur at different stages of the quarrel. From the boyish assertiveness of their earlier outbursts, for example, they proceed to the more deeply settled rivalry of the duel scene:

> *Palamon.* . . .   I shall quit you.
> *Arcite.* Defy me in these fair terms, and you show
>   More than a mistress to me. No more anger, . . .
>   We were not bred to talk, man; when we are arm'd
>   And both upon our guards, then let our fury
>   Like meeting of two tides, fly strongly from us,
>   And then to whom the birthright of this beauty
>   Truly pertains (without upbraidings, scorns,
>   Despisings of our persons, and such poutings
>   Fitter for girls and schoolboys) will be seen . . .
>   Your person I am friends with,
>   And I could wish I had not said I lov'd her,
>   Though I had died; but loving such a lady
>   And justifying my love, I must not fly from't.

> *Palamon.* Arcite, thou art so brave an enemy
> That no man but thy cousin's fit to kill thee . . .
>
> (III.vi.28–30, 32–38, 43–48)

The gallantries of this dialogue (and the ensuing episode in which the cousins arm each other) are intermediate between their angriest interchanges and the calmly elevated declarations at the beginning of the altar scene—during which each of the cousins speaks not merely for himself but both literally and figuratively as the commander of a larger force:

> *Palamon.* The glass is running now that cannot finish
> Till one of us expire. Think you but this,
> That were there aught in me which strove to show
> Mine enemy in this business, were't one eye
> Against another, arm oppress'd by arm,
> I would destroy th'offender; coz, I would,
> Though parcel of myself. Then from this gather
> How I should tender you.
> *Arcite.* I am in labor
> To push your name, your ancient love, our kindred,
> Out of my memory; and i'th'selfsame place
> To seat something I would confound. So hoist we
> The sails that must these vessels port even where
> The heavenly Limiter pleases.
> *Palamon.* You speak well.
> Before I turn, let me embrace thee, cousin;
> This I shall never do again. . . .
>
> (V.i.20–36)

The composure of these lines, remarkable in itself, seems the more impressive for engaging and developing so much of the language that precedes it; in the prison scene, for example, the cousins complained they would "never . . . again . . . feel our fiery horses/ Like proud seas under us"; in the duel scene Arcite spoke of the depth of natural force, "like meeting of two tides," in the "fury" he and his cousin were learning to contain; and here Arcite's comparison of himself and his cousin to proud ships about to make their final voyage "even where/ The heavenly Limiter pleases" becomes the appropriate expression of the effortless formal poise and equanimity that the combatants have achieved at the time of their return to Athens.[26]

---

[26] A point about authorship might be inserted here. It concerns second-person pronouns. Observation of their dramatic use is more rewarding than the usual tabulation of their numbers without attention to context. In both the dialogues (from III.vi and V.i) cited above, Palamon begins by addressing Arcite as *you*, but is moved by

The quarrel between Palamon and Arcite, which began as a young man's question over "title" to Emilia, is developed throughout Acts II and III into a contest embracing every chivalric virtue. When the kinsmen dedicate their fortunes to Emilia near the end of Act III they present themselves as the representative champions of all lovers, all soldiers (III.vi.339–342). The descriptions in the portrait scene of those qualities which "nature . . . sows into the births of noble bodies" (IV.ii.9) raise heroic expectations among the auditors:

> *Theseus.* Now as I have a soul I long to see 'em.
> Lady, you shall see men fight now.
> *Hippolyta.* I wish it,
> But not the cause, my lord. They would show
> Bravely about the titles of two kingdoms . . .
>
> (IV.ii.160–164)

Later, before the altars of Mars and Venus, it is clear that it *is* "two kingdoms" for which Arcite and Palamon contend. And when in the final combat "The two bold Titlers at this instant are/ Hand to hand at it" (V.iii. 95–96), they have become the embodiment of "Those best affections that the heavens infuse/ In their best temper'd pieces" (I.iii.11–12); they are proving their "title" to "the name of men."

The meaning of the contest, in effect, consists of the viewer's entire experience of the play, his sense of the heroic and human values arising from all the lesser conflicts and confrontations in the preceding acts, his sense of the cumulative gathering of these values and of the way in which they are drawn together in the final act. The source of these values lies in the stream of comparisons—between men and gods, men and other men—which runs

---

Arcite's impressive replies then to adopt the intimate *thou*. We must assume an artist, not e.g. a compositor, was responsible. And if this assumption leads us to examine *all* the dialogues between the two cousins—filling most of I.ii, II.ii, III.i, III.iii, and parts of III.vi, V.i, V.iv—we find such surprising consistency in the transitions between *thou, thy,* and *thee* on the one hand and *you* and *your* on the other that they can be reduced to a few rules. The reader is urged to turn to these dialogues and check the following points for himself (it takes only a few minutes). The usual form is *you.* It is used consistently throughout I.ii, and in II.ii until the start of the quarrel. *Thou* and *thee* are of course ambiguous and may register contempt as well as unusual warmth. Shortly after Emilia's entrance in II.ii Palamon adopts *thou* in his first speech expressing outrage at Arcite (cf. p. 273); thereafter he uses whichever form best accords with his feelings at the moment (there is nothing circular in this assertion, since in each case his feelings are easily inferred from the context without reference to the pronoun). Most of his uses of *thou* and *thee* are contemptuous, but there are rare occasions on which they are quite the opposite—on which they follow *you* with as telling an effect as in the dialogues cited from III.vi and V.i. Any of the cousins third-act scenes, for example, illustrates a sequence in which

through the action and dialogue of the entire play. While the one unqualifiedly bad character in the play, Creon, "only attributes/ The faculties of other
instruments/ To his own nerves and act" (I.ii.74–76), the other characters
continuously create value as they observe, admire, and seek to emulate one
another. Theseus' warm admiration for the valor of Palamon and Arcite
is perhaps the central fact that emerges from the Theban episode; since
Theseus himself "earns a deity equal with Mars," he might be thought less
in need of a model than other men, but he nevertheless tells us after the
battle that the kinsmen were so impressive "a mark/ Worth a god's view"
that "I fix'd my note/ Constantly on them." Admiration-turning-to-emula-
tion is the pattern which in I.iii links Hippolyta's account of the friendship
between Theseus and Pirithous with Emilia's beautiful narrative about her
childhood love for Flavina—a narrative concerning imitation at its simplest
and most innocent: "On my head no toy/ But was her pattern; her affections . . . I follow'd/ For my most serious decking" (I.iii.81–84). Her lines
treat imitation as the given condition for action, taking it to the very limits
of explanation:

> I
>
> And she I sigh and spoke of, were things innocent,
> Lov'd for we did, and like the elements
> That know not what nor why, yet do effect
> Rare issues by their operance, our souls
> Did so to one another. . . .

(I.iii.69–74)

The excellence of Palamon and Arcite, each "an endless mine to one another" (II.ii.86), is similarly imagined throughout as a consequence of emu-
lation—for example, in the episode in which they arm each other, as they
think back to the battle that took place before the opening of Act I:

Palamon first adopts *thou* expressing hostility, then *you,* and finally *thou* expressing
warmth. Arcite on the other hand almost constantly keeps to *you;* and his attempts
to maintain a certain respectfulness toward his cousin break down only twice, when
particularly sharp remarks by Palamon (II.ii.264–266 & III.vi.161–162) provoke him
to reply in kind; equally rare (only at III.vi.133 & V.iv.105) is his use of the affectionate form. To generalize in this way about such changes of tone is admittedly
odd, but the reasons for doing so must be clear. These generalizations account for
hundreds of pronouns spread throughout the text, and the five exceptional instances
in which the cousins address one another with *ye* are too few to be worth the
bother of writing or reading the explanations. No compositor or transcriber could
have done much tampering with such a text. He who would argue that the sprinkling
of *ye*'s in the play is evidence of the unconscious linguistic habits of Fletcher, furthermore, cannot argue at the same time that two authors came to conscious agreement
about the consistent practices adopted, or that Fletcher changed his stripes, or that
one author corrected the other, or that some scribe or printer took out Fletcher's missing *ye*'s!

> *Palamon.* Methinks this armor's very like that, Arcite,
> Thou wor'st that day the three kings fell, but lighter.
> *Arcite.* That was a very good one, and that day,
> I well remember, you outdid me, cousin;
> I never saw such valor. . . .
> You outwent me,
> Nor could my wishes reach you; yet a little
> I did by imitation.
> *Palamon.* More by virtue;
> You are modest, cousin.
> *Arcite.* When I saw you charge first,
> Methought I heard a dreadful clap of thunder
> Break from the troop. . . .
>
> (III.vi.92–96, 103–110)

This "imitation" is the cause of Theseus' dilemma when he tries to express to Emilia what he saw in the tournament:

> I have heard
> Two emulous Philomels beat the ear o'th'night
> With their contentious throats, now one the higher,
> Anon the other, then again the first,
> And by-and-by outbreasted, that the sense
> Could not be judge between 'em. So it far'd
> Good space between these kinsmen. . . .
>
> (V.iii.141–147)

"The sense could not be judge between 'em"; the figure of the nightingales suggests the mixed pain and pleasure of the beholder who, without recourse to vulgar distinctions between appearance and reality (their absence is a mark of the late Shakespeare), would attempt to distinguish between such extravagant excellences.

Theseus' difficulty is much like Emilia's in the portrait scene:

> What a mere child is fancy,
> That having two fair gauds of equal sweetness,
> Cannot distinguish, but must cry for both!

Moved by the most admirably selfless intentions, Emilia had tried to invent reasons for preferring one knight above the other; but her muddle only grew worse. The ability to see different things as different may be the source of all our knowledge (as the Greek schoolmaster said), and comparison may be the source of all the standards we make up or inquire into, but rare occasions do arise on which one set of excellences is so equally poised against another that no criteria present themselves to support a strong preference for one or

the other. There are certainly no rational or moral or esthetic grounds for preferring one knight above the other in their contest (preferences for Venus
over Mars notwithstanding), and Arcite's victory, and his later mortal accident as well, are presented so entirely as matters of chance that only the
most arrant sophistry could succeed in rationalizing them.

The general likeness of Palamon and Arcite to one another is obviously
deliberate. Sometimes one of them is even given lines that resemble lines
given elsewhere to the other (compare, for example, II.ii.289–291 with II.iii.
8–10 or III.vi.132–133 with V.i.35–36). Over a century ago Charles Knight
observed that "the two friends are energetic alike: we do not precisely see
which is . . . the more daring, the more resolved, the more generous." Many
critics from Knight to the present day have complained that they are therefore not sufficiently distinguished from each other. The grounds for this
complaint, however, lie in the critical search for distinctions in energy,
daring, resolution, generosity, and so forth. Apart from physical and tem-
peramental differences (Palamon is the more languorous, Arcite the more
fiery), the heroes are quite effectively distinguished in the play, and the
distinction is one that anyone beholding the play on stage would apprehend
immediately, whether he were capable of articulating it in words or not.
Experience is always more difficult to describe than to apprehend. Despite
the careful and necessary balance in sympathy, there is no question but that
we are made to take greater interest in Palamon. Apart from subtler distinctions in their roles, there is an immediate disparity in focus; the cousins are
"twins of honor" when they appear together, but almost everywhere else
our attention is directed primarily toward Palamon. For example, we observe Arcite in his soliloquies (in II.iii and III.i) speak more of Palamon
than Palamon in his soliloquies (II.ii and III.vi) does of Arcite. Palamon's
part, too, is longer than Arcite's (and in fact the longest in the play). Much
more important, the whole of the Daughter's underplot is oriented about
Palamon: "By him, like a shadow,/ I'll ever dwell." The Daughter and
Arcite both look up to Palamon, Palamon looks up only to the gods. An
audience consciously reflecting on the moral character of the cousins might
be hard put to decide on its preference; the dramatist meanwhile ensures
that Palamon absorbs far more of its attention. And if Palamon is implicitly
the protagonist in the first four acts, he is explicitly so in Act V—where he is
given the richest speeches in the play, the prayer to Venus in V.i and the
farewell speech as he is led to execution in V.iv. Many of Shakespeare's
young heroes start out by being mainly interested in themselves and are
then gradually forced to see themselves in relation to more and more of
their fellow men—to learn that "I" and "we" are a mere verbal distinction,

so to speak—and thus it is with Palamon; his speech on being led to execution ("There's many a man alive that hath outliv'd/ The love o'th'people . . .") shows how Shakespeare uses breadth of social reference to enhance, indeed to create, individual human dignity. By the time Arcite has become the apparent victor, Palamon has become the obvious hero.

In a recent note on *The Two Noble Kinsmen,* Frank Kermode has decided that "although he probably wrote a great deal of the play Shakespeare had nothing to do with its plot." [27] (To write "a great deal" of a play but have "nothing" to do with its plot? Surely this argues a strange conception of plot!) As reasons to "support this view" Kermode lists the following:

The failure to distinguish Palamon from Arcite (Tweedledum and Tweedledee, Professor Muir calls them) and the weak conception of Emilia; the absence of any attempt to develop, as Shakespeare would once have done, Chaucer's potent conclusion:

> Thanne may men by this ordre well discerne
> That thilke Moevere stable is and eterne—

Shakespeare probably had everything to do with the plot, but whatever he might "once have done" with the tale, Kermode is quite right about the absence of Christian homily; every trace of it is carefully expurgated in the this-worldly wisdom of Theseus' final speech before the Epilogue:

>   Never fortune
> Did play a subtler game: the conquer'd triumphs,
> The victor has the loss; yet in the passage
> The gods have been most equal. . . .
>   Oh you heavenly charmers,
> What things you make of us! For what we lack,
> We laugh; for what we have, are sorry still,
> Are children in some kind. Let us be thankful
> For that which is, and with you leave dispute
> That are above our question. Let's go off,
> And bear us like the time.   *Flourish. Exeunt.*

[27] Kermode, *Shakespeare: The Final Plays* (1963), p. 51. (But a more constructive discussion of structural elements in the play has also recently appeared: Philip Edwards, "On the Design of *The Two Noble Kinsmen,*" *Rev. of Eng. Lit.,* Vol. V [1964], no. 4, pp. 89–105.)

APPENDIX A

The Date of the Play

Princess Elizabeth, the daughter of King James, was married to Prince Frederick, Elector Palatine and later King of Bohemia, on 14 February 1613. Among the lavish entertainments given before the royal couple prior to their departure from England in April, one of the most successful was *The Masque of the Inner Temple and Grayes Inn*. The *Masque,* which Sir Francis Bacon had helped to arrange for the occasion and for which Beaumont had written the libretto, was presented on 20 February at Whitehall; the text, accompanied by a descriptive commentary on the performance, was published in quarto shortly thereafter. The description of the second anti-masque provides us with evidence relevant to the date of *The Two Noble Kinsmen*. After Iris calls for the entrance of "all the Rurall company,/ Which decke the May-games with their Countrey sports," the commentator identifies the cast:

> The second Anti-masque rush in, daunce their Measure, and as rudely depart, consisting of a Pedant.

May Lord,	May Lady.
Servingman,	Chambermaide.
A Countrey Clowne, or Shepheard,	Countrey Wench.
An Host,	Hostesse.
A Hee Baboone,	Shee Baboone.
A Hee Foole,	Shee Foole ushering them in.

> All these persons apparelled to the life, the Men issuing out of one side of the Boscage, and the Woemen from the other: the Musicke was extremely well fitted, having such a spirit of Countrey jolitie, as can hardly be imagined, but the perpetuall laughter and applause was above the Musicke.

The dance likewise was of the same strain. . . . It pleased his Majestie to call for it againe at the end . . .[1]

Other witnesses present on 20 February 1613 also testify that the *Masque* was happily received and that the second anti-masque was particularly "strange . . . and delightful."[2]

May games and sports figure prominently in Acts II and III of *The Two Noble Kinsmen,* and at the opening of Act III scene v we find the Schoolmaster Gerrold instructing his band of country yokels about the morris dance they intend to perform before Duke Theseus and his bride Hippolyta. Gerrold tells the others they are to wait "close in the Thicket" and, when he signals, to "break comly out" before the Duke and his train. The Countrymen and their wenches leave the stage at line 96; Gerrold remains behind, waiting for Theseus and his hunting party to pass. Theseus and his friends come on stage. Gerrold catches their attention—"Stay, and edifie"—and they stop and listen to his doggerel prologue for the "mighty morris" about to be performed. Part of that prologue names several of the characters in the dance:

> The body of our sport of no small study
> I first appeare, though rude, and raw, and muddy . . .
> The next the Lord of May, and Lady bright,
> The Chambermaid, and Servingman by night
> That seeke out silent hanging: Then mine Host
> And his fat Spowse, that welcomes to their cost
> The gauled Traveller, and with a beckning
> Informes the Tapster to inflame the reckning:
> Then the beast eating Clowne, and next the foole,
> The *Bavian* with long tayle, and eke long toole,
> *Cum multis aliijs* that make a dance,
> Say I, and all shall presently advance.
>
> (III.v.127–128, 131–140)

As Kökeritz has pointed out, *beast* (line 137) is a variant spelling for *beest* (beestings), and a modern edition should read "beest-eating clown," a rude country clown.[3] The Bavian is a baboon, a he-baboon. The roles in the

---

[1] Cambridge Beaumont and Fletcher, X (1912), 383. This text of the *Masque* was licensed on 27 February 1613; another text, printed in the 1647 Beaumont and Fletcher Folio (also reprinted in the Cambridge edition), does not contain the prose commentary.

[2] From the description by Howes in his continuation of Stow's *Annales* (1615), p. 917. Additional contemporary comments on the *Masque* appear in three of the *Letters of John Chamberlain,* ed. N. E. McClure (1939), I, 425–431.

[3] Helge Kökeritz, "The Beast-eating Clown," *MLN,* LXI (1946), 532–535.

morris dance obviously duplicate most of those in the second anti-masque of the show at Whitehall.[4] The correspondences, publicized by A. H. Thorndike about sixty years ago, have led most critics to agree that—just as *The Winter's Tale* evidently borrowed its dance of satyrs from Jonson's masque *Oberon*—*The Two Noble Kinsmen* borrowed its morris dance from the Beaumont *Masque,* and that this borrowing establishes the earlier limit for the date of the play.[5]

The following lines from *Bartholomew Fair* IV.iii are usually cited as evidence for the later limit:

> *Quarlous.* . . . Well, my word is out of the *Arcadia,* then: *Argalus.*
> *Win-wife.* And mine out of the play, *Palemon.*

If Winwife's allusion is to the hero of *The Two Noble Kinsmen,* it suggests that the play was well known in late 1613 or 1614. *Bartholomew Fair* was first acted on 31 October 1614, and there is reason to believe Jonson was at work on it almost a year before.[6]

One objection has been raised to treating the Jonson line as an allusion to *The Two Noble Kinsmen.* Daniel's *The Queen's Arcadia* also has a Palæmon, and the title of this rhymed pastoral led Fleay to declare in 1891 that it must be to him, and not to the Palamon of the play, that the line referred.[7] Although Fleay's several theories concerning the date of *The*

---

[4] Some discussions of the borrowing attempt also to match the number of actors on stage in *TNK* III.v.1–96 with the number of performers in the morris dance (who enter in costume at l. 143), but the departure and subsequent entrance render such attempts unnecessary, and *"Cum multis al[ij]s"* at l. 139 would seem to render them futile.

[5] Although a note to the *Masque* in Weber's 1812 edition of Beaumont and Fletcher (XIV, 337) hinted at a connection, the duplications were first clearly noted by Skeat in his 1875 edition of *TNK* and by Littledale in his 1876 edition for the New Shakspere Society, but they were not considered as evidence for the date until Littledale published his Introduction to the N.S.S. edition in 1885 (pp. 53*–55*, 68*–69*). In *The Influence of Beaumont and Fletcher on Shakspere* (1901) A. H. Thorndike expanded Littledale's argument, adding the example from *Oberon* and *The Winter's Tale,* and elaborating Littledale's point on the unlikelihood that masques at Court would borrow dances that had been staled on the public stages. The freshness of the *Masque of the Inner Temple,* and the elaborate arrangements undertaken for its production, are stressed in the contemporary descriptions, and there seems to be no doubt about the direction of the borrowing.

[6] Cf. Art. 88, *Henslowe Papers,* ed. Greg (1907), pp. 77–78. A letter by Daborne to Henslowe, 13 November 1613, refers to a new play on which Jonson is at work. This would probably be *Bartholomew Fair;* and without the letter we might still assume Jonson to be at work on the play in the winter of 1613–14.

[7] F. G. Fleay, *Biographical Chronicle of the English Drama* (1891), I, 377–378. In the same volume Fleay suggested a 1611 date for *TNK* (p. 191), and in none of his other discussions of the date (cf. n. 13 below) did he consider 1613 or refer to the evidence of the Beaumont *Masque.*

Two Noble Kinsmen failed to take into account the evidence of the borrowed morris dance, his assertion that the Jonson allusion was to Daniel may, of course, have been right. On the other hand, *The Queen's Arcadia* was performed only once (the place was Oxford and the year 1605),[8] Daniel's Palæmon is a minor character, and—if we wish to assume that Jonson would not care to have had his reference to the "word . . . out of the play" recognized—it seems a bit odd that Quarlous should identify his book but that Winwife should not identify his play. The probability, in short, is that Winwife's play is *The Two Noble Kinsmen,* although the strength of this probability will naturally depend on our consideration of all the dating evidence taken together.

There may be some additional evidence in *Bartholomew Fair* itself. A number of details other than Winwife's line suggest that Jonson in 1614 had already become acquainted with *The Two Noble Kinsmen;* there are, for example, these lines from the Induction:

If there bee neuer a *Seruant-monster* i'the *Fayre,* who can helpe it? he [the Author] sayes; nor a nest of *Antiques?* Hee is loth to make Nature afraid in his *Playes,* like those that beget *Tales, Tempests,* and such like *Drolleries,* to mixe his head with other mens heeles; let the concupisence of *Iigges* and *Dances,* raigne as strong as it will amongst you.

It is commonly assumed that these lines allude to *The Tempest* and *The Winter's Tale.* Perhaps it would be reading "such like *Drolleries*" too literally if we were to suppose that Jonson had at least one more play in the back of his mind as well, but the "nest of *Antiques*" would apply to Gerrold and his odd country crew more readily perhaps than to any group of characters in the other plays; the word *Tale* itself might have applied, in 1614, both to *The Winter's Tale* and *The Two Noble Kinsmen;*[9] and the reference to interpolated dances—if that is what Jonson meant—would be appropriate to each of these plays, although perhaps not to *The Tempest.* Were it not for the lead given by Winwife's line, however, the passage from the Induction would no doubt be of little evidential value, and a few other suggestive details in the text of *Bartholomew Fair* are perhaps equally ten-

[8] Daniel's text was published in 1606 and Jonson may have read it. The other references in *Bartholomew Fair* (e.g. to *"Ieronimo,* or *Andronicus"* in the Induction) are, nevertheless, usually to works his audience might know either directly or by reputation.

[9] *Tale* (cf. *TNK* Epilogue 12–13, p. 294 below) seems to have been used as a more or less generic term—as opposed e.g. to a "true history" like *Henry VIII*—much as we sometimes call *The Winter's Tale* a "romance."

uous and may be relegated to the notes.[10] But the remaining evidence for public performance of *The Two Noble Kinsmen* in 1613, to be found mainly in the Prologue and Epilogue, would appear to support the evidence in Jonson's play, even though their testimony again consists of allusions open inevitably to more than one interpretation.

Cut loose from the play, the Prologue is still enlivened by the intricacy of its rhythms and the variety of inflection in its tone. The surface difficulties— the ellipses in lines 11 and 24—recede as we hear how distinctly the writer imagines the speaking voice and endows it with a marked habit of converting expected statement into unexpected drama. At the same time that we attend to the Prologue as a theatrical speech, however, we might note more prosaically that it is also an unusually informative theatrical document:

Florish.

> *NEw Playes, and Maydenheads, are neare a kin,*
> *Much follow'd both, for both much mony g'yn,*
> *If they stand sound, and well: And a good Play*
> *(Whose modest Sceanes blush on his marriage day,*
> *And shake to loose his honour) is like hir* [5
> *That after holy Tye, and first nights stir*
> *Yet still is Modestie, and still retaines*
> *More of the maid to sight, than Husbands paines;*
> *We pray our Play may be so; For I am sure*
> *It has a noble Breeder, and a pure,* [10
> *A learned, and a Poet never went*
> *More famous yet twixt Po and silver Trent.*
> *Chaucer (of all admir'd) the Story gives,*
> *There constant to Eternity it lives;*
> *If we let fall the Nobleness of this,* [15
> *And the first sound this child heare, be a hisse,*
> *How will it shake the bones of that good man,*
> *And make him cry from under ground, O fan*
> *From me the witles chaffe of such a wrighter*
> *That blastes my Bayes, and my fam'd workes makes lighter* [20

---

[10] Among the classical pomposities of Gerrold in *TNK* III.v and of Justice Overdo in *BF* II.iv appears the identical quotation from Ovid, *Metamorphoses* xv.871 (a famous line, however); in Jonson's puppet-show episode in V.iv, Damon and Pythias quarrelling over Hero may incorporate some burlesque of Palamon and Arcite quarrelling over Emilia in *TNK* II.ii, III.i, III.iii, and III.vi; several jokes in the same Jonson scene (such as the bull with two pizzles and the dogs that dance the morris) may glance at the morris dancers and the Bavian, the baboon "with long tayle and eke long toole," in *TNK* III.v, recalling the chaffing in Jonson's Induction; and so forth.

> *Then Robin Hood? This is the feare we bring;*
> *For to say Truth, it were an endlesse thing,*
> *And too ambitious to aspire to him;*
> *Weake as we are, and almost breathlesse swim*
> *In this deepe water. Do but you hold out*   [25
> *Your helping hands, and we shall take about,*
> *And something doe to save us: You shall heare*
> *Sceanes though below his Art, may yet appeare*
> *Worth two houres travell. To his bones sweet sleepe:*
> *Content to you. If this play doe not keepe,*   [30
> *A little dull time from us, we perceave*
> *Our losses fall so thicke, we must needs leave.*

Florish.

26 *take* = tack

The Prologue is evidently intended for a first performance (line 16) in a theater charging admission; clearly it is not intended for a revival nor for a Court audience. No Jacobean prologues are more explicit on the newness of the plays they introduce; few are so obviously suggestive of a commercial performance—a suggestion emphatically confirmed by such phrases as *"let him* [who dislikes the play] *hisse, and kill/ Our market . . ."* in the Epilogue (cf. page 293 below).

The reference to "our losses" in the last line is probably to be regarded —given the verbal context, and given the common theatrical conventions of address between speaker and audience in a prologue—as an allusion to some public misfortune that befell the acting company. It is unlikely that a dramatist would go out of his way to be unintelligible in a Prologue designed to court the favor of his audience, and the "losses" would presumably have to be well enough known for the audience to recognize the reference and respond to it. Two identifications have been proposed in the past.

One explanation (first offered by Littledale in 1885) is that the lines refer to the destruction of the Globe theater in the fire set off during the performance of the banquet scene (I.iv) of *Henry VIII* on 29 June 1613.[11]

---

[11] Littledale: cf. n. 5 above. Regarding the related question of the date of *Henry VIII*, see the new Arden edition by R. A. Foakes (1957), pp. xxvi–xxxiii. The famous letter of Sir Henry Wotton to Sir Edmund Bacon on 2 July is the source of the information that the Globe fire began during the scene of Wolsey's banquet in Act I. Since Wotton refers to *Henry VIII* as a "new" play, it has sometimes been assumed that the première took place on 29 June. Foakes gives many reasons for dating that performance earlier in the spring of 1613, and Wotton's letter itself, as a matter of fact, makes clear that "new" can mean only "new this season": Wotton mentions the presence in the play of "the Knights of the Order, with their Georges and Garter"

Common sense suggests—and numerous contemporary references to the Globe fire confirm the suggestion—that the fire must have been known to virtually every London theatergoer in 1613. The shareholders in the King's company who were also "housekeepers" were required to lay out considerable expenditures for the construction of a new theater,[12] and the company no doubt suffered other losses as well. Littledale's explanation, especially since it complements the other evidence for a performance in 1613 (evidence of which Littledale was only partially aware), is therefore quite tempting; it will be given further consideration later.

Another explanation of the "losses," however, has occasionally been offered, in one variant form or another, since it was originally worked out by Fleay—as part of a more elaborate theory about the play—in 1883. Fleay noted that an actor's name is printed in the stage direction at IV.ii.74: *"Enter Messengers. Curtis."* Identifying the actor who played a messenger as Curtis Greville (a member of the King's company in the later 1620's), Fleay then produced an intricate argument into which the following assertions were fitted:

1. The play had been completed by Fletcher, long after Shakespeare's death, from an unfinished dramatic fragment left behind by the elder writer.

2. The first performance of the play took place before Fletcher died in the plague of 1625, and "the Prologue was clearly one of Fletcher's own modest compositions; for, had it been written after his death, there would have been a flourish about him in it [as in] . . . the prologues to *The Elder Brother, Lover's Progress*, and others written after that event. . . ."

3. Since the Prologue calls the play new, the manuscript in which Greville's name appeared, and from which the 1634 quarto was printed, must have been the prompt-copy for the original production.

4. Greville entered the King's company at some time between 27 March 1625, the date on which King James died, and 24 June 1625, the date on which (Fleay assumed) the theaters were closed because of the plague. The first performance of the play must have occurred between those dates.

5. The "losses" to which the Prologue refers, then, would be (a) the death of James on 27 March, and (b) "the small attendance" at the theater as the plague increased in virulence during the following weeks.[18]

---

and must therefore be referring to the coronation procession in Act IV (where the Knights of the Garter would appear and where the stage directions specify heraldic "Collars of Esses")—a scene Wotton could hardly have watched on the day the fire consumed "within less then an hour the whole House to the very grounds"!

[12] Cf. E. K. Chambers, *The Elizabethan Stage* (1923), II, 423–424.

[18] Fleay presented his arguments in a communication to W. J. Rolfe, printed in Rolfe's edition of *TNK* (1883), pp. 39–41. Three years later Fleay found it impossible to believe "that a play begun by Shakespeare was left unnoticed for some dozen

Most of these assertions, as we shall see, have subsequently proved to be untenable, but Fleay's suggested identification for the "losses" has nevertheless been repeated by later scholars without reference to Fleay's original reasons for it.

As Bentley has pointed out, the London theaters were almost certainly closed when James died on 27 March, and they would not have been able to reopen after his funeral in early May because the number of deaths from the plague had by then risen to more than forty a week, the point at which theatrical performances were then forbidden.[14] Greville, moreover, probably did not enter the King's company until performances were resumed near the end of the year.[15] It should be mentioned that actors' names appear in another stage direction; at the opening of V.iii we find *"Enter . . . some Attendants, T. Tucke: Curtis."* The first name has been identified as Thomas Tuckfield, of whom all we know is that he was a hired man in the King's company in December 1624.[16] The second would again refer to Curtis Greville, whose presence in the company may be dated, roughly, from about the end of 1625 to about 1632 or 1633 (cf. note 15). The date of the performance for which the book-keeper inserted the actors' names in the manuscript would have to fall within Greville's tenure in the company, although our bias should be toward the earlier limit to accommodate Tuckfield (i.e. the later the year, the less certain is Tuckfield's continuance with the company). "About 1626" will perhaps be satisfactory, although the precise date is of little present consequence, for this performance appears to

---

years"; reluctant, however, to abandon his own dating arguments (which were the sole ground for that belief), he concluded that Shakespeare had nothing to do with the play (cf. Fleay, *Chronicle History of the Life and Work of William Shakespeare* [1886], p. 254). But by 1891 he had abandoned those dating arguments (cf. n. 7 above).

[14] G. E. Bentley, *The Jacobean and Caroline Stage*, II (1940), 654–656. Statistics on deaths from the plague (on p. 668) indicate that the theaters could not have reopened until some time after 24 November 1625, the last day of the first week since May in which there were fewer than forty deaths.

[15] Cf. Bentley, I, 14–19, and II, 451–452. Greville is known to have been a member of the Palsgrave's company in 1622, a member of the King's company by October 1626, still a member of the King's in 1631, and again a member of a rival company in 1634. Since his name does not appear in any of the documents which identify most of the members of the King's company in late 1624 or early 1625, Bentley believes that he probably remained with the Palsgrave's until that company was dissolved in 1625 and that he joined the King's men at the time performances were resumed after the plague.

[16] His name appears on the list of "necessary attendantes" of the company whom Sir Henry Herbert granted protection from arrest on 27 December 1624. Cf. Bentley, II, 606–607.

have been a revival and there are indications that the actors' names were merely added to an older manuscript.

The possibility that the first performance of the play was the one in which Tuckfield and Greville took minor parts was ruled out by evidence first brought to light in 1925. Play-lists from James's Revels Office survive on scraps of paper bound into Cotton MS Tiberius E. X. One of these lists mentions "The 2. Noble Kinesmen"; analyzed by Frank Marcham and E. K. Chambers, the list has been dated c.1619, and—as both Chambers and Bentley agree—it indicates that the play was considered for a performance at Court in that year.[17] Whether or not the Court performance actually took place, the listing signifies that the play was probably in the company repertory at that time, and it makes it extremely difficult to see how a Prologue introducing a new play could allude to anything that took place in the mid-1620's.

The Prologue, however, appears to raise one further difficulty in the eyes of some critics. It refers, in line 19, to a single writer. Since the word appears at the end of a line, it is sometimes explained as due to "the mere exigency of the rhyme." The merits of this explanation need not be considered at this time. It was not mentioned by Chambers when, in 1930, he summarized the dating evidence in what is still perhaps the most influential discussion of the subject. Part of Chambers' analysis adopts a modified form of Fleay's explanation for the "losses":

The Globe fire of 1613 need not, of course, be the explanation of prol. 30:

> If this play doe not keepe
> A little dull time from us, we perceave
> Our losses fall so thicke, we must needs leave.

In fact the prologue is probably of later date than the play, since it speaks of 'a writer', although there are clearly two. There was probably a court performance about 1619 [Chambers here inserts a reference to the Revels Office fragment]. But Littledale's inquiry for a date at which the King's men's losses fell so thick as in 1613 may perhaps point us to 1625, when the death of James was followed by a heavy plague, and the theatres were closed.[18]

Chambers' failure to note any difficulty in squaring the Revels Office fragment with the suggested date for the "losses" will probably have to be put

[17] Frank Marcham, *The King's Office of the Revels, 1610–1622* (1925), p. 13. Cf. review of Marcham by Chambers in *RES,* I (1925), 479–484. The information also appears in Bentley, I, 95, 114.

[18] Chambers, *William Shakespeare* (1930), I, 530. Despite his suggestion that the Prologue is "of later date," Chambers accepts 1613 as the date of the play itself.

down to oversight; he neglects to mention the fact (and had therefore perhaps temporarily overlooked it as he wrote his summary) that the Prologue introduces a new play.

No one has suggested any date other than 1613 or 1625 for the "losses." As far as we know, the only striking loss suffered by the King's men that might have been attended by wide publicity (in the range of years open to us) would be the death of Burbadge in 1619, but the lines in the Prologue would be a curious tribute to Burbadge, just as they might seem indecorous as a reference to the death of James and to the appalling number of casualties in the plague of 1625. The Prologue speaker's *we* and *our,* in any case, apparently mean the company of actors, and in connection with the Globe fire his words sound modestly appropriate. There is, moreover, some further evidence pointing to a 1613 performance. But before we proceed to that evidence (in the Epilogue), a few miscellaneous points must be summarized rapidly.

The 1634 quarto has only recently begun to attract close bibliographical study. One critic, F. O. Waller, has called attention to evidence that the printer's copy consisted of authorial manuscript and has noted several indications that at least part of it was in Shakespeare's own hand. With regard to the date of the play, Waller mentions only one piece of evidence, the borrowing from the Beaumont *Masque,* and he uses it to suggest that the manuscript dates from early 1613. Sir Walter Greg has also referred occasionally to the play; his most recent comment (1956) is that it "was produced about 1613, . . . and was printed in 1634 from what was almost certainly the original prompt-book." The bibliographical evidence itself is presented in Chapter II; it is mentioned here only because a few details bear upon our interpretation of the Prologue and Epilogue. Spellings are generally consistent throughout Prologue, text, and Epilogue—whether of common words (e.g. *loose* for *lose* occurs in the Prologue and sixteen times in the text) or of uncommon (e.g. *take* for *tack* occurs in the Prologue and twice in the text)—suggesting that all were probably written in the same hand. The stage directions for these speeches, moreover, look as if they had been added by a book-keeper at the same time that the manuscript as a whole was prepared for use as a prompt-book (cf. pages 94–95 above).

Another matter that should be mentioned—although again the extent and complexity of the evidence permit only a hasty summary of points more fully dealt with elsewhere—is that the play shows unusually strong signs of having been written specifically for performance at an indoor theater. The text calls frequently, for example, for the use of cornets rather than trumpets (cf. pages 95–96), it is unusually specific in its indications of scenery and scenic effects (cf. page 102), and it is exceptionally lavish in its use of music.[19]

The King's men are known to have given provincial performances after the burning of the Globe; they returned to London in the fall and gave the customary performances at Court, the earliest of which is recorded for 1 November.[20] The new Globe was not ready until mid-1614, and the company would have used Blackfriars, the usual site for October or November performances anyway, for all its public appearances during the 1613–14 season. An attempt at precision about the date *The Two Noble Kinsmen* was first performed will perhaps be uncomfortably reminiscent of Fleay. Nevertheless, a date sometime in October or early November for the first performance would allow time for the play to be written, it would accommodate the borrowing from the *Masque,* it would follow the première of *Henry VIII* by an appropriate interval of perhaps six or seven months, it would accord with the inference that the play was designed with performance at Blackfriars in mind, it would satisfy the possible allusions in *Bartholomew Fair;* and if the play were the first to be presented by the company to a London theater audience after the Globe fire, the Prologue would be particularly apposite to the occasion. The Epilogue would be even more apposite.

The Epilogue, as strange and original in its movement as the Prologue, appears to have been ignored in most scholarly discussions of the play. The speaker starts out with the same embarrassed and halting manner, proceeds with the same hesitant delicacies of tone as in the latter half of the Prologue, and appeals to the gallants in the audience (lines 5–9) not to be hypocritical or hypercritical:

> *I Would now aske ye how ye like the Play,*
> *But as it is with Schoole Boyes, cannot say,*
> *I am cruell fearefull: pray yet stay a while,*
> *And let me looke upon ye: No man smile?*
> *Then it goes hard I see; He that has* [5
> *Lov'd a yong hansome wench then, show his face:*
> *Tis strange if none be heere, and if he will*
> *Against his Conscience let him hisse, and kill*
> *Our Market: Tis in vaine, I see to stay yee,*
> *Have at the worst can come, then; Now what say ye?* [10

---

[19] In addition to the frequent ceremonial flourishes throughout the play and the unusual musical effects directed in the altar scene (V.i)—all of which are described in Chap. II—there is music to accompany formal processions in I.i and I.v, there is the morris dance in III.v, and there are no less than eight songs or fragments of songs scattered throughout the play.

[20] The performance records are reprinted in Chambers, *William Shakespeare,* II, 344–345.

> *And yet mistake me not: I am not bold*
> *We have no such cause. If the tale we have told*
> *(For tis no other) any way content ye*
> *(For to that honest purpose it was ment ye)*
> *We have our end; and ye shall have ere long*   [15
> *I dare say many a better, to prolong*
> *Your old loves to us: we, and all our might,*
> *Rest at your service, Gentlemen, good night.*
>
> Florish.

Our present purpose again requires that we confine our attention merely to theatrical reference in the lines. The speaker moves away from particular reference to the play just ended to a more inclusive reference to the relationship between the players and their audience. In the last lines there would appear to be a fairly distinct allusion, although it has never, apparently, elicited comment. The promise that *"ye shall have ere long/. . . many a better* [play]*, to prolong/ Your old loves to us"* sounds like precisely the right note to strike at a resumption of London performances three or four months after the Globe fire brought them to a halt; the curtailed activity would be part of the point of the reference, and a London re-opening before a familiar audience would be the fitting occasion for the reassurance that *"we, and all our might,/ Rest at your service . . ."*

Although in the absence of strong evidence to the contrary it seems natural to assume that prologues and epilogues were written by the authors of the plays to which they were fitted, and although both literary and bibliographical considerations seem to indicate that such was the case with the Prologue and Epilogue of *The Two Noble Kinsmen,* it has sometimes been supposed—for example, it is implied by Chambers (cf. page 291 above)—that these speeches were written neither by Shakespeare nor by Fletcher. Presumably that supposition rests on the presence of the word *writer.* No other reason, in any case, has been suggested, and in the absence of any evidence or argument for a third hand, we shall have to trace out the thinking behind this supposition for ourselves. Chambers presumably meant that whoever wrote the Prologue was unaware of the facts of dramatic authorship (though presumably aware at the same time that the source lay in Chaucer). Marginal and insignificant as the play may have seemed to various scholars, however, it was once very much in the minds of the King's men; the play requires (as the altar scene in Act V should alone make clear) a most expensive and lavish production, and it requires a cast to fill more than thirty speaking roles. To assume that the actor-shareholders of the company could be ignorant of its authorship is patently absurd, even

if we assume that Shakespeare was unaccountably detached from preparations for its performance. If we were to try to imagine a first performance
after Shakespeare's death (even though that would make most of the dating
evidence unintelligible) we should have to note that Burbadge lived until
1619, Condell until 1627, and Heminge until 1630; after Shakespeare's death,
these were the men with most authority in the company, and if they farmed
out the task of writing the Prologue to a writer otherwise unconnected with
the play—merely the handling of tone in these speeches argues a professional
writer of considerable ability—it is surely strange that they would keep him
in the dark, or fail to correct him, about the matter of authorship. To attribute the Prologue to a writer ignorant of the circumstances of dramatic
composition would make of the tribute to Chaucer an even more baffling
anomaly. If we assume a strange hand, we are evidently faced with far more
difficulties than before and we seem to be left without any credible means
of explaining them.

Apart perhaps from the word *writer,* it is, hopefully, clear enough that all
the evidence bearing on the date can be brought readily to agreement by
assuming that the play was probably first performed near the beginning of
the 1613–14 theatrical season. For those who assume dual authorship in the
play, the fact that *writer* occurs in a rhyme position will conceivably suffice
to resolve the small-scale puzzle it creates.

The distinguished stage historian W. J. Lawrence, however, once attempted a different explanation. On the strength of the borrowed morris
dance, the allusion in Winwife's line, the fact that the Prologue introduced
a new play, and the allusion to "losses" (which he called "clearly a reference
to the burning of the Globe"), Lawrence in 1921 proposed that the play had
first been performed in the autumn of 1613, the same date suggested in these
pages.[21] But his familiarity with the customary ways in which Jacobean
playwrights addressed audiences at Blackfriars in their prologues and epilogues constrained him to interpret the word *writer* quite literally; he therefore worked out an ingenious theory of authorship in which he argued that
Fletcher alone had written the original play in 1613 (with its present Prologue), and that the extant play had been revised by Massinger in the 1620's.
Later, however, Lawrence became more familiar with the construction and
the texture of the play itself, and in 1937 he rejected his own earlier theory
of authorship and announced that he was "happy" to indorse the view that
Shakespeare must have been responsible for much of the play.[22] He referred

[21] Lawrence outlined his theory in a long letter to *TLS,* XX (14 July 1921), 450.
[22] Lawrence, *Speeding up Shakespeare* (1937), p. 48.

again to 1613 as the date of the play, but he made no further reference either to the word *writer* or to the historical evidence (cf. pages 259–260 above) that had formerly led him to give that word such weight. The word *writer* could also be accounted for, of course, by assuming that the play had been written by Shakespeare alone. But this discussion deals merely with the date; the question of authorship is treated elsewhere.

APPENDIX B

Checklist of Editions

1634 QUARTO. *The Two Noble Kinsmen.* Printed by Thomas Cotes for John Waterson. London, 1634.

1679 FOLIO. *Fifty Comedies and Tragedies . . . by Francis Beaumont and John Fletcher, Gentlemen.* London, 1679. The Beaumont and Fletcher Second Folio.

1711 TONSON. *The Works of Mr. Francis Beaumont, and Mr. John Fletcher.* Printed for Jacob Tonson. 7 vols. London, 1711. *TNK* in vol. VII. Reprint of 1679 Folio text.

1750 SEWARD. *The Works of Mr. Francis Beaumont, and Mr. John Fletcher.* Edited by Seward, Sympson, and Theobald. 10 vols. London, 1750. *TNK* in vol. X, edited by Thomas Seward.

1778 COLMAN. *The Dramatick Works of Beaumont and Fletcher.* Edited by George Colman *et al.* 10 vols. London, 1778. *TNK* in vol. X.

1811 STOCKDALE. *The Dramatic Works of Ben Jonson, and Beaumont and Fletcher.* Printed for John Stockdale. 4 vols. London, 1811. *TNK* in vol. IV. Colman's text and notes.

1811 MILLER. *The Modern British Drama.* Printed for William Miller. 5 vols. London, 1811. *TNK* in vol. I. Colman's text.

1812 WEBER. *The Works of Beaumont and Fletcher.* Edited by Henry Weber. 14 vols. Edinburgh, 1812. *TNK* in vol. XIII.

1840 DARLEY. *The Works of Beaumont and Fletcher.* Edited by George Darley. 2 vols. London, 1840. *TNK* in vol. II. Weber's text.

1841 KNIGHT. *The Pictorial Edition of the Works of Shakspere.* Edited by Charles Knight. 8 vols. London, c.1839–41. *TNK* in vol. VII. Bowdlerized text. 2nd Pictorial Edition, slightly revised, 1866.

1846 DYCE BEAUMONT & FLETCHER. *The Works of Beaumont and Fletcher.* Edited by Alexander Dyce. 11 vols. London, 1843–46. *TNK* in vol. XI.

1848. SIMMS. *A Supplement to the Plays of William Shakspeare.* Edited by William Gilmore Simms. New York, 1848. Bowdlerized text.

1851 TYRRELL. *The Doubtful Plays of Shakspere.* Edited by Henry Tyrrell. London, c.1851.

1866 DYCE SHAKESPEARE. *The Works of William Shakespeare.* Edited by Alexander Dyce; 2nd edition, revised. 9 vols. London, 1864–67. *TNK* in vol. VIII. Much revised from Dyce's earlier text of *TNK* (in his 1846 Beaumont and Fletcher). Republished with further slight revisions in vol. IX of Dyce's 3rd (1876) and subsequent editions of Shakespeare.

1875 SKEAT. *The Two Noble Kinsmen.* Edited by Walter W. Skeat. Cambridge, 1875. Bowdlerized text.

1876 QUARTO REPRINT. *The Two Noble Kinsmen. Reprint of the Quarto, 1634.* Prepared by Harold Littledale for The New Shakspere Society. London, 1876. An exact type-facsimile, with line-numbers added.

1876 LITTLEDALE. *The Two Noble Kinsmen.* Edited by Harold Littledale for The New Shakspere Society. Part I, Revised Text and Notes. London, 1876. (Part II, General Introduction, published in 1885.)

1877 LEOPOLD. *The Leopold Shakspere.* Introduction by F. J. Furnivall. London, 1877. (Republished as *The Royal Shakspere,* 3 vols., in 1882; *TNK* in vol. III.) Littledale's text of *TNK.*

1878 COLLIER. *The Plays and Poems of William Shakespeare.* Edited by John Payne Collier. 8 vols. London, 1878. *TNK* in vol. VII.

1881 HUDSON. *The Complete Works of William Shakespeare.* Harvard Edition, edited by Henry N. Hudson. 20 vols. Boston, 1881. (Republished in London as the Windsor Edition in 1900.) *TNK* in vol. XIX.

1883 ROLFE. *The Two Noble Kinsmen.* Edited by William J. Rolfe. New York, 1883. Slightly bowdlerized text. The Rolfe text was republished in 1884 (in vol. XIX of Rolfe's Friendly Edition of Shakespeare), in 1898 (with addenda), and in 1906 (with revised Introduction).

1890 FITZGIBBON. *Famous Elizabethan Plays.* Edited by H. Macaulay Fitzgibbon. London, 1890. Drastically bowdlerized text.

1890 THAYER. *The Best Elizabethan Plays.* Edited by William R. Thayer. Boston, 1890. Bowdlerized text.

1894 HOPKINSON. *Shakespeare's Doubtful Plays.* Edited by A. F. Hopkinson. 3 vols. London, 1891–95. *TNK* in vol. III.

1897 HERFORD. *The Two Noble Kinsmen.* Edited by C. H. Herford for *The Temple Dramatists* series. London, 1897.

1901 NEW CENTURY. *The New Century Shakespeare.* Edited by W. A. Wright *et al.;* printed for Dana Estes and Co. of Boston. 24 vols. Boston, 1900–01. *TNK* in vol. XX. Herford's text; Herford's and Dyce's notes.

1904 RALEIGH. *The Works of Shakespeare.* Edinburgh Folio Edition, edited by W. E. Henley and Walter Raleigh; printed at Edinburgh for Grant Richards, London. 10 vols. in 40 parts. London, 1904. *TNK* in part 38 (vol. X), edited by Raleigh.

1908 BROOKE. *The Shakespeare Apocrypha.* Edited by C. F. Tucker Brooke. Oxford, 1908. A "critical edition" that does not always record departures from the 1634 text.

1910 WALLER. *The Works of Beaumont and Fletcher.* Edited by Arnold Glover and A. R. Waller, 10 vols. Cambridge, 1905–12. *TNK* in vol. IX, 1910, edited by Waller. Reprint of 1679 Folio text.

1910 FARMER FACSIMILE. *The Two Noble Kinsmen.* Photographic facsimile of 1634 Quarto prepared by John S. Farmer for *Tudor Facsimile Texts* series. London, 1910.

1933 NONESUCH. *The Works of Shakespeare.* Edited by Herbert Farjeon for The Nonesuch Press. 7 vols. London, 1929–33. *TNK* in vol. VII. A literatim reprint of the 1634 text with emendations noted in the margin. The Nonesuch edition was republished as *The Complete Works of William Shakespeare,* 4 vols., in 1953; *TNK* in vol. III.

1935 PARKS & BEATTY. *The English Drama, 900–1642.* Edited by Edd Winfield Parks and Richmond Croom Beatty. New York, 1935.

1936 KITTREDGE. *The Complete Works of Shakespeare.* Edited by George Lyman Kittredge. Boston, 1936.

A text prepared by Peter Ure is reportedly soon to be published in the New Cambridge edition of Shakespeare.

There is no very satisfactory modern edition of the play. The most accurate text is the Nonesuch. Of the critical editions, Littledale's is less misleading than Brooke's. Perhaps the best of the student editions is Parks & Beatty.

INDEX

Inclusive of all persons, other than Shakespeare and Fletcher, mentioned in text, quotations, and notes. A raised B after a number indicates a key bibliographical reference.